Principles of Accoun
the Caribbean

Fourth edition

Frank Wood B.Sc.(Econ.), F.C.A.

and

Sheila Robinson B.A., F.M.A.A.T., Cert. Ed.

LONGMAN
Publishing for the Caribbean

Pearson Education Limited
Edinburgh Gate, Harlow,
Essex CM20 2JE, England
and Associated Companies throughout the World.

Carlong Publishers (Caribbean) Ltd
33 Second Street,
Newport West,
PO Box 489,
Kingston 10,
Jamaica.

Lexicon Trinidad Ltd,
Boundary Road,
San Juan,
Trinidad

First published 2000
Fifth impression 2002

Printed in Singapore (B & JO)

ISBN 0 582 40539 4

Preface to the Fourth Edition

This edition covers two syllabuses of the Caribbean Examinations Council: (1) Principles of Accounts – Basic Proficiency, and (2) Principles of Accounts – General Proficiency.

Students taking the Basic Proficiency examination will be able to leave out the study of various chapters. Their teachers will advise which.

The main changes between this and the previous edition are (1) The inclusion of material for the Schools-Based Assessment and (2) The introduction of the vertical style of final accounts to supplement the traditional horizontal style of those accounts.

In addition there have been a number of changes in the text to make it easier for students to understand. There is also now a separate chapter on 'Accounts for Cooperatives', the last chapter in the book. This is to illustrate the importance of cooperatives in the Caribbean.

We have had tremendous support from Ruth Owen-Wright of the University of Technology, Jamaica. The chapter on cooperatives has been contributed by her.

Frank Wood & Sheila Robinson

Contents

Syllabus for the Examination in Principles of Accounts

The Caribbean Examination Council (CXC) produces a comprehensive syllabus for Principles of Accounts. Centres involved in the teaching and assessment of this subject should ensure that they have an up-to-date copy of the specific requirements.

The authors have reviewed the requirements of the syllabus and have presented these in an abbreviated form (below) to give an indication of the differences between the Basic and General Proficiency levels.

Structure of the Syllabus

The present syllabus for Principles of Accounts has been developed for examination and certification at two proficiency levels, namely Basic and General.

Distinction between the Basic and General Proficiency Levels

Area of Study	Basic	General
1. Number of Units (see below)	8	8 + 4 (Additional)
2. Number of Objectives	48	70
3. Number of Profiles	Knowledge Application } 2	Knowledge Application Interpretation } 3

Syllabus Units	**Basic**	**General**	**Paper1 — Multi-Choice**	
			No. of Items tested:	
			Basic	**General**
1. Introduction to Principles of Accounts	*	*	8	5
2. The Balance Sheet	*	*	12	6
3. Books of Original Entry	*	*	12	10
4. The Ledger	*	*	12	7
5. Simple Manufacturing Accounts	*	*	5	4
6. The Payroll	*	*	4	2
7. Accounts for Non-Trading Organizations	*	*	4	4
8. Further Uses of The General Ledger	*	*	3	4
9. Treatment of Incomplete Records and Control Accounts		*		4
10. Partnership Accounts		*		6
11. Company Accounts		*		4
12. Accounts of Cooperative Societies		*		4
Total	8	12	60	60

Format of the Examination

Paper 1 (1½ hours) A 60-item multiple-choice paper testing the profiles of Knowledge, Application and Understanding (principles and practices) in the ratios of 1:1 for the Basic Proficiency and 1:2:1 for the General Proficiency. Refer also to the above table for areas tested.

	Basic	**General**
Number of Questions	60	60
Areas Tested (Principles and Practices)	Knowledge Application	Knowledge Application Understanding
Ratio	1 :1	1 : 2 : 1
Distribution of Areas	See Table	See Table

Paper 2 (3 hours) This is a problem solving paper divided into two sections:

Section 1	**Basic**	**General**
Number of questions (compulsory)	3	3
Areas of examination (units)	2, 3, 4 and 7	2, 3, 4, 8, 9 and 10
Section 2		
Number of questions	2 from 4	2 from 4
Areas of examination (units)	1 to 8	1 to 12
Assessment		
Marks per question	18	20

Paper 3 School Based Assessment (SBA)

An accounting project	Refer to Chapter 44

Weighting of the examination components

The syllabus states the weightings of Knowledge and Application at Basic Proficiency level and the weighting of Knowledge, Application and Interpretation at General Proficiency level. For details of these refer to the tables in the syllabus.

Requirements of the syllabus

OBJECTIVES	CONTENTS	MAIN CHAPTER REFERENCES IN TEXT
UNIT 1: Introduction to Principles of Accounts The student should be able to:		
1. State the purpose of accounting	Discussion of accounting as a business practice Purpose of accounting	1
2. Define accounting	Simple definition of the terms 'accounting', and 'Principles of Accounts'.	1
3. State the various forms of business organizations	Accounting for sole traders	1
	(For General Proficiency you also need to study partnerships, companies, cooperatives and other specialized bodies e.g. banks, state enterprises, insurance companies, statutory corporations.)	34, 39, 43

OBJECTIVES	CONTENTS	MAIN CHAPTER REFERENCES IN TEXT
4. Identify the major components of the final accounts and balance sheets of the various forms of business organizations		8, 9, 34, 39, 43
5. Recognize the different types of accounts	**Classification of accounts:** Nominal, e.g. wages, discounts Real, e.g. stock, machinery Personal, e.g. debtors, creditors	11
6. Draw up simple account formats neatly and accurately	Simple format, debit and credit sides: meaning of debit and credit	3
7. Explain the significance of debit and credit in each type of account		
8. Use double entry	Meaning of double entry	3
9. Describe the accounting cycle (General Proficiency only)	The accounting cycle	18
10. Give a diagrammatic presentation of the accounting cycle (General Proficiency only)		3
11. Define accounting concepts and conventions (General Proficiency only)	Concepts: duality, going concern, accrual, etc. Conventions: materiality, consistency, prudence (conservatism)	33
12. State some accounting processes which could be readily performed by use of the computer	Use of computers for the preparation of accounting records Definition of components, e.g. diskette, menu, hardware, software, etc.	40

UNIT 2: The Balance Sheet

The student should be able to:

OBJECTIVES	CONTENTS	MAIN CHAPTER REFERENCES IN TEXT
1. Define a balance sheet and identify its components	Definition of a balance sheet; components (assets, liabilities, capital)	2, 9
2. Construct a simple balance sheet in basic format	Simple examples of a balance sheet of a sole trader	2, 3, 9
3. Use and interpret the balance sheet equation	The balance sheet equation: C = A – L	2
4. Identify examples of different types of assets and liabilities and arrange them in order of liquidity and permanency	*Assets:* Fixed, e.g. land, building Current, e.g. cash, debtors, inventory	

OBJECTIVES	CONTENTS	MAIN CHAPTER REFERENCES IN TEXT
	Liabilities: current (short-term): e.g. bank over-draft, creditors Long-term e.g. debentures, mortgage, bank loans	2, 3, 9
5. Define liquidity; (General Proficiency only)	Definition of liquidity; order of liquidity	9
6. State the significance of liquidity; (General Proficiency only)		
7. Define and calculate working capital and show its significance for the operation of the business	Definition and calculation of working capital The working capital approach to the balance sheet	24
8. Determine which items in a balance sheet will change as a result of various transactions		2, 3, 4, 9

UNIT 3: Books of Original Entry
The student should be able to:

OBJECTIVES	CONTENTS	MAIN CHAPTER REFERENCES IN TEXT
1. State the reason for using the various books of original entry	The use of journal, cash book, purchases book, sales book, returns inward book, returns outward book	11
2. Distinguish between cash and credit transactions	Interpret transactions (cash and credit)	4
3. Define and use documents related to books of original entry	*Source documents:* vouchers, receipts, bank statements, invoice, credit notes, debit notes, petty cash vouchers	12, 13, 14, 25, 26
4. Make entries in the books of original entry		12, 13, 14, 16, 17, 26
5. Distinguish between discounts received and discounts allowed	*Discounts:* cash and trade discounts, discounts received and discounts allowed	17
6. Distinguish between cash and trade discounts and record them		17
7. Balance the cash book	Balancing and posting the cash book	16, 17
8. Total other books of original entry	Totalling and posting other books of original entry	12, 13, 14, 26
9. Reconcile the cash book balance with the bank statement balance	Bank reconciliation statement	25

OBJECTIVES	CONTENTS	MAIN CHAPTER REFERENCES IN TEXT
10. Define and record imprest cash and record payments therefrom	Definition of petty cash and imprest system: recording of entries in petty cash book	26

UNIT 4: The Ledger
The student should be able to:

OBJECTIVES	CONTENTS	MAIN CHAPTER REFERENCES IN TEXT
1. Make detailed entries in the ledger from the journal and other books of original entry	*Meaning of posting:* Posting from the journal and other books of original entry to the ledger	12, 13, 14, 16, 17, 26
2. Extract a trial balance	Extracting a trial balance from accounting records	7
3. State the uses of the trial balance	Uses of the trial balance	7
4. Use the trial balance to detect errors in the ledger		7
5. Balance and close all classes of accounts	*Balancing accounts:* taking trial balance of the balances; closing accounts	6
6. Calculate the value of stock (General Proficiency only)	Stock taking and valuation, LIFO, FIFO, average cost method, stock cards (simple treatment)	41
7. Prepare simple final statements of trading account, profit and loss account and balance sheet	Preparation of trading account; profit and loss account and balance sheets using horizontal and vertical presentation formats	5, 8, 9, 10
8. State the relationship of assets, liabilities, capital, working capital to the balance sheet and interpret their implications for the financial position (General Proficiency only)	*Basic ratio analysis in relation to business objectives, e.g. ratio:* Current ratio, liquidity ratio return on capital invested	29, 42
9. Analyze and interpret the financial position of a business as regards rate of turnover, average stock and simple ratios; (General Proficiency only)	*Trading results:* simple ratios, e.g. rate of turnover, average stock, gross profit percentage, net profit percentage, return on investment	29, 42
10. Distinguish between the accounts receivable (debtors) and accounts payable (creditors) ledger	Accounts receivable (debtors) and accounts payable (creditors)	11, 12, 13

UNIT 5: Simple Manufacturing Accounts
The student should be able to:

OBJECTIVES	CONTENTS	MAIN CHAPTER REFERENCES IN TEXT
1. Identify and define elements of cost	The elements of cost	37 (items 1–2)
2. Establish the cost of manufactured products	Accounting procedures for recording costs	

OBJECTIVES	CONTENTS	MAIN CHAPTER REFERENCES IN TEXT
3. Calculate the gross and net profit for a manufacturing concern	Preparation of accounts for a manufacturing concern: (a) manufacturing account (b) trading account (c) profit and loss account (d) balance sheet (General Proficiency only)	37
4. Prepare a balance sheet for a manufacturing concern (General Proficiency only)		

UNIT 6: The Payroll
The student should be able to:

OBJECTIVES	CONTENTS	MAIN CHAPTER REFERENCES IN TEXT
1. Fill out particulars on time cards/sheets	Time cards/sheets, employee earnings records; deductions, e.g. income tax, social security, etc.	38
2. Transfer particulars from time cards/sheets to payroll	Preparation of payroll and wage documents, from time cards/sheets	38
3. Calculate employees' gross earnings		38
4. Make the necessary deductions from employees' earnings and calculate employees' net pay	Recording deductions and calculations of net pay	38

UNIT 7: Accounts for Non-trading Organizations
The student should be able to:

OBJECTIVES	CONTENTS	MAIN CHAPTER REFERENCES IN TEXT
1. Distinguish between capital expenditure and revenue expenditure	Capital expenditure and revenue expenditure	31
2. Distinguish the differences in accounting procedures for trading and non-trading organizations	Accounting procedures for trading and non-trading organizations.	32
3. Prepare a receipts and payments account	Receipts and payments account	32
4. Prepare an income and expenditure account and balance sheet	Income and expenditure account and balance sheet including simple accruals and prepayments	32

UNIT 8: Further Uses of the General Journal
The student should be able to:

OBJECTIVES	CONTENTS	MAIN CHAPTER REFERENCES IN TEXT
1. State uses of the general journal	general journal	18
2. Recognise and record opening entries, intermediate entries and (General Proficiency only) closing entries	Opening entries, intermediate entries and (General Proficiency only) closing entries	18

OBJECTIVES	CONTENTS	MAIN CHAPTER REFERENCES IN TEXT
3. State why adjustments arise	The treatment of adjusting entries	18, 23
4. Make simple calculations and entries for depreciation	Depreciation: (straight line, reducing balance)	20, 21
5. Make entries for prepayment and accruals (General Proficiency only)	Prepayments, accruals (General Proficiency only)	23
6. Calculate and make entries for provision for bad debts and discounts (General Proficiency only)	Bad debts, provision for bad debts and provision for discounts	22
7. Record adjustments in the final accounts and the balance sheet (General Proficiency only)	Effects of adjustments on the final accounts and balance sheet (General Proficiency only)	23
8. Correct errors by making journal entries (General Proficiency only)	Correction of errors; suspense accounts	27, 28

SECTION TWO:
This section of the syllabus, comprising units 9, 10, 11 and 12, are for GENERAL PROFICIENCY ONLY

UNIT 9: Treatment of Incomplete Records and Control Accounts
The student should be able to:

1. Identify single entry records	Incomplete records	30
2. Draw up a statement of affairs from such records so as to show capital		30
3. State disadvantages of single entry recording	Disadvantages of single entry recording	30
4. Convert single entry into double entry	Conversion to double entry	18
5. State the reasons for control accounts	Control accounts	19
6. Prepare simple control accounts		19

UNIT 10: Partnership Accounts
The student should be able to:

1. Define a partnership business	Partnership as a form of business; structure of a partnership; comparison of a partnership with a sole proprietorship	34
2. State the reasons for establishing partnerships	Reasons for a partnership	34
3. State the essential legal provisions of the Partnerships Act (1890) and apply them	The legal implications of a partnership with respect to: (a) sharing profits and losses (b) interest on capital (c) salaries of partners (d) interest on drawings	34

OBJECTIVES	CONTENTS	MAIN CHAPTER REFERENCES IN TEXT
4. Apply the special accounting procedures involved in (a) recording capital (b) setting up current accounts (c) appropriating profits (d) drawing up balance sheets	Recording transactions of a partnership: raising capital and recording current account of partners; appropriation of profits; preparation of a balance sheet	34
5. Define goodwill	Goodwill in a partnership	35
6. Make entries for admission of a new partner	Admission of a partner, goodwill and premiums	35
7. Define premium		35

UNIT 11: Company Accounts
The student should be able to:

OBJECTIVES	CONTENTS	MAIN CHAPTER REFERENCES IN TEXT
1. Define the legal status of a company	Limited liability company/llc	39
2. State reasons for establishing a limited liability company as opposed to a partnership or sole proprietorship		39
3. Define different ways of raising capital	Types of shares — ordinary, preference; debentures	39
4. Define and state the use of bonds and treasury bills	Bonds and treasury bills	43
5. Apply accounting procedures in companies for: (a) recording capital (b) appropriating profits (c) drawing up the balance sheet	Issue of shares and debentures at par dividends; reserves	39

UNIT 12: Accounts of Cooperative Societies
The student should be able to:

OBJECTIVES	CONTENTS	MAIN CHAPTER REFERENCES IN TEXT
1. Define the legal status and types of cooperative societies	Definition of cooperative societies; definition of credit unions; agricultural cooperatives, etc.	43 (items 1–4)
2. State the six cooperative principles		
3. Define different ways of raising capital	Shares and deposits	
4. Apply accounting procedures in cooperatives for: (a) recording contributions/loans (b) distribution of surplus (c) drawing up the balance sheet and income statement (profit and loss account) of a cooperative society	Shares and deposits, repayments and interest; reserves, bonuses, dividends, patronage	

CHAPTER **1**

Introduction to Accounting

Learning Objectives

- To provide a general overview of what accounting is and the business environment in which it operates.
- To distinguish between bookkeeping and accounting.
- To know the main users of accounting information.

1.1 Being in Business

When someone decides to start a business, they do so with the aim of making money. To make money they will have to trade with other people and businesses.

Trading means selling goods and/or services with the aim of making a profit. It can be seen immediately that money plays a very important role in business. It is the means by which a value is given to goods or services that are offered to potential customers.

Controlling money in a business is vital if it is to be successful and a profit is to be made. The owner(s) of the business need to know how much money is coming into the business from the sale of goods and/or services. They also need to know how much it is costing to run the business. In other words, they need to 'account' for every dollar coming into and going out of the business. This process is known as accounting and this book describes the basic methods used by accountants in the financial control of a business.

The basis of business is shown in exhibit 1.1.

Exhibit 1.1 The basis of business

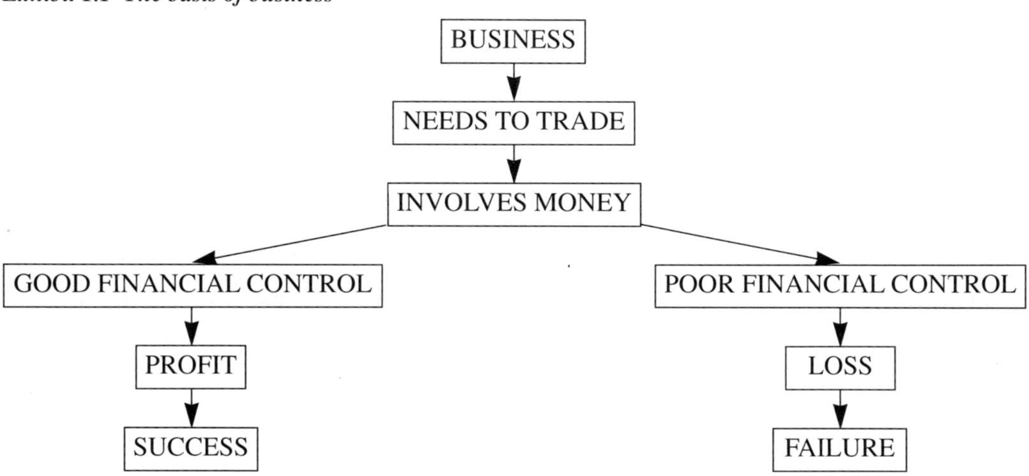

Financial control is a major function in a business but there are other aspects which are needed to ensure success:

- a competitive product and/or service
- a good sales strategy
- a competent workforce.

None of these would be of any use unless there was a market (people or businesses willing to buy).

It is, however, a fact that businesses making it their practice to keep good records of financial data will have the information they need to make sound management decisions with a far better chance of success than those that do not do this.

1.2 What is Accounting?

People and Businesses

Accounting is something that affects people in their personal lives just as much as it affects very large businesses. We all use accounting ideas when we plan what we are going to do with our money. We have to plan how much of it we will spend and how much we will save. We may write down a plan, known as a **budget**, or we may simply keep it in our minds.

Recording Accounting Data

However, when people normally talk about accounting they mean the type used by businesses and other organizations. They cannot keep all the details in their minds so they have to write it all down.

They will not only record cash received and paid out: they will also record goods bought and sold, items bought to use rather than to sell, and so on. This part of accounting is usually called the *recording of data*.

Classifying and Summarizing

When the data are being recorded they have to be sorted out in order to be most useful to the business. This is known as *classifying* and *summarizing data.*

Following such classifications and summaries, it will be possible to work out how much profit or loss has been made by the business during a period of time. It will also be possible to show what resources are owned by the business, and what is owed by it, on the closing date of the period.

Communicating Information

From the data, anyone skilled in accounting should be able to tell whether or not the business is performing well financially. They should be able to work out what are the strengths and weaknesses of the business.

Finally, they should be able to tell or *communicate* their results to the owners of the business, or to others allowed to receive this information. Accounting is therefore concerned with:

- recording of data
- classifying and summarizing data
- communicating what has been learned from the data.

1.3 Definition of Accounting

There have been many definitions of accounting. The following is the most widely used definition: 'The process of identifying, measuring and communicating economic information to permit informed judgements and decisions by users of the information.'

1.4 The Purpose of Accounting

The definition in Section 1.3 starts with the words 'The process of …'. To enable that process to be carried out, the right data has to be available. It is accounting that provides that information, and therefore we can say that it is the provision of the right data for the decision process that is the purpose of accounting.

1.5 What is Bookkeeping?

The part of accounting that is concerned with recording data is often known as bookkeeping. Until about one hundred years ago all accounting data were recorded in books, hence the term 'bookkeeping'.

Nowadays, although books may be used, quite obviously a lot of accounting data is recorded by using computers.

1.6 Users of Accounting Information

The possible users can be the following.

- **Owner(s) of the business** they want to be able to see whether or not the business is profitable. In addition, they want to know what the financial resources of the business are.
- **A prospective buyer** when the owner wants to sell the business the buyer will want to see such information.
- **The bank** if the owner wants to borrow money for use in the business then the bank will need such information.
- **Tax inspectors** they need such information to be able to calculate the taxes payable.
- **A prospective partner** if the owner wants to share ownership with someone else, then the would-be partner will want such information.

There could also be other users. It is obvious that without recorded accounting data a business would have many difficulties.

New Terms

Budget (p. 2): A written plan of how to spend a certain amount of money, expressed in dollars or some other currency.

Bookkeeping (p. 3): The recording of accounting data.

Summary

1. Accounting is concerned with the recording, classifying and summarizing of data, and then communicating what has been learned from it.
2. It may not be only the owners of a busines who will need the accounting information, as they may need it to show to others, e.g. the bank or the Inspector of Taxes.

CHAPTER **2**

The Accounting Equation and the Balance Sheet

Learning Objectives

- To understand the accounting equation.
- To understand what is meant by assets, liabilities and capital.
- To be able to draw up balance sheets after different transactions have occurred.
- To understand the difference between 'horizontal' and 'vertical' style balance sheets.

2.1 The Accounting Equation

The whole of accounting is based upon a very simple idea. This is called the *accounting equation*. It sounds complicated, but in fact it is easy to understand.

It can be explained by saying that if a firm is to set up, and start trading, then it needs resources. Let us assume that in the first place it is the owner of the business who has supplied all of the resources. This can be shown as:

Resources in the business = Resources supplied by the owner

In accounting, terms are used to describe things. The amount of the resources supplied by the owner is called **capital**. The actual resources that are then in the business are called **assets**. This means that the accounting equation above, when the owner has supplied all of the resources, can be shown as:

Assets = Capital

Usually, however, someone other than the owner has supplied some of the assets. The owner may have borrowed these things, or may have bought them and promised to pay at a later date. In both cases he or she owes the money for them. **Liabilities** is the name given to the amount owing to these people for these assets. The equation has now changed to:

Assets = Capital + Liabilities

It can be seen that the two sides of the equation will have the same totals. This is because we are dealing with the same thing from two different points of view. It is:

Resources: what they are = Resources: who supplied them
(Assets) (Capital + Liabilities)

It is a fact that the totals of each side will always equal each other, and that this will always be true no matter how many transactions there may be. The actual assets, capital and liabilities may change, but the total of the Assets will always equal the total of Capital + Liabilities.

Assets consist of property of all kinds, such as buildings, machinery, stocks of goods and motor vehicles; also benefits such as debts owed by customers and money in the bank.

Liabilities consist of money owing for goods supplied to the firm and for expenses; also loans made to the firm.

Capital is often called the owner's **equity** or net worth.

Please note that in this book all the years will be shown as 2000, 2001, 2002 and so on up to 2009. Even though some of these years may be in the future, it will make it easier for students to compare years in accounts than using those years before 2000, e.g. 1997, 1998 or 1999.

2.2 The Balance Sheet

The accounting equation is shown in a statement called the **balance sheet**. It is not the first bookkeeping record to be made, but it is a good place to start to consider accounting.

The Introduction of Capital

On 1 May 2000 B. Blake started in business; and put $5,000 into a bank account for the business. The balance sheet would appear:

B. Blake
Balance Sheet as at 1 May 2000

Assets	$		$
Cash at bank	5,000	Capital	5,000
	5,000		5,000

The Purchase of an Asset by Cheque

When Blake has a bank account, he can use cheques as payment. On 3 May 2000 Blake buys fixtures for $3,000, paying by cheque. The effect of this transaction is that the cash at the bank is reduced and a new asset, Fixtures, appears:

B. Blake
Balance Sheet as at 3 May 2000

Assets	$		$
Fixtures	3,000	Capital	5,000
Cash at bank	2,000		
	5,000		5,000

The Purchase of and Asset and the Incurring of a Liability

On 6 May 2000 Blake buys some goods for $500 from D. Smith and agrees to pay for them some time within the following two weeks. There is now a new asset, the **stock** of goods, and there is also a new liability because Blake owes money to Smith for the goods.

A person to whom money is owed for goods is known in accounting language as a **creditor**.

B. Blake
Balance Sheet as at 6 May 2000

Assets	$	*Capital and liabilities*	$
Fixtures	3,000	Capital	5,000
Stock of goods	500	Creditor	500
Cash at bank	2,000		
	5,500		5,500

Sale of an Asset on Credit

On 10 May 2000 goods that had cost $100 were sold to J. Brown for the same amount, the money to be paid later. This means a reduction in the stock of goods and there will now be a new asset. A person who owes money to the firm is known in accounting language as a **debtor**. The balance sheet now appears as:

B. Blake
Balance Sheet as at 10 May 2000

Assets	$	*Capital and liabilities*	$
Fixtures	3,000	Capital	5,000
Stock of goods	400	Creditor	500
Debtor	100		
Cash at bank	2,000		
	5,500		5,500

Sale of an Asset for Immediate Payment

On 13 May 2000 goods that had cost $50 were sold to D. Daley for the same amount, Daley paying for them immediately by cheque. Here one asset, Stock of goods, is reduced, while another asset, Cash at bank, is increased. The balance sheet now appears:

B. Blake
Balance Sheet as at 13 May 2000

Assets	$	*Capital and liabilities*	$
Fixtures	3,000	Capital	5,000
Stock of goods	350	Creditor	500
Debtor	100		
Cash at bank	2,050		
	5,500		5,500

The Payment of a Liability

On 15 May 2000 Blake pays a cheque for $200 to D. Smith in part payment of the amount owing. The asset of Cash at bank is therefore reduced, and the liability of the creditor is also reduced. The balance sheet now appears:

B. Blake
Balance Sheet as at 15 May 2000

Assets	$	*Capital and liabilities*	$
Fixtures	3,000	Capital	5,000
Stock of goods	350	Creditor	300
Debtor	100		
Cash at bank	1,850		
	5,300		5,300

Collection of an Asset

On 31 May 2000 J. Brown, who owes Blake $100, makes a part payment of $75 by cheque. The effect is to reduce one asset, Debtor, and to increase another asset, Cash at bank. This results in a balance sheet as follows:

B. Blake
Balance Sheet as at 31 May 2000

Assets	$	*Capital and liabilities*	$
Fixtures	3,000	Capital	5,000
Stock of goods	350	Creditor	300
Debtor	25		
Cash at bank	1,925		
	5,300		5,300

It can be seen that every transaction has affected two items. Sometimes it has changed two assets by reducing one and increasing the other. Other times things have changed differently. A summary of the effect of transactions upon assets, liabilities and capital is shown in Exhibit 2.1. Each transaction has therefore maintained the same total for assets as that of capital + liabilities. This is shown in Exhibit 2.2.

Exhibit 2.1

Example of transaction	Effects	
1 Owner buys goods on credit	⇧ Increase asset (Stock of goods)	⇧ Increase liability (Creditors)
2 Owner buys goods by cheque	⇧ Increase asset (Stock of goods)	⇩ Decrease asset (Bank)
3 Owner pays creditor by cheque	⇩ Decrease asset (Bank)	⇩ Decrease liability (Creditors)
4 Owner pays more capital into the bank	⇧ Increase asset (Bank)	⇧ Increase capital
5 Owner takes money out of the business bank account for own use	⇩ Decrease asset (Bank)	⇩ Decrease capital
6 Owner pays creditor from private money outside the firm	⇩ Decrease liability (Creditors)	⇧ Increase capital

Exhibit 2.2

Number of transactions as above	Assets	Capital and liabilities	Effect on balance sheet totals
1	+	+	Each side added to equally
2	+ –		A *plus* and a *minus* both on the assets side, *cancelling* out each other
3	–	–	Each side has equal deductions
4	+	+	Each side has equal additions
5	–	–	Each side has equal deductions
6		+ –	A plus and a minus both on the liabilities side, cancelling out each other

2.3 Alternative Form of Balance Sheet Presentation

Earlier in this chapter you have been shown balance sheets presented in the following manner:

K. King
Balance Sheet as at (date)

Assets	$	*Capital and liabilities*	$
Details of all assets	xxx	Details of capital	xxx
		Details of liabilities	xxx
	xxx		xxx

This is called a 'horizontal' or side-by-side form of presentation. There is no law saying that balance sheets have to be in a horizontal form. However, the author of this book is of the opinion that it is easier for students to learn accounting if the horizontal balance sheet is used at the start.

We could have shown the balance sheet in another way. This is called the 'vertical' form of presentation. In a simple form it would appear as follows:

K. King
Balance Sheet as at (date)

Assets	$
Details of all assets	xxx
Less Liabilities	
Details of all liabilities	xxx
	xxx
Financed by:	
Capital	
Details of capital	xxx

All the figures for assets, liabilities and capital would be exactly the same as when the horizontal style is used. It is only the way it is shown that is different. We will look at this in more detail in later chapters.

New Terms

Capital (p. 4): The total of resources supplied to a business by its owner.
Assets (p. 4): Resources owned by the business.
Liabilities (p. 4): Total of money owed for assets supplied to the business.
Equity (p. 5): Another name for the capital of the owner.
Balance sheet (p. 5): A statement showing the assets, capital and liabilities of a business.
Stock (p. 5): Unsold goods.
Creditor (p. 5): A person to whom money is owed for goods or services.
Debtor (p. 6): A person who owes money to the business for goods or services supplied to him.

Summary

1 The accounting equation is: Assets = Capital + Liabilities.
2 The total of each side of the balance sheet should always be equal to the other side.
3 Every transaction affects two items in the balance sheet.

Notes

- Generally, the figures used for exhibits and exercises have been kept down to relatively small amounts. This has been done deliberately to make the work of the user of this book that much easier. Constantly handling large figures does not add anything to the study of the principles of accounting; instead it simply wastes a lot of the students' time, and they will probably make far more errors if larger figures are used. It could lead to the authors being accused of not being 'realistic' with the figures given, but we believe that it is far more important to make learning easier for the student.
- Multiple-choice questions are included in the book. See Section 7.6 on p. 57.

Exercises

Note: Questions with the letter X shown after the question number do *not* have answers shown at the back of the book. Answers to the others are shown on p. 420 onwards.

2.1 You are to complete the gaps in the following table.

	Assets	*Liabilities*	*Capital*
	$	$	$
(*a*)	12,500	1,800	?
(*b*)	28,000	4,900	?
(*c*)	16,800	?	12,500
(*d*)	19,600	?	16,450
(*e*)	?	6,300	19,200
(*f*)	?	11,650	39,750

2.2X You are to complete the gaps in the following table.

	Assets	*Liabilities*	*Capital*
	$	$	$
(*a*)	55,000	16,900	?
(*b*)	?	17,200	34,400
(*c*)	36,100	?	28,500
(*d*)	119,500	15,400	?
(*e*)	88,000	?	62,000
(*f*)	?	49,000	110,000

2.3 Distinguish from the following list the items that are liabilities from those that are assets.

(*a*) Office machinery.
(*b*) Loan from C. Shirley.
(*c*) Fixtures and fittings.
(*d*) Motor vehicles.
(*e*) We owe for goods.
(*f*) Cash at bank.

2.4X Classify the following items into assets and liabilities.

Motor vehicles.
Premises.
Creditors for goods.
Stock of goods.
Debtors.
Owing to bank.
Cash in hand.
Loan from D. Jones.
Machinery.

2.5 State which of the following are shown under the wrong classification for J. Wong's business.

Assets	*Liabilities*
Loan from C. Smith	Stock of goods
Cash in hand	Debtors
Machinery	Money owing to bank
Creditors	
Premises	
Motor vehicles	

2.6X Which of the following are shown under the wrong headings?

Assets	*Liabilities*
Cash at bank	Loan from J. Graham
Fixtures	Machinery
Creditors	Motor vehicles
Building	
Stock of goods	
Debtors	
Capital	

2.7 A. Smart sets up a new business. Before he actually sells anything he has bought motor vehicles $2,000, premises at a cost of $5,000 and goods $1,000. He did not pay in full for his stock of goods and still owes $400 in respect of them. He had borrowed $3,000 from D. Bevan. After the events just described, and before trading starts, he has $100 cash in hand and $700 cash at bank. You are required to calculate the amount of his capital.

2.8X T. Chin starts a business. Before he actually starts to sell anything he has bought fixtures at $2,000, motor vehicles at $5,000 and a stock of goods at $3,500. Although he has paid in full for the fixtures and the motor vehicles, he still owes $1,400 for some of the goods. J. Preston had lent him $3,000. Chin, after the above, has $2,800 in the business bank account and $100 cash in hand. You are required to calculate his capital.

2.9 Draw up A. Foster's balance sheet from the following as at 31 December 2001.

	$
Capital	23,750
Debtors	4,950
Motor vehicles	5,700
Creditors	2,450
Fixtures	5,500
Stock of goods	8,800
Cash at bank	1,250

2.10X Draw up Kelly's balance sheet as at 30 June 2002 from the following items.

	$
Capital	13,000
Office machinery	9,000
Creditors	900
Stock of goods	1,550
Debtors	275
Cash at bank	5,075
Loan from C. Smith	2,000

2.11 Complete the columns to show how much the assets, liabilities and capital have been changed by the following transactions.

	Effect upon		
	Assets	*Liabilities*	*Capital*
(*a*) We pay a creditor in cash $70.			
(*b*) Bought fixtures paying by cheque $200.			
(*c*) Bought goods on credit $275.			
(*d*) The proprietor introduces another $500 cash into the firm.			
(*e*) J. Walker lends the firm cash $200.			
(*f*) A debtor pays us by cheque $50.			
(*g*) We return goods costing $60 to a supplier whose bill we had not paid.			
(*h*) Bought additional shop premises paying by cheque $5,000.			

2.12X Complete the columns to show how much the assets, liabilities and capital have been changed by the following transactions.

	Effect upon		
	Assets	*Liabilities*	*Capital*
(*a*) Bought a motor van on credit $500.			
(*b*) Repaid by cash a loan owed to P. Smith $1,000.			
(*c*) Bought goods for $150 paying by cheque.			
(*d*) The owner puts a further $5,000 cash into the business.			
(*e*) A debtor returns to us $80 goods. We agree to make an allowance for them.			
(*f*) Bought goods on credit $220.			
(*g*) The owner takes out $100 cash for his personal use.			
(*h*) Paid a creditor $190 by cheque.			

2.13 C. Sangster has the following items in his balance sheet as on 30 April 2004. Capital $18,900; Loan from T. Sasso $2,000; Creditors $1,600; Fixtures $3,500; Motor vehicle $4,200; Stock of goods $4,950; Debtors $3,280; Cash at bank $6,450; Cash in hand $120.
During the first week of May 2004, Sangster:

1 Bought extra stock of goods on credit $770.
2 Got paid in cash $280 by a debtor.
3 Bought extra fixtures by cheque $1,000.

You are to draw up a balance sheet as on 7 May 2004 after the above transactions have been completed.

2.14X C. Samuels has the following balance sheet as at 31 March 2005.

Balance Sheet as at 31 March 2005

Assets	$	*Capital and liabilities*	$
Buildings	6,000	Capital	14,400
Motor vehicles	4,000	Loan from L. Stennett	2,000
Stock of goods	2,000	Creditors	1,600
Debtors	2,800		
Cash at bank	3,200		
	18,000		18,000

The following transactions occur:

(*a*) April 2 Paid a cheque of $500 to a creditor.
(*b*) April 8 A debtor paid C. Samuels $300 by cheque.
(*c*) April 10 L. Stennett is repaid $1,000 by cheque.

Draw up a balance sheet on 10 April 2005 after the transactions have been completed.

CHAPTER **3**

The Double Entry System for Assets, Liabilities and Capital

Learning Objectives

- To explain the recording and layout of financial transactions using the double-entry system.
- To explain the meaning of debit and credit in bookkeeping terms.
- To state the rules of the double-entry system and to provide worked examples to illustrate the use of these rules.

3.1 Nature of a Transaction

In Chapter 2 we saw how various events changed two items in the balance sheet. Events which do result in such changes are known as 'transactions'. This means that if the propreitor asks the price of some goods, but does not buy them, there is no transaction as no balance sheet item would have changed. If he later asks the price of some goods, and then buys these for cash, in this second case there would be a transaction as it would mean that balance sheet items had changed, i.e. stock of goods and cash.

3.2 The Double Entry System

We have seen that every transaction affects two items. If we want to show the effect of every transaction when we are doing our bookkeeping, we will have to show the effect of a transaction on each of the two items. For each transaction this means that a bookkeeping entry will have to be made to show an increase or decrease of that item, and another entry to show the decrease or increase of the other item. From this you will probably be able to see that the term **double entry system** of bookkeeping is a good one, as each transaction is entered twice (double entry).

In Chapter 2 we drew up a new balance sheet after each transaction. You could do this easily if you had only a few transactions per day, but if there were hundreds of transactions each day it would become impossible for you to draw up hundreds of different balance sheets. You simply would not have enough time.

Instead of constantly drawing up amended balance sheets after each transaction, what we have instead is the double entry system. The basis of this system is that the transactions which have occurred are entered in a set of 'accounts'. An **account** is a place in our books where all the information referring to a particular asset, liability or for capital, is entered. Thus there will be an account for motor vans, where all the transactions concerning motor vans will be entered. Likewise, there will be an account for buildings, where all the transactions concerned with buildings will be shown. This will be extended so that every asset, every liability and capital will have its own account, for transactions in that item.

3.3 The Accounts for Double Entry

Each account should be shown on a separate page. The double entry system divides each page into two halves. The left-hand side is called the **debit** side, while the right-hand side is called the **credit** side. The title of each account is written across the top of the account at the centre.

You must not think that the words 'debit' and 'credit' in bookkeeping mean the same as the words 'debit' and 'credit' in normal language. If you do, you will become very confused.

Exhibit 3.1 shows a page of an accounts book. If you have to make an entry of $10 on the debit side of the account, the instructions could say 'debit the account with $10' or 'the account needs debiting with $10'.

Exhibit 3.1

Title of account written here					
Date	*Details*	$	*Date*	*Details*	$
	↑			↑	

Left-hand side of the page.
This is the 'debit' side.

Right-hand side of the page.
This is the 'credit' side.

Debit is abbreviated as Dr.
Credit is abbreviated as Cr.
In Chapter 2 transactions were to increase or decrease assets, liabilities or capital. Double entry rules for accounts are shown in Exhibit 3.2.

Exhibit 3.2

Accounts	To record	Entry in the account
Assets	An increase A decrease	Debit Credit
Liabilities	An increase A decrease	Credit Debit
Capital	An increase A decrease	Credit Debit

Let us look once again at the accounting equation:

	Assets	=	Liabilities	and	Capital
To increase each item	Debit		Credit		Credit
To decrease each item	Credit		Debit		Debit

The double entry rules for liabilities and capital are the same, but they are the opposite of those for assets. This is because assets are on the opposite side of the equation and therefore follow opposite rules.

We haven't enough space in this book to put each account on a separate page, so we will have to list the accounts under each other. In a real firm at least one full page would be taken for each account.

To help students having difficulty deciding on which side of each account the items should be entered, a useful hint is to think of the debit side being *in* to the account and the credit side being *out* of the account. To give two examples of the use of this approach we will look at the following.

1 **Paid cash $200 to buy machinery** The double entry for this transaction would be as follows:
  - cash goes *out* – a credit entry in the cash account
  - machinery comes *in* – a debit entry in the machinery account.

2 **Took $500 out of the cash till of the business and paid it into the bank account of the business** The double entry for this transaction would be as follows:
  - money comes *in* to the bank – a debit entry in the bank account
  - cash goes *out* of the cash till – a credit entry in the cash account.

3.4 Worked Examples

The entry of a few transactions can now be attempted.

1 The proprietor starts the firm with $1,000 in cash on 1 August 2000.

Effect	*Action*
1 Increases the *asset* of cash	Debit the cash account – cash goes *in*
2 Increases the capital	Credit the capital account – cash comes *out* of the owner's money

These are entered as follows:

Cash

2000	$			
Aug 1	1,000			

Capital

		2000	$
		Aug 1	1,000

The date of the transaction has already been entered. Now there remains the description which is to be entered alongside the amount. What we now need is a reference to the other account in which the other aspect of the transaction has been shown. Otherwise in future we would not be able to see easily which accounts had been affected by the transaction. The double entry to the item in the cash account is completed by an entry in the capital account, therefore the word 'Capital' will appear in the cash account. Similarly, the double entry to the item in the capital account is completed by an entry in the cash account, therefore the word 'Cash' will appear in the capital account.

The completed accounts are therefore:

Cash

2000	$		
Aug 1 Capital	1,000		

Capital

		2000	$
		Aug 1 Cash	1,000

This method of entering transactions fulfils the requirements of the double entry rules as shown on p. 16. Now let us look at the entry of some more transactions.

2 A motor van is bought for $275 cash on 2 August 2000.

Effect	*Action*
1 Increases the *asset* of motor van	Debit the motor van account – motor van comes *in*
2 Decreases the *asset* of cash	Credit the cash account – cash goes *out*

Motor Van

2000		$			
Aug 2	Cash	275			

Cash

			2000		$
			Aug 2	Motor van	275

3 Fixtures are bought on credit from Shop Fitters for $115 on 3 August 2000.

Effect	*Action*
1 Increases the *asset* of fixtures	Debit the fixtures account – fixtures come *in*
2 Increases the *liability* to Shop Fitters	Credit Shop Fitters' account – fixtures comes *out* of the supplier's account

Fixtures

2000		$			
Aug 3	Shop Fitters	115			

Shop Fitters

			2000		$
			Aug 3	Fixtures	115

4 We paid the amount owing in cash to Shop Fitters on 17 August 2000.

Effect	*Action*
1 Decreases the *liability* to Shop Fitters	Debit Shop Fitters' account – cash goes *in* to the supplier's account
2 Decreases the *asset* of cash	Credit the cash account – cash goes *out*

Shop Fitters

2000	$		
Aug 17 Cash	115		

Cash

		2000	$
		Aug 17 Shop Fitters	115

5 Transactions to date: taking the transactions numbered (1)–(4) above, the records will now appear as follows:

Cash

2000	$	2000	$
Aug 1 Capital	1,000	Aug 2 Motor van	275
		Aug 17 Shop Fitters	115

Capital

		2000	$
		Aug 1 Cash	1,000

Motor Van

2000	$		
Aug 1 Cash	275		

Shop Fitters

2000	$	2000	$
Aug 17 Cash	115	Aug 3 Fixtures	115

Fixtures

2000	$		
Aug 3 Shop Fitters	115		

Before you read further, you are required to work through questions 3.4, 3.5 and 3.8 at the end of this chapter.

3.5 A Further Worked Example

Now you have actually made some entries in accounts you are to go carefully through the following example. Make certain you can understand every entry.

Transactions			*Effect*	*Action*	*In* / *Out*
2004 May 1 (A)	J. Charles started an engineering business, putting $1,000 into a business bank account		↑ Increases **asset** of bank ↑ Increases **capital** of owner	**Debit** bank account **Credit** capital account	*In* *Out*
May 3 (B)	Bought works machinery on credit from Unique Machines $275		↑ Increases **asset** of machinery ↑ Increases **liability** to Unique Machines	**Debit** machinery account **Credit** Unique Machines' account	*In* *Out*
May 4 (C)	Withdrew $200 cash from the bank and placed it in the cash box		↑ Increases **asset** of cash ↓ Decreases **asset** of bank	**Debit** cash account **Credit** bank account	*In* *Out*
May 7 (D)	Bought a motor van paying in cash $180		↑ Increases **asset** of motor van ↓ Decreases **asset** of cash	**Debit** motor van account **Credit** cash cash account	*In* *Out*
May 10 (E)	Sold some of the machinery for $15 on credit to B. Barnes		↑ Increases **asset** of money owing from B. Barnes ↓ Decreases **asset** of machinery	**Debit** B. Barnes account **Credit** machinery account	*In* *Out*
May 21 (F)	Returned some of the machinery, value $27 to Unique Machines		↓ Decreases **liability** to Unique Machines ↓ Decreases **asset** of machinery	**Debit** Unique Machines **Credit** machinery account	*In* *Out*
May 28 (G)	B. Barnes pays the firm the amount owing, $15, by cheque		↑ Increases **asset** of bank ↓ Decreases **asset** of money owing by B. Barnes	**Debit** bank account **Credit** B. Barnes account	*In* *Out*
May 30 (H)	Bought another motor van paying by cheque $420		↑ Increases **asset** of motor vans ↓ Decreases **asset** of bank	**Debit** motor van account **Credit** bank account	*In* *Out*
May 31 (I)	Paid the amount of $248 to Unique Machines by cheque		↓ Decreases **liability** to Unique Machines ↓ Decreases **asset** of bank	**Debit** Unique Machines **Credit** bank account	*In* *Out*

The accounts for the transactions are now shown. The letters (A) to (I) correspond with the transactions (A) to (I) in the table opposite.

Bank

2004			$	2004			$
May 1	Capital	(A)	1,000	May 4	Cash	(C)	200
May 28	B. Barnes	(G)	15	May 30	Motor van	(H)	420
				May 31	Unique Machines	(I)	248

Cash

2004			$	2004			$
May 4	Bank	(C)	200	May 7	Motor van	(D)	180

Capital

				2004			$
				May 1	Bank	(A)	1,000

Machinery

2004			$	2004			$
May 3	Unique Machines	(B)	275	May 10	B. Barnes	(E)	15
				May 21	Unique Machines	(F)	27

Motor Van

2004			$				
May 7	Cash	(D)	180				
May 30	Bank	(H)	420				

Unique Machines

2004			$	2004			$
May 21	Machinery	(F)	27	May 3	Machinery	(B)	275
May 31	Bank	(I)	248				

B. Barnes

2004			$	2004			$
May 10	Machinery	(E)	15	May 28	Bank	(G)	15

3.6 Abbreviation of 'Limited'

In this book when we come across transactions with limited companies the letters 'Ltd' are used as the abbreviation for 'Limited Company'. So we will know that, if we see the name of a firm as T. Lee Ltd, then that firm will be a limited company. In our books the transactions with T. Lee Ltd will be entered the same as for any other customer or supplier. Later in the book we will examine the nature and status of a limited company.

New Terms

Double entry bookkeeping (p. 14): A system where each transaction is entered twice, once on the debit side and once on the credit side.

Account (p. 15): Part of double entry records, containing details of transactions for a specific item.

Debit (p. 15): The left-hand side of the accounts in double entry.

Credit (p. 15): The right-hand side of the accounts in double entry.

Summary

1 Double entry maintains the principle that every debit entry has a corresponding credit entry.

2 Every different kind of asset and liability each has its own separate account.

Exercises

Note: Questions with the letter X shown after the question number do *not* have answers shown at the back of the book. Answers to the others are shown on p. 434.

3.1 Complete the following table showing which accounts are to be debited and which to be credited.

	Account to be debited	*Account to be credited*
(*a*) Bought motor van for cash.		
(*b*) Bought office machinery on credit from J. Grant & Son.		
(*c*) Introduced capital in cash.		
(*d*) A debtor, J. Beach, pays us by cheque.		
(*e*) Paid a creditor, A. Barrett, in cash.		

3.2 The following table is also to be completed, showing the accounts to be debited and credited.

	Account to be debited	*Account to be credited*
(*a*) Bought machinery on credit from A. Jackson & Son.		
(*b*) Returned machinery to A. Jackson & Son.		
(*c*) A debtor, J. Brown, pays us in cash.		
(*d*) J. Smith lends us money, giving it to us by cheque.		
(*e*) Sold office machinery for cash.		

3.3X Complete the following table.

	Account to be debited	*Account to be credited*
(*a*) Bought office machinery on credit from D. Isaacs Ltd.		
(*b*) Paid a creditor, C. Jones, from owner's private monies outside the firm.		
(*c*) A debtor, N. Fox, paid us in cash.		
(*d*) Repaid part of loan from P. Exeter by cheque.		
(*e*) Returned some of office machinery to D. Isaacs Ltd.		
(*f*) A debtor, N. Lyn, pays us by cheque.		
(*g*) Bought motor van by cash.		

3.4 Complete the following table showing which accounts are to be debited and which to be credited.

	Account to be debited	*Account to be credited*
(*a*) Bought motor lorry for cash.		
(*b*) Paid creditor, T. Lue, by cheque.		
(*c*) Repaid P. Lopez's loan by cash.		
(*d*) Sold motor lorry for cash.		
(*e*) Bought office machinery on credit from Ultra Ltd.		
(*f*) A debtor, A. Hill, pays us by cash.		
(*g*) A debtor, J. Cross, pays us by cheque.		
(*h*) Put a further amount into the business by cheque.		
(*i*) A loan of $200 in cash is received from L. Lowe.		
(*j*) Paid a creditor, D. Lord, by cash.		

3.5 Write up the asset and liability accounts in the records of D. Coy to record these transactions.

2002
May 1 Started business with $1,000 cash.
May 3 Bought a motor lorry on credit from Speed & Sons for $698.
May 14 Bought office machinery by cash from Duplicators Ltd for $60
May 31 Paid Speed & Sons the amount owing to them, $698, in cash.

3.6 Write up the asset and liability and capital accounts to record the following transactions in the records of G. Powell.

2003
July 1 Started business with $2,500 in the bank.
July 2 Bought office furniture by cheque $150.
July 3 Bought machinery $750 on credit from Planers Ltd.
July 5 Bought a motor van paying by cheque $600.
July 8 Sold some of the office furniture – not suitable for the firm – for $60 on credit to J. Walker & Sons.
July 15 Paid the amount owing to Planers Ltd $750 by cheque.
July 23 Received the amount due from J. Walker $60 in cash.
July 31 Bought more machinery by cheque $280.

3.7 You are required to open the asset and liability and capital accounts and record the following transactions for June 2004 in the records of C. Williams.

2004
June 1 Started business with $2,000 cash.
June 2 Paid $1,800 of the opening cash into a bank account for the business.
June 5 Bought office furniture on credit from Betta-Built Ltd for $120.
June 8 Bought a motor van, paying by cheque $950.
June 12 Bought works machinery from Evans & Sons on credit $560.
June 18 Returned faulty office furniture costing $62 to Beta-Built Ltd.
June 25 Sold some of the works machinery for $75 cash.
June 26 Paid amount owing to Beta-Built Ltd $58 by cheque.
June 28 Took $100 out of the bank and put it in the cash till.
June 30 J. Smith lent us $500, giving us the money by cheque.

3.8X Write up the asset, capital and liability accounts in the records of C. Williams to record the following transactions.

2005
June 1 Started business with $5,000 cash in bank.
June 2 Bought motor van, paying by cheque $1,200.
June 5 Bought office fixtures $400 on credit from Young Ltd.
June 8 Bought motor van on credit from Super Motors $800.

Cont'd

June 12 Took $100 out of the bank and put it into the cash till.
June 15 Bought office fixtures paying by cash $60.
June 19 Paid Super Motors a cheque for $800.
June 21 A loan of $1,000 cash is received from J. Jarvis.
June 25 Paid $800 of the cash in hand into the bank account.
June 30 Bought more office fixtures, paying by cheque $300.

3.9X Write up the accounts to record the following transactions.

2003
Mar 1 Started business with $1,000 cash.
Mar 2 Received a loan of $5,000 from M. Chow by cheque, a bank account being opened and the cheque paid into it.
Mar 3 Bought machinery for cash $60.
Mar 5 Bought display equipment on credit from Better-View Machines $550.
Mar 8 Took $300 out of the bank and put it into the cash till.
Mar 15 Repaid part of Chow's loan by cheque $800.
Mar 17 Paid amount owing to Better-View Machines $550 by cheque.
Mar 24 Repaid part of Chow's loan by cash $100.
Mar 31 Bought additional machinery, this time on credit from D. Smith for $500.

3.10X Write up the asset, capital and liability accounts in the books of N. Morris to record the following transactions.

2003
May 1 Started business with $14,000 cash.
May 2 Paid $13,600 of the opening cash into a bank account for the business.
May 3 Bought shop fittings on credit from Lawrence Ltd for $600.
May 4 Bought a motor van, paying by cheque $4,000.
May 6 A. Lee lent us $500 by cheque.
May 7 Bought another motor van on credit from Pear Tree Garage $2,800.
May 10 Bought shop fittings for cash $350.
May 14 Returned some of shop fittings costing $150 to Lawrence Ltd as they were unsuitable.
May 16 Took $300 out of the bank and put it into the cash till.
May 18 Bought machinery for cash $280.
May 21 Paid Lawrence Ltd the amount owing to them by cheque.
May 23 Repaid part of Lee's loan by cheque $200.
May 28 Bought machinery on credit from Better Built Ltd $1,300.
May 31 Paid Pear Tree Garage by cheque $2,800.

CHAPTER **4**

The Asset of Stock

Learning Objectives

- To explain the various accounts used in recording the movement of stocks.
- To show how the purchase and sale of goods by both cash and credit are dealt with in the double entry system.
- To show how the return of goods is recorded in the double entry system.

4.1 Stock Movements

In a business on any date we will normally have goods, bought previously, which so far have not yet been sold. These unsold goods are known as our 'stock' of goods.

The stock of goods in a business is constantly changing because some of it is bought, some is sold, some is returned to the suppliers and some is returned by the firm's customers.

To keep a check on the movements of stock, an account is opened for each type of dealing in goods. Thus we will have the following accounts:

Account	Reason
Purchases account	For the purchase of goods
Sales account	For the sale of goods
Returns inwards account	For goods returned to the firm by its customers
Returns outwards account	For goods returned by the firm to its suppliers

As stock is an asset, and these four accounts are all connected with this asset, the double entry rules are those used for assets.

We shall now look at some entries in the following sections.

4.2 Purchase of Stock on Credit

On 1 August 2004, goods costing $165 are bought on credit from D. Henry.

First, the twofold effect of the transaction must be considered so that the bookkeeping entries can be worked out.

1 **An increase in the asset of stock** An increase in an asset needs a debit entry in an account. Here the account is a stock account showing the particular movement of stock; in this case it is the 'purchases' movement, so the account must be the purchases account.

2 **An increase in a liability** This is the liability of the firm to D. Henry because the goods bought have not yet been paid for. An increase in a liability needs a credit entry, so that to enter this part of the transaction a credit entry is made in D. Henry's account.

Purchases

2004	$		
Aug 1 D. Henry	165		

D. Henry

		2004	$
		Aug 1 Purchases	165

Here again, we can use the idea of the debit side being *in* to the account, and the credit side being *out* of the account. In this case, purchases have come *in* – thus creating a debit in the Purchases account; whereas the goods have come *out* of D. Henry – needing a credit in the account of D. Henry.

4.3 Purchases of Stock for Cash

On 2 August 2004, goods costing $22 were bought, cash being paid for them immediately.

1 **The asset of stock was increased** Thus a debit entry will be needed. The movement of stock is that of a purchase, so that it is the Purchases account which needs debiting. (Purchases have come *in* – debit the Purchases account)

2 **The asset of cash was decreased** To reduce an asset a credit entry is called for, and the asset is that of cash so that the Cash account needs crediting. (Cash has gone *out* – credit the Cash account.)

Purchases

2004	$		
Aug 2 Cash	22		

Cash

		2004	$
		Aug 2 Purchases	22

4.4 Sales of Stock on Credit

On 3 August 2004, goods were sold on credit for $250 to J. Lee.

1 **An asset account was increased** This is the account showing that J. Lee is a debtor for the goods. The increase in the asset of debtors requires a debit and the debtor is J. Lee, so the account concerned is that of J. Lee. (Goods have gone *in* to J. Lee – debit J. Lee's account.)

2 **The asset of stock was decreased** For this a credit entry to reduce an asset is needed. The movement of stock is that of 'Sales', so the account credited is the Sales account. (Sales have gone *out* – credit the Sales account.)

J. Lee

2004		$		
Aug 3	Sales	250		

Sales

		2004		$
		Aug 3	J. Lee	250

4.5 Sales of Stock for Cash

On 4 August 2004, goods were sold for $55, the cash being received at once upon sale.

1 **The asset of cash was increased** A debit in the Cash account is needed to show this. (Cash has come *in* – debit the Cash account.)

2 **The asset of stock was reduced** The reduction of an asset requires a credit and the movement of stock is represented by 'Sales'. So the entry needed is a credit in the Sales account. (Sales have gone *out* – credit the Sales account.)

Cash

2004		$		
Aug 4	Sales	55		

Sales

		2004		$
		Aug 4	Cash	55

4.6 Returns Inwards

Returns inwards represent goods sold that have now been returned by a customer. This could be for various reasons, such as we have sent the customer goods of the wrong size or the wrong colour; the goods may have been damaged; the goods were of poor quality, and so on. Just as the original sale was entered in a double entry fashion, so is the return of those goods.

On 5 August 2004, goods that had previously been sold to F. Lowe for $29 were returned by her.

1 **The asset of stock was increased by the goods returned** So a debit representing an increase of an asset is needed, and this time the movement of stock is that of 'Returns Inwards'. The entry required therefore is a debit in the Returns Inwards account. (The goods have come *in* – debit the Returns Inwards account.)

2 **A decrease in an asset** The debt of F. Lowe to the firm is now reduced, and to record this a credit is needed in F. Lowe's account. (The goods have come *out* of F. Lowe – credit F. Lowe's account.)

Returns Inwards

2004		$		
Aug 5	F. Lowe	29		

F. Lowe

			2004	$
			Aug 5 Returns Inwards	29

An alternative name for a returns inwards account is a **sales returns account**.

4.7 Returns Outwards

These represent goods that were purchased, and are now being returned to the supplier. As the original purchase was entered in a double entry fashion, so also is the return to the supplier of those goods.

On 6 August 2004, goods previously bought for $96 were returned by the firm to K. Hogan.

1 **The liability of the firm to K. Hogan was decreased** by the value of the goods returned to him. The decrease in a liability needs a debit, this time in K. Hogan's account. (The goods have gone *in* to K. Hogan – debit K. Hogan's account.)

2 **The asset of stock is decreased** by the goods sent out. So a credit representing a reduction in an asset is needed, and the movement of stock is that of 'Returns Outwards' so that the entry will be a credit in the Returns Outwards account. (The returns have gone *out* – credit the Returns Outwards account.)

K. Hogan

2004	$			
Aug 6 Returns outwards	96			

Returns Outwards

			2004	$
			Aug 6 K. Hogan	96

An alternative name for a returns outwards account is a **purchases returns account**.

4.8 A Worked Example

2005

May 1 Bought goods on credit $68 from D. Small.
2 Bought goods on credit $77 from A. Lyon & Son.
5 Sold goods on credit to D. Hughes for $60.
6 Sold goods on credit to M. Spencer for $45.
10 Returned goods $15 to D. Small.
12 Goods bought for cash $100.
19 M. Spencer returned $16 goods to us.
21 Goods sold for cash $150.
22 Paid cash to D. Small $53.
30 D. Hughes paid the amount owing by him $60 in cash.
31 Bought goods on credit $64 from A. Lyon & Son.

Purchases

2005	$		
May 1 D. Small	68		
May 2 A. Lyon & Son	77		
May 12 Cash	100		
May 31 A. Lyon & Son	64		

Sales

		2005	$
		May 5 D. Hughes	60
		May 6 M. Spencer	45
		May 21 Cash	150

Returns Outwards

		2005	$
		May 10 D. Small	15

Returns Inwards

2005	$		
May 19 M. Spencer	16		

D. Small

2005	$	2005	$
May 10 Returns outwards	15	May 1 Purchases	68
May 22 Cash	53		

A. Lyon & Son

		2005	$
		May 2 Purchases	77
		May 31 Purchases	64

D. Hughes

2005	$	2005	$
May 5 Sales	60	May 30 Cash	60

M. Spencer

2005	$	2005	$
May 6 Sales	45	May 19 Returns inwards	16

Cash

2005	$	2005	$
May 21 Sales	150	May 12 Purchases	100
May 30 D. Hughes	60	May 22 D. Small	53

4.9 Special Meaning of 'Sales' and 'Purchases'

It must be emphasized that 'Sales' and 'Purchases' have a special meaning in accounting language.

'Purchases' in accounting means *the purchase of those goods that the firm buys with the prime intention of selling*. Sometimes the goods may be altered, added to or used in the manufacture of something else, but it is the element of *resale* that is important. To a firm that deals in computers, for instance, computers are purchases. If something else is bought, such as a motor van, such an item cannot be called purchases, even though in ordinary language it may be said that a motor van has been purchased. The prime intention of *buying* the motor van is for use by the company and not for resale.

Similarly, 'Sales' means the *sale of those goods in which the firm normally deals and which were bought with the prime intention of resale*. The word 'Sales' must never be given to the disposal of other items.

If we did not keep to these meanings, it would result in the different kinds of stock accounts containing something other than goods sold or for resale.

4.10 Comparison of Cash and Credit Transactions for Purchases and Sales

The difference between the records needed for cash and credit transactions can now be seen.

The complete set of entries for purchases of goods where they are paid for immediately by cash would be:

1 debit the purchases account
2 credit the cash account.

On the other hand, the complete set of entries for the purchase of goods on credit can be broken down into two stages: first, the purchase of the goods and second, the payment for them. The first part is:

1 debit the purchases account
2 credit the supplier's account.

The second part is:

1 debit the supplier's account
2 credit the cash account.

The difference can now be seen; with the cash purchase no record is kept of the supplier's account. This is because cash passes immediately and therefore there is no need to keep a check of indebtedness (money owing) to a supplier. On the other hand, in the credit purchase the records should show to whom money is owed until payment is made.

A study of cash sales and credit sales will reveal a similar difference.

Cash sales	*Credit sales*
Complete entry:	First part:
debit cash account	debit customer's account
credit sales account	credit sales account
	Second part:
	debit cash account
	credit customer's account

New Terms

Purchases (p. 25): Goods bought by the business for the purpose of selling them again.
Sales (p. 25): Goods sold by the business.
Returns inwards (p. 25): Goods returned to the business by its customers.
Returns outwards (p. 25): Goods returned by the business to its suppliers.

Summary

1 Separate accounts are kept for each different type of movement of stock, i.e. sales account, purchases account, returns inwards account and returns outwards account.
2 Credit sales are entered on the debit side of the customer's personal account.
3 Credit purchases are entered on the credit side of the supplier's personal account.
4 Returns inwards are entered on the credit side of the customer's personal account.
5 Returns outwards are entered on the debit side of the supplier's personal account.
6 Cash sales require only two entries for the whole transaction. Credit sales require four entries for the whole transaction, being two entries for the sale and two entries for the receipt of money.
7 Cash purchases require only two entries for the whole transaction. Credit purchases require four entries for the whole transaction, being two entries for the purchase and two entries for the payment of money.

Exercises

Note: Questions with the letter X shown after the question number do *not* have answers shown at the back of the book. Answers to the others questions are shown on p. 434 onwards.

4.1 Complete the following table showing which accounts are to be credited and which are to be debited.

	Account to be debited	*Account to be credited*
(*a*) Goods bought, cash being paid immediately.		
(*b*) Goods bought on credit from E. Flynn.		
(*c*) Goods sold on credit to C. Grant.		
(*d*) A motor van sold for cash.		
(*e*) Goods sold for cash.		

4.2 Similarly, complete this next table.

	Account to be debited	*Account to be credited*
(*a*) Goods returned to H. Fong.		
(*b*) Goods bought on credit from P. Franklin.		
(*c*) Goods sold on credit to S. Mullings.		
(*d*) M. Patterson returns goods to us.		
(*e*) Goods bought being paid for by cheque immediately.		

4.3X Complete the following table showing which accounts are to be credited and which are to be debited.

	Account to be debited	*Account to be credited*
(*a*) Goods bought on credit from J. Reid.		
(*b*) Goods sold on credit to B. Perkins.		
(*c*) Motor vans bought on credit from H. Quarrie.		
(*d*) Goods sold, a cheque being received immediately.		
(*e*) Goods sold for cash.		
(*f*) Goods we returned to H. Hardy.		
(*g*) Machinery sold for cash.		
(*h*) Goods returned to us by J. Nelson.		
(*i*) Goods bought on credit from D. Singh.		
(*j*) Goods we returned to H. Forbes.		

4.4X Complete the following table.

	Account to be debited	*Account to be credited*
(*a*) Goods bought on credit from T. Morgan.		
(*b*) Goods returned to us by J. Thomas.		
(*c*) Machinery returned to L. Jones Ltd.		
(*d*) Goods bought for cash.		
(*e*) Motor van bought on credit from D. Davies Ltd.		
(*f*) Goods returned by us to I. Prince.		
(*g*) D. Picton paid us his account by cheque.		
(*h*) Goods bought by cheque.		
(*i*) We paid creditor, B. Henry, by cheque.		
(*j*) Goods sold on credit to J. Mullings.		

4.5 Enter up the following transactions in the requisite accounts.

2003
June 1 Bought goods on credit $72 from C. Blake.
June 3 Bought goods on credit $90 from C. Foster.
June 5 Returned goods to C. Blake $15.
June 19 Sold goods for cash $25.
June 21 Sold goods on credit $64 to E. Rose.
June 30 Bought goods on credit from A. Price $145.

4.6 You are to write up the following in the books.

2004
July 1 Started business with $500 cash.
July 3 Bought goods for cash $85.
July 7 Bought goods on credit $116 from E. Morgan.
July 10 Sold goods for cash $42.
July 14 Returned goods to E. Morgan $28.
July 18 Bought goods on credit $98 from A. Moses.
July 21 Returned goods to A. Moses $19.
July 24 Sold goods to A. Knight $55 on credit.
July 25 Paid E. Morgan's account by cash $88.
July 31 A. Knight paid us his account in cash $55.

4.7 You are to enter the following in the accounts needed.

2006
Aug 1 Started business with $1,000 cash.
Aug 2 Paid $900 of the opening cash into the bank.

Aug 4 Bought goods on credit $78 from s. Holmes.
Aug 5 Bought a motor van by cheque $500.
Aug 7 Bought goods for cash $55.
Aug 10 Sold goods on credit $98 to D. Moore.
Aug 12 Returned goods to S. Holmes $18.
Aug 19 Sold goods for cash $28.
Aug 22 Bought fixtures on credit from Kingston Equipment Co. $150.
Aug 24 D. Watson lent us $100 paying us the money by cheque.
Aug 29 Paid S. Holmes his account by cheque $60.
Aug 31 Paid Kingston Equipment Co. by cheque $150.

4.8 Enter up the following transactions in the records of E. Sangster.
2007
July 1 Started business with $10,000 in the bank.
July 2 T. Cooper lent us $400 in cash.
July 3 Bought goods on credit from F. Jones $840 and S. Chang $3,600.
July 4 Sold goods for cash $200.
July 6 Took $250 of the cash and paid it into the bank.
July 8 Sold goods on credit to C. Chin $180.
July 10 Sold goods on credit to J. Newman $220.
July 11 Bought goods on credit from F. Jones $370.
July 12 C. Chin returned goods to us $40.
July 14 Sold goods on credit to H. Morgan $190 and J. Peat $320.
July 15 We returned goods to F. Jones $140.
July 17 Bought motor van on credit from Montego Motors $2,600.
July 18 Bought office furniture on credit from Faster Supplies Ltd $600.
July 19 Returned goods to S. Chang $110.
July 20 Bought goods for cash $220.
July 24 Sold goods for cash $70.
July 25 Paid money owing to F. Jones by cheque $1,070.
July 26 Goods returned to us by H. Morgan $30.
July 27 Returned some of office furniture costing $160 to Faster Supplies Ltd.
July 28 E. Sangster put a further $500 into the business in the form of cash.
July 29 Paid Montego Motors $2,600 by cheque.
July 31 Bought office furniture for cash $100.

4.9 Enter up the following transactions in the records.
2005
May 1 Started business with $2,000 in the bank.
May 2 Bought goods on credit from C. Shaw $900.
May 3 Bought goods on credit from F. Hughes $250.
May 5 Sold goods for cash $180.
May 6 Returned goods to C. Shaw $40.
May 8 Bought goods on credit from F. Hughes $190.
May 10 Sold goods on credit to G. Wood $390.
May 12 Sold goods for cash $210.
May 18 Took $300 of the cash and paid it into the bank.
May 21 Bought machinery by cheque $550.
May 22 Sold goods on credit to L. Moore $220.
May 23 G. Wood returned goods to us $140.
May 25 L. Moore returned goods to us $10.
May 28 Returned goods to F. Hughes $30.
May 29 Paid Shaw by cheque $860.
May 31 Bought machinery on credit from D. Lee $270.

4.10X You are to enter the following in the accounts needed.

2007

June 1 Started business with $1,000 cash.
June 2 Paid $800 of the opening cash into a bank account for the firm.
June 3 Bought goods on credit from H. Grant $330.
June 4 Bought goods on credit from D. Clark $140.
June 8 Sold goods on credit to B. Miller $90.
June 8 Bought office furniture on credit from Barrett's Ltd $400.
June 10 Sold goods for cash $120.
June 13 Bought goods for credit from H. Grant $200.
June 14 Bought goods for cash $60.
June 15 Sold goods on credit to H. Sangster $180.
June 16 Returned goods $50 to H. Grant.
June 17 Returned some of the office furniture $30 to Barrett's Ltd.
June 18 Sold goods on credit to B. Miller $400.
June 21 Paid H. Grant's account by cheque $480.
June 23 B. Miller paid us the amount owing in cash $490.
June 24 Sangster returned to us $50 goods.
June 25 Goods sold for cash $150.
June 28 Bought goods for cash $370.
June 30 Bought motor van on credit from J. Kelly $600.

4.11X The following transactions are to be entered up in the records of C. Williams.

2006

Aug 1 Started business with $7,500 in cash.
Aug 2 Paid $6,800 of the opening cash into a bank account.
Aug 2 Bought goods on credit from E. Mills $880, D. Thomas $540, C. Orane $300.
Aug 3 Bought office equipment on credit from Hamilton & Co. $188.
Aug 4 Sold goods for cash $120.
Aug 5 Sold goods on credit to Marshall Ltd $144, Green & Co. $57, Coke Ltd $680.
Aug 6 Bought motor van paying by cheque $2,400.
Aug 7 Sold goods on credit to Marshall Ltd $76, H. White $150.
Aug 8 We returned goods to D. Thomas $40.
Aug 10 Bought office equipment, paying by cheque $70.
Aug 11 Goods returned to us by Coke Ltd $60, Green & Co. $7.
Aug 13 Paid by cheque D. Thomas $500, C. Orane $300.
Aug 15 Paid by cheque Hamilton & Co. $188.
Aug 18 Marshall paid us by cash $144.
Aug 21 D. Groves lent us $1,000 giving us the money by cheque.
Aug 22 Bought goods on credit from C. Orane $296.
Aug 23 Sold goods for cash $145.
Aug 25 Some office equipment $28 returned to Hamilton & Co. as it was faulty.
Aug 26 Goods returned to us by H. White $16.
Aug 27 Hamilton & Co. paid us cash $28.
Aug 28 C. Williams put another $1,000 into the business bank account from his private monies outside the business.
Aug 31 Repaid part of D. Grove's loan by cheque $300.

CHAPTER **5**

The Effect of Profit or Loss on Capital: The Double Entry System for Expenses

Learning Objectives

- To understand the nature of profit and loss.
- To see the effects of profits and losses on capital.
- To show how expenses are recorded using the double entry system.
- To understand the term 'revenues' and be able to record them in the double entry system.
- To understand drawings, be able to record them and recognize the effects of drawings on capital.

5.1 The Nature of Profit or Loss

To an accountant, **profit** means the amount by which revenues are greater than expenses for a set of transactions. The term 'revenues' means the value of goods and services that have been supplied to customers. The term 'expenses' means the value of all the assets that have been used up to obtain those revenues.

If, therefore, we had supplied goods and services valued at $100,000 to customers, and the expenses incurred by us to be able to supply those goods and services amounted to $70,000, then the result would be a profit, calculated as follows.

	$
Revenues (goods and services supplied to our customers for the sum of)	100,000
Less Expenses (value of all the assets used up to enable us to supply the above goods and services)	70,000
Profit is therefore	30,000

On the other hand, it could also be possible that our expenses may exceed our revenues for a set of transactions. In this case the result is a **loss**. For instance, a loss would be incurred given the following details.

	$
Expenses (value of all the assets used up to supply goods and services to our customers)	80,000
Less Revenues (what we have charged our customers in respect of all the goods and services supplied to them)	60,000
Loss is therefore	20,000

5.2 The Effects of Profit or Loss on Capital

We can now look at the effects of profit on capital by the use of an example. On 1 January the assets and liabilities of a firm are:

Assets: Fixtures, $10,000; stock, $7,000
Cash at bank, $3,000
Liabilities: Creditors, $2,000

The capital is found by the formula:

Assets – Liabilities = Capital

In this case capital works out at $10,000 + $7,000 + $3,000 – $2,000 = $18,000.

On 2 January the whole of the $7,000 stock is sold for $11,000 cash. On 2 January the assets and liabilities have become:

Assets: Fixtures, $10,000; stock, nil; cash at bank, $14,000
Liabilities: Creditors, $2,000

The capital can be calculated:

Assets $10,000 + $14,000 – Liabilities $2,000 = $22,000

It can be seen that capital has increased from $18,000 to $22,000, a $4,000 increase, because the $7,000 stock was sold for $11,000, a profit of $4,000. Profit therefore increases capital:

Old capital + Profit = New capital
$18,000 + $4,000 = $22,000

On the other hand, a loss would reduce the capital so that it would become:

Old capital – Loss = New capital

5.3 Profit or Loss and Expenses

While the firm is selling its goods, there will be other **expenses** on top of the cost of the goods being sold. Every firm has other expenses such as rent, salaries, pay, telephone expenses, motor expenses and so on. Every extra $1 of expenses will mean $1 less profit.

It would be possible simply to have one account with the title 'Expenses Account'. However, rather than just know that the total expenses were $50,000, it would be more useful if we knew exactly how much of that figure was for rent, how much for motor expenses and so on. An expenses account is therefore opened for each type of expense.

5.4 Debit or Credit

We have to decide whether expenses accounts are to be debited or credited with the amounts involved. Assets involve expenditure by the firm and are shown as debit entries. Expenses also involve expenditure by the firm, and therefore should also be debit entries.

An alternative explanation may also be used for expenses. Every expense results in a decrease in an asset or an increase in a liability, and because of the accounting equation this means that the capital is reduced by each expense. The decrease of capital needs a debit entry and therefore expenses accounts contain debit entries for expenses.

5.5 Effect of Transactions

A few illustrations will demonstrate the double entry required.

1 The rent of $200 is paid in cash. Here the twofold effect is as follows.

  1 **The total of the expense of rent is increased** – the benefit goes *in*. As expense entries are shown as debits, and the expense is rent, so the action required is the debiting of the rent account.

  2 **The asset of cash is decreased** – money goes *out*. This means crediting the cash account to show the decrease of the asset.

  Summary: Debit the rent account with $200 – *in*
  Credit the cash account with $200 – *out*

2 Motor expenses are paid with a cheque for $550. The twofold effect is as follows.

  1 **The total of the motor expenses paid is increased** – a benefit is received *in*. To increase an expenses account needs a debit, so the action required is to debit the motor expenses account – *in*.

  2 **The asset of money in the bank is decreased** – money goes *out*. This means crediting the bank account to show the decrease of the asset – *out*.

  Summary: Debit the motor expenses account with $550 – *in*
  Credit the bank account with $550 – *out*

3 $260 cash in paid for telephone expenses.

  1 **The total of telephone expenses is increased** – a benefit received goes *in*. Expenses are shown by a debit entry, therefore, to increase the expense account in question, the action required is to debit the telephone expenses account.

  2 **The asset of cash is decreased** – money goes *out*. This needs a credit in the cash account to decrease the asset.

  Summary: Debit the telephone expenses account with $260 – *in*
  Credit the cash account with $260 – *out*

It is now possible to study the effects of some more transactions showing the results in the form of a table. See Exhibit 5.1.

Exhibit 5.1

		Increase	Action	Decrease	Action
2006 June 1	Paid for postage stamps by cash $50	Expense of postage	Debit postage account (*in*)	Asset of cash	Credit cash account (*out*)
June 2	Paid for advertising by cheque $290	Expense of advertising	Debit advertising account (*in*)	Asset of bank	Credit bank account (*out*)
June 3	Staff pay, in cash, $960	Expense of staff pay	Debit staff pay account (*in*)	Asset of cash	Credit cash account (*out*)
June 4	Paid insurance by cheque $420	Expense of insurance	Debit insurance account (*in*)	Asset of bank	Credit bank account (*out*)

These examples can now be shown in account form.

Cash

		2006		$
		Jun 1	Postage	50
		Jun 3	Staff pay	960

Bank

		2006		$
		Jun 2	Advertising	290
		Jun 4	Insurance	420

Advertising

2006		$	
Jun 2	Bank	290	

Insurance

2006		$	
Jun 4	Bank	420	

Postage

2006		$	
Jun 1	Cash	50	

Staff pay

2006	$		
Jun 3 Cash	960		

5.6 Drawings

Sometimes the owner will want to take cash out of the business for his private use. These are known as **drawings**. Any money taken out as drawings will reduce capital.

The capital account is a very important account. To help to stop it getting full of small details, each item of drawings is not entered in the capital account. Instead a drawings account is opened, and the debits are entered there.

The following example illustrates the entries for drawings.

On 25 August 2006, the proprietor takes $50 cash out of the business for his own use.

	Effect	*Action*
1	Capital is decreased by $50	Debit the drawings account $50
2	Cash is decreased by $50	Credit the cash account 50

Drawings

2006	$		
Aug 25 Cash	50		

Cash

		2006	$
		Aug 25 Drawings	50

Sometimes good are taken for private use. These are also known as drawings. Entries for such transactions will be described later in the book on p. 202.

5.7 Revenues and Double Entry

We have just looked at instances of expenses being recorded. There will also be the need to record revenues. We will now look at an example.

2006

June 5 Part of our premises are not needed by us at the moment. We let someone else use them and receive rent of $140 by cheque.

Here the twofold effect is:

1 *The asset of the bank is increased* – money comes *in*. This means debiting the bank account to show the increase of the asset.

2 *The total of the revenue of rent received is increased* – the benefit comes *out* of rent received so the action required is the crediting of the rent received account.

Summary: Debit the bank account with $140 – *in*

Credit the rent received account with $140 – *out*

This will therefore appear as:

Bank

2006		$		
Jun 5	Rent received	140		

Rent Received

		2006		$
		Jun 5	Bank	140

New Terms

Profit (p. 35): Result of selling goods for more than they cost.

Loss (p. 35): Result of selling goods for less than they have cost the business.

Expenses (p. 36): Cost of operating the business.

Drawings (p. 39): Cash or goods taken out of a business by the owner for his private use.

Summary

1. Profit increases capital.
2. Losses reduce capital.
3. Every different type of expense will be shown in a separate account, specially named for that type of expense.
4. Expenses are shown as debit entries in the various expense accounts.

Exercises

5.1 You are to complete the following table, showing the accounts to be debited and those to be credited.

	Account to be debited	*Account to be credited*
(*a*) Paid rates by cheque.		
(*b*) Paid staff by cash.		
(*c*) Rent received by cheque.		
(*d*) Received by cheque refund of insurance previously paid.		
(*e*) Paid general expenses by cash.		

5.2 Complete the following table.

	Account to be debited	*Account to be credited*
(*a*) Paid rent by cash.		
(*b*) Paid for goods by cash.		
(*c*) Received by cheque a refund of rates already paid.		
(*d*) Paid general expenses by cheque.		
(*e*) Received commissions in cash.		
(*f*) Goods returned by us to T. Jones.		
(*g*) Goods sold for cash.		
(*h*) Bought office fixtures by cheque.		
(*i*) Paid staff in cash.		
(*j*) Took cash out of business for private use.		

5.3X Complete the following table, showing the accounts to be debited and those to be credited.

	Account to be debited	*Account to be credited*
(*a*) Paid insurance by cheque.		
(*b*) Paid motor expenses by cash.		
(*c*) Rent received in cash.		
(*d*) Paid rates by cheque.		
(*e*) Received refund of rates by cheque.		
(*f*) Paid for stationery expenses by cash.		
(*g*) Paid staff by cash.		
(*h*) Sold surplus stationery receiving proceeds by cheque.		
(*i*) Received sales commission by cheque.		
(*j*) Bought motor van by cheque.		

5.4X The following table should be completed.

	Account to be debited	*Account to be credited*
(*a*) Sold surplus stationery, receiving proceeds in cash.		
(*b*) Paid staff by cheque.		
(*c*) Rent received for premises sublet, by cheque.		
(*d*) Goods returned to us by B. Roberts.		
(*e*) Commission received by us previously in error, we now refund this by cheque.		
(*f*) Bought machinery by cheque.		
(*g*) Paid lighting expenses in cash.		
(*h*) Insurance rebate received by cheque.		
(*i*) Buildings bought by cheque.		
(*j*) Building repairs paid in cash.		

5.5 Enter the following transactions in the necessary accounts in double entry.

2008
- Jan 1 Started business with $200 in the bank.
- Jan 2 U. Surer lent us $1,000 giving us the money by cheque.
- Jan 3 Bought goods on credit $296 from T. Parkin.
- Jan 5 Bought motor van by cheque $250.
- Jan 6 Cash sales $105.
- Jan 7 Paid motor expenses in cash $15.
- Jan 8 Paid staff in cash $18.
- Jan 10 Bought goods on credit from C. Moore $85.
- Jan 12 Paid insurance by cheque $22.
- Jan 25 Received commission in cash $15.
- Jan 31 Paid electricity bill by cheque $17.

5.6 You are to enter the following transactions, completing double entry in the books for the month of May 2007.

2007
- May 1 Started business with $2,000 in the bank.
- May 2 Purchased goods $175 on credit from M. Mills.
- May 3 Bought fixtures and fittings $150 paying by cheque.
- May 5 Sold goods for cash $275.
- May 6 Bought goods on credit $114 from S. Wong.
- May 10 Paid rent by cash $15.
- May 12 Bought stationery $27, paying by cash.
- May 18 Goods returned to M. Mills $23.
- May 21 Let off part of the premises receiving rent by cheque $5.

Cont'd

May 23 Sold goods on credit to U. Henry for $77.
May 24 Bought a motor van paying by cheque $300.
May 30 Paid the month's staff pay by cash $117.
May 31 The proprietor took cash for himself $44.

5.7 Write up the following transactions in the books of L. Thompson.
2008
Mar 1 Started business with cash $1,500.
Mar 2 Bought goods on credit from A. Chang $296.
Mar 3 Paid rent by cash $28.
Mar 4 Paid $1,000 of the cash of the firm into a bank account.
Mar 5 Sold goods on credit to E. Linton $54.
Mar 7 Bought stationery $15 paying by cheque.
Mar 11 Cash sales $49.
Mar 14 Goods returned by us to A. Chang $17.
Mar 17 Sold goods on credit to S. Morgan $29.
Mar 20 Paid for repairs to the building by cash $18.
Mar 22 E. Linton returned goods to us $14.
Mar 27 Paid Chang by cheque $279.
Mar 28 Cash purchases $125.
Mar 29 Bought a motor van paying by cheque $395.
Mar 30 Paid motor expenses in cash $15.
Mar 31 Bought fixtures $120 on credit from A. Webster.

5.8X Enter the following transactions in double entry.
2009
July 1 Started business with $8,000 in the bank.
July 2 Bought stationery by cheque $30.
July 3 Bought goods on credit from I. Walsh $900.
July 4 Sold goods for cash $180.
July 5 Paid insurance by cash $40.
July 7 Bought machinery on credit from H. Morgan $500.
July 8 Paid for machinery expenses by cheque $50.
July 10 Sold goods on credit to D. Small $320.
July 11 Returned goods to I. Walsh $70.
July 14 Paid staff by cash $70.
July 17 Paid rent by cheque $100.
July 20 Received cheque $200 from D. Small.
July 21 Paid H. Morgan by cheque $500.
July 23 Bought stationery on credit from Express Ltd $80.
July 25 Sold goods on credit to N. Thomas $230.
July 28 Received rent $20 in cash for part of premises sublet.
July 31 Paid Express Ltd by cheque $80.

5.9X Write up the following transactions in the records of D. DaSilva.
2005
Mar 1 Started business with $3,000 in the bank and $500 cash.
Mar 2 Bought goods on credit from: T. Small $250; C. Todd $190; V. Ryan $180.
Mar 3 Bought goods for cash $230.
Mar 4 Paid rent in cash $10.
Mar 5 Bought stationery paying by cheque $49.
Mar 6 Sold goods on credit to: C. Crooks $140; R. Rogers $100; B. Grant $240.
Mar 7 Paid staff in cash $80.
Mar 10 We returned goods to C. Todd $60.
Mar 11 Paid rent in cash $10.
Mar 13 R. Rogers returns goods to us $20.
Mar 15 Sold goods on credit to: J. Burns $90; J. Smart $130; N. Thorn $170.

Mar 16	Paid rates by cheque $130.
Mar 18	Paid insurance in cash $40.
Mar 19	Paid rent by cheque $10.
Mar 20	Bought motor van on credit from C. White $600.
Mar 21	Paid motor expenses in cash $6.
Mar 23	Paid staff in cash $90.
Mar 24	Received part of amount owing from B. Grant by cheque $200.
Mar 28	Received refund of rates $10 by cheque.
Mar 28	Paid following by cheque: T. Small $250; C. Todd $130; C. White $600.

5.10X You are to enter the following transactions, completing double entry in the records of J. Collins for the month of June 2005.

2005	
June 1	Started business with $10,000 in the bank and $300 cash.
June 1	Bought goods on credit from: J. Carby $400; F. McIntyre $1,188; C. Morrison $1,344.
June 2	Bought shop fittings by cheque $240.
June 3	Bought shop fittings on credit from M. Johnson Ltd $575.
June 5	Paid insurance by cash $88.
June 6	Bought motor van, paying by cheque $3,200.
June 7	Sold goods for cash $140.
June 7	Sold goods on credit to: W. Graham and Co $450; F. Phillips Ltd $246; D. R. Edwards $80.
June 8	Bought office stationery $180 on credit from D. Ball and Co.
June 9	Paid rent by cheque $75.
June 10	Paid rates by cheque $250.
June 11	Returned goods to F. McIntyre $168.
June 12	Paid D. Ball and Co $180 by cheque.
June 13	Sold goods on credit to K. P. Prince and Co $220; F. Phillips Ltd $154; Kay and Edwards Ltd $270.
June 14	Goods returned to us by W. Graham and Co $40.
June 15	Paid staff by cash $120.
June 16	Loan from D. Clayton by cheque $500.
June 17	W. Graham and Co paid us the amount owing by cheque $410.
June 18	Some of office stationery bought unwisely: we sell it for cash $15.
June 20	Overpaid insurance: a refund of $8 received by cheque.
June 21	Paid motor expenses by cash $55.
June 23	Paid staff by cash $120.
June 25	Cheques received from K. P. Prince and Co $220; F. Phillips Ltd $100 (as part payment).
June 26	Some of shop fittings unsuitable and returned to M. Johnson Ltd $25.
June 28	Paid F. McIntyre $1,020 by cheque.
June 29	Paid rent by cheque $75.
June 30	J. Collins took drawings by cheque $200.

CHAPTER **6**

Balancing Off Accounts

Learning Objectives

- To demonstrate how to obtain the closing balances of personal accounts for both debtors and creditors.
- To show how to distinguish between a debit balance and a credit balance.
- To explain how to show personal ledger accounts in a three-column format instead of as 'T' accounts.

6.1 Accounts for Debtors

Where Debtors Have Paid their Accounts

What you have been reading so far is the recording of transactions in the books by means of debit and credit entries. At the end of each month we will have to look at each account to see what is shown by the entries.

Probably the most obvious reason for this is to find out how much our customers owe us for goods we have sold to them. In most firms this is done at the end of each month. Let us look at the account of one of our customers, K. Morgan, for transactions in August 2006.

K. Morgan

2006	$	2006	$
Aug 1 Sales	144	Aug 22 Bank	144
Aug 19 Sales	300	Aug 28 Bank	300

This shows that during the month we sold a total of $444 goods to Morgan, and have been paid a total of $444 by him. At the close of business at the end of August he therefore owes us nothing. His account can be closed off on 31 August 2006 by inserting the totals of each side, as follows.

K. Morgan

2006	$	2006	$
Aug 1 Sales	144	Aug 22 Bank	144
Aug 19 Sales	300	Aug 28 Bank	300
	444		444

Notice that totals in accounting are shown with a single line above them, and a double line underneath. Totals on accounts at the end of a period are always shown on a level with one another, as shown in the following completed account for C. Lee.

C. Lee

2006	$	2006	$
Aug 11 Sales	177	Aug 30 Bank	480
Aug 19 Sales	203		
Aug 22 Sales	100		
	480		480

In this account, C. Lee also owed us nothing at the end of August 2006, as she had paid us for all sales to her.

If an account contains only one entry on each side and they are equal, totals are unnecessary. Here is an example.

K. Johnson

2006	$	2006	$
Aug 6 Sales	214	Aug 12 Bank	214

Where Debtors Still Owe for Goods

On the other hand, some of our customers will still owe us something at the end of the month. In these cases the totals of each side would not equal one another. Let us look at the account of D. Thomas for August 2006.

D. Thomas

2006	$	2006	$
Aug 1 Sales	158	Aug 28 Bank	158
Aug 15 Sales	206		
Aug 30 Sales	118		

If you add the figures you will see that the debit side adds up to $482 and the credit side adds up to $158. You should be able to see what the difference of $324 (i.e. $482–$158) represents: it consists of sales of $206 and $118 not paid for and therefore owing to us on 31 August 2006.

In double entry we enter figures as totals only if the totals on both sides of the account agree. We do, however, want to close off the account for August, but showing that Thomas owes us $324. If he owes $324 at close of business on 31 August 2006, then he will still owe us that same figure when the business opens on 1 September 2006.

We show this by **balancing the account**. This is done in five stages.

1. Add up both sides to find out their totals. Do not write anything permanent in the account at this stage, but you could write the figures lightly in pencil.
2. Deduct the smaller total from the larger total to find the balance.
3. Now enter the balance on the side with the smallest total. This means the totals will now be equal.
4. Enter totals on a level with each other.
5. Now enter the balance on the line below the totals. The balance below the totals should be on the opposite side to the balance shown above the totals.

Against the balance above the totals, complete the date column by showing the last day of that period. Below the totals show the first day of the next period against the balance. The balance above the totals is described as balance *carried down*. The balance below the total is described as balance *brought down*.

Thomas' account when 'balanced off' will appear as shown in Exhibit 6.1.

Exhibit 6.1

D. Thomas

2006	$	2006	$
Aug 1 Sales	158	Aug 28 Bank	158
Aug 15 Sales	206	Aug 31 Balance carried down	324
Aug 30 Sales	118		
	482		482
Sept 1 Balance brought down	324		

Stage 5: Finally enter balance to start off entries for following month.

Stage 4: Now enter totals level with each other.

Stage 3: Enter balance here so that totals will be equal.

We can now look at another account prior to balancing.

H. Henry

2006	$	2006	$
Aug 5 Sales	300	Aug 24 Returns inwards	50
Aug 28 Sales	540	Aug 29 Bank	250

We will abbreviate 'carried down' to 'c/d' and 'brought down' to 'b/d' from now on.

H. Henry

2006	$	2006	$
Aug 5 Sales	300	Aug 24 Returns inwards	50
Aug 28 Sales	540	Aug 29 Bank	250
		Aug 31 Balance c/d	540
	840		840
Sept 1 Balance b/d	540		

Notes:

- The date given to 'Balance c/d' is the last day of the period which is finishing, and 'Balance b/d' is given the opening date of the next period.
- As the total of the debit side originally exceeded the total of the credit side, the balance is said to be a debit balance. This being a personal account (i.e. for a person), the person concerned is said to be a *debtor* – the accounting term for anyone who owes

money to the firm. The use of the term 'debtor' for a person whose account has a debit balance can again thus be seen.

If accounts contain only one entry, it is unnecessary to enter the total. A double line ruled under the entry will mean that the entry is its own total. For example:

B. Walters

2006		$	2006		$
Aug 18	Sales	51	Aug 31	Balance c/d	51
Sept 1	Balance b/d	51			

6.2 Accounts for Creditors

Exactly the same principles will apply when the balances are carried down to the credit side. We can look at two accounts of our suppliers which are to be balanced off.

E. Williams

2006		$	2006		$
Aug 21	Bank	100	Aug 2	Purchases	248
			Aug 18	Purchases	116

K. Patterson

2006		$	2006		$
Aug 14	Returns outwards	20	Aug 8	Purchases	620
Aug 28	Bank	600	Aug 15	Purchases	200

We now add up the totals and find the balance, i.e. stages 1 and 2. When balanced these will appear as shown in Exhibit 6.2.

Exhibit 6.2

E. Williams

2006		$	2006		$
Aug 21	Bank	100	Aug 2	Purchases	248
Aug 31	Balance c/d	264	Aug 18	Purchases	116
		364			364
			Sept 1	Balance b/d	264

Stage 3: Enter balance here so that totals will be equal.

Stage 4: Now enter totals level with each other.

Stage 5: Finally, enter balance to start of entries for following month.

K. Patterson

2006		$	2006		$
Aug 14	Returns outwards	20	Aug 8	Purchases	620
Aug 28	Bank	600	Aug 15	Purchases	200
Aug 31	Balance c/d	200			
		820			820
			Sept 1	Balance b/d	200

The type of accounts that have been demonstrated so far are often known as T accounts. This is because the accounts are in the shape of a T:

Account title here (the top stroke of the T)

This vertical line divides the two sides and is the downstroke of the T.

Before you read further, attempt exercises 6.1, 6.2 and 6.3 on p. 50.

6.3 Computers and Accounts

Throughout the main part of this book, the type of account used shows the left-hand side of the account as the debit side and the right-hand side as the credit side. However, when most computers are used, the style of the ledger account is different. It appears as three columns of figures, one column for debit entries, another column for credit entries and the last column for the balance. If you have a current account at a bank, your bank statements will normally be shown using this method.

The accounts used in this chapter will now be re-drafted to show the ledger accounts drawn up in this way.

K. Morgan

	Debit	*Credit*	*Balance* (and whether debit or credit)
2006	$	$	$
Aug 1 Sales	144		144 Dr.
Aug 19 Sales	300		444 Dr.
Aug 22 Bank		144	300 Dr.
Aug 28 Bank		300	0

C. Lee

	Debit	*Credit*	*Balance*
2006	$	$	$
Aug 11 Sales	177		177 Dr.
Aug 19 Sales	203		380 Dr.
Aug 22 Sales	100		480 Dr.
Aug 30 Bank		480	0

K. Johnson

	Debit	Credit	Balance
2006	$	$	$
Aug 6 Sales	214		214 Dr.
Aug 12 Bank		214	0

D. Thomas

	Debit	Credit	Balance
2006	$	$	$
Aug 1 Sales	158		158 Dr.
Aug 15 Sales	206		364 Dr.
Aug 28 Cash		158	206 Dr.
Aug 31 Sales	118		324 Dr

H. Henry

	Debit	Credit	Balance
2006	$	$	$
Aug 5 Sales	300		300 Dr.
Aug 24 Returns		50	250 Dr.
Aug 28 Sales	540		790 Dr.
Aug 29 Bank		250	540 Dr

B. Walters

	Debit	Credit	Balance
2006	$	$	$
Aug 18 Sales	51		51 Dr.

E. Williams

	Debit	Credit	Balance
2006	$	$	$
Aug 2 Purchases		248	248 Cr.
Aug 18 Purchases		116	364 Cr.
Aug 21 Bank	100		264 Cr.

K. Patterson

	Debit	Credit	Balance
2006	$	$	$
Aug 8 Purchases		620	620 Cr.
Aug 14 Returns	20		600 Cr.
Aug 15 Purchases		200	800 Cr.
Aug 28 Bank	600		200 Cr.

It will be noticed that the balance is calculated again after every entry. This can be done quite simply when using a computer because it is the machine which calculates the new balance. Because the balance is altered after every transaction this method is often known as the **running balance** method.

When manual methods are being used it is often too much work to have to calculate a new balance after each entry. It also means that the greater the number of calculations, the greater the possibility of errors. For these reasons it is usual for students to use two-sided accounts. However, it is important to note that there is no difference in principle: the final balances are the same using either method.

New Terms

Balancing an account (p. 45): Finding and entering the difference between the two sides of an account on the lesser side, so as to equalize the two sides of an account

Summary

1 Debtors are disclosed by debit balances on customers' accounts.

2 Creditors are disclosed by credit balances on suppliers' accounts.

Exercises

6.1 Enter the following items in the necessary debtors' and creditors' accounts only; do *not* write up other accounts. Then balance down each personal account at the end of the month. (Keep your answer; it will be used as a basis for question 6.4X.)

2006
May 1 Sales on credit to H. Harvey $690, N. Morgan $153, J. Lindo $420.
May 4 Sales on credit to L. Masters $418, H. Harvey $66.
May 10 Returns inwards from H. Harvey $40, J. Lindo $20.
May 18 N. Morgan paid us by cheque $153.
May 20 J. Lindo paid us $400 by cheque.
May 24 H. Harvey paid us $300 by cash.
May 31 Sales on credit to L. Masters $203.

6.2 Enter the following in the personal accounts only; do *not* write up the other accounts. Then balance down each personal account at the end of the month. (Keep your answer; it will be used as the basis of question 6.5X)

2008
June 1 Purchases on credit from J. Young $458, L. Williams $120, G. Norman $708.
June 3 Purchases on credit from L. Williams $77, T. Harris $880.
June 10 We returned goods to G. Norman $22, J. Young $55.
June 15 Purchases on credit from J. Young $80.
June 19 We paid T. Harris by cheque $880.
June 28 We paid J. Young by cash $250.
June 30 We returned goods to L. Williams $17.

6.3 Enter the following in the personal accounts only; do *not* write up the other accounts. Balance down each personal account at the end of the month. After completing this, state which of the balances represent debtors and which are creditors.

2004
Sept 1 Sales on credit to D. Williams $458, J. Moore $235, G. Grant $98.
Sept 2 Purchases on credit from A. White $77, H. Samuels $231, P. Owen $65.

Sept 8 Sales on credit to J. Moore $444, F. Franklin $249.
Sept 10 Purchases on credit from H. Samuels $12, O. Oliver $222.
Sept 12 Returns inwards from G. Grant $9, J. Moore $26.
Sept 17 We returned goods to H. Samuels $24, O. Oliver $12.
Sept 20 We paid A. White by cheque $77.
Sept 24 D. Williams paid us by cheque $300.
Sept 26 We paid O. Oliver by cash $210.
Sept 28 D. Williams paid us by cash $100.
Sept 30 F. Franklin pays us by cheque $249.

6.4X Redraft each of the accounts given in your answer to 6.1 in three-column ledger style accounts as would be produced by a computer; see Section 6.3 of the text.

6.5X Redraft each of the accounts given in your answer to 6.2 in three-column ledger style accounts, as would be produced by a computer (see Section 6.3 of the text).

6.6X Enter the following items in the necessary personal accounts; do *not* write up the other accounts. Balance down each personal account at the end of the month.

2005
May 1 Purchases on credit from M. Sinclair $249, M. Brown $188, S. Thompson $260, D. Cox $62.
May 4 Purchases on credit from S. Thompson $55, M. Brown $77, P. Moss $100.
May 7 We paid P. Moss by cheque $100.
May 10 We returned goods to M. Brown $15, M. Sinclair $19.
May 12 Purchases on credit from M. Brown $278, S. Thompson $255.
May 19 We paid S. Thompson by cheque $570.
May 22 We returned goods to M. Sinclair $14.
May 28 Purchases on credit from S. Thompson $665, M. Brown $66.
May 31 We paid M. Brown by cash $125.

6.7X Enter the following items in the necessary personal accounts; do *not* write up the other accounts. Balance each personal account at the end of the month.

2004
Aug 1 Sales on credit to L. Sterling $445, L. Lindo $480, R. Spencer $221.
Aug 4 Goods returned to us by L. Sterling $15, R. Spencer $33.
Aug 8 Sales on credit to L. Lindo $66, R. Spencer $129, L. Banks $465.
Aug 9 We received a cheque for $430 from L. Sterling.
Aug 12 Sales on credit to R. Spencer $235, L. Banks $777.
Aug 19 Goods returned to us by L. Banks $21, R. Spencer $25.
Aug 22 We received cheques as follows: R. Spencer $300, L. Lindo $414.
Aug 31 Sales on credit to L. Lindo $887, L. Banks $442.

6.8X Enter the following, personal accounts only. Bring down balances at end of the month. After completing this, state which of the balances represent debtors and those which are creditors.

2007
May 1 Credit sales to B. Flynn $241, R. Kelly $29, J. Long $887, T. Fryer $124.
May 2 Credit purchases from S. Wood $148, T. DuQuesnay $27, R. Johnson $77, G. Henriques $108.
May 8 Credit sales to R. Kelly $74, J. Long $132.
May 9 Credit purchases from T. DuQuesnay $142, G. Henriques $44.
May 10 Goods returned to us by J. Long $17, T. Fryer $44.
May 12 Cash paid to us by T. Fryer $80.
May 15 We returned goods to S. Wood $8, G. Henriques $18.
May 19 We received cheques from J. Long $500, B. Flynn $241.
May 21 We sold goods on credit to B. Flynn $44, R. Kelly $280.
May 28 We paid by cheque the following: S. Wood $140; G. Henriques $50; R. Johnson $60.
May 31 We returned goods to G. Henriques $4.

CHAPTER **7**

The Trial Balance

Learning Objectives

- To explain why trial balance totals should equal one another.
- To demonstrate how to draw up a trial balance from a given set of figures.
- To understand that when some kinds of errors are made the trial balance totals can still equal one another.

7.1 Total Debit Entries = Total Credit Entries

You have already seen that the method of bookkeeping in use is that of the double entry method. This means:

- for each debit entry there is a credit entry;
- for each credit entry there is a debit entry.

All the items recorded in all the accounts on the debit side should equal in *total* all the items recorded on the credit side of the books. We need to check that for each debit entry there is also a credit entry. To see if the two totals are equal, usually known as seeing if the two sides of the books 'balance', a **trial balance** may be drawn up at the end of a period.

A form of a trial balance could be drawn up by listing all the accounts and adding together all the debit entries, at the same time adding together all the credit entries. Using the worked exercise on p. 54, such a trial balance would appear as in Exhibit 7.1. Note that it could not be drawn up until after all the entries had been made. It will therefore be dated as at 31 May 2005.

Exhibit 7.1

J. Charles Trial Balance as at 31 May 2005		
	Dr.	*Cr.*
	$	$
Purchases	309	
Sales		255
Returns outwards		15
Returns inwards	16	
D. Small	68	68
A. Lyon and Son		141
D. Hughes	60	60
M. Spencer	45	16
Cash	210	153
	708	708

7.2 Total Debit Balances = Total Credit Balances

The method described in Section 7.1 was not the accepted method of drawing up a trial balance, but it is the easiest to understand at first. In fact, a trial balance is a list of balances only, arranged according to whether they are debit balances or credit balances. If the trial balance shown above had been drawn up using the correct method, it would appear as in Exhibit 7.2.

Exhibit 7.2

J. Charles Trial Balance as at 31 May 2005		
	Dr.	*Cr.*
	$	$
Purchases	309	
Sales		255
Returns outwards		15
Returns inwards	16	
A. Lyon and Son		141
M. Spencer	29	
Cash	57	
	411	411

Here the two sides also 'balance'. The sums of $68 in D. Small's account, $60 in D. Hughes' account, $16 in M. Spencer's account and $153 in the cash account have however been cancelled out from each side of these accounts by taking only the *balances* instead of *totals*. As equal amounts have been cancelled from each side, $297 in all, the new totals should still equal one another, as in fact they do at $411.

This form of trial balance is the easiest to extract when there are more than a few transactions during the period. Also, the balances are either used later when the profits are being calculated, or else appear in a balance sheet. Trial balances therefore are not just drawn up to find errors.

7.3 A Worked Example

K. Patterson commenced in business on 1 May 2001. He entered the following transactions in his books, but had not balanced off the accounts:

2001		
May	1	Put $9,000 into a bank account for the business as capital.
	2	Bought $900 goods, on credit, from T. Worrall,
	3	Bought $250 goods, on credit, form K. Young.
	5	Cash sales $180.
	6	Returned $40 goods to T. Worrall.
	10	Sold goods for $590, on credit, to T. Moore.
	12	Cash sales $210.
	18	Bought $190 goods, on credit, from K. Young.
	21	Machinery bought for $550, payment being made by cheque.
	22	Sold goods for $220 on credit to C. Howe.
	23	T. Moore returned $140 goods to Patterson.
	25	C. Howe returned $10 goods to Patterson.
	28	Returned goods $80 to K. Young.
	29	Paid T. Worrall $860 by cheque.
	30	Paid K. Young $170 in cash.
	30	T. Moore paid Patterson $300 by cheque.
	31	Bought machinery for $2,700, on credit, from A. B. Ltd.

Books of K. Patterson

Bank

2001	$	2001	$
May 1 Capital	9,000	May 21 Machinery	550
May 30 T. Moore	300	May 29 T. Worrall	860

Cash

2001	$	2001	$
May 5 Sales	180	May 30 K. Young	170
May 12 Sales	210		

T. Worrall

2001	$	2001	$
May 6 Returns outwards	40	May 2 Purchases	900
May 29 Bank	860		

K. Young

2001	$	2001	$
May 28 Returns outwards	80	May 3 Purchases	250
May 30 Cash	170	May 18 Purchases	190

T. Moore

2001	$	2001	$
May 10 Sales	590	May 23 Returns inwards	140
		May 30 Bank	300

C. Howe

2001	$	2001	$
May 22 Sales	220	May 25 Returns inwards	10

A. B. Ltd

		2001	$
		May 31 Machinery	2,700

Capital

		2001	$
		May 1 Bank	9,000

Purchases

2001	$		
May 2 T. Worrall	900		
May 3 K. Young	250		
May 18 K. Young	190		

Sales

		2001	$
		May 5 Cash	180
		May 10 T. Moore	590
		May 12 Cash	210
		May 22 C. Howe	220

Returns Inwards

2001	$			
May 23 T. Moore	140			
May 25 C. Howe	10			

Returns Outwards

		2001	$
		May 6 T. Worrall	40
		May 28 K. Young	80

Machinery

2001	$		
May 21 Bank	550		
May 31 A. B. Ltd	2,700		

If the above accounts are balanced off, a trial balance would appear as shown in Exhibit 7.3. It must be pointed out that we do not just balance off accounts so that a trial balance can be drawn up. Later chapters will cover the uses to which the balances are put.

Exhibit 7.3

K. Patterson
Trial Balance as at 31 May 2001

	Dr.	*Cr.*
	$	$
Bank	7,890	
Cash	220	
K. Young		190
T. Moore	150	
C. Howe	210	
A. B. Ltd		2,700
Capital		9,000
Purchases	1,340	
Sales		1,200
Returns inwards	150	
Returns outwards		120
Machinery	3,250	
	13,210	13,210

7.4 The Uses of Trial Balances

Trial balances may be used:

- to check that the books 'balance', i.e. that every debit entry has been accompanied by a credit entry
- to ascertain the net amount of the error(s), should an error(s) have been made
- as a basis from which the trading account, profit and loss account and balance sheet are prepared (these will be explained later).

7.5 Trial Balances and Errors

It may at first sight appear that the balancing of a trial balance proves that the books are correct. This, however, is quite wrong. It means that certain types of errors have not been made, but there are several other types of errors that will not affect the balancing of a trial balance, such as omitting a transaction altogether. Examples of the errors which would be revealed, provided there are no compensating errors that cancel them out, are errors in additions; using one figure for the debit entry and another figure for the credit entry; entering only one aspect of a transaction and so on. We shall consider these in greater detail in later chapters.

7.6 Multiple-choice Self-test Questions

The Caribbean Examinations Council sets multiple-choice questions in accounting.

Multiple-choice questions certainly give an examiner the opportunity to cover briefly large parts of the syllabus. Students who omit to study areas of the syllabus will be caught out by an examiner's use of multiple-choice questions. No longer will it be possible to say that it is highly probable a certain topic will not be tested – the examiner can easily cover it with a multiple-choice question.

We have deliberately set blocks of multiple-choice questions at given places in this textbook, rather than a few at the end of each chapter. Such questions are relatively easy to answer a few minutes after reading the chapter; by asking yourself the questions later, your powers of recall and understanding are far better tested. It also gives you practice at answering a few questions in one block, as in an examination.

Each multiple-choice question has a 'stem', i.e. the part that poses the problem; a 'key', which is the one correct answer, and a number of 'distractors', i.e. incorrect answers. The key plus the distractors are known as the 'options'.

If you do not know the answer you should guess. You may be right by chance, or you may remember something subconsciously. In any event, unless the examiner warns otherwise, he or she will expect you to guess if you don't know the answer.

You should now attempt Set no. 1, which contains 20 multiple-choice questions, on p. 407.

New Terms

Trial balance (p. 52): A list of account titles and their balances in the books on a specific date, shown in debit and credit columns.

Summary

1 Trial balances are one form of checking on the arithmetical accuracy of the books.

2 Errors can be made in the accounts which will not be shown up by the trial balance.

Exercises

7.1 You are to enter up the necessary accounts for the month of May from the following details, and then balance off the accounts and extract a trial balance as at 31 May 2006.

2006
May 1 Started firm with capital in cash of $250.
May 2 Bought goods on credit from the following persons: D. Ellis, $54; C. Mendez, $87; K. Gibson, $25; D. Booth, $76; L. Lowe, $64.
May 4 Sold goods on credit to: C. Bailey, $43; B. Hughes, $62; H. Spencer, $176.
May 6 Paid rent by cash, $12.
May 9 Bailey paid us his account by cheque, $43.
May 10 H. Spencer paid us $150 by cheque.
May 12 We paid the following by cheque: K. Gibson, $25; D. Ellis, $54.
May 15 Paid carriage by cash, $23.
May 18 Bought goods on credit from C. Mendez, $43; D. Booth, $110.
May 21 Sold goods on credit to B. Hughes, $67.
May 31 Paid rent by cheque, $18.

7.2 Write up the accounts from the following details for the month of March, and extract a trial balance as at 31 March 2004.

2004
Mar 1 Started business with $800 in the bank.
Mar 2 Bought goods on credit from the following persons: K. Henriques, $76; M. Hyatt, $27; T. Braham, $56.
Mar 5 Cash sales, $87.
Mar 6 Paid staff in cash, $14.
Mar 7 Sold goods on credit to: H. Elliott, $35: L. Lindo, $42; J. Carvalho, $72.
Mar 9 Bought goods for cash, $46.
Mar 10 Bought goods on credit from: M. Hyatt, $57; T. Braham, $98.
Mar 12 Paid staff in cash, $14.
Mar 13 Sold goods on credit to: L. Lindo, $32; J. Carvalho, $23.
Mar 15 Bought shop fixtures on credit from Betta Ltd, $50.
Mar 17 Paid M. Hyatt by cheque, $84.
Mar 18 Returned goods to T. Braham, $20.
Mar 21 Paid Betta Ltd a cheque for, $50.
Mar 24 J. Carvalho paid us his account by cheque, $95.
Mar 27 Returned goods to K. Henriques, $24.
Mar 30 J. King lent us $60 by cash.
Mar 31 Bought a motor van paying by cheque, $400.

7.3 The following transactions are to be entered up in the ledger for June, and a trial balance extracted as at 30 June 2008.

2008
June 1 Started business with $600 in the bank and $50 cash in hand.
June 2 Bought $500 goods on credit from C. Jones.
June 3 Credit sales: H. Henry, $66; N. Neita, $25; P. Pitter, $43.
June 4 Goods bought for cash, $23.
June 5 Bought motor van paying by cheque, $256.
June 7 Paid motor expenses by cheque, $12.
June 9 Credit sales: B. Barnes, $24; K. Lyn, $26; M. Moore, $65.

June 11 Goods bought on credit: C. Jones, $240, N. Moss, $62; O. Hue, $46.
June 13 Goods returned by us to C. Jones, $25.
June 15 Paid motor expenses by cash, $5.
June 19 Goods returned to us by N. Neita, $11.
June 20 Cash taken for own use (drawings), $10.
June 21 Paid the following by cheque: N. Moss, $62; O. Hue, $46.
June 23 H. Henry paid us in cash, $66.
June 25 P. Pitter paid us by cheque, $43.
June 26 Cash sales, $34.
June 27 Cash taken for own use, $24.
June 28 Goods returned by us to C. Jones, $42.
June 29 Paid for postage stamps by cash, $4.
June 30 Credit sales: N. Nieta, $43; M. Edgar, $67; K. Lyn, $45.

7.4X Record the following details in the ledger for the month of November 2003 and extract a trial balance as at 30 November.

2003
Nov 1 Started with $5,000 in the bank.
Nov 3 Bought goods on credit from: T. Henriques, $160; J. Smith, $230; W. Rogers, $400; P. Bonitto, $310.
Nov 5 Cash sales, $240.
Nov 6 Paid rent by cheque, $20.
Nov 7 Paid rates by cheque, $190.
Nov 11 Sold goods on credit to: L. Matthews, $48; K. Alberga, $32; R. Hall, $1,170.
Nov 17 Paid staff by cash, $40.
Nov 18 We returned goods to: T. Henriques, $14; P. Bonitto, $20.
Nov 19 Bought goods on credit from: P. Bonitto, $80; W. Rogers, $270; D. Diaz, $130.
Nov 20 Goods returned to us: K. Alberga, $2; L. Matthews, $4.
Nov 21 Bought motor van on credit from U. Z. Motors, $500.
Nov 23 Paid the following by cheque: T. Henriques, $146; J. Smith, $230; W. Rogers, $300.
Nov 25 Bought another motor van, paying by cheque immediately, $700.
Nov 26 Received a loan of $400 cash from A. Williams.
Nov 28 Received cheques from: L. Matthews, $44; L. Alberga, $30.
Nov 30 Proprietor brings a further $300 into the business, by a payment into the business bank account.

7.5X Record the following for the month of June, balance off all the accounts, and then extract a trial balance as at 30 June 2004.

2004
June 1 Started business with $3,500 cash.
June 2 Put $2,800 of the cash into a bank account.
June 3 Bought goods for cash, $150.
June 4 Bought goods on credit from: L. Coke, $360; M. Burton, $490; T. Hill, $110; C. Small, $340.
June 5 Bought stationery on credit from: Subaran Ltd, $170.
June 6 Sold goods on credit to: S. Walters, $90: T. Binns, $150; C. Howard, $190; P. Peart, $160.
June 8 Paid rent by cheque, $55.
June 10 Bought fixtures on credit from Matalon Ltd, $480.
June 11 Paid staff in cash, $120.
June 14 Returned goods to M. Burton, $40; T. Hill, $60.
June 15 Bought motor van by cheque, $700.
June 16 Received loan from J. Henry by cheque, $600.
June 18 Goods returned to us by: S. Walters, $20; C. Howard, $40.
June 21 Cash sales, $90.
June 24 Sold goods on credit to: T. Binns, $100; P. Peart, $340; J. Smart, $115.
June 26 We paid the following by cheque: M. Burton, $450; T. Hill, $50.

Cont'd

June 29	Received cheques from: J. Smart, $115; T. Binns, $250.
June 30	Received a further loan from J. Henry by cash, $200.
June 30	Received $500 cash from P. Peart.

7.6X You are required to enter up the following transactions for May 2005. The accounts are then to be balanced off and a trial balance extracted as at 31 May 2005.

2005	
May 1	R. Groves started firm by depositing $15,000 into a bank account.
May 2	Bought motor van on credit from K. Fung and Son, $3,400.
May 2	Bought shop fittings by cheque, $600.
May 3	Bought goods on credit from: K. Hollar Ltd, $1,350; C. DeSouza, $810; P. Tucker, $180; C. Ross Ltd, $440.
May 4	Paid rent by cheque, $80.
May 5	Received loan of $300 in cash from D. Kong.
May 5	Sold goods on credit to: H. Tai and Partners, $500; P. Nunes, $373; D. Price, $140; P. Wong Ltd, $390.
May 6	Bought office equipment on credit from Arthur Young and Co., $740.
May 7	Cash sales, $260.
May 8	Paid staff in cash, $90.
May 9	Bought office stationery for cash, $28.
May 11	Sold goods on credit to: D. Price, $80; L. Grant and Son, $115.
May 12	Returned goods to: C. DeSouza, $54; C. Ross Ltd, $60.
May 13	Paid K. Fung and Son $3,400 by cheque.
May 14	Bought office stationery on credit from Rowland Supplies, $150.
May 15	Bought goods on credit from: P. Tucker, $310; R. Grizzle, $770.
May 16	Goods returned to us by: P. Nunes, $11; P. Wong Ltd, $45.
May 17	Paid K. Hollar Ltd, $1,350 by cheque.
May 18	Paid staff in cash, $95.
May 19	Repaid part of D. Kong's loan by cheque, $120.
May 20	Cheques received from D. Price, $80; P. Wong Ltd, $345.
May 21	R. Groves took $100 drawings in cash.
May 22	Some of the shop fittings were unsuitable and were sold for $60 cash.
May 24	Bought another motor van paying by cheque immediately, $3,700.
May 26	Paid staff in cash, $110.
May 28	Bought goods for cash, $90.

CHAPTER **8**

Trading and Profit and Loss Accounts: An Introduction

Learning Objectives

- To understand the difference between gross profit and net profit.
- To be able to draw up a trading and profit and loss account from information given in a trial balance.
- To recognize that an adjustment is needed for the closing stock at the end of a period.
- To be able to enter up the capital account after the trading and profit and loss accounts have been drawn up.
- To be able to draw up trading and profit and loss accounts using both the horizontal and vertical methods.

8.1 Purpose of the Trading and Profit and Loss Account

People run businesses to try to make a profit. If they are not successful they may lose money. To calculate how much profit or loss has been made over a period of time, a **trading and profit and loss account** is prepared.

Normally, all businesses prepare trading and profit and loss accounts at least once a year. They could be prepared for a lesser period if required.

The main purpose of a trading and profit and loss account is for the owners to be able to see how profitably the business is being run. It is also used for other purposes; for instance, the income tax inspector will want to see it in order to work out the tax bill.

8.2 Format for the Trading and Profit and Loss Account

One of the most important uses of the trading and profit and loss accounts is that of comparing the results obtained with the results expected. In a trading organization, a lot of attention is paid to how much profit is made, before deducting expenses, for every $100 of sales. So that this can easily be seen in the profit calculations, the account in which profit is calculated is split into two sections – one in which the **gross profit** is found, and the next section in which the **net profit** is calculated.

Gross profit (calculated in the **trading account**)	This is the excess of sales over the cost of goods sold in the period.
Net profit (calculated in the **profit and loss account**)	This is what is left of the gross profit after all other expenses have been deducted.

It is possible to have one account called a trading account, and another called a profit and loss account. Normally, however, they are combined to form one account called the trading and profit and loss account.

8.3 Information Needed

Before drawing up a trading and profit and loss account you should look at the trial balance. This contains nearly all the information needed. (Later on in this book you will see that certain adjustments have to be made, but we will ignore these at this stage.)

Our first look is at the preparation of a trading and profit and loss account for K. Williams, after his first year's trading. His trial balance appears as Exhibit 8.1. We are going to assume that all the goods purchased were sold by 31 December 2003, leaving no stock at that date.

Exhibit 8.1

K. Williams
Trial Balance as on 31 December 2003

	Dr.	*Cr.*
	$	$
Sales		9,650
Purchases	7,150	
General expenses	550	
Fixtures and fittings	1,840	
Debtors	1,460	
Creditors		1,180
Capital		2,800
Drawings	1,750	
Bank	820	
Cash	60	
	13,630	13,630

8.4 Horizontal and Vertical Trading and Profit and Loss Accounts

In the following sections (8.5 and 8.7), we will look at trading and profit and loss accounts drawn up using the horizontal style. The left-hand side is the debit side, while the right-hand side is the credit side. These accounts can therefore be seen as part of the double entry system, and students should be able to understand why each item is shown as either a debit or a credit in them.

In Section 8.9 we will see how the trading and profit and loss account can be shown using a vertical style.

8.5 Preparation of a Trading and Profit and Loss Account

To Calculate Gross Profit

Remember that:

Sales – Cost of goods sold = Gross profit

We could in fact calculate this using simple arithmetic. However, we must remember that we are using double entry methods. The answer will be the same whether normal arithmetic is used or proper double entry methods. To enable you to see fully how the calculations are performed using double entry, we will show the balances for Sales and Purchases in Exhibit 8.1, and how the entries are made to transfer these items into the calculations within the trading account. The following steps are carried out.

1. Transfer the credit balance of the sales account to the credit of the trading account portion of the trading and profit and loss account.
   Debit: Sales account.
   Credit: Trading account.
2. Transfer the debit balance of the purchases account to the debit of the trading account.
   Debit: Trading account.
   Credit: Purchases account.
   Remember, in this case there is no stock of unsold goods. This means that:
   Purchases = Cost of goods sold
3. If sales are greater than the cost of goods sold, the difference is gross profit. (If not, the answer would be a gross loss.) We will carry this gross profit figure from the trading account part down to the profit and loss part. The double entry for gross profit is therefore as follows.
   Debit: Trading account.
   Credit: Profit and loss account.

Exhibit 8.2 shows this done for Exhibit 8.1. Notice that, after the trading account has been completed, there are no balances remaining in the sales and purchases accounts. They are now *closed*.

Exhibit 8.2

Sales

	$		$
2003		2003	
Dec 31 Trading a/c	9,650	Dec 31 Balance b/d	9,650

K. Williams
Trading and Profit and Loss Account for the year ended 31 December 2003

	$		$
Purchases	7,150 (2)	Sales	(1) 9,650
Gross profit c/d	2,500		
	9,650		9,650
		Gross profit b/d	(3) 2,500

Purchases

	$		$
2003		2003	
Dec 31 Balance b/d	7,150	Dec 31 Trading a/c	7,150

To Calculate Net Profit and Record It

Remember that:

Gross profit – Expenses = Net profit

Remember also that:

Old capital + Net profit = New capital

The double entry needed to carry out these calculations is as follows.

1 Transfer the debit balances on expenses accounts to the debit of the profit and loss account.

Debit: Profit and loss account.
Credit: Expenses accounts.

2 Transfer the net profit, when found, to the capital account to show the increase in capital.

Debit: Profit and loss account.
Credit: Capital account.

Exhibit 8.3 illustrates the above procedures.

Exhibit 8.3

K. Williams
Trading and Profit and Loss Account for the year ended 31 December 2003

	$		$
Purchases	7,150	Sales	9,650
Gross profit c/d	2,500		
	9,650		9,650
General expenses	550	Gross profit b/d	2,500
Net profit	1,950		
	2,500		2,500

General Expenses

2003	$	2003	$
Dec 31 Balance b/d	550	Dec 31 Profit and Loss a/c	550

Capital

		2003	$
		Dec 31 Balance b/d	2,800
		31 Net profit	1,950

8.6 Completion of Capital Account

You have seen that we credit the capital account with the amount of net profit. We have therefore recorded the increase in capital.

In the trial balance, Exhibit 8.1, we can see that there are drawings of $1,750. Drawings means withdrawals of capital.

After entering the net profit in the capital account, we can now complete the account. To do this we transfer the drawings to the capital account.

Debit: Capital account.

Credit: Drawings account.

The completed capital and drawings accounts are shown in Exhibit 8.4.

Exhibit 8.4

Drawings

2003		$	2003		$
Dec 31	Balance b/d	1,750	Dec 31	Capital	1,750

Capital

2003		$	2003		$
Dec 31	Drawings	1,750	Dec 31	Balance b/d	2,800
Dec 31	Balance c/d	3,000	Dec 31	Net profit	1,950
		4,750			4,750
			2004		
			Jan 1	Balance c/d	3,000

8.7 Stock of Unsold Goods at End of First Accounting Period

Usually some of the goods bought (purchases) have not been sold by the end of the accounting period. We have already seen that gross profit is calculated as follows:

Sales – Cost of goods sold = Gross profit

But purchases equals cost of goods sold only if there is no stock at the end of a period. We can calculate cost of goods sold as follows:

What we bought in the period:	Purchases
Less Goods bought but not sold in the period:	Closing stock
	Cost of goods sold

Remember, we are concerned here with the very first trading and profit and loss account of a business, where there is no opening stock. In Section 10.3 we will look at the later years of a business.

Let us look at the drawing up of a trading and profit and loss account for L. Sands. Her trial balance is shown as Exhibit 8.5 and was drawn up after her first year of trading.

Exhibit 8.5

L. Sands
Trial Balance as on 31 December 2005

	Dr.	*Cr.*
	$	$
Sales		3,850
Purchases	2,900	
Rent	240	
Lighting	150	
General expenses	60	
Fixtures and fittings	500	
Debtors	680	
Creditors		910
Bank	1,510	
Cash	20	
Drawings	700	
Capital		2,000
	6,760	6,760

Note: On 31 December 2005, at the close of trading, L. Sands had goods costing $300 which were unsold. The cost of goods sold figure will be:

	$
Purchases	2,900
Less Closing stock	300
Cost of goods sold	2,600

Given the figure of sales $3,850, the gross profit can be calculated:

Sales – Cost of goods sold = Gross profit
$3,850 – $2,600 = $1,250

The net profit will be:

Gross profit – Expenses = Net profit
$1,250 – $(240 + 150 + 60 = 450) = $800

We will now see this shown in double entry in Exhibit 8.6.

Exhibit 8.6

Sales

2005	$	2005	$
Dec 31 Trading a/c	3,850	Dec 31 Balance b/d	3,850

Purchases

2005	$	2005	$
Dec 31 Balance b/d	2,900	Dec 31 Trading a/c	2,900

Rent

2005	$	2005	$
Dec 31 Balance b/d	240	Dec 31 Profit and loss a/c	240

Lighting

2005	$	2005	$
Dec 31 Balance b/d	150	Dec 31 Profit and loss a/c	150

General Expenses

2005	$	2005	$
Dec 31 Balance b/d	60	Dec 31 Profit and loss a/c	60

Stock

2005	$		
Dec 31 Trading a/c	300		

L. Sands
Trading and Profit and Loss Account for the year ended 31 December 2005

	$		$
Purchases	2,900	Sales	3,850
Gross profit c/d	1,250	Closing stock	300
	4,150		4,150
Rent	240	Gross profit b/d	1,250
Lighting	150		
General expenses	60		
Net profit	800		
	1,250		1,250

To record the stock we have entered the following.

Debit: Stock a count.

Credit: Trading account.

This means that there is now a balance on the stock account. We had to record it there because at 31 December 2005 we had an asset, $300 of stock, but there was no record of that fact in our books. We have now brought our records up to date by showing the stock in our accounts. Without the stock accounts at 31 December 2005, our records would have been incomplete.

8.8 The Capital Account

The capital account can now be completed.

Capital

2005		$	2005		$
Dec 31	Drawings	700	Jan 1	Cash	2,000
Dec 31	Balance c/d	2,100	Dec 31	Net profit from profit and loss a/c	800
		2,800			2,800
			2006		
			Jan 1	Balance b/d	2,100

Drawings

2005		$	2005		$
Dec 31	Balance b/d	700	Dec 31	Capital	700

8.9 The Vertical Style for Trading and Profit and Loss Accounts

We will now use the vertical style for drawing up a trading and profit and loss account in Exhibit 8.7, using the information in Exhibit 8.6. It looks as follows.

Exhibit 8.7

L. Sands
Trading and Profit and Loss Account for the year ended 31 December 2005

	$	$
Sales		3,850
Less Cost of goods sold:		
Purchases	2,900	
Less Closing stock	300	2,600
Gross profit		1,250
Less Expenses		
Rent	240	
Lighting expenses	150	
General expenses	60	450
Net profit		800

You can see that the figures used are exactly the same using either the horizontal or vertical methods of display.

This is a more modern method of presentation. It would make more sense to someone who knew very little about accounting, as it does not show it in a debit/credit way.

However, showing the horizontal style first probably makes it easier for students to see how the double entry system is used to calculate profits.

8.10 The Balances Still in Our Books

Taking Exhibit 8.6, but including the adjustment for closing stock of $300, we can now see which balances still exist. We can do this by drawing up a trial balance as it would appear once the trading and profit and loss account was completed. This is shown in Exhibit 8.7.

Accounts Closed

Sales Purchases	} transferred to trading account
Rent Lighting General expenses	} transferred to profit and loss account
Drawings	transferred to capital account

Accounts not Closed

The one account that was not in the original trial balance was the stock account. It was not brought into our books until the trading account was prepared. These balances will be used by us when we look at the balance sheets.

Exhibit 8.8

L. Sands
Trial Balance as on 31 December 2005
(after Trading and Profit and Loss Accounts completed)

	Dr.	*Cr.*
	$	$
Fixtures and fittings	500	
Debtors	680	
Creditors		910
Stock	300	
Bank	1,510	
Cash	20	
Capital		2,100
	3,010	3,010

New Terms

Trading and profit and loss account (p. 61): Combined account in which both gross and net profits are calculated.
Gross profit (p. 62): The figure of sales, less the cost of goods sold.
Net profit (p. 62): Gross profit less expenses.
Trading account (p. 62): Account in which gross profit is calculated.
Profit and loss account (p. 62): Account in which net profit is calculated.

Summary

1 Stocks of unsold goods needs to be brought into the calculations in the trading account.
2 The net profit is added to capital by crediting it in the capital account.
3 Balances on accounts not closed off are carried forward to the following period.

Exercises

8.1 From the trial balance of B. Charles, who has been in business for one year, extract a trading and profit and loss account for the year ended 31 December 2006. A balance sheet is not required.

Trial Balance as at 31 December 2006

	Dr.	*Cr.*
	$	$
Sales		18,462
Purchases	14,629	
Pay	2,150	
Motor expenses	520	
Rent and rates	670	
Insurance	111	
General expenses	105	
Premises	1,500	
Motor vehicles	1,200	
Debtors	1,950	
Creditors		1,538
Cash at bank	1,654	
Cash in hand	40	
Drawings	895	
Capital		5,424
	25,424	25,424

Stock at 31 December 2006 was $2,548.
(Keep your answer; it will be used later in question 9.1.)

8.2 From the following trial balance of C. Wynter, who has been trading for one year, you are required to draw up a trading and profit and loss account for the year ended 30 June 2004. A balance sheet is not required.

Trial Balance as at 31 June 2004

	Dr.	*Cr.*
	$	$
Sales		28,794
Purchases	23,803	
Rent and rates	854	
Lighting expenses	422	
Pay	3,164	
Insurance	105	
Shop buildings	50,000	
Shop fixtures	1,000	
Debtors	3,166	
Trade expenses	506	
Creditors		1,206
Cash at bank	3,847	
Drawings	2,400	
Motor vans	5,500	
Motor running expenses	1,133	
Capital		65,900
	95,900	95,900

Cont'd

Stock at 30 June 2004 was $4,166.
(Keep your answer; it will be used later in question 9.2.)

8.3X From the following trial balance of F. Chaplin, draw up a trading and profit and loss account for the year ended 31 December 2008. A balance sheet is not required. She has been in business for one year only.

Trial Balance as at 31 December 2008

	Dr.	*Cr.*
	$	$
General expenses	210	
Rent and rates	400	
Motor expenses	735	
Pay	3,560	
Insurance	392	
Purchases	18,385	
Sales		26,815
Motor vehicle	2,800	
Creditors		5,160
Debtors	4,090	
Premises	20,000	
Cash at bank	1,375	
Cash in hand	25	
Capital		24,347
Drawings	4,350	
	56,322	56,322

Stock at 31 December 2008 was $4,960.
(Keep your answer; it will be used later in question 9.3X.)

8.4X Extract a trading and profit and loss account for the year ended 30 June 2004 for F. Kidd. The business has been in existence for one year. The trial balance as at 30 June 2004 was as follows.

	Dr.	*Cr.*
	$	$
Rent and rates	1,560	
Insurance	305	
Lighting expenses	516	
Motor expenses	1,960	
Pay	4,850	
Sales		35,600
Purchases	30,970	
Trade expenses	806	
Motor vans	3,500	
Creditors		3,250
Debtors	6,810	
Shop fixtures	3,960	
Shop buildings	28,000	
Cash at bank	1,134	
Drawings	6,278	
Capital		51,799
	90,649	90,649

Cont'd

Stock at 30 June 2004 was $9,960.
(Keep your answer; it will be used later in question 9.4X.)

CHAPTER **9**

Balance Sheets

Learning Objectives

- To be able to draw up a balance sheet from information given in a trial balance.
- To understand that balance sheets are not part of the double entry system.
- To appreciate the need for showing balances under the headings 'fixed assets', 'current assets', 'current liabilities' and 'capital'.
- To be able to draw up balance sheets using both the horizontal and the vertical methods.

9.1 Contents of the Balance Sheet

You saw in Chapter 2 that balance sheets contain details of assets, liabilities and capital. These details have to be found in our records and then written out as a balance sheet.

It is easy to find these details. They consist of all the balances remaining in our records once the trading and profit and loss account for the period has been completed. All balances remaining have to be assets, capital or liabilities. All the other balances should have been closed off when the trading and profit and loss account was completed.

9.2 Drawing up a Balance Sheet

Let us now look again at the trial balance of L. Sands (Exhibit 8.7) as on 31 December 2005 *after* the trading and profit and loss account had been prepared. This is presented in Exhibit 9.1.

Exhibit 9.1

L. Sands Trial Balance as at 31 December 2005 (after Trading and Profit and Loss Accounts completed)		
	Dr.	*Cr.*
	$	$
Fixtures and fittings	500	
Debtors	680	
Creditors		910
Stock	300	
Bank	1,510	
Cash	20	
Capital		2,100
	3,010	3,010

We can now draw up a balance sheet as at 31 December 2005 (Exhibit 9.2). You saw examples of balance sheets in Chapter 2. As you saw in Chapter 2, assets are shown on the left-hand side, and capital and liabilities are on the right-hand side.

Exhibit 9.2

L. Sands Balance Sheet as at 31 December 2005			
Assets	$	*Capital and liabilities*	$
Fixtures and fittings	500	Capital	2,100
Stock	300	Creditors	910
Debtors	680		
Bank	1,510		
Cash	20		
	3,010		3,010

This balance sheet could, in fact, be drawn up using a better style. We will see how this can be done later in the chapter.

9.3 No Double Entry in Balance Sheets

It may seem very strange to you to learn that balance sheets are *not* part of the double entry system.

When we draw up accounts such as cash account, rent account, sales account, trading and profit and loss account and so on, we are writing up part of the double entry system. We make entries on the debit and credit sides of these accounts.

In drawing up a balance sheet we do not enter anything in the various accounts. We do not actually transfer the fixtures balance or the stock balance, or any of the others, to the balance sheet.

All we do is *list* the asset, capital and liabilities balances so as to form a balance sheet. This means that none of these accounts have been closed off. *Nothing is entered in the accounts.*

When the next accounting period starts, these accounts are still open containing balances. As a result of business transactions, entries are then made in them to add to, or deduct from, the amounts shown in the accounts using normal double entry.

If you see the word 'account' you will know that it is part of the double entry system, and will include debit and credit entries. If the word 'account' cannot be used, it is not part of double entry. For instance the following are not 'accounts', and are therefore *not* part of double entry:

- **trial balance** this is simply a proof of the equality of debits and credits in the accounts;
- **balance sheet** this is a list of balances arranged according to whether they are asset, capital or liabilities, to show the financial position of the firm on a specific date.

9.4 Balance Sheet Layout: 'Order of Permanence' Method

You would not expect to go into a department store and see goods for sale all mixed up and not laid out properly. You would expect the goods to be displayed so that you could easily find them. Similarly, in balance sheets we do not want all the items shown in just any order: we want them displayed so that useful information can easily be seen.

For people such as bank managers, accountants and investors who look at a lot of different balance sheets, we want to keep to one method so as to make a comparison of balance sheets easier. What you are going to look at now is a method for showing items in balance sheets. This first method is the one used in the United Kingdom and the majority of Commonwealth countries, and is known as the 'order of permanence'. In North America a completely different method is used, known as the 'order of liquidity'. This will be looked at later, in Section 9.5.

Assets

Let us look at the assets side first. We are going to show the assets under two headings, **fixed assets** and **current assets**.

Assets are called fixed assets when they:

- are of long life
- are to be used in the business
- were not bought only for the purposes of resale.

Examples: buildings, machinery, motor vehicles, fixtures and fittings.

Fixed assets are listed starting with those the business will keep the longest, down to those which will not be kept so long. We can say the same thing simply as starting with the most permanent asset, and continuing down the list of assets in the 'order of permanency', finishing with the least permanent asset. For instance:

- land and buildings
- fixtures and fittings
- machinery
- motor vehicles.

Current assets are cash in hand, cash at bank, debtors, items held for resale at a profit or items that have a short life. These are listed starting with the asset furthest away from being turned into cash and finishing with cash itself. For instance:

- stock
- debtors
- cash at bank
- cash in hand.

Capital and Liabilities

The order on the other side of the balance sheet is:

- capital
- **long-term liabilities**: for instance, loans that do not have to be repaid in the near future
- **current liabilities**: items to be paid for in the near future.

9.5 Balance Sheet Layout: Order of Liquidity Method

The term 'liquid' is used to describe how easily or quickly an asset may be turned into cash. This means that the most **liquid asset** is cash itself, while the most difficult asset to turn into cash is something held not for purposes of turning into cash, but to keep for permanent use in the business, and which may take quite some time to turn into cash even if it came to be sold. These least liquid assets can therefore be seen to be fixed assets, with land and buildings probably being the fixed assets that would take longest to turn into cash.

In North America, as well as in many other countries, balance sheets are shown in the 'order of liquidity', so that the most liquid asset is shown first, i.e. cash, and so on until the least liquid asset is shown, last of all. This method is therefore the complete opposite of the 'permanency' method.

In North America the term 'accounts receivable' is used instead of 'debtors', while 'accounts payable' means the same as 'creditors'. There are other slight differences, but the general principles of accounting are exactly the same whether it is accounting in the Caribbean, North America or the United Kingdom. Former Communist countries such as Russia and Poland are now starting to use the same methods of accounting as you are now studying.

9.6 A Properly Drawn Up Balance Sheet (Horizontal Style)

Exhibit 9.3 shows Exhibit 9.2 drawn up in better style using the 'order of permanence' method. Also read the notes following the exhibit.

Exhibit 9.3

L. Sands
Balance Sheet as at 31 December 2005

	$	$		$	$
Fixed assets			*Capital*		
Furniture and fittings		500	Cash introduced	2,000	
			Add Net profit		
Current assets			for the year	800	
Stock	300			2,800	
Debtors	680		*Less* Drawings	700	
Bank	1,510				2,100
Cash	20		*Current liabilities*		
		2,510	Creditors		910
		3,010			3,010

Notes:

- A total for capital and for each class of assets and liabilities should be shown. An example of this is the $2,510 total of current assets. To do this, the figures for each asset are listed, and only the total is shown in the end column.
- You do not have to write the word 'account' after each item.
- The owner will be most interested in the amount of capital. To show only the final balance of $2,100 means that the owner will not know how it was calculated. So we show the full details of the capital account.
- Look at the date on the balance sheet. Now compare it with the dates put on the top of the trading and profit and loss account. The balance sheet is a position statement; it is shown as being at one point in time, i.e. as at 31 December 2005. The trading and profit and loss account is different. It is for a period of time, in this case for a whole year.

9.7 Vertical-Style Balance Sheets

Exhibit 9.3 is now shown in Exhibit 9.4 using the more modern vertical style.

Exhibit 9.4

L. Sands Balance Sheet as at 31 December 2005		
	$	$
Fixed assets		
Fixtures and fittings		500
Current assets		
Stock	300	
Debtors	680	
Bank	1,510	
Cash	20	
	2,510	
Less current liabilities		
Creditors	910	
Working capital		1,600
		2,100
Financed by:		
Capital		
Cash introduced		2,000
Add Net profit for the year		800
		2,800
Less Drawings		700
		2,100

In a vertical-style balance sheet the terms of fixed assets, current assets, current liabilities and capital mean exactly the same as for a horizontal balance sheet. All we have done is to show them in a different way, vertically instead of side by side (horizontally).

It is also usual to show the total of the current liabilities deducted from the total of the current assets. The figure thus shown is known as *working capital.*

If there were any long-term liabilities, e.g. a loan which does not have to be repaid within the next twelve months, then that would be deducted from the total of fixed assets plus net current assets. We will see an example of this in the next chapter in Exhibit 10.8 on p. 87.

9.8 Examinations and Horizontal- and Vertical-style Final Accounts

Up to the time of writing this edition, the examinations set by the CXC for the Basic and General Proficiency examinations have used the horizontal style for final accounts. This will probably change over the next few years, some questions being asked using the vertical style as well.

This will reflect what is happening in the world of business. More and more businesses now produce their final accounts using the vertical style. This style is easier to understand for those who do not know a lot about accounts.

New Terms

Fixed assets (p. 76): Assets bought which have a long life and are to be used in the business.

Current assets (p. 77): Assets consisting of cash, goods for resale or items having a short life.

Long-term liabilities (p. 77): Liabilities not having to be paid for in the near future, which is taken to be one year.

Current liabilities (p. 77): Liabilities to be paid for in the near future, which is taken to be one year.

Liquid assets (p. 77): Assets that can easily or quickly be turned into cash.

Summary

1 All balances remaining on a trial balance after the trading and profit and loss account for a period has been drawn up are displayed in a balance sheet dated the last day of the period.

2 The balance sheet is *not* part of double entry.

3 Fixed assets are shown before current assets in a balance sheet when working in order of permanence.

4 Capital is shown before liabilities in a horizontal balance sheet.

Exercises

9.1 Complete question 8.1 by drawing up a balance sheet as at 31 December 2006.

9.2 Complete question 8.2 by drawing up a balance sheet as at 30 June 2004.

9.3X Complete question 8.3X by drawing up a balance sheet as at 31 December 2008.

9.4X Complete question 8.4X by drawing up a balance sheet as at 30 June 2004.

CHAPTER **10**

Trading and Profit and Loss Accounts and Balance Sheets: Further Considerations

Learning Objectives

- To be able to record returns inwards and returns outwards in the final accounts.
- To understand that carriage inwards on goods is treated to be part of the cost of the goods.
- To realise that carriage outwards is an expense to be entered in the profit and loss account.
- To be able to adjust the final accounts properly for both the opening and closing stocks of the periods.
- To appreciate that costs of putting goods into a saleable condition should be charged to the trading account in a merchandising firm.

10.1 Carriage Inwards

Carriage (cost of transport of goods) into a firm is called **carriage inwards**.

When you buy goods, the cost of carriage inwards may either be included as part of the price, or you may have to pay separately for it. Suppose you were buying certain goods. One supplier might sell them to you for $100, and would deliver the goods and not bill you for carriage. Another supplier might sell exactly the same goods to you for $95, but you would have to pay $5 to a haulage firm for carriage inwards, i.e. a total cost of $100.

To keep the cost of buying goods shown on the same basis, carriage inwards is always added to the purchases in the trading account. The following transfer is made.

Debit: Trading account.
Credit: Carriage inwards account.

10.2 Carriage Outwards

Carriage from a firm out to its customers is called **carriage outwards**.

This is always treated as an expense to be transferred to the debit of the profit and loss account. The following transfer is made.

Debit: Profit and loss account.

Credit: Carriage outwards account.

Exhibit 10.1 shows the items in a trial balance necessary for the trading and profit and loss account for the year ended 31 December 2005 for G. Grant.

Exhibit 10.1

G. Grant
Trial Balance as at 31 December 2005 (extracts)

	Dr.	*Cr.*
	$	$
Sales		6,000
Purchases	4,000	
Carriage inwards	350	
Carriage outwards	280	
Other expenses	220	

The closing stock on 31 December 2005 was $650.

We can now show the trading and profit and loss account completed.

G. Grant
Trading and Profit and Loss Account for the year ended 31 December 2005

	$		$
Purchases	4,000	Sales	6,000
Carriage inwards	350	Closing stock	650
	4,350		
Gross profit c/d	2,300		
	6,650		6,650
Carriage outwards	280	Gross profit b/d	2,300
Other expenses	220		
Net profit	1,800		
	2,300		2,300

10.3 The Second Year of a Business

Following on from Exhibit 9.3 in the last chapter, L. Sands carries on his business for another year. He then extracts a trial balance as on 31 December 2006, shown as Exhibit 10.2.

Exhibit 10.2

L. Sands
Trial Balance as at 31 December 2006

	Dr. $	*Cr.* $
Sales		6,700
Purchases	4,260	
Lighting	190	
Rent	240	
Pay: store assistant	520	
General expenses	70	
Carriage outwards	110	
Shop premises	2,000	
Fixtures and fittings	750	
Debtors	1,200	
Creditors		900
Bank	120	
Cash	40	
Loan from T. Wright		1,000
Drawings	900	
Capital		2,100
Stock (at 31 December 2005)	300	
	10,700	10,700

Closing stock at 31 December 2006 was $550.

Adjustments Needed for Stock

Previously we have done the accounts for new businesses only. These started without stock and therefore had closing stock only, as we were doing the first trading and profit and loss account.

When we prepare the trading and profit and loss account for the second year, we can now see the difference. Looking at Exhibits 9.1 and 10.2 for L. Sands, we can see the stock figures needed for the trading accounts.

Trading account for period	*Year to 31 December 2005*	*Year to 31 December 2006*
Opening stock 1.1.2005	None	
Closing stock 31.12.2005	$300	
Opening stock 1.1.2006		$300
Closing stock 31.12.2006		$550

This means that calculations for the first year of trading, to 31 December 2005, had only one stock figure included in them. This was the closing stock. For the second year of trading, to 31 December 2006, both opening and closing stock figures will be in the calculations.

The stock shown in the trial balance, Exhibit 10.2, is that brought forward from the previous year on 31 December 2005, it is therefore the opening stock of 2006. The closing stock at 31 December 2006 can be found only by stocktaking. Assume it amounts at cost to $550.

Let us first of all calculate the cost of goods sold for 2006.

	$
Stock of goods at start of year	300
Add Purchases	4,260
Total goods available for sale	4,560
Less What remains at the end of the year: i.e. stock of goods at close	550
Therefore cost of goods that have been sold	4,010

We illustrate this diagrammatically in Exhibit 10.3.

Exhibit 10.3

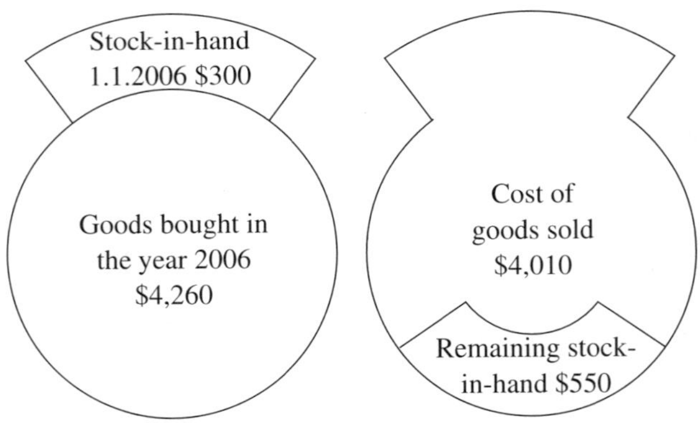

The sales were $6,700, so:

Sales $6,700 – Cost of goods sold $4,010 = Gross profit $2,690

Now the trading and profit and loss accounts can be drawn up using double entry (see Exhibit 10.4). For purposes of illustration, the stock account will also be shown. The gross profit using double entry methods is also obviously $2,690, as calculated already by ordinary arithmetic.

Exhibit 10.4

Stock

2005	$	2006	$
Dec 31 Balance b/d	300	Dec 31 Trading a/c	300
2006			
Dec 31 Trading a/c	550		

L. Sands
Trading and Profit and Loss Account for the year ended 31 December 2006

	$		$
Opening stock	300	Sales	6,700
Purchases	4,260	Closing stock	550
Gross profit c/d	2,690		
	7,250		7,250
Pay	520	Gross profit b/d	2,690
Carriage outwards	110		
Lighthing expenses	190		
Rent	240		
General expenses	70		
Net profit	1,560		
	2,690		2,690

The stock which at 31 December 2006 is $550, and has not been previously shown in the accounts, has been entered using double entry.

Debit: Stock account $550.
Credit: Trading account $550.

Display of Cost of Goods Sold in the Trading Account

Accountants like to see a figure for **cost of goods sold** actually shown in the trading account. This is because they use it for various calculations to be described later in this course.

Exhibit 10.4 shows a trading account where the normal double entry is shown. However, although the stock account would stay exactly as in Exhibit 10.4, accountants would prefer to show the trading account part as in Exhibit 10.5. The figures of gross profit and net profit stay the same. The only difference is in display. You can see that the 'Cost of goods sold' figure of $4,010 is the same as that shown in Exhibit 10.3. In future we will show trading accounts displayed by this method. This is the method you should use in your examinations.

The balances remaining in the books, including the new balance on the stock account, are now drawn up in the form of a balance sheet (see Exhibit 10.6).

Exhibit 10.5 Horizontal-style trading and profit and loss account

L. Sands
Trading and Profit and Loss Account for the year ended 31 December 2006

	$		$
Opening stock	300	Sales	6,700
Add Purchases	4,260		
	4,560		
Less Closing stock	550		
Cost of goods sold	4,010		
Gross profit c/d	2,690		
	6,700		6,700
Pay	520	Gross profit b/d	2,690
Carriage outwards	110		
Lighting expenses	190		
Rent	240		
General expenses	70		
Net profit	1,560		
	2,690		2,690

Exhibit 10.6 Horizontal-style balance sheet

L. Sands
Balance Sheet as at 31 December 2006

Fixed assets	$	$	*Capital*	$	$
Shop premises		2,000	Balance 1 Jan 2006	2,100	
Fixtures and fittings		750	*Add* Net profit for year	1,560	
		2,750		3,660	
			Less Drawings	900	
Current assets					2,760
Stock	550		*Long-term liability*		
Debtors	1,200		Loan from T. Wright		1,000
Bank	120		*Current liabilites*		
Cash	40		Creditors		900
		1,910			
		4,660			4,660

Exhibits 10.5 and 10.6 are now redrafted using the vertical style as Exhibits 10.7 and 10.8.

Exhibit 10.7 Vertical-style trading and profit and loss account

L. Sands
Trading and Profit and Loss Account for the year ended 31 December 2006

	$	$
Sales		6,700
Less Cost of goods sold:		
Opening stock	300	
Add Purchases	4,260	
	4,560	
Less Closing stock	550	4,010
Gross profit		2,690
Less Expenses:		
Pay	520	
Carriage outwards	110	
Lighting expenses	190	
Rent	240	
General expenses	70	1,130
Net profit		1,560

Exhibit 10.8 Vertical-style balance sheet

L. Sands
Balance Sheet as at 31 December 2006

	$	$
Fixed assets		
Shop premises	2,000	
Fixtures and fittings	750	2,750
Current assets		
Stock	550	
Debtors	1,200	
Bank	120	
Cash	40	
	1,910	
Less Current liabilities		
Creditors	900	
Working capital		1,010
		3,760
Less Long-term liability		
Loan from T. Wright		1,000
		2,760

	$	$
Financed by:		
Capital		
Balance at 1 January 2006		2,100
Add Net profit for the year		1,560
		3,660
		900
Less Drawings		2,760

Notice that, as described in section 9.7, the long-term liability, loan from T. Wright of $1,000 is deducted from the total of fixed assets plus working capital = $3,760.

10.4 Final Accounts

The term **final accounts** is often used to mean the trading and profit and loss accounts and the balance sheet. The term can be misleading, as the balance sheet is not an account. In examinations, if the question requires final accounts to be prepared, you should draw up trading and profit and loss accounts and also the balance sheet.

10.5 Other Cost Items in the Trading Account

Sometimes the goods you buy to sell have to have something done to them before they can be sold. An example of this is a trader who sells clocks packed in boxes. To do this, she:

- buys clocks from one supplier
- buys boxes from a different supplier
- pays someone to pack the clock into the boxes.

Expenses of each of these stages will be transferred to the trading account when calculating gross profit. This is because they have to be bought, and packed in boxes, before they can be sold.

- The pay received by the sales person selling the clocks will *not* be transferred to the trading account. Instead, it will be transferred to the profit and loss account.

For goods imported from abroad, it is usual to find that the cost of import duty, marine insurance and freight, etc., are also treated as part of the cost of goods sold and are therefore debited to the trading account.

10.6 Treatment of Returns

In the trading account:

- Returns inwards should be deducted from Sales;
- Returns outwards should be deducted from Purchases.

In Exhibit 10.5, if Sales had been $7,200 and Returns inwards $500, and Purchases $4,460 and Returns outwards $200, then the trading account would have appeared as in Exhibit 10.9.

Exhibit 10.9

L. Sands
Trading Account for the year ended 31 December 2006

	$	$		$	$
Opening stock		300	Sales	7,200	
Add Purchases	4,460		*Less* Returns inwards	500	6,700
Less Returns outwards	200	4,260			
		4,560			
Less Closing stock		550			
Cost of goods sold		4,010			
Gross profit c/d		2,690			
		6,700			6,700

The term often used for the figure of sales less returns inwards is that of **net sales** – in Exhibit 10.9 this is $6,700. The figure of purchases less returns outwards is often called **net purchases**.

The trading account is now shown using the vertical style in Exhibit 10.10.

Exhibit 10.10

L. Sands
Trading Account for the year ended 31 December 2006

	$	$	$
Sales		7,200	
Less Returns inwards		500	6,700
Less Cost of goods sold:			
Opening stock		300	
Add Purchases	4,460		
Less Returns outwards	200	4,260	
		4,560	
Less Closing stock		550	4,010
Gross profit			2,690

New Terms

Carriage inwards (p. 81): Cost of transport of goods into a business.

Carriage outwards (p. 81): Cost of transport of goods to the customers of a business.

Cost of goods sold (p. 84): Cost of goods sold to customers during an accounting period.

Final accounts (p. 88): Term that includes the trading and profit and loss accounts and balance sheet.

Summary

1. Carriage inwards is shown as a cost item in the trading account.
2. Carriage outwards is shown as an expense in the profit and loss account.
3. In the second and later years of a business, both opening and closing stocks are brought into the trading account.
4. It is normal practice to show cost of goods sold as a separate figure in the trading account.
5. Cost items concerned with getting the goods into a saleable condition are charged in the trading account.
6. Returns inwards should be deducted from sales in the trading account.
7. Returns outwards should be deducted from purchases in the trading account.

Exercises

10.1 From the following details, draw up J. Grant's trading account for the year ended 31 December 2003.

	$
Carriage inwards	670
Returns outwards	495
Returns inwards	890
Sales	38,742
Purchases	26,409
Stock of goods: 1 January 2003	6,924
31 December 2003	7,489

10.2X The following details for the year ended 31 March 2008 for C. Black are available. Draw up the trading account for that year.

	$
Stock: 1 April 2007	16,492
31 March 2008	18,504
Returns inwards	1,372
Returns outwards	2,896
Purchases	36,905
Carriage inwards	1,122
Sales	54,600

10.3 From the following trial balance of R. Mendez, draw up a trading and profit and loss account for the year ended 30 September 2005, and a balance sheet as at that date.

	Dr.	*Cr.*
	$	$
Stock 1 October 2005	2,368	
Carriage outwards	200	
Carriage inwards	310	
Returns inwards	205	
Returns outwards		322
Purchases	11,874	
Sales		18,600
Staff pay	3,862	
Rent and rates	304	
Insurance	78	
Motor expenses	664	

Office expenses	216	
Lighting expenses	166	
General expenses	314	
Premises	5,000	
Motor vehicles	1,800	
Fixtures and fittings	350	
Debtors	3,896	
Creditors		1,731
Cash at bank	482	
Drawings	1,200	
Capital		12,636
	33,289	33,289

Stock at 30 September 2006 was $2,946.

10.4 The following trial balance was extracted from the books of B. Rousseau on 30 April 2007. From it, prepare her trading and profit and loss account for the year ended 30 April 2007, and a balance sheet as at that date.

	Dr. $	*Cr.* $
Sales		18,600
Purchases	11,556	
Stock 1 May 2006	3,776	
Carriage outwards	326	
Carriage inwards	234	
Returns inwards	440	
Returns outwards		355
Staff pay	2,447	
Motor expenses	664	
Rent	456	
Rates	120	
Sundry expenses	1,202	
Motor vehicles	2,400	
Fixtures and fittings	600	
Debtors	4,577	
Creditors		3,045
Cash at bank	3,876	
Cash in hand	120	
Drawings	2,050	
Capital		12,844
	34,844	34,844

Stock at 30 April 2007 was $4,998.

10.5X The following is the trial balance of J. Singh as at 31 March 2006. Draw up a set of final accounts for the year ended 31 March 2006.

	Dr. $	*Cr.* $
Stock 1 April 2005	18,160	
Sales		92,340
Purchases	69,185	
Carriage inwards	420	
Carriage outwards	1,570	
Returns outwards		640

Cont'd

Staff pay	10,240	
Rent and rates	3,015	
Communication expenses	624	
Commissions payable	216	
Insurance	405	
Sundry expenses	318	
Buildings	20,000	
Debtors	14,320	
Creditors		8,160
Fixtures	2,850	
Cash at bank	2,970	
Cash in hand	115	
Loan from K. Blake		10,000
Drawings	7,620	
Capital		40,888
	152,028	152,028

Stock at 31 March 2006 was $22,390.

10.6X L. Binns drew up the following trial balance as at 30 September 2008. You are to draft trading and profit and loss accounts for the year to 30 September 2008 and a balance sheet as at that date.

	Dr. $	*Cr.* $
Loan from P. Parkin		5,000
Capital		25,955
Drawings	8,420	
Cash at bank	3,115	
Cash in hand	295	
Debtors	12,300	
Creditors		9,370
Stock 30 September 2007	23,910	
Motor van	4,100	
Office equipment	6,250	
Sales		130,900
Purchases	92,100	
Returns inwards	550	
Carriage inwards	215	
Returns outwards		307
Carriage outwards	309	
Motor expenses	1,630	
Rent	2,970	
Telephone charges	405	
Staff pay	12,810	
Insurance	492	
Office expenses	1,377	
Sundry expenses	284	
	171,532	171,532

Stock at 30 September 2008 was $27,475.

10.7X From the information below, you are required to extract the necessary details to work out the gross profit on September's trading of David Tomms (Wholesalers) Ltd.

	$
Stock 1 September	620
Stock 30 September	640
Cash balance	120
Drawings	150
Purchases for month	2,160
Sales for month	3,275
Carriage inwards	30

(*Pitman Examinations Institute*)

CHAPTER **11**

Books of Original Entry and Ledgers

Learning Objectives

- To know the need for books of original entry.
- To understand what each book is used for.
- To appreciate how the books of original entry are used alongside the ledgers.
- To be able to list accounts as either personal or impersonal accounts.

11.1 The Growth of the firm

While the firm is very small, all the double entry accounts can be kept in one book, which we would call the ledger. As the firm grows, it will become impossible to use just one book, as the large number of pages needed for a lot of transactions would mean that the book would be too big to handle. Also, suppose we have several bookkeepers: they could not all do their work properly if there was only one ledger.

The answer to this problem is for us to use more books. When we do this we put similar types of transactions together and have a book for each type. We do not mix together transactions that are different from each other.

11.2 Books of Original Entry

Books of original entry are the books in which we record transactions first of all. As mentioned above, we have a separate book for each different kind of transaction. The nature of the transaction affects which book it is entered into: sales will be entered in one book, purchases in another book, cash in another book, and so on. We enter the transactions in these books giving the following details:

- date – the transactions should be shown in chronological order;
- details column completed;
- folio column – for cross-referencing purposes;
- money column completed.

11.3 Types of Books of Original Entry

These are:

- **sales journal** for credit sales
- **purchases journal** for credit purchases

- **returns inwards journal** for returns inwards
- **returns outwards journal** for returns outwards
- **cash book** for receipts and payments of cash and cheques
- **general journal** for other items.

11.4 Using More than One Ledger

Although we have lists of which transactions are entered in which books of original entry, we still have more work to do. We have got to show the effects of the transactions by putting them into double entry accounts. Instead of keeping all the double entry accounts in one ledger, we have several ledgers. This makes it easier to divide the work between different bookkeepers.

11.5 Types of Ledgers

The different types of ledgers are:

- **sales ledger** this is kept just for customers' personal accounts
- **purchases ledger** this is kept just for suppliers' personal accounts
- **general ledger** this contains the remaining double entry accounts such as expenses, fixed assets, capital, etc.

11.6 Diagram of Books Used

Exhibit 11.1 shows in a diagram how the various books of original entry are used. In the next few chapters we will look at the books used in more detail.

Exhibit 11.1

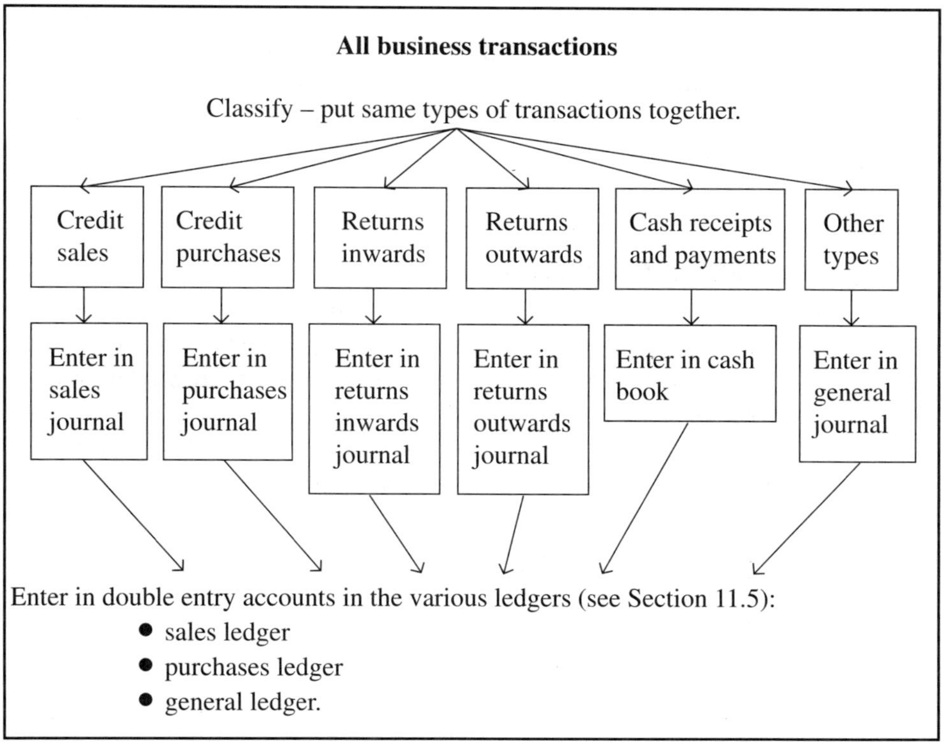

11.7 Types of Accounts

Some people describe all accounts as either personal accounts or impersonal accounts.

- **Personal accounts** accounts for debtors and creditors.
- **Impersonal accounts** divided between real accounts and nominal accounts.
- **Real accounts** accounts in which property is recorded: examples are buildings, machinery, fixtures and stock.
- **Nominal accounts** accounts in which expenses, income and capital are recorded.

Exhibit 11.2 may enable you to understand it better.

Exhibit 11.2

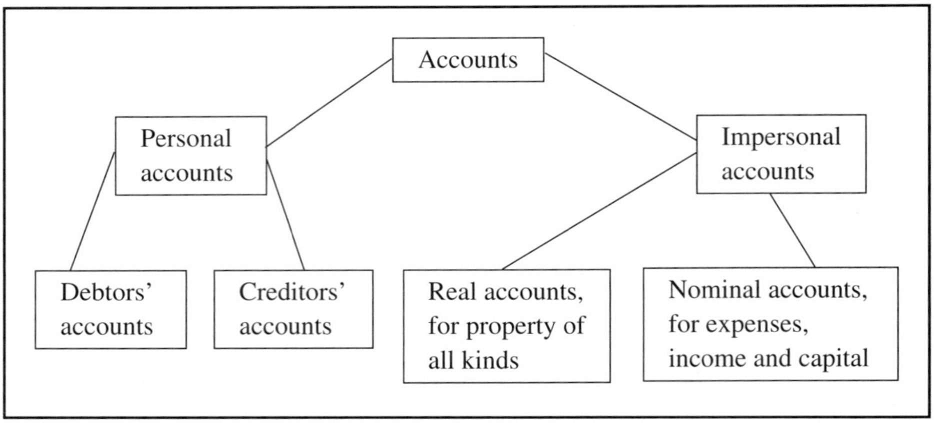

11.8 Nominal and Private Ledgers

The ledger in which the impersonal accounts are kept is known as the **nominal** (or general) **ledger**. Very often, to ensure privacy for the proprietor(s), the capital and drawings accounts and similar accounts are kept in a **private ledger**. In this way, office staff cannot see details of items which the proprietors want to keep a secret.

11.9 Computers and Accounting

So far we have been describing the whole set of accounting records of a business as the 'books' of a business. However, you will probably be aware that computers do not use bound books, and you may wonder whether or not what we have been looking at is relevant to accounting when computers are used.

In fact, the term 'book' or 'journal' is simply a convenient way of describing what is in effect a 'collection point' for a particular type of information. The principles of accounting can therefore be more easily discussed if we keep to standard terms. The principles remain exactly the same no matter whether manual, computerized or other methods are in use.

New Terms

Books of original entry (p. 94): Books where the first entry of a transaction is made.

Sales journal (p. 94): Book of original entry for credit sales.

Purchases journal (p. 94): Book of original entry for credit purchases.

Returns inwards journal (p. 95): Book of original entry for goods returned by customers.

Returns outwards journal (p. 95): Book of original entry for goods returned to suppliers.

Cash book (p. 95): Book of original entry for cash and bank receipts and payments.

General journal (p. 95): Book of original entry for all items other than those for cash or goods.

Sales ledger (p. 95): A ledger for customers' personal accounts.

Purchases ledger (p. 95): A ledger for suppliers' personal accounts.

General ledger (p. 95): All accounts other than those for customers and suppliers.

Personal accounts (p. 96): Accounts for both creditors and debtors.

Impersonal accounts (p. 96): All accounts other than debtors' and creditors' accounts.

Real accounts (p. 96): Accounts in which property of all kinds is recorded.

Nominal accounts (p. 96): Accounts in which expenses, revenue and capital are recorded.

Nominal ledger (p. 96): Another name for the general ledger.

Private ledger (p. 96): Ledger for capital and drawings accounts.

Summary

1 Trasanctions are classified and listed in the appropriate book of original entry.

2 The books of original entry are used as a basis for posting the transactions to the double entry accounts in the various ledgers.

CHAPTER **12**

The Sales Journal and the Sales Ledger

Learning Objectives

- To be able to draw up a sales invoice.
- To be able to enter up a sales journal and post to the sales ledger.
- To appreciate the need for credit control.

12.1 Introduction

In Chapter 11 we saw that the ledger had been split up into a set of journals and ledgers. This chapter deals with sales journals and sales ledgers.

12.2 Cash Sales

When goods are paid for immediately by cash, there is no need to enter such sales in the sales journal. In such cases we do not need to know the names and addresses of customers and what has been sold to them.

12.3 Credit Sales

In many businesses, however, most of the sales will be made on credit rather than for immediate cash. In fact, the sales of some business will consist entirely of credit sales.

For each credit sale, the selling firm will send a document to the buyer showing full details of the goods sold and the prices of the goods. This document is known as an invoice, and to the seller it is known as a **sales invoice**. The seller will keep one or more copies of each sales invoice for their own use. Exhibit 12.1 is an example of an invoice.

Exhibit 12.1

Your Purchase Order 10/A/980

J. Blake
7 Over Warehouse
Kingston 5
1 September 2005

INVOICE NO. 16554

To: D. Prendergast
45 Charles Street
Montego Bay

	Per unit	*Total*
	$	$
21 cases McBrand Pears	20	420
5 cartons Kay's Flour	4	20
6 cases Joy's Vinegar	20	120
		560

12.4 Copies of Sales Invoices

As soon as the sales invoices for the goods sold have been made out, they are sent to the customer. The selling firm will keep copies of all these sales invoices. These copies will have been made at the same time as the original, usually by some kind of carbon paper or special copying paper.

12.5 Entering into the Sales Journal

From the copy of the sales invoice, the seller enters up the sales journal. This book is merely a list, showing the following:

- date
- name of customer
- invoice number
- folio column
- final amount of invoice.

There is no need to give details of the goods sold in the sales journal. This can be found by looking at the copy invoices. The folio column will be completed when the items are entered in the sales ledger

Because the sales invoice represents the *source* from which the sales journal is written up, it is often known as a *source document*. We will see other source documents in later chapters.

Now look at Exhibit 12.2, which is a sales journal, starting with the record of the sales invoice already shown in Exhibit 12.1. Let us assume that the entries are on p. 26 of the journal.

Exhibit 12.2

Sales Journal	Invoice no.	Folio	(p. 26) Amount
2005			$
Sept 1 D. Prendergast	16554		560
Sept 8 T. Cardoza	16555		1,640
Sept 28 C. Chin	16556		220
Sept 30 D. Singh and Co.	16557		1,100
Transferred to sales account			3,520

12.6 Posting Credit Sales to the Sales Ledger

Instead of having one ledger for all accounts, we now have a general ledger and a sales ledger. The sales ledger was described in Chapter 11.

1 The credit sales are now posted, one by one, to the debit side of each customer's account in the sales ledger.
2 At the end of each period, the total of the credit sales is posted to the credit of the sales account in the general ledger. This is illustrated in Exhibit 12.3.

You will have noticed the use of the word 'posting'. This is what we call the act of using one book as a means of entering the items in the other accounts.

Exhibit 12.3

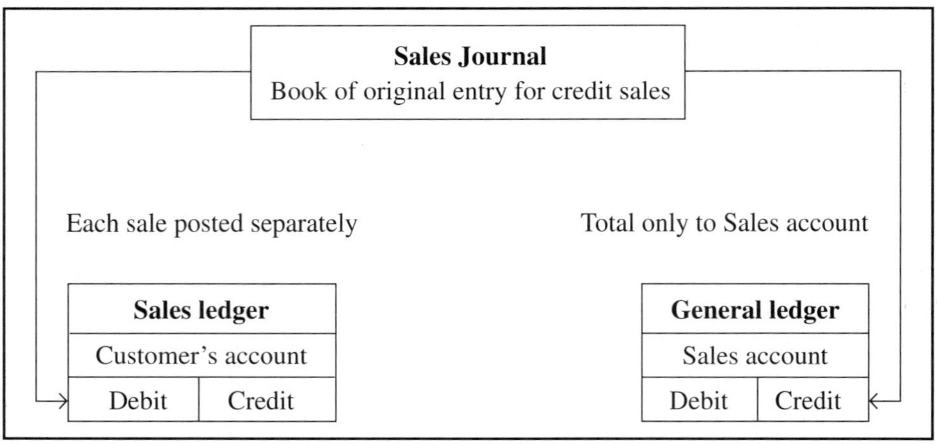

12.7 An Example of Posting Credit Sales

The sales journal in Exhibit 12.2 is now looked at again. This time posting is made to the sales ledger and the general ledger. Notice the completion of the folio columns with the reference numbers in Exhibit 12.4. SL is the abbreviation for Sales Ledger; GL is for General Ledger.

Exhibit 12.4

Sales Journal

	Invoice no.	*Folio*	*(p. 26) Amount*
2005			$
Sept 1 D. Predergast	16554	SL 12	560
Sept 8 T. Cardoza	16555	SL 39	1,640
Sept 28 C. Chin	16556	SL 125	220
Sept 30 D. Singh and Co.	16557	SL 249	1,100
Transferred to sales account		GL 44	3,520

Sales Ledger

D. Prendergast *(p. 12)*

2005		$	
Sept 1 Sales	SJ 26	560	

T. Cardoza *(p. 39)*

2005		$	
Sept 8 Sales	SJ 26	1,640	

C. Chin *(p. 125)*

2005		$	
Sept 28 Sales	SJ 26	220	

D. Singh and Co. *(p. 249)*

2005		$	
Sept 30 Sales	SJ 26	1,100	

General Ledger

Sales *(p. 44)*

	2005		$
	Sept 30 Credit sales for the month	SJ 26	3,520

Alternative names for the sales journal are 'sales book' and 'sales day book'.

Before you continue, you should attempt exercise 12.1.

12.8 Trade Discounts

Suppose you are the proprietor of a business. You are selling to three different kinds of customers:

1 traders who buy a lot of goods from you;
2 traders who buy only a few items from you;
3 the general public.

The traders themselves have to sell the goods to the general public in their own areas. They have to make a profit to help finance their businesses, so they will want to pay you less than retail price.

The traders who buy in large quantities will not want to pay as much as traders who buy in small quantities. You want to attract such large customers, and so you are happy to sell to such traders at a lower price.

This means that your selling prices are at three levels: to traders buying large quantities, to traders buying small quantities, and to the general public.

So that your staff does not need three different price lists, all goods are shown at the same price. However, a reduction (discount), called a **trade discount**, is given to the traders. Exhibit 12.5 gives an example.

Exhibit 12.5

You are selling a make of food mixing machine. The basic price is \$200. Traders (1) are given 25% trade discount, traders (2) 20%, and the general public get no trade discount. The prices paid by each type of customer would be:

		Trader (1)		**Trader (2)**	**General public**
		\$		\$	\$
Basic price		200		200	200
Less trade discount	(25%)	50	(20%)	40	nil
Price to be paid by customer		150		160	200

12.9 Sales Invoice with Trade Discount

Exhibit 12.6 shows an invoice for goods sold to D. Prendergast. It is for the same items as were shown in Exhibit 12.1, but this time the seller is R. Grant and he uses trade discounts to get to the price paid by his customers.

Exhibit 12.6

Your Purchase Order 11/A/G80	R. Grant Higher Side Kingston 5 2 September 2005	
INVOICE NO. 30756		
To: D. Prendergast 45 Charles Street Montego Bay	*Per unit*	*Total*
	$	$
21 cases McBrand Pears	25	525
5 cartons Kay's Flour	5	25
6 cases Joy's Vinegar	25	150
		700
Less 20% trade discount		140
		560

By comparing Exhibit 12.1 and 12.6 you can see that the prices paid by D. Prendergast were the same. It is simply the method of calculating the price that is different.

12.10 No Double Entry for Trade Discounts

As trade discount is simply a way of calculating sales prices, no entry for trade discount should be made in the double entry records or in the sales journal. The recording of Exhibit 12.6 in Grant's sales journal and Prendergast's personal account will appear as follows:

Sales Journal

	Invoice no.	*Folio*	*(p. 87)* *Amount*
2005			$
Sept 2 D. Prendergast	30756	SL 32	560

Sales Ledger
D. Prendergast *(p. 32)*

2005		$	
Sept 2 Sales	SJ 87	560	

12.11 Credit Control

Any organization that sells goods on credit should keep a close check to ensure that debtors pay their accounts on time. If this is not done properly, the debtors can come to owe an amount that will make the business short of money.

The following procedures should be carried out.

- For each debtor a limit should be set. The debtor should then not be allowed to owe more than this limit. The amount of the limit will depend on the circumstances. Such things as the size of the customer's firm and the amount of business done with it, as well as its past record of payments, will help in the deciding the limit figure.
- As soon as the payment date has been reached, it should be checked whether or not payment has been made. Failure to pay on time may mean that you will refuse to supply any more goods unless payment is made quickly.
- Where payment is not forthcoming, after investigation it may be necessary to take legal action to sue the customer for the debt. This will depend on the circumstances.
- It is important that the customer is aware as to what will happen if the account is not paid by the correct date.

New Terms

Sales invoices (p. 98): A document showing details of goods sold and the prices of those goods.

Trade discount (p. 102): A reduction given to a customer when calculating the selling prices of goods.

Source documents (p. 99): Documents that contain original evidence of a transaction.

Summary

1 Cash sales are not entered in the sales journal.
2 The sales journal is a list recording all credit sales for each period.
3 The sales journal is used for posting credit sales to the sales ledger.
4 The total of the sales journal for the period is posted to the credit of the sales account.
5 No entry is made for trade discounts in the double entry accounts.
6 All firms should have an adequate system of credit control over their debtors.

Exercises

12.1 You are to enter up p. 54 of the sales journal from the following details. Post the items to the relevant accounts in the sales ledger and then show the transfer to the sales account on p. 98 in the general ledger. Show folio numbers against all items to complete the posting process.

2006		
Mar 1	Credit sales to J. Gordon (89)	$187
Mar 3	Credit sales to G. Abrahams (76)	$166
Mar 6	Credit sales to V. White (107)	$12
Mar 10	Credit sales to J. Gordon (199)	$55
Mar 17	Credit sales to F. Williams (105)	$289
Mar 19	Credit sales to U. Richards (66)	$66
Mar 27	Credit sales to V. Wong (14)	$28
Mar 31	Credit sales to L. Singh (63)	$78

The page number of the various ledger accounts in the sales ledger are shown in brackets.

12.2X Enter up p. 209 of the sales journal from the following, then post the items to the relevant accounts in the sales ledger. Then show the transfer to the sales account on p. 115 in the general ledger. Show folio numbers against all items to compete the posting process.

2008		
May 1	Credit sales to J. Johnson (377)	$305
May 3	Credit sales to T. Royes (406)	$164
May 5	Credit sales to B. Ho (22)	$45
May 7	Credit sales to M. Lee (89)	$100
May 16	Credit sales to J. Jureidini (95)	$308
May 23	Credit sales to A. Vendryes (164)	$212
May 30	Credit sales to J. Samuels (207)	$1,296

The page number of the various ledger accounts in the sales ledger are shown in brackets.

12.3 F. Benjamin of 10 Lower Street, San Fernando, is selling the following items, the recommended retail prices as shown: white tape at $10 per roll, green baize at $4 per metre, blue cotton at $6 per sheet, black silk at $20 per dress length. He makes the following sales.

2007

May 1 To F. Gomez, 3 Keswick Road, Port-of-Spain: 3 rolls white tape, 5 sheets blue cotton, 1 dress length black silk. *Less* 25% trade discount (ledger p.105).

May 4 To A. Gray, 1 Shilton Road, Pointe-à–Pierre: 60 rolls white tape, 30 metres green baize. *Less* 33⅓% trade discount (ledger p. 277).

May 8 To E. Hosein, 1 High Road, Marabella: 1 dress length black silk. No trade discount (ledger p. 84).

May 20 To M. Ali, 1 Knott Road, Port-of-Spain: 10 rolls white tape, 6 sheets blue cotton, 3 dress lengths black silk, 11 metres green baize. *Less* 25% trade discount (ledger p. 77).

May 31 To B. Cooper, 1 Tops Lane, St. Augustine: 12 rolls white tape, 14 sheets blue cotton, 9 metres green baize. *Less* 33⅓% trade discount (ledger p. 211).

You are to (*a*) draw up a sales invoice for each of the above sales; (*b*) enter them up on p. 163 in the sales journal, post to the personal accounts; (c) transfer the total to the sales account on p. 66 in the general ledger; (*d*) show all folio numbers.

12.4X J. Fisher, White House, Bridgetown, is selling the following items, the retail prices as shown: plastic tubing at $1 per metre, polythene sheeting at $2 per length, vinyl padding at $5 per box, foam rubber at $3 per sheet. She makes the following sales.

2005

June 1 To A. Portsmouth, 5 Rockley Road, Worthing: 22 metres plastic tubing, 6 sheets foam rubber, 4 boxes vinyl padding. *Less* 25% trade discount (ledger p. 222).

June 5 To B. Butler, 1 Wembley Road, Freshwater Bay: 50 lengths polythene sheeting, 8 boxes vinyl padding, 20 sheets foam rubber. *Less* 20% trade discount (ledger p. 16).

June 11 To A. Gate, 1 Bristol Road, Hastings: 4 metres plastic tubing, 33 lengths of polythene sheeting, 30 sheets foam rubber. *Less* 25% trade discount (ledger p. 88).

June 21 To L. Mackeson, 5 Maine Road, Bathsheba: 29 metres plastic tubing. No trade discount is given (ledger p. 14).

June 30 To M. Alison, Daley Road, Gun Hill: 32 metres plastic tubing, 24 lengths polythene sheeting, 20 boxes vinyl padding. *Less* 33⅓% trade discount (ledger p. 17).

(*a*) Draw up a sales invoice for each of the above sales; (*b*) then enter up on p. 312 of the sales journal and post to the personal accounts; (*c*) transfer the total to the sales account on p. 54 of the general ledger; (*d*) show all folio numbers.

CHAPTER **13**

The Purchases Journal and the Purchases Ledger

Learning Objectives

- To be able to enter purchases invoices into the purchases journal.
- To be able to post the purchases journal to the purchases ledger.

13.1 Purchase Invoices

An invoice is a **purchases invoice** when it is entered in the books of the firm purchasing the goods. The same invoice, in the books of the seller, would be a sales invoice.

For example for Exhibit 12.1 which is an invoice:

- in the books of D. Prendergast it is a purchases invoice
- in the books of J. Blake it is a sales invoice.

13.2 Entering into the Purchases Journal

From the purchases invoices for goods bought on credit, the purchaser enters the details in his purchases journal. This book is merely a list, showing the following:

- date
- name of supplier
- reference number of the invoice
- folio column
- final amount of invoice.

There is no need to show details of the goods bought in the purchases journal. This can be found by looking at the invoices themselves. Exhibit 13.1 is an example of a purchases journal.

Exhibit 13.1

Purchases Journal	*Invoice no.*	*Folio*	*(p. 49) Amount*
2005			$
Sept 2 R. Simpson	9/101		670
Sept 8 B. Hamilton	9/102		1,380
Sept 19 C. Brown	9/103		120
Sept 30 K. Gabriel	9/104		510
			2,680

In the same way that sales invoices are used as the source for entering up the sales journal, the purchases invoices are used as the source for entering up the purchases journal. These are also known as **source documents**.

13.3 Posting Credit Purchases to the Purchases Ledger

We now have a separate purchases ledger. The double entry is as follows:

1 the credit purchases are posted, one by one, to the credit of each supplier's account in the purchases ledger;

2 at the end of each period, the total of the credit purchases is posted to the debit of the purchases account in the general ledger, as illustrated in Exhibit 13.2.

Exhibit 13.2

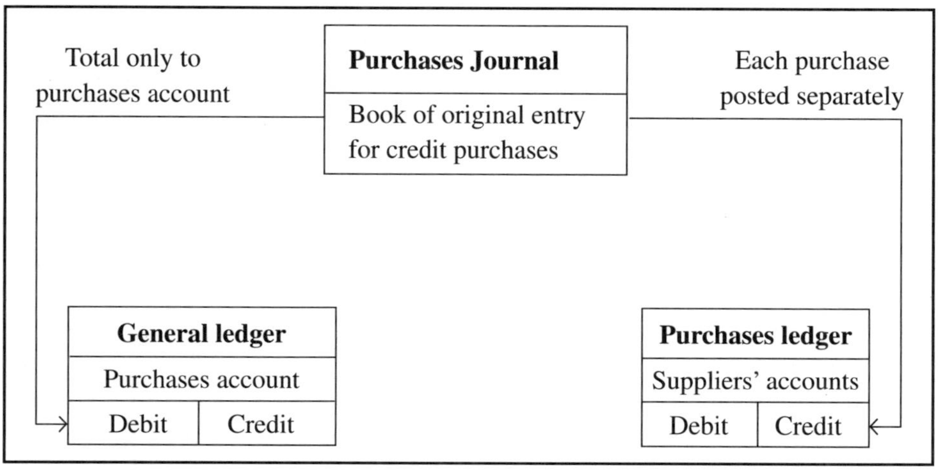

13.4 An Example of Posting Credit Purchases

The purchases journal in Exhibit 13.1 is now show again in Exhibit 13.3. This time posting is made to the purchases ledger and the general ledger. Notice the completion of the folio columns.

Exhibit 13.3

Purchases Journal

	Invoice no.	*Folio*	*(p. 49)* *Amount*
2005			$
Sept 2 R. Simpson	9/101	PL 16	670
Sept 8 B. Hamilton	9/102	PL 29	1,380
Sept 19 C. Brown	9/103	PL 55	120
Sept 30 K. Gabriel	9/104	PL 89	510
Transferred to purchases account		GL 63	2,680

Purchases Ledger

R. Simpson *(p. 16)*

			2005		$
			Sept 2 Purchases	PJ 49	670

B. Hamilton *(p. 29)*

			2005		$
			Sept 8 Purchases	PJ 49	1,380

C. Brown *(p. 55)*

			2005		$
			Sept 19 Purchases	PJ 49	120

K. Gabriel *(p. 89)*

			2005		$
			Sept 30 Purchases	PJ 49	510

General Ledger

Purchases *(p. 63)*

2005		$			
Sept 30 Credit purchases for the month	PJ 49	2,680			

The purchases journal is often known also as the 'purchases book' or the 'purchases day book'.

New Terms

Purchases invoice (p. 106): A document received by purchaser showing details of goods bought and their prices.

Summary

1 Cash purchases are not entered in the purchases journal.
2 The purchases journal is a list of all credit purchases.
3 The purchases journal is used to post the items to the double entry personal accounts in the purchases ledger.
4 The total of credit purchases for the period is posted to the debit of the purchases account.

Exercises

13.1 B. Mann has the following purchases for the month of May 2004.

2004

May 1 From K. Khan: 4 radios at \$30 each, 3 music centres at \$160 each. *Less* 25% trade discount (ledger p. 84).

May 3 From A. Bell: 2 washing machines at \$200 each, 5 vacuum cleaners at \$60 each, 2 dish dryers at \$150 each. *Less* 20% trade discount (ledger p.208).

May 15 From J. Kelly: 1 Music centre at \$300 each, 2 washing machines at \$250 each. *Less* 25% trade discount (ledger p. 11).

May 20 From B. Powell: 6 radios at \$70 each, *less* 33⅓% trade discount (ledger p. 187).

May 30 From B. Lewis: 4 dish dryers at \$200 each, *less* 20% trade discount (ledger p. 66).

Required:

(*a*) Enter up the purchases journal for the month on p. 177.
(*b*) Post the transactions to the suppliers' accounts.
(*c*) Transfer the total to the purchases account on p. 99 of the general ledger.
(*d*) Show all folio numbers.

13.2X A. Rowland has the following purchases for the month of June 2009

2009

June 2 From C. Lee: 2 sets golf clubs at \$250 each, 5 footballs at \$20 each. *Less* 25% trade discount (ledger p. 300).

June 11 From M. Elliott: 6 cricket bats at \$20 each, 6 roller skates at \$30 each, 4 rugby balls at \$25 each. *Less* 25% trade discount (ledger p. 215).

June 18 From B. Wong: 6 sets golf trophies at \$100 each, 4 sets golf clubs at \$300. *Less* 33⅓% trade discount (ledger p. 89).

June 25 From B. Parkinson: 5 cricket bats at \$40 each. *Less* 25% trade discount (ledger p. 75).

June 30 From N. Francis: 8 goal posts at \$70 each. *Less* 25% trade discount (ledger p. 184).

Required:

(*a*) Enter up p. 207 of the purchases journal for the month.
(*b*) Post the items to the suppliers' accounts.
(*c*) Transfer the total to the purchases account, p. 33 of the general ledger.
(*d*) Show all folio numbers.

13.3 C. Phillips, a sole trader, has the following purchases and sales for March 2005.

2005

Mar 1	Bought from Smith Stores: silk $40, cotton $80, all *less* 25% trade discount (purchases ledger p. 105).
Mar 8	Sold to A. Grantley: linen goods $28, woollen items $44. No trade discount (sales ledger p. 241).
Mar 15	Sold to A. Henry: silk $36, linen $144, cotton goods $120. All *less* 20% trade discount (sales ledger p. 126).
Mar 23	Bought from C. Kelly: cotton $88, linen $52. All *less* 25% trade discount (purchases ledger p. 70).
Mar 24	Sold to D. Sangster: linen goods $42, cotton $48. *Less* 10% trade discount (sales ledger p. 99).
Mar 31	Bought from J. Hamilton: linen goods $270. *Less* 33⅓% trade discount (purchases ledger p. 122).

Required:

(*a*) Prepare p. 55 of the purchases journal and page 62 of sales journal of C. Phillips from the above.

(*b*) Post the items to the personal accounts.

(*c*) Post the totals of the journals to the sales and purchases accounts, on p. 88 and 146 of the general ledger.

(*d*) Show all folio numbers.

13.4X A. Henriques has the following purchases and sales for May 2006.

2006

May 1	Sold to M. Marshall: brass goods $24, bronze items $36. *Less* 25% trade discount (sales ledger p. 88).
May 7	Sold to R. Richards: tin goods $70, lead items $230. *Less* 33⅓% trade discount (sales ledger p. 177).
May 9	Bought from C. Clarke: tin goods $400. *Less* 40% trade discount (purchases ledger p. 206).
May 16	Bought from A. Charles: copper goods $320. *Less* 50% trade discount (purchases ledger p. 14).
May 23	Sold to T. Young: tin goods $50, brass items $70, lead figures $80. All *less* 20% trade discount (sales ledger p. 111).
May 31	Bought from M. Nelson: brass figures $100. *Less* 50% trade discount (purchases ledger p. 122).

Required:

(*a*) Write up p. 216 of the sales journal and p. 119 of the purchases journal.

(*b*) Post the items to the personal accounts.

(*c*) Post the totals of the journals to the sales accounts, on p. 322 of the general ledger and the purchases account on p. 166 of the general ledger.

(*d*) Show all folio numbers.

CHAPTER **14**

The Returns Journals

Learning Objectives

- To be able to enter up the returns inwards and returns outwards journals from source documents.
- To be able to post the journal entries to the sales and purchases ledgers.
- To be able to make out statements.
- To understand the use of statements.
- To be able to enter up the accounts for credit card transactions.

14.1 Returns Inwards and Credit Notes

Sometimes we will agree to customers returning goods to us. This might be for reasons such as the following:

- goods were of the wrong type
- they were the wrong colour
- goods were faulty
- customer had bought more than was needed.

We might ask the customers to return the goods. Sometimes they may agree to keep the goods if an allowance is made to reduce their price.

In each of these cases a document known as a **credit note** will be sent to the customer, showing the amount of the allowance given by us for the returns or the faulty goods. It is called a credit note because the customer's account will be credited with the amount of the allowance, to show the reduction in the amount owed. Exhibit 14.1 shows an example of a credit note. To stop them being mistaken for invoices, credit notes are often printed in red.

Exhibit 14.1

To: D. Prendergast 45 Charles Street Montego Bay CREDIT NOTE NO. 9/37		R. Grant Higher Side, Kingston 5 8 September 2005
	Per unit	*Total*
	$	$
2 cases McBrand Pears	25	50
Less 20% trade discount		10
		40

14.2 Returns Inwards Journal

The credit notes are listed in a returns inwards journal. This is then used for posting the items, as follows:

1. **Sales ledger:** credit the amount of credit notes, one by one, to the accounts of the customers in the sales ledger;
2. **General ledger:** at the end of the period, the total of the returns inwards journal is posted to the debit of the returns inwards account.

Credit notes are *source documents* for entering up the returns inwards journal.

14.3 Example of a Returns Inwards Journal

An example of a returns inwards journal showing the items posted to the sales ledger and the general ledger, is shown in Exhibit 14.2.

Exhibit 14.2

Returns Inwards Journal

	Invoice no.	*Folio*	*(p. 10) Amount*
2005			$
Sept 8 D. Prendergast	9/37	SL 12	40
Sept 17 A. Brewster	9/38	SL 58	120
Sept 19 C. Vickers	9/39	SL 99	290
Sept 29 M. Nelson	9/40	SL 122	160
Transferred to returns inwards account		GL 114	610

Sales Ledger

D. Prendergast *(p. 12)*

	2005			$
	Sept 8	Returns inwards	RI 10	40

A. Brewster *(p. 58)*

	2005			$
	Sept 17	Returns inwards	RI 10	120

C. Vickers *(p. 99)*

	2005			$
	Sept 19	Returns inwards	RI 10	290

M. Nelson *(p. 122)*

	2005			$
	Sept 29	Returns inwards	RI 10	160

General Ledger

Returns Inwards *(p. 114)*

2005			$	
Sept 30	Returns for the month	RI 10	610	

Alternative names in use for the returns inwards journal are 'returns inwards book' or 'sales returns book', the latter name arising from the fact that it is the sales that are returned at a later date.

14.4 Returns Outwards and Debit Notes

If the supplier agrees, goods bought previously may be returned. When this happens a **debit note** is sent to the supplier giving details of the goods and the reason for their return. The credit note received from the supplier will simply be evidence of the supplier's agreement, and the amounts involved.

Also, an allowance might be given by the supplier for any faults in the goods. Here too, a debit note should be sent to the supplier. Exhibit 14.3 show an example of a debit note.

Exhibit 14.3

W. Lee,
High Street,
Marabella
11 September 2005

To: B. Hamilton
10 Manley Road,
Port-of-Spain

DEBIT NOTE NO. 9/34

	Per unit	*Total*
	$	$
4 cases Heinz Beans	60	240
Less 25% trade discount		60
		180

14.5 Returns Outwards Journal

The debit notes are listed in a returns outwards journal. This is then used for posting the items, as follows:

1 **Purchases ledger:** debit the amounts of debit notes, one by one, to the accounts of the suppliers in the purchases ledger;
2 **General ledger:** at the end of the period, the total of the returns outwards journal is posted to the credit of the returns outwards account.

Debit notes are *source documents* for entering up the returns outwards journal.

14.6 Example of a Returns Outwards Journal

An example of a returns outwards journal, showing the items posted to purchases ledger and the general ledger, is shown in Exhibit 14.4.

Exhibit 14.4

Returns Outwards Journal

	Note no.	*Folio*	*(p. 7) Amount*
2005			$
Sept 11 B. Hamilton	9/34	PL 29	180
Sept 16 B. Rose	9/35	PL 46	100
Sept 28 C. Blake	9/36	PL 55	30
Sept 30 S. Saunders	9/37	PL 87	360
Transferred to returns outwards account		GL 116	670

Purchases Ledger

B. Hamilton *(p. 29)*

2005		$	
Sept 11	Returns outwards RO 7	180	

B. Rose *(p. 46)*

2005		$	
Sept 16	Returns outwards RO 7	100	

C. Blake *(p. 55)*

2005		$	
Sept 28	Returns outwards RO 7	30	

S. Saunders *(p. 87)*

2005		$	
Sept 30	Returns outwards RO 7	360	

General Ledger

Returns Outwards *(p. 116)*

	2005			$
	Sept 30	Returns for the month	RO 7	670

Other names in use for the returns outwards journal are 'returns outwards book' or 'purchases returns book'.

14.7 Double Entry and Returns

Exhibit 14.5 shows how double entry is made for both returns inwards and returns outwards.

Exhibit 14.5

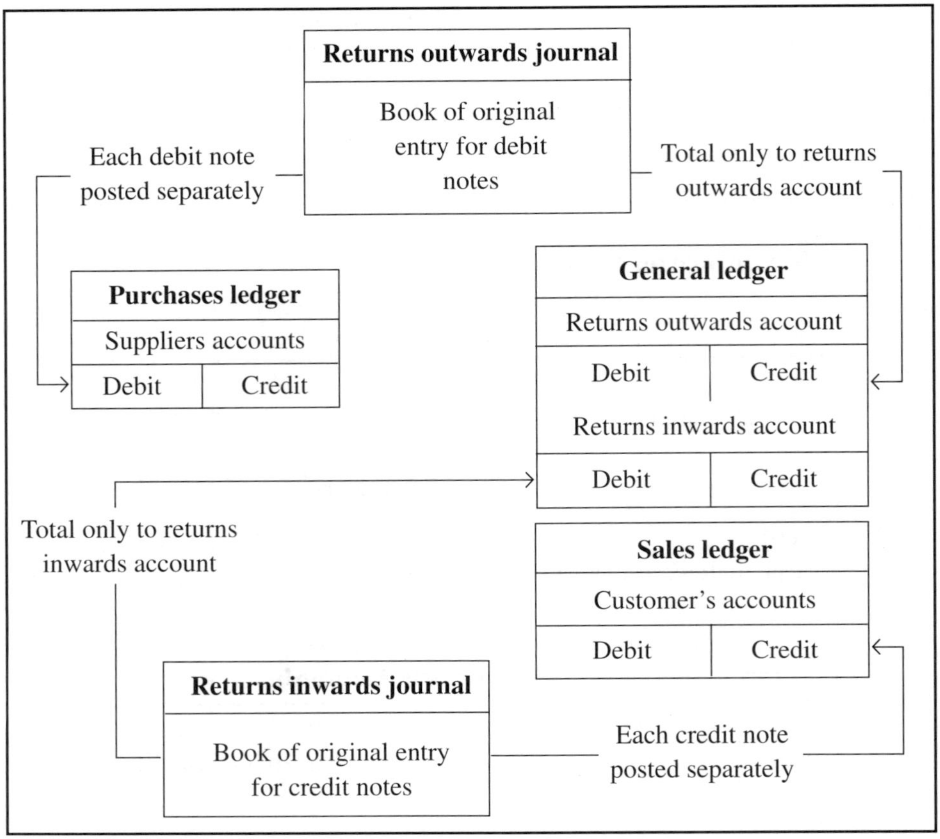

14.8 Reasons For Keeping Separate Returns Accounts

It might be thought that the returns inwards could have been debited to the sales account rather than to a separate returns inwards account. This, however, would have meant that it would only be the net figure of sales that appeared in the trading account.

It is important for the owners of a business to check on how much in sales is being returned. This may show that too many faulty goods are being sold, thus needing to be returned. This would involve the business in a lot of unnecessary costs, such as carriage outwards, packing expenses and so on. Showing the figures separately will highlight an excessive amount of returns.

Similar considerations will apply with returns outwards, and therefore a separate returns outwards account will be kept.

14.9 Statements

At the end of each month, a **statement** should be sent to each customer (debtor) who owes money on the last day of that month. It is really a copy of the customer's account in our books. It should show:

1 amount owing at start of month;
2 amount of each sales invoice sent during the month;

3 credit notes sent during the month;
4 cash and cheques received from customer during the month;
5 finally, the amount due from debtor at the end of the month.

Debtors will use these statements to see if the accounts in their own accounting records agree with their accounts in our records. If in our books a debtor is shown as owing $798, then, depending on items in transit between us, his books should show us as a creditor for $798. The statement also acts as a reminder to the debtor that money is owed, and will show the date by which payment should be made.

An example of a statement might be as shown in Exhibit 14.6.

Exhibit 14.6

STATEMENT OF ACCOUNT

R. GRANT
Higher Side
Marabella
Tel 012 345
Fax 012 789

Accounts Dept
D. Poole & Co.
45 Charles Drive,
Port-of-Spain

Date	*Details*	*Debit*	*Credit*	*Balance*
2005		$	$	$
Sept 1	Balance b/f			880
Sept 2	Invoice 30756	560		1,440
Sept 8	Returns 9/37		40	1,400
Sept 25	Bank		880	520
Sept 30	Balance owing c/f			520
All accounts due and payable within 1 month				

14.10 Sales and Purchases via Credit Cards

Various banks, building societies and other financial organizations issue credit cards to their customers. Examples are Visa, Access and American Express. The holder of the credit card purchases items or services without giving cash or cheques, but simply signs a special voucher used by the store or selling organization. Later on, usually several weeks later, the credit card holder pays the organization issuing the card, e.g. Visa, for all of the previous month's outgoings.

The sellers of the goods or services then present the vouchers to the credit card company and the total of the vouchers less commission is paid to them by that credit card company.

In effect, the sales are 'cash sales', for as far as the purchaser is concerned the goods (or obtained services) have been purchased and received, and have been paid for by credit card. Such sales are very rarely sales to anyone other than members of the general public, rather than professionals in a specific trade.

Once the customer has departed with the goods, or has had the necessary services, she does not become a debtor needing an entry in a sales ledger. All the selling company is then interested in, from a recording point of view, is collecting the money from the credit card company. The double entry needed is as follows.

Sales of items via credit cards
Debit: Credit card company.
Credit: Cash sales.

Receipt of money from credit card company
Debit: Bank.
Credit: Credit card company.

Commission charged by credit card company
Debit: Selling expenses.
Credit: Credit card company.

14.11 E. & O.E.

One some invoices and other documents you will see the initials 'E. & O.E.' printed at the bottom of the invoice. This abbreviation sands for 'Errors and Omissions Excepted'. Basically, this is a warning that there may possibly be errors or omissions which could mean that the figures shown could be incorrect, and that the recipient should carefully check the figures before taking any action concerning them.

14.12 Multiple-choice Questions

Now attempt Set No. 2, consisting of questions MC 21–MC 40; see p. 410.

New Terms

Credit note (p. 111): A document received showing allowance given by supplier in respect of unsatisfactory goods.

Debit note (p. 113): A document sent to a customer showing allowance given for unsatisfactory goods.

Statement (p. 116): A copy of a customer's personal account taken from the supplier's books.

Summary

1 Goods returned to us by our customers are all entered in a returns inwards journal.
2 The returns inwards journal is used to post each item to the credit of the account of the customer concerned in the sales ledger.
3 The total of returns inwards journal is debited at the end of the period to the returns inwards account in the general ledger.
4 Goods returned by us to our suppliers are all entered in a returns outwards journal.
5 The returns outwards journal is used to debit the account of each supplier concerned in the purchases ledger.
6 The total of returns outwards journal is credited at the end of the period to the returns outwards account in the general ledger.

Exercises

14.1 You are to enter up the purchases journal and the returns outwards journal from the following details, then to post the items to the relevant accounts in the purchases ledger and to show the transfers to the general ledger at the end of the month. Make up your own folio numbers and show against every item.

2007

May 1	Credit purchase from H. Lloyd, $119.
May 4	Credit purchases from the following: D. Scott, $98; A. Simpson, $114; A. Williams, $25; S. Wood, $56.
May 7	Goods returned by us to the following: H. Lloyd, $16; D. Scott, $14.
May 10	Credit purchase from A. Simpson, $59.
May 18	Credit purchases from the following: M. White, $89; J. Wong, $67; H. Miller, $196; H. Lewis, $119.
May 25	Goods returned by us to the following: J. Wong, $5; A. Simpson, $11.
May 31	Credit purchases from: A. Williams, $56; C. Cooper, $98.

14.2X Enter up the sales journal and the returns inwards journal from the following details. Then post to the customers' accounts and show the transfers to the general ledger. Make up your own folio numbers and record against each item.

2004

June 1	Credit sales to: A. Singh, $188; P. Tulloch, $60; J. Flynn, $77; B. Lopez, $88.
June 6	Credit sales to: M. Hosein, $114; S. Thompson, $118; J. Flynn, $66.
June 10	Goods returned to us by: A. Singh, $12; B. Lopez, $17.
June 20	Credit sales to M. Barrow, $970.
June 24	Goods returned to us by S. Thompson, $5.
June 30	Credit sales to M. Parkin, $91.

14.3 You are to enter up the sales, purchases and the returns inwards and returns outwards journals from the following details, then to post the items to the relevant accounts in the sales and purchases ledgers. The total of the journals are then to be transferred to the accounts in the general ledger. Make up your own folio numbers and record against each item.

2006

May 1	Credit sales: T. Thompson, $56; L. Rodriguez, $148; K. Barton, $145.
May 3	Credit purchases: P. Potter, $144; H. Harris, $25; B. Spencer, $76.
May 7	Credit sales: K. Kelly, $89; N. Mendes, $78; N. Lee, $257.
May 9	Credit purchases: B. Perkins, $24; H. Harris, $58; H. Miles, $123.
May 11	Goods returned by us to: P. Potter, $12; B. Spencer, $22.
May 14	Goods returned by us by: T. Thompson, $5; K. Barton, $11; K. Kelly, $14.
May 17	Credit purchases: H. Harris, $54; B. Perkins, $65; L. Nixon, $75.
May 20	Goods returned by us to B. Spencer, $14.
May 24	Credit sales: K. Mohammed, $57; K. Kelly, $65; O. Green, $112.
May 28	Goods returned to us by N. Mendes, $24.
May 31	Credit sales: N. Lee, $55.

14.4 Write up the journals for June 2002 from the following credit transactions.

2002

June 1	Sold goods to K. King, $196.
June 6	Sold goods to R. Jones for $700 *less* 30% trade discount.
June 11	Bought goods from E. T. Ltd for $1,800 *less* 20% trade discount.
June 16	K. King returned $21 of goods sold to him on 1 June.
June 20	Sent an invoice to N. English for $500 goods *less* 20% trade discount.
June 24	We returned $200 of goods *less* 20% discount to E. T. Ltd.
June 30	Bought goods for $400 from A. Richards.

You are also required to:

(*a*) Post the transactions to the sales and purchases ledgers and to the general ledger.

(*b*) Balance the personal accounts.

(*c*) Use the accounts to draw up a trial balance as on 30 June 2002.

(*CXC style*)

14.5X You are to enter the following items in the books, post to personal accounts, and show transfers to the general ledger. Make up your own folio numbers and record against each item.

2005	
July 1	Credit purchases from: K. Hill, $380; M. Norman, $500; N. Senior, $106.
July 3	Credit sales to: E. Rigby, $510; E. Phillips, $246; F. Thompson, $356.
July 5	Credit purchases from: R. Morton, $200; J. Cook, $180; D. Edwards, $410; C. Davies, $66.
July 8	Credit sales to: A. Green, $307; H. George, $250; J. Ferguson, $185.
July 12	Returns outwards to: M. Norman, $30; N. Senior, $16.
July 14	Returns inwards from: E. Phillips, $18; F. Thompson, $22.
July 20	Credit sales to: E. Phillips, $188; F. Powell, $310; E. Lee, $420.
July 24	Credit purchases from: C. Ferguson, $550; K. Ennevor, $900.
July 31	Returns inwards from E. Phillips, $27; E. Rigby, $30.
July 31	Returns outwards to: J. Cook, $13; C. Davies, $11.

14.6X Post the following transactions from the sales day book and the sales returns day book to the ledgers.

Sales Day Book

2006		*Folio*	*Details*	*$*
January 3	M. Jones	L2		60
January 7	B. Buston	L3	200	
	less 10%		20	180
January 10	M. Jones	L2		70
January 15	M. White	L4	180	
	less 10%		18	162
January 21	M. Jones			70
				542

Sales Returns Day Book

January 20	M. Jones	L2	12
			12

(*Pitman Examination Institute*)

14.7X

STATEMENT

J. Hunt
24 Richards Road
St John's
Antigua
31 March 2004

Mr R. J. Cook
14 Nelson Street
St John's

		$	$	$
February 1	Balance			130.42
February 6	Invoice 512	140.64		271.06
February 8	Cheque		127.16	
	Discount		3.26	140.64
February 12	Returns		16.30	124.34
February 26	Invoice 540	184.42		308.76
February 28	Undercharge	3.60		312.36

Study the statement.

(*a*) Name the person who is supplying goods.

(*b*) Explain in simple terms the meaning of each item in the statement from 1 to 26 February and state the document used for the item on 28 February and the names of the sender and the receiver.

(*c*) Give the names of the debtor and the creditor and the amount owed on 28 February 2004.

CHAPTER **15**

The Banking System

Learning Objectives

- To know the difference between current accounts and deposit accounts.
- To be able to make out cheques.
- To understand the effect of various kinds of crossing on cheques.
- To be able to endorse a cheque over to someone else.
- To be able to fill in bank paying-in slips.
- To understand what a bill of exchange is.
- To realize the timing differences between entries in a cash book and those on a bank statement.

15.1 Introduction

We will be looking at payments into and out of bank accounts in Chapters 16 and 17. You therefore need to know some details about bank accounts.

15.2 Types of Account

There are two main types of bank account.

Current Accounts

These are used for regular payments into and out of a bank. A **cheque book** is given by the bank to the holder of the account. The account holder can write a cheque to make payments.

For paying money into the current account, the holder is given a paying-in book.

Current accounts do not usually earn interest.

Deposit Accounts

A deposit account is for putting money into the bank and not taking it out quickly.

Usually interest is given by the bank on money kept in deposit accounts.

15.3 Cheques

1 When the bank has agreed to let you open a current account, it will ask you for a signature. This allows the bank to prove that your cheques are in fact signed by you, and have not been forged. You will then be issued with a cheque book.

2 You can then use the cheques to make payments out of the account. Normally you must make sure that you have more money in the account than the amount paid out. If you wish to pay out more money than you have banked, you will have to see the bank

manager. You will then discuss the reasons for this, and if he or she agrees permission will be given for you to 'overdraw' your account. This is known as a **bank overdraft**. The person filling in the cheque and using it for payment, is known as the **drawer**. The person to whom the cheque is paid is known as the **payee**.

We can now look at Exhibit 15.1, which is a blank cheque form before it is filled in. On the face of the cheque are various sets of numbers. These are:

- 914234 — Every cheque printed for the Country Bank will be given a different number, so that individual items can be traced.
- 09-07-99 — Each branch of each bank has a different number given to it. Thus this branch has a 'code' number 09-07-99.
- 0599 — Each account with the bank is given a different number. This particular number is kept only for the account of J. Woodstock at the Montego Bay branch.

When we fill in the cheque we copy the details on the counterfoil which we then detach and keep for our records.

We can now look at the completion of a cheque. Let us assume that we are to pay seventy-two dollars and eighty-five cents to K. Marshall on 22 May 2005. Exhibit 15.2 shows the completed cheque. In Section 15.4 we will learn why we have drawn two parallel lines across the face of the cheque.

Exhibit 15.1

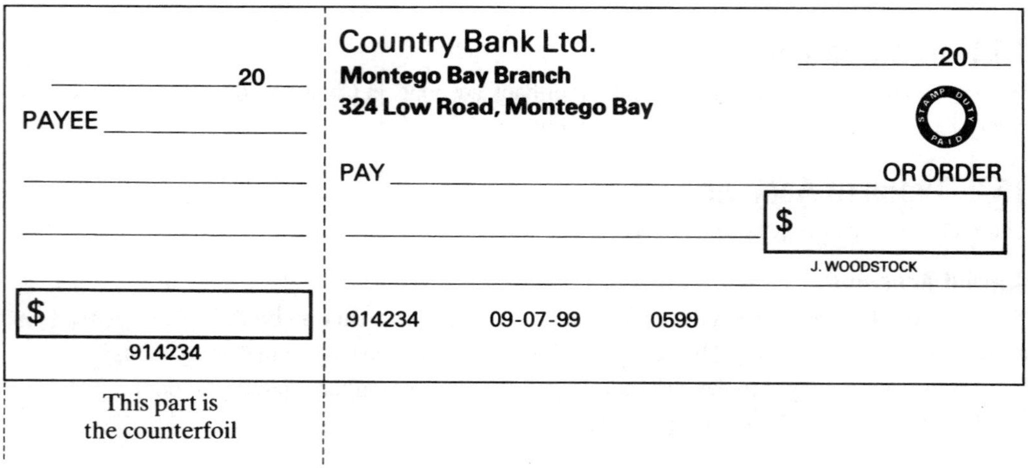

Exhibit 15.2

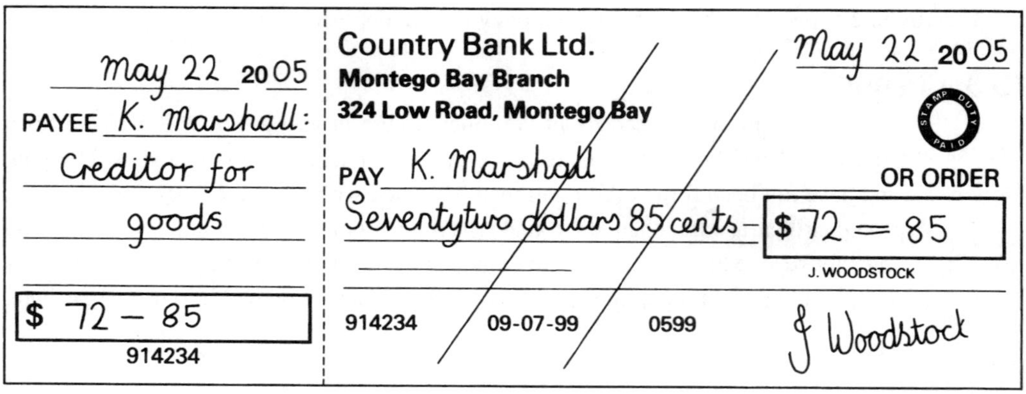

In Exhibit 15.2:

- the drawer is: J. Woodstock
- the payee is: K. Marshall.

15.4 Cheque Crossings

The two parallel lines across the face of a cheque as in Exhibit 15.2 are drawn as a safeguard. If we had not done this the cheque would have been an 'uncrossed cheque'. If someone had stolen an uncrossed cheque he or she could have gone to the Montego Bay branch of the Country Bank and obtained cash in exchange for the cheque. When the cheque is crossed it means it *must* be paid into a bank account.

The cheque shown has a crossing known as a 'general crossing', as there are no specific instructions given to the bank in writing within the lines of the crossing.

Cheques can be further safeguarded by using specific crossings, i.e. writing a form of instruction within the crossing on the cheque as shown in Exhibit 15.3. These are called 'special crossings'.

Exhibit 15.3

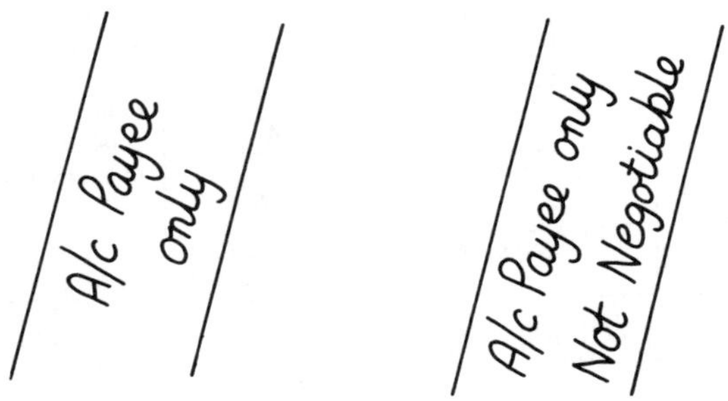

Special crossings are specific instructions to the banks about the use of the cheque. The use of 'Account Payee only' means the cheques should be paid only into the account of the payee named. If cheques are lost or stolen, the drawer must advise his bank immediately and confirm by letter. These cheques will be 'stopped'; i.e., payment will not be made on the cheques, provided you act swiftly. The safest crossing is that of 'A/c Payee only; Not Negotiable'. If the cheque is lost or stolen it will be of no use to the thief or finder. This is because it is impossible for this cheque to be paid into any bank account other than that of the named payee.

15.5 Cheque Endorsements

If a cheque does not have a crossing forbidding the payee to do so, the payee may pass the cheque over to someone else. Should James receive a cheque from Campbell, and then wish to use it as a payment to Scott, he can do so.

In doing this he must 'endorse' the cheque to Scott. This is done by James writing 'Pay A. Scott or order' on the reverse side of the cheque, and then adding his own (i.e. James') signature.

15.6 Paying-in Slips

When we want to pay money into our current accounts, either cash or cheques, or both, we use a **paying-in slip**. One of these is shown as Exhibit 15.4.

J. Woodstock has banked the following items:

Four	\$20 notes	
Three	\$10 notes	
One	\$5 note	
Four	\$1 notes	
Coins	\$2.30	
Cheques received from:		*Code numbers:*
E. Khouri	\$184.20	02–58–76
J. Gordon	\$ 65.40	05–77–85

Exhibit 15.4

Face of paying-in slip

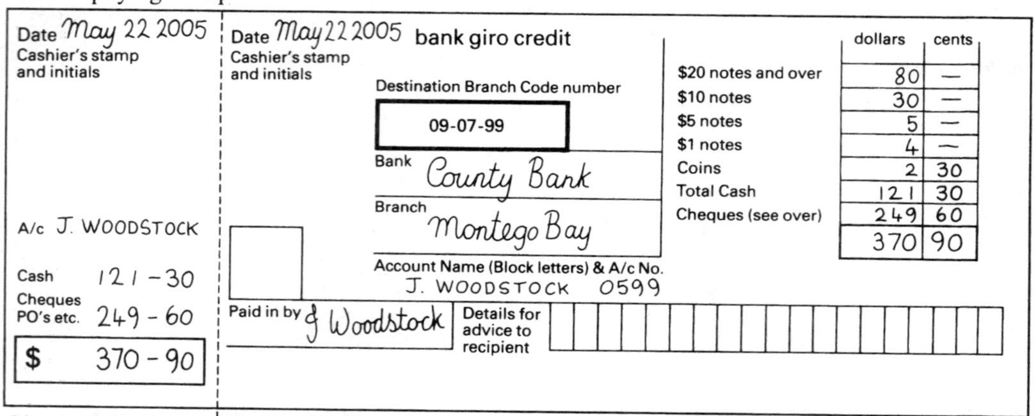
Date May 22 2005
Cashier's stamp and initials
A/c J. WOODSTOCK
Cash 121 – 30
Cheques PO's etc. 249 – 60
\$ 370 – 90

Date May 22 2005 bank giro credit
Cashier's stamp and initials
Destination Branch Code number
09-07-99
Bank County Bank
Branch Montego Bay
Account Name (Block letters) & A/c No. J. WOODSTOCK 0599
Paid in by J Woodstock
Details for advice to recipient

	dollars	cents
\$20 notes and over	80	—
\$10 notes	30	—
\$5 notes	5	—
\$1 notes	4	—
Coins	2	30
Total Cash	121	30
Cheques (see over)	249	60
	370	90

Counterfoil retained by Woodstock

Paying-in slip and cash and cheques handed in to bank

Reverse side of paying-in slip

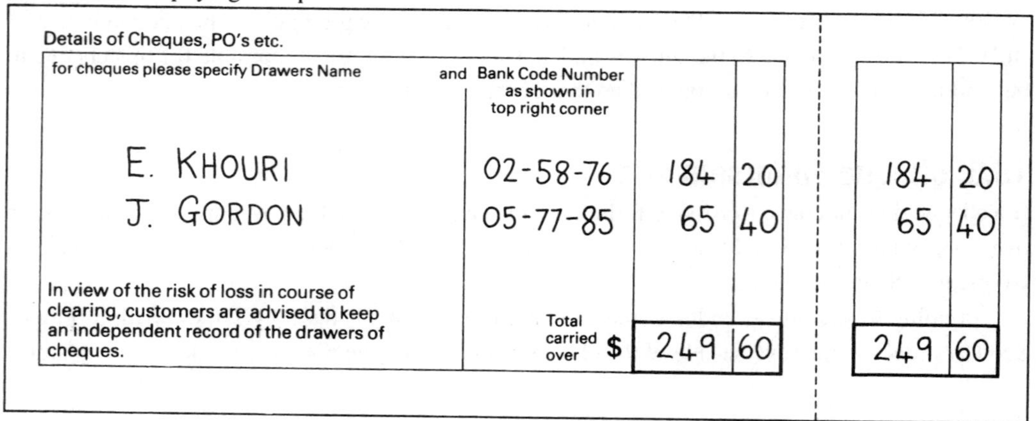
Details of Cheques, PO's etc.

for cheques please specify Drawers Name and	Bank Code Number as shown in top right corner				
E. KHOURI	02-58-76	184	20	184	20
J. GORDON	05-77-85	65	40	65	40
In view of the risk of loss in course of clearing, customers are advised to keep an independent record of the drawers of cheques.	Total carried over \$	249	60	249	60

Reverse of counterfoil

15.7 Cheque Clearings

We will now consider how cheques paid from one person's bank account pass into another person's bank account.

Let us look at the progress of the cheque in Exhibit 15.2. We will assume that the Post Office is being very efficient and delivering all letters the following day after being posted.

2005

May 22 Woodstock, in Montego Bay, sends the cheque to K. Marshall, who lives in Spanish Town. Woodstock enters the payment in his cash book.

May 23 Cheque received by Marshall. He banks it the same day in his bank account at National Bank in Spanish Town. Marshall shows the cheque in his cash book as being received and banked on 23 May.

May 24 National Bank in Kingston receive it. They exchange it with the Head Office of the Country Bank in Kingston.
The Country Bank send the cheque to their Montego Bay branch.

May 25 The Montego Bay branch of the Country Bank examine the cheque. If there is nothing wrong with it, the cheque can now be debited by the bank to J. Woodstock's account.

This illustrates the fact that different organizations will make entries for a particular transaction on different dates:

2005

May 22 This is the day on which Woodstock has made the entry in his cash book.

May 25 This is the day when the bank makes an entry in Woodstock's account in respect of the cheque.

15.8 Bills of Exchange

A cheque is a very common form of payment used in business. Another form of payment met with is a **bill of exchange**.

Particularly when trading with customers in distant countries, the supplier would have to wait a long time before the goods shipped arrive at a customer's business and the customer would then be prepared to pay for them. One way that can give the supplier quicker use of the money owing to him is for him to draw a bill of exchange on the debtor. This means that a document is drawn up requiring the debtor to pay the amount owing to the creditor, or to anyone nominated by him at any time, on or by a particular date. The creditor sends this document to the debtor who, if agreeing to it, is said to 'accept' it by writing on the document that she will comply with it and appending her signature. The debtor then returns the bill of exchange to the creditor. This document is then legal proof of the debt. The debtor is not then able to contest the correctness of the debt but only for any fault in the bill of exchange itself. The creditor can now act in one of three ways.

1. He can give the bill to another person in payment of a debt. That person may also then give it to someone else. The person who possesses the bill at maturity, i.e. the date for payment of the bill, will present it to the debtor for payment.
2. He may 'discount' it with a bank. 'Discount' here means that the bank will take the bill of exchange and treat it in the same manner as money deposited in the bank account. The bank will then hold the bill unit maturity, when it will present it to the

debtor for payment. The bank will make a charge to the creditor for this service known as a *discounting charge*.

3 He may hold the bill until maturity, when he will present it to the debtor for payment. In this case, apart from having a document which is legal proof of the debt and could therefore save legal costs if a dispute arose, no quicker benefit has been gained from having a bill of exchange. However, action 1 or 2 could have been taken if the need had arisen.

On 'accepting' the bill of exchange, the customer will be given shipping documents enabling her to claim the goods as her own when they arrive.

The supplier who draws up the bill of exchange is known as the **drawer**. The debtor on whom it is drawn is the **drawee**; when accepted she becomes the **acceptor**, while the person to whom the bill is to be paid is the **payee**.

New Terms

Current account (p. 121): Bank account used for regular payments into and out of the bank.

Deposit account (p. 121): Bank account for money to be kept in for a long time; interest is given on money deposited.

Cheque book (p. 121): Book containing forms (cheques) used to pay money out of a current account.

Bank overdraft (p. 122): When we have drawn cheques on our bank account for amounts in excess of what we have paid into it.

Drawer (p. 122): The person making out a cheque and using it for payment.

Payee (p. 122): The person to whom a cheque is paid.

Paying-in slip (p. 123): Form used for paying money into a bank account.

Bill of exchange (p. 125): A document in which the acceptor promises to pay the holder of the bill a stated sum of money at a stated future date.

Summary

1 A current account will be accompanied by the use of a cheque book, while a deposit account will not.

2 Crossings on cheques indicate that they must be banked before cash can be collected for them.

3 Special crossings on cheques act as instructions to the banker, and are usually used to ensure that the cheque cannot be used by anyone other than its rightful owner.

4 Cheque endorsements are to enable a rightful owner of the cheque to give it to someone else.

5 Cheque clearing is the way in which a cheque goes through the banking system and is credited to its rightful owner and charged against the drawer's bank account.

6 Bills of exchange are most commonly used in foreign trade.

CHAPTER **16**

Two-column Cash Books

Learning Objectives

- To be able to enter up and balance off two-column cash books.

16.1 Introduction

So far in this book, when you have been asked to record cash transactions and bank transactions, you have made entries either in a cash account or in a bank account. These two accounts have until now been shown on two separate pages of the ledger.

Now that we have decided to have a completely separate book for all *receipts* of money, whether cash or bank items, and for all cash and bank *payments*, we will find it easier to put the two sets of account columns together. This means that we can show all money received and paid out, whether by cash or by cheques, on the same page of the cash book.

In the cash book the debit column for cash is put next to the debit column for bank. The credit column for cash is put next to the credit column for bank.

16.2 Drawing up a Cash Book

We can now look at a set of items concerning both cash and bank receipts, and cash and bank payments:

- in Exhibit 16.1: using a separate cash account and bank account
- in Exhibit 16.2: using a two-column cash book, showing cash receipts and payments in the cash columns, and cheque receipts and payments in the bank columns.

List of transactions:

2005

Aug 1 Started business by putting $1,000 into a business bank account.
Aug 2 Received cash from T. Moore, $33.
Aug 3 Received a cheque from I. Powell Ltd, $244.
Aug 5 Received cash from G. Bernard, $25.
Aug 7 Paid rates by cheque, $105.
Aug 8 Paid rent by cash, $20.
Aug 12 Paid M. Prince by cash, $19.
Aug 13 Paid cheque to D. Soares Ltd, $95.
Aug 15 Received cash from B. Hussey, $37.
Aug 16 Received cheque from G. Polack, $408.
Aug 26 Paid N. Foster by cheque, $268.
Aug 28 Paid staff by cash, $25.

Aug 30 Received cheque from B. Singh, $20.
Aug 30 Received cash from H. Howe, $18.

The balances are to be carried down as at 31 August 2005.

Exhibit 16.1

Cash

2005	$	2005	$
Aug 2 T. Moore	33	Aug 8 Rent	20
Aug 5 G. Bernard	25	Aug 12 M. Prince	19
Aug 15 B. Hussey	37	Aug 28 Pay	25
Aug 30 H. Howe	18	Aug 31 Balance c/d	49
	113		113
Sept 1 Balance b/d	49		

Bank

2005	$	2005	$
Aug 1 Capital	1,000	Aug 7 Rates	105
Aug 3 I. Powell Ltd	244	Aug 13 D. Soares Ltd	95
Aug 16 G. Polack	408	Aug 26 N. Foster	268
Aug 30 B. Singh	20	Aug 31 Balance c/d	1,204
	1,672		1,672
Sept 1 Balance b/d	1,204		

Exhibit 16.2

Cash Book

	Cash	*Bank*		*Cash*	*Bank*
2005	$	$	2005	$	$
Aug 1 Capital		1,000	Aug 7 Rates		105
Aug 2 T. Moore	33		Aug 8 Rent	20	
Aug 3 I. Powell Ltd		244	Aug 12 M. Prince	19	
Aug 5 G. Bernard	25		Aug 13 D. Soares Ltd		95
Aug 15 B. Hussey	37		Aug 26 N. Foster		268
Aug 16 G. Polack		408	Aug 26 Pay	25	
Aug 30 B. Singh		20	Aug 31 Balance c/d	49	1,204
Aug 30 H. Howe	18				
	113	1,672		113	1,672
Sept 1 Balances b/d	49	1,204			

16.3 Cash Paid into the Bank

In Exhibit 16.2 the payments into the bank have been *cheques* received by the firm which have been banked immediately. We must now consider *cash* being paid into the bank.

Part Payment of Cash into Bank

Let us look at the position when a customer pays the account in cash, and later a part of this cash is paid into the bank. The receipt of the cash is debited to the cash column on the date received, the credit entry being in the customer's personal account. The cash banked has the following effect, needing action as shown:

Effect	*Action*
1 Asset of bank is increased	Debit the asset account, i.e. the bank account, which is represented by the bank column in the cash book.
2 Asset of cash is decreased.	Credit the asset account, i.e. the cash account, which is represented by the cash column in the cash book.

A cash receipt of $100 from J. Diaz on 1 August 2005, later followed by the banking on 3 August of $80 of this account, would appear in the cash book as follows.

Cash Book

	Cash	*Bank*		*Cash*	*Bank*
2005	$	$	2005	$	$
Aug 1 J. Diaz	100		Aug 3 Bank	80	
Aug 3 Cash		80			

The details column shows entries against each item stating the name of the account in which the completion of double entry has taken place. Against the cash payment of $80 appears the word 'bank', meaning that the debit $80 is to be found in the bank column; and the opposite applies.

Whole Payment into Bank

Where the whole of the cash received is banked immediately, the receipt can be treated in exactly the same manner as a cheque received; i.e., it can be entered directly in the bank column.

Withdrawal of Cash from Bank

If the firm requires cash, it may withdraw cash from the bank. This is done by making out a cheque to pay itself a certain amount in cash. The bank will give cash in exchange for the cheque.

The twofold effect and the action required may be shown as follows.

Effect	*Action*
1 Asset of cash is increased	Debit the asset account, i.e. the cash column in the cash book.
2 Asset of bank is decreased.	Credit the asset account, i.e. the bank column in the cash book.

A withdrawal of $75 cash on 1 June 2005 from the bank would appear in the cash book as follows.

Cash Book

	Cash	*Bank*		*Cash*	*Bank*
2005	$	$	2005	$	$
June 1 Bank	75		June 1 Cash		75

Both the debit and credit entries for this item are in the same book. When this happens it is known as a **contra** item. In such a case a capital C should be entered in the folio column to show that it is a contra.

16.4 Dollars and Cents

In this book, to save you unnecessary arithmetic, we do not give examples in both dollars and cents. Obviously this is not true of a real business. There will therefore be a cents column as well as a dollar column in all the books and journals of a business.

When entering up items, if the sum involved does not include any cents, then there are two methods of filling up the cents column:

	$	¢
F. Barker	208	00
or		
F. Barker	208	—

New Terms

Contra (p. 130): A contra item is where both the debit and credit entries are made in the cash book.

Summary

1 A cash book consists of a cash account and a bank account put together into one book.

Exercises

16.1 Write up a two-column cash book from the following details, and balance off as at the end of the month.

2005	
May 1	Started business with capital in cash, $100.
May 2	Paid rent by cash, $10.
May 3	F. Lai lent us $500, paying by cheque.
May 4	Paid B. McKenzie by cheque, $65.
May 5	Cash sales, $98.
May 7	N. Miller paid us by cheque, $62.
May 9	Paid B. Burton in cash, $22.
May 11	Cash sales paid direct into the bank, $53.
May 15	G. Motta paid us in cash, $65.
May 16	Took out of the cash till and paid into the bank account, $50.
May 19	Repaid F. Lai by cheque, $100.
May 22	Cash sales paid direct into the bank, $66.
May 26	Paid motor expenses by cheque, $12.
May 30	Withdrew cash from the bank for business use, $100.
May 31	Paid staff in cash, $97.

16.2 Write up a two-column cash book from the following details, and balance off as at the end of the month.

2006	
Mar 1	Balances brought down from last month: cash in hand, $56. cash in bank, $2,356.
Mar 2	Paid rates by cheque, $156.
Mar 3	Paid for postage stamps in cash, $5.
Mar 5	Cash sales, $74.
Mar 7	Cash paid into bank, $60.
Mar 8	Paid T. Lee by cheque, $75.
Mar 10	Paid C. Brooks in cash, $2.
Mar 12	J. Moores pays us $150, $50 being in cash and $100 by cheque.
Mar 17	Cash drawings by proprietor, $20.
Mar 20	P. Jones pays us by cheque, $79.
Mar 22	Withdrew from the bank for business use, $200.
Mar 24	Bought a new motor van for cash, $195.
Mar 28	Paid rent by cheque, $40.
Mar 31	Cash sales paid direct into the bank, $105.

16.3X A two-column cash book is to be written up from the following, carrying the balances down to the following month.

2004	
Jan 1	Started business with $4,000 in the bank.
Jan 2	Paid for fixtures by cheque, $660.
Jan 4	Cash sales, $225.
Jan 5	Paid rent by cash, $140.
Jan 6	T. Thomas paid us by cheque, $188.
Jan 8	Cash sales paid direct into the bank, $308.
Jan 10	J. Khaleel paid us in cash, $300.
Jan 12	Paid staff in cash, $275.
Jan 14	J. Walters lent us $500 paying by cheque.
Jan 15	Withdrew $200 from the bank for business use.
Jan 20	Bought stationery paying by cash, $60.
Jan 22	Paid J. Fung by cheque, $166.
Jan 28	Cash drawing, $100.
Jan 30	J. Scott paid us by cheque, $277.
Jan 31	Cash sales, $66.

16.4X Write up a two-column cash book from the following.

2006	
Nov 1	Balance brought forward from last month: cash, $105; bank, $2,164.
Nov 2	Cash sales, $605.
Nov 3	Took out of the cash till and paid into the bank, $500.
Nov 4	J. Matthews paid us by cheque, $217.
Nov 5	Paid for postage stamps in cash, $60.
Nov 6	Bought office equipment by cheque, $189.
Nov 7	Paid J. Lindo by cheque, $50.
Nov 9	Received rates refund by cheque, $72.
Nov 11	Withdrew from the bank for business use, $250.
Nov 12	Paid staff in cash, $239.
Nov 14	Paid motor expenses by cheque, $57.
Nov 16	L. Levy lent us cash, $200.
Nov 20	R. Norman paid us by cheque, $112.
Nov 28	We paid general expenses in cash, $22.
Nov 30	Paid insurance by cheque, $74.

16.5X Roger Groves runs a small store. The records he keeps are of cash received and paid, also cheques received. His bank statement and cheque counterfoils act as his bank record. All cheques received are banked immediately.

He did not sell anything or buy anything on credit in May 2003.

You know the following for May 2003.

		$
May 1	Cash in till brought forward	160
May 8	Sales for week:	
	cheques	975
	cash	206
	Banked all cash except for $200.	
May 15	Sales for week:	
	cheques	547
	cash	896
	Banked all cash except for $300 kept as cash balance.	
May 31	Sales for remainder of month:	
	cheques	2,590
	cash	1,724
	Bought office equipment for cash	500
	Paid insurance by cash	600
	Banked all cash except for float of	300

On 1 May 2003 both the bank statement and the cash book showed a balance of $3,725. Cheques drawn for month were as follows.

			$
No. 164	May 7	J. Jackson for stock	647
165	May 12	Rent for business premises	900
166	May 16	Repairs to office equipment	166
167	May 21	Cheque for private use	220
168	May 27	T. Towers for stock	724
169	May 31	Motor running expenses	307

You are to:

(*a*) write up a two-column cash book for the month and balance down

(*b*) write up purchases and sales accounts and show totals

(*c*) calculate the total expenses for the month.

(*CXC style*)

CHAPTER **17**

Cash Discounts and the Three-column Cash Book

Learning Objectives

- To be able to enter discounts received and discounts allowed in double entry records.
- To write up a three-column cash book.
- To understand the difference between a cash discount and a trade discount.

17.1 Cash discounts

It is better if customers pay their accounts quickly. A firm may accept a smaller sum in full settlement if payment is made within a certain period of time. The amount of the reduction of the sum to be paid is known as a *cash discount*. The term 'cash discount' thus refers to the allowance given for quick payment. It is still called cash discount, even if the account is paid by cheque.

The rate of cash discount is usually stated as a percentage. Full details of the percentage allowed, and the period within which payment is to be made, are quoted on all sales documents by the selling company. A typical period during which discount may be allowed is one month from the date of the original transaction.

17.2 Discounts Allowed and Discounts Received

A firm may have two types of cash discounts in its books:

1. It may allow cash discounts to its customers when they pay quickly: we call this type **discounts allowed**;
2. It may receive discounts from its suppliers when it pays them quickly: we call this type **discounts received**.

We can now see the effect of discounts by looking at two examples.

Example 1

W. Charles owes us \$100. He pays on 2 September 2005 by cash within the time limit laid down, and the firm allows him 5% cash discount. So he pays \$100 – \$5 = \$95 in full settlement of his account. This means that W. Charles' debt of \$100 has now been shown as fully settled; also, it has been recorded exactly how the settlement took place (see Exhibit 17.1).

Exhibit 17.1

Effect	Action
1 *Of cash*	
Cash is increased by $95.	Debit cash account; i.e., enter $95 in debit column of cash book.
Asset of debtors is decreased by $95.	Credit W. Charles $95
2 *Of discounts*	
Expenses of discounts allowed increased by $5.	Debit discounts allowed account $5.
Asset of debtors is decreased by $5. (After the cash was paid the balance of $5 still appeared. As the account has been fully settled, this asset must now be cancelled.)	Credit W. Charles $5.

Example 2

The firm owes S. Smith $400. It pays her on 3 September 2005 by cheque within the time limit laid down by her and she allows 2½% cash discount. Thus, the firm pays $400 – $10 = $390 in full settlement of the account. This means that our indebtedness to S. Smith has been shown as fully settled; also, it has been recorded exactly how the settlement took place (see Exhibit 17.2).

Exhibit 17.2

Effect	Action
1 *Of cheque*	
Liability of creditors is reduced by $390.	Debit S. Smith's account $390.
Asset of bank is reduced by $390.	Credit bank, i.e. enter in credit bank column, $390.
2 *Of discounts*	
Liability of creditors is reduced by $10. (After the cheque was paid the balance of $10 remained. As the account has been fully settled the liability must now be cancelled.)	Debit S. Smith's account $10.
Revenue of discounts received increased by $10.	Credit discounts received account $10.

The accounts in the firm's books would appear as follows.

Cash Book *(p. 32)*

	Folio	*Cash*	*Bank*		*Folio*	*Cash*	*Bank*
2005		$	$	2005		$	$
Sept 2 W Charles	SL 12	95		Sept 3 S Smith	PL 75		390

General Ledger
Discounts Received *(p. 18)*

			2005	*Folio*	$
			Sept 2 S Smith	PL 75	10

General Ledger
Discounts Allowed *(p. 17)*

2005	*Folio*	$			
Sept 2 W Charles	SL 12	5			

Sales Ledger
W. Charles *(p. 12)*

2005	*Folio*	$	2005	*Folio*	$
Sept 1 Balance	b/d	100	Sept 2 Cash	CB 32	95
			Sept 2 Discount	GL 17	5
		100			100

Purchases Ledger
S. Smith *(p. 75)*

2005	*Folio*	$	2005	*Folio*	$
Sept 3 Bank	CB 32	390	Sept 1 Balance	b/d	400
Sept 3 Discounts	GL 18	10			
		400			400

17.3 Discount Columns in Cash Book

The discounts allowed account and the discounts received account are in the general ledger along with all the other revenue and expense accounts. It has already been stated that every effort should be made to avoid too much reference to the general ledger.

In the case of discounts this is done by adding an extra column on each side of the cash book in which the amounts of discounts are entered. Discounts received are entered in the discounts column on the credit side of the cash book, and discounts allowed in the discounts column on the debit side of the cash book.

The cash book, if completed for the two examples so far dealt with, would appear as follows.

Cash Book

	Folio	Disc't	Cash	Bank		Folio	Disc't	Cash	Bank
2005		$	$	$	2005		$	$	$
Sept 2 W. Charles	SL 12	5	95		Sept 3 S. Smith	PL 75	10		390

There is no alteration to the method of showing discounts in the personal accounts.

To Make Entries in the Discounts Accounts

- Total of discounts column on receipts side of cash book: post to debit side of discounts allowed account in total, at end of month.
- Total of discounts column on payments side of cash book: post to credit side of discounts received account in total, at end of month.

17.4 A Worked Example

2005		$
May 1	Balances brought down from April:	
	cash balance	29
	bank balance	654
	Debtors accounts:	
	B. Kahn	120
	N. Campbell	280
	D. Shand	40
	Creditors accounts:	
	U. Barrow	60
	A. Azar	440
	R. Long	100
May 2	B. Kahn paid us by cheque, having deducted 2½% cash discount of $3.	117
May 8	We paid R. Long his account by cheque, deducting 5% cash discount of $5.	95
May 11	We withdrew $100 cash from the bank for business use.	100
May 16	N. Campbell paid us his account by cheque, deducting 2½% discount of $7.	273
May 25	We paid staff in cash.	92
May 28	D. Shand paid us in cash after having deducted 2½% cash discount.	38
May 29	We paid U. Barrow by cheque less 5% cash discount of $3.	57
May 30	We paid A. Azar by cheque less 2½% cash discount of $11.	429

Exhibit 17.3 depicts the above transactions as entered into the cash book.

Exhibit 17.3

Cash Book *(p. 64)*

	Folio	*Disc't*	*Cash*	*Bank*		*Folio*	*Disc't*	*Cash*	*Bank*
2005		$	$	$	2005		$	$	$
May 1 Balance	b/d		29	654	May 8 R. Long	PL 58	5		95
May 2 B. Kahn	SL 13	3		117	May 11 Cash	C			100
May 11 Bank	C		100		May 25 Pay	GL 12		92	
May 16 N. Campbell	SL 84	7		273	May 29 U. Barrow	PL 15	3		57
May 28 D. Shand	SL 91	2	38		May 30 A. Azar	PL 98	11		429
					May 31 Balances	c/d		75	363
	GL 101	12	167	1,044		GL 88	19	167	1,044
Jun 1 Balances	b/d		75	363					

Sales Ledger

B. Kahn *(p. 13)*

2005	*Folio*	$	2005	*Folio*	$
May 1 Balance	b/d	120	May 2 Bank	CB 64	117
			May 2 Discount	CB 64	3
		120			120

N. Campbell *(p. 84)*

2005	*Folio*	$	2005	*Folio*	$
May 1 Balance	b/d	280	May 16 Bank	CB 64	273
			May 16 Discount	CB 64	7
		280			280

D. Shand *(p. 91)*

2005	*Folio*	$	2005	*Folio*	$
May 1 Balance	b/d	40	May 28 Bank	CB 64	38
			May 28 Discount	CB 64	2
		40			40

Purchases Ledger

U. Barrow *(p. 15)*

2005	*Folio*	$	2005	*Folio*	$
May 29 Bank	CB 64	57	May 1 Balance	b/d	60
May 29 Discount	CB 64	3			
		60			60

R. Long *(p. 58)*

2005	*Folio*	$	2005	*Folio*	$
May 8 Bank	CB 64	95	May 1 Balance	b/d	100
May 8 Discount	CB 64	5			
		100			100

A. Azar *(p. 98)*

2005	*Folio*	$	2005	*Folio*	$
May 30 Bank	CB 64	429	May 1 Balance	b/d	440
May 30 Discount	CB 64	11			
		440			440

General Ledger

Pay *(p. 77)*

2005	*Folio*	$			
May 25 Cash	CB 64	92			

Discounts Received *(p. 88)*

			2005	*Folio*	$
			May 31 Total for the month	CB 64	19

Discounts Allowed *(p. 101)*

2005	*Folio*	$			
May 31 Total for the month	CB 64	12			

Is the above method of entering discounts correct? You can easily check. In Exhibit 17.4, you can see that proper double entry has been carried out. Equal amounts, in total, have been entered on each side of the accounts.

Exhibit 17.4

Discounts in ledger accounts	Debits		Credits	
		$		$
Discounts received	U. Barrow	3	Discounts	
	R. Long	5	received	
	A. Azar	11	account	19
		19		
Discounts allowed	Discounts			$
	allowed		B. Kahn	3
	account	12	N. Campbell	7
			D. Shand	2
				12

17.5 Cash Discounts and Trade Discounts Compared

- **Cash discounts** discounts for speedy payment; entered in double entry accounts.
- **Trade discounts** simply a method of calculating selling prices; *not* entered in double entry accounts.

17.6 The Importance of Cash Discounts

Where a business is offered the chance to obtain cash discounts by paying their bills quickly, then normally it is well worth doing so. For instance, suppose that K. Wallace buys $200 goods from C. Charles. Cash discount of 2½% is allowable if payment is made within one month.

Wallace may not bother to pay until after two months, thereby not getting the discount. He thinks that 2½% is a very small figure. He has however lost 2½% of $200 because he was one month late in paying. He has lost far more than he thinks if it is put in terms of a rate of interest per annum. This works out as follows:

$$\frac{\text{Amount lost \$5}}{\text{Payment delayed \$200}} \times \frac{100}{1} \times 12 = 30\% \text{ per annum}$$

Try it for yourself. If you borrowed $200 for 30% for one year you would pay interest of $60. For one month you would pay $60 ÷ 12 = $5.

This means that leaving the account unpaid for one month extra was like borrowing money at 30% per annum. If a 5% discount had been lost it would have been like borrowing money at 60% per annum. These are very high rates of interest in normal conditions.

Of course, it may well be that Mr Wallace was so short of cash that he was unable to pay, and his bank may also not have wanted to lend him any money. However, as a general rule it is not very sensible to lose cash discounts by delaying payment for a short time.

17.7 Bank Overdrafts

A firm may borrow money from a bank by means of a bank overdraft. This means that the firm is allowed to pay more out of the bank account, by paying out cheques, for a total amount greater than that which it has placed in the account.

Up to this point the bank balances have all represented money at the bank; thus they have all been assets; i.e. debit balances. When the account is overdrawn, the firm owes money to the bank, the account is a liability and the balance becomes a credit one.

Taking the cash book last illustrated, suppose that the amount payable to A. Azar was $1,429 instead of $429. Thus the total amount of balance brought forward plus bankings, $1,044, is exceeded by the amount withdrawn. The cash book would appear as shown in Exhibit 17.5. On a balance sheet, a bank overdraft will be shown as an item under 'Current Liabilities'.

Exhibit 17.5

Cash Book

	Discount	Cash	Bank		Discount	Cash	Bank
2005	$	$	$	2005			
May 1 Balances b/d		29	654	May 8 R. Long	5		95
May 2 B. Kahn	3		117	May 11 Cash			100
May 11 Bank		100		May 25 Pay		92	
May 16 N. Campbell	7		273	May 29 U. Barrow	3		57
May 28 D. Shand	2	38		May 30 A. Azar	11		1,429
May 31 Balance c/d			637	May 31 Balance c/d		75	
	12	167	1,681		19	167	1,681
Jun 1 Balance b/d		75		June 1 Balance b/d			637

New Terms

Discounts allowed (p. 133): A reduction given to customers who pay their accounts within the time allowed.

Discounts received (p. 133): A reduction given to us by a supplier when we pay his account within the discount period given.

Summary

1 Cash discounts are given to encourage people to pay their accounts within a stated time limit.

2 'Cash discount' is the name given for discount for quick payment even though in fact the payment may be made by cheque.

3 The discounts columns in the cash book make it easier to enter up the books. They act as a collection point for discounts allowed and discounts received, for which double entry is completed when the totals are transferred to the discounts accounts in the general ledger, usually at the end of each month.

Exercises

17.1 Enter up a three-column cash book from the details following. Balance off at the end of the month, and post to the relevant discount accounts in the general ledger.

2007

May 1 Started business with $6,000 in the bank.
May 1 Bought fixtures paying by cheque, $950.
May 2 Bought goods paying by cheque, $1,240.
May 3 Cash sales, $407.
May 4 Paid rent in cash, $200.
May 5 N. Morgan paid us his account of $220 by a cheque for $210; we allowed him $10 discount.
May 7 Paid S. Thompson and Co. $80 owing to him by means of a cheque $76; they allowed us $4 discount.

May 9 Received a cheque for $380 from S. Cooper, discount having been allowed $20.
May 12 Paid rates by cheque, $410.
May 14 L. Curtis paid us a cheque for $115.
May 16 Paid M. Monroe his account of $120 by cash $114, having deducted $6 cash discount.
May 20 P. Exeter paid us a cheque for $78, having deducted $2 cash discount.
May 31 Cash sales paid direct into the bank, $88.

17.2 A three-column cash book is to be written up from the following details, balanced off and posted to the relevant discount accounts in the general ledger.

2005
Mar 1 Balances brought forward: cash, $230; bank, $4,756.
Mar 2 The following paid their accounts by cheque, in each case deducting 5% cash discounts: accounts: R. Burton, $140; E. Taylor, $220; R. Harris, $300.
Mar 4 Paid rent by cheque, $120.
Mar 6 J. Cotton lent us $1,000 paying by cheque.
Mar 8 We paid the following accounts by cheque in each case deducting a 2½% cash discount: N. Black, $360; P. Towers, $480; C. Rowse, $800.
Mar 10 Paid motor expenses in cash, $44.
Mar 12 H. Hankins paid his account of $77 by cheque $74, deducting $3 cash discount.
Mar 15 Paid staff in cash, $160.
Mar 18 The following paid their accounts by cheque, in each case deducting 5% cash discount: accounts: C. Winston, $260; R. Wilson and Son, $340; H. Winter, $460.
Mar 21 Cash withdrawn from the bank $350 for business use.
Mar 24 Cash drawings, $120.
Mar 25 Paid T. Briers his account of $140, by cash $133, having deducted $7 cash discount.
Mar 29 Bought fixtures paying by cheque, $650.
Mar 31 Received commission by cheque, $88.

17.3 From the following details write up a three-column cash book, balance off at the end of the month, and post to the relevant discount accounts in the general ledger:

2003
Mar 1 Balances brought forward:
cash in hand, $211
cash at bank, $3,984
Mar 2 We paid each of the following accounts by cheque, in each case deducting a 5% discount: T. Adams, $80; C. Bibby, $260; D. Clarke, $440.
Mar 4 C. Potts paid us a cheque for $98.
Mar 6 Cash sales paid direct into the bank, $49.
Mar 7 Paid insurance by cash $65.
Mar 9 The following persons paid us their accounts by cheque, in each case deducting a discount of 2½%: R. Smiley, $160; J. Turner, $640; R. Pimlott, $520.
Mar 12 Paid motor expenses by cash, $100.
Mar 18 Cash sales, $98.
Mar 21 Paid staff by cheque, $120.
Mar 23 Paid rent by cash, $60.
Mar 28 Received a cheque for $500 being a loan from R. Godfrey.
Mar 31 Paid for stationery by cheque, $27.

17.4X Enter the following in a three-column cash book. Balance off the cash book at the end of the month and post to the discount accounts in the general ledger.

2008
June 1 Balances brought forward: cash, $97; bank, $2,186.
June 2 The following paid us by cheque, in each case deducting a 5% cash discount: R. Harty, $1,000; C. White, $280; P. Peers, $180; O. Hardy, $600.
June 3 Cash sales paid direct into the bank, $134.

June 5 Paid rent by cash, $88.
June 6 We paid the following accounts by cheque, in each case deducting 2½% cash discount: J. Charlton, $400; H. Sobers, $640; D. Shallcross, $200.
June 8 Withdrew cash from the bank for business use, $250.
June 10 Cash sales, $206.
June 12 D. Deeds paid us their account of $89 by cheque less $2 cash discount.
June 14 Paid staff by cash, $250.
June 16 We paid the following accounts by cheque: L. Lucas, $117 less cash discount of $6; D. Fisher, $206 less cash discount of $8.
June 20 Bought fixtures by cheque, $8,000.
June 24 Bought motor lorry paying by cheque, $7,166.
June 29 Received $169 cheque from D. Steel.
June 30 Cash sales, $116.
June 30 Bought stationery paying by cash, $60.

17.5X You are to write up a three-column cash book for M. Pinero from the details that follow. Then balance off at the end of the month and post to the discount accounts in the general ledger.

2006
May 1 Balances brought forward:
cash in hand, $58
bank overdraft, $1,470
May 2 M. Pinero paid further capital into the bank, $1,000.
May 3 Bought office fixtures by cheque, $780.
May 4 Cash sales, $220.
May 5 Banked cash, $200.
May 6 We paid the following by cheque, in each case deducting 2½% cash discount: B. Barnes, $80; T. Horton, $240; T. Jacklin, $400.
May 8 Cash sales, $500.
May 12 Paid motor expenses in cash, $77.
May 15 Cash withdrawn from the bank, $400.
May 16 Cash drawings, $120.
May 18 The following firms paid us their accounts by cheque, in each case deducting a 5% discount: L. Graham, $80; B. Crenshaw, $140; H. Green, $220.
May 20 Staff paid in cash, $210.
May 22 T. Weiskopf paid us his account in cash, $204.
May 26 Paid insurance by cheque, $150.
May 28 We banked all the cash in our possession except for $20 in the cash till.
May 31 Bought motor van, paying by cheque, $4,920.

CHAPTER **18**

The Journal

Learning Objectives

- To be able to enter up the journal.
- To be able to post from the journal to the ledgers.
- To be able to complete opening entries for a set of books.
- To understand the accounting cycle.

18.1 Main Books of Original Entry

We have seen in earlier chapters that most transactions are entered in one of the following special books of original entry:

- cash book
- sales journal
- purchases journal
- returns inwards journal
- returns outwards journal.

These books have grouped together similar things; for example, all credit sales are in the sales journal. Tracing any of them is relatively easy, as we know exactly which book would contain the item.

18.2 The Journal: The Other Book of Original Entry

The items that do not pass through the above books are much less common, and sometimes much more complicated. It is easy for a bookkeeper to forget the details of these transactions.

If the bookkeeper left the firm, it could be impossible to understand such bookkeeping entries.

What is needed is a form of diary to record such transactions, before the entries are made in the double entry accounts. This book is called **the journal**. It contains, for each transaction:

- the date
- the name of account(s) to be debited and the amount(s)
- the name of the account(s) to be credited and the amount(s)
- a description and explanation of the transaction (this is called a '**narrative**')
- a reference number for the source documents giving proof of the transaction.

The use of the journal makes fraud by bookkeepers more difficult. It also reduces the risk of entering the item once only instead of having double entry. Despite these advantages, there are many firms that do not have such a book.

18.3 Typical Uses of the Journal

Some of the main uses of the journal are listed below. It must not be thought that this list is a fully detailed one:

- **opening entries** – the entries needed to open a new set of books
- the purchase and sale of fixed assets on credit
- the correction of errors
- the writing off of bad debts
- other items: closing entries and adjusting entries.

The layout of the journal can now be shown. You can see that on the first line we put the account to be debited. The second line gives the account to be credited. We do not write the name of the account to be credited directly under the name of the account to be debited, but indent it. This makes it easier to see which is the debit and which is the credit.

The Journal

Date	*Details*	*Folio*	*Dr.*	*Cr.*
			$	$
	The name of the account to be debited. The name of the account to be credited. The narrative.			

We should remember that the journal is not a double entry account. It is a form of diary, and entering an item in the journal is not the same as recording an item in an account. Once the journal entry is made, the entry in the double entry accounts can then be made.

18.4 Journal Entries in Examination Questions

If you were to ask examiners what type of bookkeeping and accounting questions are always answered badly by a lot of students, they would certainly include 'questions involving journal entries'. This is not because they are difficult, but a lot of students seem to get some sort of a mental block when answering such questions. The author, who has been an examiner for a large number of accounting bodies around the world, thinks that it is because students think of the information in terms of the debits and credits in accounts, and not of it as a form of written instruction, which is what a journal is, stating which account is to be debited, which account is to be credited, plus describing the transaction.

To try to help you to avoid this sort of problem with journal entries, we will first of all show what the entries are in the accounts and then write up the journal for those entries. We will now look at a few examples, which include folio numbers.

Purchase and Sale on Credit of Fixed Assets

1 A machine is bought on credit from Toolmakers for $550 on 1 July 2005.

From what you have learned in earlier chapters, you will know that the double entry accounts would be as follows.

Machinery (Folio GL 1)

2005			$	
Jul 1 Toolmakers		PL 55	550	

Toolmakers (Folio PL 55)

			2005			$
			Jul 1 Machinery		GL 1	550

Now what we have to do is to record those entries in the journal. Remember, the journal is simply a kind of diary, not in account form, but in ordinary written form. It says which account has been debited, which account has been credited, and then gives the narrative simply describing the nature of the transaction. For the transaction above, the journal entry will appear as follows.

Date	*Details*	*Folio*	*Dr.*	*Cr.*
2005			$	$
Jul 1	Machinery	GL 1	550	
	Toolmakers	PL 55		550
	Purchase of milling machine on credit,			
	Capital Purchases invoice no. 7/159			

2 Sale of stationery not now needed for $300 on credit to K. King on 2 July 2005.

Here again it is not difficult to work out what entries are needed in the double entry accounts. They are as follows.

K. King (Folio SL 79)

2005			$			
Jul 1 Stationery		GL 51	300			

Stationery (Folio GL 51)

			2005			$
			Jul 2 K. King			300

These are shown in journal form as set out below.

Date	*Details*	*Folio*	*Dr.*	*Cr.*
2005			$	$
Jul 2	K. King	SL 79	300	
	Stationery	GL 51		300
	Sale of some stationery not now needed,			
	see letter 1/55/68			

Bad Debts

3 A debt of $78 owing to us from H. Marshall is written off as a bad debt on 31 August 2005.

As the debt is now of no value, we have to stop showing it as an asset. This means that we will credit H. Marshall to cancel it out of his account. A bad debt is an expense, and so we will debit it to a Bad Debts account. In double entry form, this is shown as follows.

Bad Debts (Folio GL 16)

2005			$			
Aug 31 H. Marshall		SL 99	78			

H. Marshall (Folio SL 99)

2005		$	2005		$
Aug 1 Balance b/d		78	Aug 31 Bad debts	GL 16	78

The journal entry showing this is as follows.

Date	*Details*	*Folio*	*Dr.*	*Cr.*
2005			$	$
Aug 31	Bad debts	GL 16	78	
	H. Marshall	SL 99		78
	Debt written off as bad. See letter in file 7/8906			

Other Items

These can be of many kinds and it is impossible to write out a complete list. Several examples are now follow.

1 S. Blake, a debtor, owed $200 on 1 July 2006. He was unable to pay his account in cash, but offers a motor car in full settlement of the debt. The offer is accepted on 5 July 2006.

The personal account is therefore not now owed and needs crediting. On the other hand, the firm now has an extra asset, a motor car, therefore the motor car account needs to be debited. The double entry records are therefore as set out below.

The double entry records are therefore as set out below.

S. Blake (SL 333)

2006		$	2006		$
Jul 1 Balance	b/d	200	Jul 5 Motor car	GL 171	200

Motor Car (GL 171)

2006		$			
Jul 5 S. Blake	SL 333	200			

This is shown in the journal as follows.

The Journal

Date	*Details*	*Folio*	*Dr.*	*Cr.*
2006			$	$
Jul 5	Motor car	GL 171	200	
	S. Blake	SL 333		200
	Accepted motor car in full settlement of debt per letter dated 5.7.2006			

2 G. Grant is a creditor. On 10 July 2006, his business is taken over by A. Lee, to whom the debt is now to be paid.

Here it is a case of one creditor being exchanged for another one. The action needed is to cancel the amount owing to G. Grant by debiting his account, and to show it owing to Lee by opening an account for Lee and crediting it.

The double entry records are as follows.

G. Grant (SL 92)

2006			$	2006			$
Jul 10	A. Lee	SL 244	150	Jul 1	Balance	b/d	150

A. Lee (SL 244)

				2006			$
				Jul 10	G. Grant	SL 92	150

The journal entries are as set out below.

The Journal

Date	*Details*	*Folio*	*Dr.*	*Cr.*
2006			$	$
Jul 10	G. Grant	SL 92	150	
	A. Lee	SL 244		150
	Transfer of indebtedness as per letter ref. G/1335			

3 We had previously bought an office typewriter for $310, which has not yet been paid for. It is faulty. On 12 July 2006 we return it to the supplier, R. S. Ltd. An allowance of $310 is agreed, so that we will not have to pay for it.

The double entry records are as follows.

R. S. Ltd (PL 124)

2006			$	2006			$
Jul 12	Office machinery	GL 288	310	Jul 1	Balance	b/d	310

Office Machinery (GL 288)

				2006			$
				Jul 12	R. S. Ltd		310

The journal entries are the following.

The Journal

Date	*Details*	*Folio*	*Dr.*	*Cr.*
2006			$	$
Jul 12	R. S. Ltd	PL 124	310	
	Office machinery	GL 288		310
	Faulty typewriter returned to supplier			
	Full allowance given. See letter 10.7.2006			

18.5 Opening Entries

J. Brown, after being in business for some years without keeping proper records, now decides to keep a double entry set of books. On 1 July 2006 he establishes that his assets and liabilities are as follows.

Assets: Motor van, $840; fixtures, $700; stock, $390; *Debtors:* B. Nunez, $95, D. Blake, $45, Bank, $80, Cash, $20.

Liabilities: *Creditors:* M. Lee, $129, C. Shaw, $41.

The assets therefore total $840 + $700 + $390 + $95 + $45 + $80 + $20 = $2,170; and the liabilities total $129 + $41 = $170.

The capital consists of: Assets – Liabilities = $2,170 – $170 = $2,000.

We must start the writing up of the books on 1 July 2006 (see Exhibit 18.1).

1. We open asset accounts, one for each asset. Each opening asset is shown as a debit balance.
2. We open liability accounts, one for each liability. Each opening liability is shown as a credit balance.
3. We open an account for the capital, showing it as a credit balance.

The journal records what you are doing, and why.

Exhibit 18.1 shows:

- the journal;
- the opening entries in the double entry accounts.

Exhibit 18.1

The Journal *(p. 1)*

Date	*Details*	*Folio*	*Dr.*	*Cr.*
2006			$	$
Jul 1	Motor van	GL 8	840	
	Fixtures	GL 13	700	
	Stock	GL 19	390	
	Debtors: B. Nunez	SL 45	95	
	D. Blake	SL 49	45	
	Bank	CB 12	80	
	Cash	CB 12	20	
	Creditors: M. Lee	PL 81		129
	C. Shaw	PL 86		41
	Capital	GL 50		2,000
	Assets and liabilities at this date entered to open the books.			
			2,170	2,170

General Ledger

Motor Van *(p. 8)*

2006			$				
July 1	Balance	J 1	840				

Fixtures *(p. 13)*

2006			$				
July 1	Balance	J 1	700				

Stock *(p. 19)*

2006			$				
July 1	Balance	J 1	390				

Capital *(p. 50)*

				2006			$
				July 1	Balance	J 1	2,000

Sales Ledger

B. Nunez *(p. 45)*

2006			$				
July 1	Balance	J 1	95				

D. Blake *(p. 49)*

2006			$				
July 1	Balance	J 1	45				

Purchases Ledger

M. Lee *(p. 81)*

				2006			$
				July 1	Balance	J 1	129

C. Shaw *(p. 86)*

				2006			$
				July 1	Balance	J 1	41

Cash Book *(p. 12)*

			Cash	*Bank*	
2006			$	$	
July 1	Balances	J 1	20	80	

Once these opening balances have been recorded in the books, the day-to-day transactions can be entered in the normal manner. The need for opening entries will not occur very often. They will not be needed each year, as the balances from last year will have been brought forward.

18.6 Closing Entries

At the end of an accounting year, when the various expense and revenue items are transferred to the trading account or the profit and loss account, entries in respect of every such transfer should be made in the journal. Collectively, these journal entries are known as the **closing entries**, as they close off the accounts as at the end of the accounting year.

In addition, the items that need transferring to the capital account should also be entered in the journal. These will be such items as drawings and net profit (or net loss).

To illustrate closing entries, we will take just four items out of a much larger number of items needing closing entries. These are:

	Folio	$
Sales	GL 27	295,600 (*Cr.*)
Carriage inwards	GL 49	3,450 (*Dr.*)
Rent expense	GL 45	7,700 (*Dr.*)
Discounts received	GL 66	6,470 (*Cr.*)

The final accounts are shown in the nominal ledger, folio NL 33. They are for the year ended 31 December 2005. The journal entries will therefore appear as shown in Exhibit 18.2.

Exhibit 18.2

The Journal (*p. 22*)

Date	*Details*	*Folio*	*Dr.*	*Cr.*
2005			$	$
Dec 31	Sales	GL 27	295,600	
	Trading account	NL 33		295,600
	Transfer of sales to trading account			
Dec 31	Trading account	NL 33	3,450	
	Carriage inwards	GL 49		3,450
	Transfer of carriage inwards to trading account			
Dec 31	Profit and loss account	NL 33	7,700	
	Rent expense			7,700
	Transfer of rent expense to profit and loss account			
Dec 31	Discount received	GL 66	6,470	
	Profit and loss account	NL 33		6,470
	Transfer of discounts received to profit and loss account			

Drawings needed to be transferred to the capital account would be shown as follows.

Debit: capital account.
Credit: drawings account.

18.7 Correction of Errors

Journal entries for these will be found in Chapters 27 and 28.

18.8 Examination Guidance

In section 18.4 the difficulties that many students have in examinations were pointed out to the reader. Later on in this book, especially when dealing with journal entries for errors in Chapter 27 and 28, journal entries become more difficult to sort out.

Other than for opening and closing entries shown in Sections 18.5 and 18.6, where the double entry accounts are too numerous, the best way for most students to tackle journal entry questions is as follows.

1. On your examination answer paper write a heading 'Workings'. Then, under that, show the double entry accounts.
2. Now put a heading 'Answer', and show the answer in the form of the Journal, as shown in this chapter.

If you are already confident in dealing with these questions, and you feel that you can manage them without showing your workings, then you may wish to leave out your workings from your answer.

If the question asks for journal entries you must *not* fall into the trap of *just* showing the double entry accounts, as you could get no marks at all, even though your double entry records are correct. The examiner wants to see the *journal* entries, so you must show them as your answer.

18.9 The Accounting Cycle

Each accounting period sees a cycle of recording transactions, these being completed when the trading and profit and loss account and the balance sheet are prepared. The **accounting cycle** through which all accounting transactions pass can be shown in the form of a diagram (see Exhibit 18.3).

Exhibit 18.3

The Accounting Cycle for a Profit-making Organization

Source documents

Where original information is to be found

– Sales and purchases invoices
– Debit and credit notes for returns
– Bank paying-in slips and cheque counterfoils
– Receipts for cash paid out and received
– Correspondence containing other financial information

↓

Original entry

What happens to it

Classified and then entered in books of prime entry
– Sales and purchases journals
– Returns inwards and outwards journals
– Cash books*
– The journal

↓

Double entry accounts

Double entry

How the dual aspect of each transaction is recorded

General ledger	*Sales ledger*	*Purchases ledger*	*Cash books**
Real and nominal accounts	Debtors' accounts	Creditors' accounts	Cash book and petty cash book

(**Note:* Cash books fulfil both the roles of books of prime entry and double entry accounts)

↓

Check arithmetic

Checking the arithmetical accuracy of double entry records

Trial balance

↓

Profit or loss

Calculation of profit or loss for the accounting period

Trading and profit and loss accounts

↓

Closing financial position

Financial statement showing liabilities, assets and capital at the end of the accounting period

Balance sheet

Each period will see the same cycle performed. The connection between one period and the next are the balances remaining on the balance sheet which are carried forward to start the next period's recording.

New Terms

The Journal (p. 143): A book that details the bookkeeping entries needed for items that do not pass through other books of original entry.

Narrative (p. 143): An explanation of the bookkeeping entries required that have to pass through the journal.

Opening entries (p. 144): Entries needed to open up a double entry set of books.

Closing entries (p. 144): Entries showing transfers to the trading and profit and loss account.

Accounting cycle (p. 151): The cycle by which all transactions are recorded in a double entry set of books.

Summary

1 The journal is the collection place for items that do not pass fully through the other main books of original entry.

2 Opening entries are made on opening a set of books using double entry.

3 The main parts of the accounting cycle are as follows:

- collect source documents
- enter transactions in books of prime entry
- post to ledgers
- extract trial balance
- prepare trading and profit and loss accounts
- draw up balance sheet.

Exercises

18.1 You are to open the books of K. Mullings, a trader, via the journal to record the assets and liabilities. Record the daily transactions for the month of May in appropriate journals, then post to ledgers. A trial balance is to be extracted as on 31 May 2006.

2006

May 1 *Assets:* premises, $2,000; motor van, $450; fixtures, $600; stock, $1,289; debtors – N. Hardy, $40; M. Nelson, $180; cash at bank, $1,254; cash in hand, $45. *Liabilities:* creditors; B. Blake, $60; V. Rodriguez, $200.

May 1 Paid rent by cheque, $15.

May 2 Bought goods on credit from B. Blake, $20; C. Harris, $56; H. Gordon, $38; N. Lopez, $69.

May 3 Sold goods on credit to: K. O'Connor, $56; M. Benjamin, $78; L. Singh, $98; N. Duffy, $48; B. Green, $118; M. Nelson, $40.

May 4 Paid for motor expenses in cash, $13.

May 7 Cash drawings by proprietor, $20.

May 9 Sold goods on credit to: M. Benjamin, $22; L. Pearson, $67.

May 11 Goods returned to Mullings by: K. O'Connor, $16; L. Singh, $18.

May 14	Bought another motor van on credit from Better Motors Ltd, $300.
May 16	The following paid Mullings their accounts by cheque less 5% cash discount: N. Hardy; M. Nelson; K. O'Connor; L. Singh.
May 19	Returned goods to N. Lopez, $20.
May 22	Bought goods on credit from: J. Johnson, $89; T. Baptiste, $72.
May 24	The following accounts were settled by Mullings by cheque less 5% cash discount: B. Blake; V. Rodriguez; N. Lopez.
May 27	Paid staff by cheque, $56.
May 30	Paid rates by cheque, $66.
May 31	Paid Better Motors Ltd by cheque, $300.

18.2 You are to show the journal entries necessary to record the following items.

2005

(i)	May 1	Bought a motor vehicle on credit from Kingston Garage for $6,790.
(ii)	May 2	Bought machinery $980 on credit from Systems Accelerated.
(iii)	May 8	Office furniture bought by us for $490 was returned to the supplier Unique Offices, as it was unsuitable. Full allowance will be given us.
(iv)	May 12	We are owed $150 by W. Charles. He is unable to pay in cash: we receive office equipment to the value of $150 in full settlement of the debt.
(v)	May 14	We take $45 goods out of the business stock for private use without paying for them.
(vi)	May 28	Some time ago we paid an insurance bill thinking that it was all in respect of the business. We now discover that $76 of the amount paid was in fact insurance of our private house.

18.3X Show the journal entries necessary to record the following items.

(i) We bought fixtures on credit from J. Harper, $1,809.

(ii) We take $500 goods out of the business stock without paying for them.

(iii) $28 of the goods taken by us on 4 April are now returned back into stock by us. We do not take any money for the return of the goods.

(iv) K. Lamb owes us $500. He is unable to pay his debt. We agree to take a motor vehicle from him at that value and so cancel the debt.

(v) Some of the fixtures bought from J. Harper, $65 worth, are found to be unsuitable and are returned to him for full allowance.

(vi) Office equipment is bought on credit from Super Offices for $2,190.

18.4X (*a*) J. Green's financial position at 1 May 2008 was as follows.

		$
Bank		2,910
Cash		160
Equipment		5,900
Premises		25,000
Creditors:	R. Smith	890
	T. Thomas	610
Debtors:	J. Carnegie	540
Loan from:	J. Higgins	4,000

(i) Show the opening entries needed to open a double entry set of books for Mr Green as at 1 May 2008.

(ii) Open up the necessary accounts in J. Green's ledger to record the above as well as the succeeding transactions.

(*b*) During May 2008 J. Green's transactions were as follows.

2008

May 2	Bought goods from T. Thomas on credit, $2,100.
May 5	Paid R. Smith on account by cheque, $500.
May 12	Repaid J. Higgins by cheque, $1,000.
May 24	Sold goods to J. Carnegie on credit, $2,220.
May 31	Total cash sales for the month $8,560, of which $8,000 banked on 31 May.

May 31 J. Carnegie returned goods to us, $400.
May 31 Paid loan interest to Higgins by cheque, $200.
You are required to post all accounts and to extract a trial balance as at 31 May 2008, but only the cash book needs balancing down.
Note: Sales, purchases and returns journals are not needed.

18.5X Show the entries in the journal for J. Small, including narrative, on 16 September 2003 in respect of the following occurring on that date.

(i) J. Jones, a debtor for $720, was unable to pay his account in full. As settlement in full we were given cash $220 and a motor van, $500.
(ii) Small sold some of his office equipment for cash, $1,000.
(iii) Small took goods for his own use valued at $290 cost price.
(iv) Closing entries (final accounts being drawn up) to be made for:

	$
Purchases	29,470
Rent expense	540
Discounts received	800
Drawings	3,500
Net profit	4,170

(*CXC style*)

CHAPTER **19**

Control Accounts

Learning Objectives

- To be able to draw up sales ledger control accounts.
- To be able to draw up purchases ledger control accounts.
- To know the sources of information for control accounts.

19.1 The Need for Control Accounts

When all the accounts were kept in one ledger, a trial balance could be drawn up as a test of the arithmetical accuracy of the accounts. It must be remembered that certain errors were not revealed by such a trial balance. If the trial balance totals disagreed, for a small business the books could easily and quickly be checked so as to find the errors.

However, when the firm has grown and the accounting work has been divided up so that there are several or many ledgers, any errors could be very difficult to find. We could have to check every item in every ledger. What is required is a type of trial balance for each ledger, and this requirement is met by the **control account**. This ensures that it is only the ledgers whose control accounts do not balance that need detailed checking to find errors.

19.2 The principle of Control Accounts

The principle on which the control account is based is simple, and is as follows. If the opening balance of an account is known, together with the information of the additions and deductions entered in the account, the closing balance can be calculated.

This idea can be applied to a complete ledger. Suppose that there were only four accounts in the sales ledger, and for the month of May 2002, the accounts were as follows.

Sales Ledger
T. Sangster

2002		$	2002		$
May 1	Balance b/d	850	May 7	Bank	820
May 4	Sales	900	May 7	Discounts allowed	30
May 30	Sales	350	May 31	Balance c/d	1,250
		2,100			2,100
Jun 1	Balance b/d	1,250			

P. Mayall

2002		$	2002		$
May 1	Balance b/d	1,500	May 9	Returns inwards	200
May 28	Sales	400	May 14	Bank	900
			May 14	Discounts allowed	20
			May 31	Balance c/d	780
		1,900			1,900
Jun 1	Balance b/d	780			

K. Wingfield

2002		$	2002		$
May 1	Balance b/d	750	May 20	Returns inwards	110
May 15	Sales	600	May 31	Balance c/d	1,240
		1,350			1,350
Jun 1	Balance b/d	1,240			

C. Shenton

2002		$	2002		$
May 1	Balance b/d	450	May 28	Bad debts	450

A control account, in this case a *sales ledger control account*, would consist only of the totals of each of the items in the sales ledger.

Let us first list the totals for each type of item.

May 1 Balances b/d:	\$850 + \$1,500 + \$750 + \$450 = \$3,550
Sales in May:	\$900 + \$350 + \$400 + \$600 = \$2,250
Cheques received in May:	\$820 + \$900 = \$1,720
Discounts allowed in May:	\$30 + \$20 = \$50
Returns inwards in May:	\$200 + \$110 = \$310
Bad debts written off in May:	\$450

Now, looking at the totals only, it is possible to draw up a sales ledger control account. Debits are shown as usual on the left-hand side, and credits on the right-hand side.

Sales Ledger Control Account

2002		$	2002		$
May 1	Balance b/d	3,550	May 31	Bank	1,720
May 31	Sales for the month	2,250	May 31	Discounts allowed	50
			May 31	Returns inwards	310
			May 31	Bad debts	450
			May 31	Balance c/d (A)	?
		5,800			5,800
Jun 1	Balance b/d (B)	?			

From your studies so far of double entry, you should be able to see that the Balance c/d (A) is the figure needed to balance the account, i.e. the difference between the two sides. It works out to be $3,270.

We can now look at the ledger and see if that is correct. The balances are $1,250 + $780 + $1,240 = $3,270. As this has now been proved to be correct, the figure of $3,270 can be shown in the Sales Ledger Control Account as the Balance carried down (A) and the Balance brought down (B).

In the above, very simple, example, there were only four ledger accounts. Suppose instead that there were 400 or 4,000 or 40,000 ledger accounts. In these cases the information concerning the totals of each type of item cannot be obtained so easily.

Remember that the main purpose of a control account is to act as a check on the accuracy of the entries in the ledgers. The total of a list of all the balances extracted from the ledger should equal the balance on the control account. If not, a mistake, or even many mistakes, may have been made and will have to be found.

19.3 Information for Control Accounts

Exhibits 19.1 and 19.2 list where information is obtained with which to draw up control accounts.

Exhibit 19.1

Sales ledger control	**Source**
1 Opening debtors	List of debtors balances drawn up at end of previous period.
2 Credit sales	Total from sales journal.
3 Returns inwards	Total of returns inwards journal.
4 Cheques received	Cash book: bank column on received side. List extracted or total of a special column which has been included in the cash book.
5 Cash received	Cash book: cash column on received side. List extracted or total of a special column which has been included in the cash book.
6 Closing debtors	List of debtors balances drawn up at end of the period.

Exhibit 19.2

Purchases ledger control	Source
1 Opening creditors	List of creditors balances drawn up at end of previous period.
2 Credit purchases	Total from purchases journal.
3 Returns outwards	Total of returns outwards journal.
4 Cheques paid	Cash book: bank column on payments side. List extracted or total of a special column which has been included in the cash book.
5 Cash paid	Cash book: cash column on payments side. List extracted or total of a special column which has been included in the cash book.
6 Closing creditors	List of creditors balances drawn up at end of the period.

19.4 Form of Control Accounts

It is usual to find control accounts in the same form as an account, with the totals of the debit entries in the ledger on the left-hand side and the totals of the various credit entries in the ledger on the right-hand side of the account.

Exhibit 19.3 shows an example of a sales ledger control account for a sales ledger in which all the entries are arithmetically correct. We have proved the ledger to be arithmetically correct because the totals of the control account equal each other. If the totals are not equal, then this proves there is an error somewhere.

Exhibit 19.4 shows an example where an error is found to exist in a purchases ledger. The ledger will have to be checked in detail, the error found, and the control account then corrected. There is a $40 error in this ledger. We will have to check the ledger in detail to find the error.

Notice that a double line does not appear under the totals figures. We will not 'rule off' the account until the error is traced and corrected.

Exhibit 19.3

Sales ledger	$
Debit balances on 1 January 2006	1,894
Total credit sales for the month	10,290
Cheques received from customers in the month	7,284
Cash received from customers in the month	1,236
Returns inwards from customers during the month	296
Debit balances on 31 January as extracted from the sales ledger	3,368

Sales Ledger Control

2006		$	2006		$
Jan 1	Balance b/d	1,894	Jan 31	Bank	7,284
Jan 31	Sales	10,290	Jan 31	Cash	1,236
			Jan 31	Returns inwards	296
			Jan 31	Balance c/d	3,368
		12,184			12,184

Exhibit 19.4

Purchases ledger	$
Credit balances on 1 January 2006	3,890
Cheques paid to suppliers during the month	3,620
Returns outwards to suppliers in the month	95
Bought from suppliers in the month	4,936
Credit balances on 31 January as extracted from the purchases ledger	5,151

Purchases Ledger Control

2006		$	2006		$
Jan 31	Bank	3,620	Jan 31	Balances b/d	3,890
Jan 31	Returns outwards	95	Jan 31	Purchases	4,936
Jan 31	Balances c/d	5,151			
		*8,866			*8,826

*Show an error of $40

19.5 Other Transfers

Transfers to bad debts accounts will have to be recorded in the sales ledger control account as they involve entries in the sales ledgers.

Similarly, a contra account, whereby the same firm is both a supplier and a customer and interindebtedness is set off, will also need entering in the control accounts. An example of this is as follows.

1 The firm has sold A. Hope $600 goods on 1 May 2005.
2 Hope has supplied the firm with $880 goods on 12 May 2005.
3 The $600 owing by Hope is set off against $600 owing to him on 30 May 2005.
4 This leaves $280 owing to Hope on 31 May 2005.

Sales Ledger
A. Hope

2005		$				
May 1 Sales	(1)	600				

Purchases Ledger
A. Hope

			2005		$
			May 12 Purchases	(2)	880

The set-off now takes place.

Sales Ledger
A. Hope

2005		$	2005		$
May 1 Sales	(1)	600	May 30 Set-off: purchases ledger	(3)	600

Purchases Ledger
A. Hope

2005		$	2005		$
May 30 Set-off: sales ledger	(3)	600	May 12 Purchases	(2)	880
May 31 Balance c/d	(4)	280			
		880			880
			Jun 1 Balance b/d	(4)	280

The transfer of the $600 will therefore appear on the credit side of the sales ledger control account and on the debit side of the purchases ledger control account. Relevant entries must be made in the journal.

Students often find it difficult to work out which side of each control account contra items (set-offs) are shown. Think of it as cash received and cash paid, for the entries go on the same sides of the control accounts as these items. Thus a contra item will appear on the credit side of the sales ledger control account (the same side as cash received from debtors) and will appear on the debit side of the purchases ledger control account (the same side as cash paid to creditors would appear). Remember this and you won't get it wrong.

19.6 A More Complicated Example

Exhibit 19.5 shows a worked example of a more complicated control account.

You will see that there are sometimes credit balances in the sales ledger as well as debit balances. Suppose for instance we sold $500 goods to W. Young; he paid in full for them, and then afterwards he returned $40 goods to us. This would leave a credit balance of $40 on the account, whereas usually the balances in the sales ledger are debit balances.

Exhibit 19.5

2006		$
Aug 1	Sales ledger: debit balances	3,816
Aug 1	Sales ledger: credit balances	22
Aug 31	Transactions for the month:	
	Cash received	104
	Cheques received	6,239
	Sales	7,090
	Discounts allowed	298
	Returns inwards	164
	Cash refunded to a customer who had overpaid her account	37
	At the end of the month:	
	Sales ledger: debit balances	4,156
	Sales ledger: credit balances	40

Sales Ledger Control Account

2006		$	2006		$
Aug 1	Balance b/d	3,816	Aug 1	Balances b/d	22
Aug 31	Sales	7,090	Aug 31	Cash	104
	Cash refunded	37		Bank	6,239
	Balances c/d	40		Discounts allowed	298
				Returns inwards	164
				Balance c/d	4,156
		10,983			10,983

New Terms

Control account (p. 156): An account that checks the arithmetical accuracy of a ledger.

Summary

1 Control accounts enable errors to be traced down to the ledger that does not balance; thus there will be no need to check all the books in full to find an error.

2 Transfers between sales and purchases ledgers should be shown in the control accounts.

Exercises

19.1 You are required to prepare a sales ledger control account from the following.

2004		$
May 1	Sales ledger balances	4,560
	Total of entries for May:	
	Sales journal	10,870
	Returns inwards journal	460
	Cheques and cash received from customers	9,615
	Discounts allowed	305
May 31	Sales ledger balances	5,050

19.2 You are to prepare a sales ledger control account from the following. Deduce the closing figure of sales ledger balances as at 31 March 2008.

2008		$
Mar 1	Sales ledger balances	6,708
	Total for March:	
	Discounts allowed	300
	Cash and cheques received from debtors	8,970
	Sales journal	11,500
	Bad debts written off	115
	Returns inwards journal	210
Mar 31	Sales ledger balances	?

19.3X Draw up a purchases ledger control account from the following.

2002		$
June 1	Purchases ledger balances	3,890
	Total for June:	
	Purchases journal	5,640
	Returns outwards journal	315
	Cash and cheques paid to creditors	5,230
	Discounts received	110
June 30	Purchases ledger balances	?

19.4X You are to prepare a purchases ledger control account from the following. As the final figure of purchases ledger balances at 30 November is missing, you will have to deduce that figure.

2004		$
Nov 1	Purchases ledger balances	7,560
	Total for November:	
	Discounts received	240
	Returns outwards journal	355
	Cash and cheques paid to creditors	9,850
	Purchases journal	11,100
Nov 30	Purchases ledger balances	?

19.5 Prepare a sales ledger control account from the following.

2005		$
May 1	Debit balances	6,420
	Total for May:	
	Sales journal	12,800

	Cash and cheques received from debtors	10,370
	Discounts allowed	395
	Debit balances in the sales ledger set off against credit balances in the purchases ledger	145
May 31	Debit balances	?
	Credit balances	50

19.6X Draw up a sales ledger control account from the following.

2006		$
Apr 1	Debit balances	4,960
	Credit balances	120
	Total for April:	
	Sales journal	8,470
	Cash and cheques received from debtors	7,695
	Discounts allowed	245
	Debit balances in the sales ledger set off against credit balances in the purchases ledger	77
Apr 30	Debit balances	?
	Credit balances	46

CHAPTER **20**

Depreciation of Fixed Assets: Nature and Calculations

Learning Objectives

- To be able to explain the need for a charge for depreciation expense.
- To understand the causes of depreciation.
- To be able to calculate depreciation using either the straight line or reducing balance methods.
- To know how to calculate depreciation on assets bought or sold within an accounting period.

20.1 Nature of Fixed Assets

Fixed assets are those assets that are:

- of long life, and
- to be used in the business, and
- not bought with the main purpose of resale.

20.2 Depreciation of Fixed Assets

However, fixed assets such as machinery, motor vans, fixtures and even buildings do not last forever. If the amount received (if any) on disposal is deducted from the cost of buying them, the difference is called **depreciation**.

The only time that depreciation can be calculated accurately is when the fixed asset is disposed of, and the difference between the cost to its owner and the amount received on disposal is then calculated. If a motor van was bought for $1,000 and sold five years later for $20, then the amount of depreciation is $1,000 – $20 = $980.

20.3 Depreciation is an Expense

Depreciation is the part of the original purchase price of the fixed asset consumed during its period of use by the firm. It is an expense for services consumed just like expenses for items such as pay, rent or electricity. Because it is an expense, depreciation will have to be charged to the profit and loss account, and therefore will reduce net profit.

You can see that the only real difference between the expense of depreciation for a motor vehicle, and the expense of petrol for the motor vehicle is that the petrol expense is used up in a day or two, whereas the expense of the motor vehicle is spread over several years. Both are expenses of the business.

20.4 Causes of Depreciation

These can be divided up between:

- physical deterioration
- economic factors
- the time factor
- depletion.

Let us look at these in more detail.

Physical Depreciation

Wear and tear

When a motor vehicle or machinery or fixtures and fittings is used it will eventually wear out. Some last many years, others only a few years. This is true even of buildings, although some may last for a very long time.

Erosion, rust, rot and decay

Land may be eroded or wasted away by the action of wind, rain, sun and other elements of nature. Similarly, the metals in motor vehicles or machinery will rust or corrode. Wood will rot eventually. Decay is another process that will occur due to the elements of nature and a lack of proper attention.

Economic Factors

Sometimes an asset is put out of use even though it is in good physical condition. The two main economic factors at work here are usually:

- obsolescence
- inadequacy.

Obsolescence

This is the process of becoming out of date. For instance, over the years there has been great progress in the development of synthesizers and electronic devices used by leading commercial musicians. The old equipment will therefore have become obsolete and much of it will have been taken out of use by such musicians.

This does not mean that the equipment is worn out. Other people may well take over the old equipment and use it, possibly because they cannot afford to buy new up-to-date equipment.

Inadequacy

This arises when an asset is no longer used because of growth and changes in the size of firm. For instance, a small ferryboat that is operated by a firm at a coastal resort will become entirely inadequate when the resort becomes more popular. Then it will be found that it would be more efficient and economical to operate a large ferryboat, and so the smaller boat will be put out of use by the firm.

In this case also, it does not mean that the ferryboat is no longer in good working order. It may be sold to a firm at a smaller resort.

The Time Factor

Obviously, time is needed for wear and tear, erosion, obsolescence and inadequacy to occur. However, there are fixed assets to which the time factor is connected in a different way. These are assets that have a legal life fixed in terms of years.

For instance, you may agree to rent some buildings for 10 years. This is normally called a 'lease'. When the years are finished the lease is worth nothing to you, as it has finished. Whatever you paid for the lease is now of no value.

A similar asset is a patent purchased with complete rights so that only you are able to produce something. When the patent's time has finished, it no longer has any value.

Instead of using the term 'depreciation', *amortization* is often used for these assets.

Depletion

Other assets are of wasting character, perhaps as a result of the extraction of raw materials from them. These materials are then either used by the firm to make something else, or sold in their raw state to other firms. Natural resources such as mines, quarries and oil wells come under this heading. Providing for the consumption of an asset of a wasting character is called providing for **depletion**.

20.5 Methods of Calculating Depreciation Charges

The two main methods in use are the straight line method and the reducing balance method. Most accountants think that, although other methods may be needed in certain cases, the straight line method is the one that is generally most suitable.

Straight Line Method

By this method, sometimes also called the 'fixed instalment method', the number of years of use is estimated. The cost price of the asset is then divided by that number of years, to give the depreciation charge each year.

For instance, if a motor lorry was bought for \$22,000 and we thought we would keep it for four years and then sell it for \$2,000, the depreciation to be charged would be:

$$\frac{\text{Cost price (22,000)} - \text{Disposal value (2,000)}}{\text{Number of years of use (4)}} = \frac{\$20,000}{4}$$

$$= \$5,000 \text{ depreciation each year for 4 years}$$

If, after four years, the motor lorry had no disposal value, the charge for depreciation would be:

$$\frac{\text{Cost price (22,000)}}{\text{Number of years of use (4)}} = \frac{\$22,000}{4}$$

$$= \$5,500 \text{ depreciation each year for 4 years.}$$

Reducing Balance Method

By this method, a fixed percentage for depreciation is deducted from the cost price in the first year. In the second or later years the same percentage is taken of the reduced balance (i.e. cost price *less* depreciation already charged). This method is also known as the 'diminishing balance' method.

If a machine is bought for $10,000, and depreciation is to be charged at 20%, the calculations for the first three years would be as follows.

	$
Cost price	10,000
First year: depreciation (20%)	2,000
	8,000
Second year: depreciation (20% of $8,000)	1,600
	6,400
Third year: depreciation (20% of $6,400)	1,280
Book value at each of third year	5,120

Using this method, much larger amounts are charged in the earlier years of use compared with the final years of use. It is often said that repairs and upkeep in the early years will not cost as much as when the asset becomes old. This means that:

In the early years		*In the later years*
A higher charge for depreciation + a lower charge for repairs and upkeep	will tend to be fairly equal to	a lower charge for depreciation + a higher charge for repairs and upkeep

Exhibit 20.1 gives a comparison of the calculations using the two methods, if the same cost is given for the two methods.

Exhibit 20.1

A firm has just bought a machine for $8,000. It will be kept in use for four years, and then it will be disposed of for an estimated amount of $500. The firm asks for a comparison of the amounts charged as depreciation using both methods.

For the straight line method, a figure of ($8,000 – $500) ÷ 4 = $7,500 ÷ 4 = $1,875 per annum is to be used. For the reducing balance method, a percentage figure of 50% will be used.

	Method 1: Straight line		**Method 2: Reducing balance**
	$		$
Cost price	8,000		8,000
Depreciation: year 1	1,875	(50% of $8,000)	4,000
	6.125		4,000
Depreciation: year 2	1,875	(50% of $4,000)	2,000
	4,250		2,000
Depreciation: year 3	1,875	(50% of $2,000)	1,000
	2,375		1,000
Depreciation: year 4	1,875	(50% of $1,000)	500
Disposal value	500		500

This illustrates the fact that when using the reducing balance method there is a much higher charge for depreciation in the early years, and lower charges in the later years.

20.6 Other Methods of Calculating Depreciation

There are many more methods of calculating depreciation but they are outside the scope of this book. Special methods are often used in particular industries where there are circumstances that are peculiar to that industry.

New Terms

Depreciation (p. 165): The part of the cost price of the fixed asset consumed during its period of use by the firm.

Obsolescence (p. 166): Becoming out of date.

Depletion (p. 167): The wasting away of an asset as it is used up.

Straight line method (p. 167): Depreciation calculation which remains at an equal amount each year.

Reducing balance method (p. 168): Depreciation calculation which is at a lesser amount every following period.

Summary

1 Depreciation is an expense of the business and has to be charged against any period during which depreciation occurs.
2 The main causes of depreciation are: physical depreciation, economic factors, the time factor and depletion.
3 There are other methods of depreciation in addition to the straight line and reducing balance methods. Special methods are used in particular industries.

Exercises

20.1 D. Jones, a manufacturer, purchases a lathe for the sum of $4,000. It has an estimated life of five years and a scrap value of $500.

Jones is not certain whether she should use the 'straight line' or 'reducing balance' basis for the purpose of calculating depreciation on the machine.

You are required to calculate the depreciation on the lathe using both methods, showing clearly the balance remaining in the lathe account at the end of each of the five years for each method. (Assume that 40% per annum is to be used for the reducing balance method.)

(Calculations to nearest $.)

20.2 A machine costs $12,500. It will be kept for four years, and then sold for an estimated figure of $5,120. Show the calculations of the figures for depreciation for each of the four years using (*a*) the straight line method, (*b*) the reducing balance method, for this method using a depreciation rate of 20%.

20.3 A motor vehicle costs $6,400. It will be kept for five years, and then sold for scrap for $200. Calculate the depreciation for each year using (*a*) the reducing balance method, using a depreciation rate of 50%; (*b*) the straight line method.

20.4X A machine costs $5,120. It will be kept for five years, and then sold at an estimated figure of $1,215. Show the calculations of the figures for depreciation each year using (*a*) the straight line method, (*b*) the reducing balance method using a depreciation rate of 25%.

20.5X A mechanical digger costs $12,150. It will be kept in use for five years. At the end of that time agreement has already been made that it will be sold for $1,600. Show your calculation of the amount of depreciation each year if (*a*) the reducing balance method at a rate of 33⅓% was used. (*b*) the straight line method was used.

20.6X A tractor is bought for $6,000. It will be used for three years, and then sold back to the supplier for $3,072. Show the depreciation calculations for each year using (*a*) the reducing balance method with a rate of 20%, (*b*) the straight line method.

CHAPTER **21**

Double Entry Records for Depreciation

Learning Objectives

- To incorporate depreciation calculations into the accounting records.
- To record the disposal of fixed assets and the adjustments needed to the provision for depreciation accounts.

21.1 The Old Method Of Recording Depreciation

It used to be normal to show depreciation in the fixed asset accounts. This will be the first method to be shown, as it is the easiest for a student to understand.

Here the double entry for each year's depreciation charge is as follows.

1 **Debit**: Depreciation expense account.
2 **Credit**: Asset account.

This is then transferred to the profit and loss account.

1 **Debit**: Profit and loss account.
2 **Credit**: Depreciation expense account.

Exhibit 21.1 shows the entries that would be needed during the first three years of use of a fixed asset. A machine is bought by J. Green on 1 January 2005 for $2,000. It is to be depreciated at the rate of 20% using the reducing balance method. The asset account, depreciation account, profit and loss account and balance sheet in respect of the first three years are shown.

Exhibit 21.1

Machinery

2005		$	2005		$
Jan 1	Cash	2,000	Dec 31	Depreciation expense	400
			Dec 31	Balance c/d	1,600
		2,000			2,000
2006		$	2006		$
Jan 1	Balance b/d	1,600	Dec 31	Depreciation expense	320
			Dec 31	Balance c/d	1,280
		1,600			1,600

Cont'd

2007		$	2007		$
Jan 1	Balance b/d	1,280	Dec 31	Depreciation expense	256
			Dec 31	Balance c/d	1,024
		1,280			1,280
2008		$			
Jan 1	Balance b/d	1,024			

Depreciation Expense Account

2005		$	2005		$
Dec 31	Machinery	400	Dec 31	Profit and loss account	400
2006			2006		
Dec 31	Machinery	320	Dec 31	Profit and loss account	320
2007			2007		
Dec 31	Machinery	256	Dec 31	Profit and loss account	256

J. Green
Profit and Loss Account for the year ended 31 December (extracts)

	$	
2005 Depreciation	400	
2006 Depreciation	320	
2007 Depreciation	256	

This is usually shown on the balance sheet as follows.

J. Green
Balance Sheets (extracts)

	$	$
As at 31 December 2005		
Machinery at cost	2,000	
Less Depreciation for the year	400	
		1,600
As at 31 December 2006		
Machinery as at 1 January 2006	1,600	
Less Depreciation for the year	320	
		1,280
As at 31 December 2007		
Machinery as at 1 January 2007	1,280	
Less Depreciation for the year	256	
		1,024

In larger firms, the old method is not often found now. It is regarded as being out of date.

21.2 The Modern Method of Recording Depreciation

In the method now normally used, the fixed assets accounts are always kept for showing the assets at cost price. The depreciation is shown in a separate 'provision for depreciation' account. This method has been used by most limited companies for many years. This is because company balance sheets show fixed assets at cost less total depreciation to date.

When the depreciation calculations have taken place, the depreciation is then to be shown in a separate account. The double entry is as follows.

1 **Debit**: Profit and loss account.

2 **Credit**: Provision for depreciation account.

Notice that no entry is made in the asset account for depreciation. This means that the fixed asset accounts will normally be shown at cost price.

The first example of the modern method uses the same figures as Exhibit 21.1. In a business belonging to L. Hart with financial years ended 31 December a machine is bought for $2,000 on 1 January 2005. It is to be depreciated at the rate of 20% using the reducing balance method. The records for the first three years are now shown in Exhibit 21.2.

Exhibit 21.2

Machinery

	$		
2005	$		
Jan 1 Cash	2,000		

Provision for Depreciation — Machinery

2005	$	2005	$
Dec 31 Balance c/d	400	Dec 31 Profit and loss a/c	400
2006		2006	
Dec 31 Balance c/d	720	Jan 1 Balance b/d	400
		Dec 31 Profit and loss a/c	320
	720		720
2007		2007	
Dec 31 Balance c/d	976	Jan 1 Balance b/d	720
		Dec 31 Profit and loss a/c	256
	976		976
		2008	
		Jan 1 Balance b/d	976

L. Hart
Profit and Loss Account for the year ended 31 December (extracts)

	$	
2005 Depreciation	400	
2006 Depreciation	320	
2007 Depreciation	256	

Cont'd

Now the balance on the machinery account is shown on the balance sheet at the end of each year less the balance on the provision for depreciation account.

L. Hart
Balance Sheets (extracts)

	$	$
As at 31 December 2005		
Machinery at cost	2,000	
Less Depreciation to date	400	
		1,600
As at 31 December 2006		
Machinery at cost	2,000	
Less Depreciation to date	720	
		1,280
As at 31 December 2007		
Machinery at cost	2,000	
Less Depreciation to date	976	
		1,024

By comparing Exhibit 21.1 with Exhibit 21.2, you can see that the amount charged for depreciation in the profit and loss account is the same under both methods. Similarly, the final balancing figures for machinery in each of the balance sheets, i.e. $1,600, $1,280 and $1,024, are also the same. The main difference lies in the accumulation of figures in separate accounts for the asset and for provision for depreciation under the modern method.

As modern balance sheets demand the disclosure as separate figures of the cost of each type of asset and the depreciation to date on each type of asset, keeping this information in separate accounts makes that task easier to perform.

The terms **aggregate depreciation** and **net book value** are often used. What this means in the above example is now shown:

	31.12.2005	31.12.2006	31.12.2007
	$	$	$
Machinery at cost	2,000	2,000	2,000
Less aggregate depreciation	400	720	976
Net book value	1,600	1,280	1,024

The term **accumulated depreciation** means the same as aggregate depreciation.

Another example is now given in Exhibit 21.3. This is of a business belonging to J. Hood with financial years ended 30 June. A motor lorry is bought on 1 July 2001 for $8,000. Another motor lorry is bought on 1 July 2002 for $11,000. Each lorry is expected to be in use for five years, and the disposal value of the first lorry is expected to be $500 and the second lorry is expected to fetch $1,000 disposal value. The method of depreciation to be used is the straight line method. The first two years' accounts are shown.

Exhibit 21.3

Motor Lorries

2001	$	2003	$
Jul 1 Bank	8,000	Jun 30 Balance c/d	19,000
2002			
Jul 1 Bank	11,000		
	19,000		19,000

Provision for Depreciation – Motor Lorries

2002	$	2002	$
Jun 30 Balance c/d	1,500	Jun 30 Profit and loss a/c	1,500
		Jul 1 Balance b/d	1,500
2003		2003	
Jun 30 Balance c/d	5,000	Jun 30 Profit and loss a/c	3,500
	5,000		5,000
		Jul 1 Balance b/d	5,000

J. Hood
Profit and Loss Account for the year ended 31 June (extracts)

	$	
2002 Depreciation	1,500	
2003 Depreciation	3,500	

J. Hood
Balance Sheet as at 30 June 2002

	$	$
Motor lorry at cost	8,000	
Less Depreciation to date	1,500	6,500

J. Hood
Balance Sheet as at 30 June 2003

	$	$
Motor lorries at cost	19,000	
Less Depreciation to date	5,000	14,000

21.3 The Sale of an Asset

Reason for Accounting Entries

Upon the sale of an asset, we will want to delete if from our accounts. This means that the cost of that asset needs to be taken out of the asset account. In addition, the depreciation of the sold asset will have to be taken out of the depreciation provision. Finally, the profit or loss on sale, if any, will have to be calculated.

When we charge depreciation on a fixed asset we are having to make guesses. We cannot be absolutely certain how long we will keep the asset in use, nor can we be certain at the date of purchase how much the asset will be sold for when we dispose of it. We will not often guess correctly. This means that when we dispose of an asset the cash received for it is usually different from our original guess.

Accounting Entries Needed

On the sale of a fixed asset, for instance machinery, the following entries are needed.

1 Transfer the cost price of the asset sold to an assets disposal account (in this case a machinery disposals account).
Debit machinery disposals account.
Credit machinery account.

2 Transfer the depreciation already charged to the assets disposal account.
Debit provision for depreciation – machinery.
Credit machinery disposals account.

3 For remittance received on disposal.
Debit cash book.
Credit machinery disposal account.

4 Transfer difference (amount to balance the account) to the profit and loss account.
If the machinery disposals account shows a credit balance, it is a profit on sale.
Debit machinery disposals account.
Credit profit and loss account.
If the machinery disposals account shows a debit balance, it is a loss on sale.
Debit profit and loss account.
Credit machinery disposals account.

As examples, we can look at what would happen if the machine shown in Exhibit 21.2 were sold in 2008. To 31 December 2007 it is shown as having cost $2,000 and $976 had been written off for depreciation. In Exhibit 21.4 we can show the entries necessary if it was sold at a profit, for $1,070 on book value, and in Exhibit 21.5 the entries necessary where a loss on book value is shown.

Exhibit 21.4

Machinery

2005		$	2008		$
Jan 1 Cash		2,000	Jan 2 Machinery disposals	(1)	2,000

Provision for Depreciation: Machinery

2008		$	2008		$
Jan 2 Machinery disposals	(2)	976	Jan 1 Balance b/d		976

Machinery Disposals

2008			$	2008			$
Jan 2	Machinery	(1)	2,000	Jan 2	Provision for depreciation	(2)	976
Dec 31	Profit and loss a/c	(4)	46	Jan 2	Cash	(3)	1,070
			2,046				2,046

Profit and Loss Account for the year ended 31 December 2008

					$
			Profit on sale of machinery	(4)	46

Exhibit 21.5 now shows the entries if, instead of being sold at a profit, the same asset had been sold for only $950, which would mean that a loss was incurred on sale.

Exhibit 21.5

Machinery

2005			$	2008			$
Jan 1	Cash		2,000	Jan 2	Machinery disposals	(1)	2,000

Provision for Depreciation: Machinery

2008			$	2008			$
Jan 2	Machinery disposals	(2)	976	Jan 1	Balance b/d		976

Machinery Disposals

2008			$	2008			$
Jan 2	Machinery	(1)	2,000	Jan 2	Provision for depreciation	(2)	976
				Jan 2	Cash	(3)	950
				Dec 31	Profit and loss	(4)	74
			2,000				2,000

Profit and Loss Account for the year ended 31 December 2008

		$	
Loss on sale of machinery	(4)	74	

New Terms

Accumulated depreciation (p. 174): Total depreciation provided on asset from date of purchase to date of current balance sheet.

Aggregate depreciation (p. 174): Alternative term for accumulated depreciation.

Net book value (p. 174): Cost price of asset less accumulated depreciation to date of balance sheet.

Summary

1 The method of showing depreciation in the assets account is now used only by some small organizations.
2 Using the modern method, asset accounts are kept at cost price, while the depreciation is credited to a provision for depreciation account.
3 When we sell a fixed asset, we must transfer both the cost and the accumulated depreciation to a separate disposal account.
4 Profit on disposal is transferred to the credit of the profit and loss account.
5 Loss on disposal is transferred to the debit of the profit and loss account.

Exercises

21.1 On 1 July 2002 R. Bryan, a trader, purchased a motor delivery van for $4,000. Using the old method only, with calculations to the nearest $, you are required to do the following.

(*a*) Show how the motor delivery van account would appear in the books of R. Bryan for the four years ending 30 June 2006.
Depreciation is written off at the rate of 20% on a reducing balance basis.

(*b*) Explain the difference between the straight line method and the reducing balance method of depreciation.

21.2 John Miller, who is a sole trader, decides to purchase a motor van for the sum of $7,500 on 1 January 2003. He cannot decide whether to write off depreciation of the new van on the straight line method or the diminishing balance method.

Required (using old method only)
In order to assist Miller in reaching a decision, draw up the motor van account for the first three years, taking a rate of 20% for depreciation, as it would appear:
(*a*) under the straight line method;
(*b*) under the diminishing balance method.

21.3X Harvey DaCosta, a sole trader, purchases on 1 November 2007 a new machine for $18,000. His business year end is 31 October but he cannot decide which method of depreciation he should use in respect of the machine – the straight line method or the reducing balance method.

Required
In order to assist him in making his decision, draw up the machine account, and provision for depreciation account, for the three years from 1 November 2007, using:
(*a*) the straight line method;
(*b*) the reducing balance method.
Each account must indicate which method is being used and must be balanced at the end of each of the three years.

Notes:
(i) In both cases the rate of depreciation is to be 10%.
(ii) Calculations should be made to the nearest $.

21.4X (*a*) What is meant by depreciation, and why is it important that a business person should provide for depreciation in his accounts?
(*b*) On 1 January 2006 A. Simpson, a haulage contractor, purchased three tipper lorries for $48,000 each. Mr Simpson estimated that his lorries would have an effective working life of five years with a disposal value of $3,000 each. The straight line method of depreciation is to be used. The financial year ends on 31 December. One of the lorries kept breaking down and was sold on 1 January 2008 for $25,000.

You are required to show the relevant entries for the years 2006, 2007 and 2008 in the following ledger accounts (use modern method only):
(i) lorries
(ii) lorries disposal
(iii) provision for depreciation on lorries.
All workings are to be shown.

21.5X Reconstruct in good form the following balance sheet after taking into account the transactions for December:

Balance Sheet as at 30 November

Assets	$	*Liabilities*	$
Cash	500	Capital	3,000
Machinery	1,000	*Add* Net profit	1,000
Vans	2,000		
Debtors	1,500		4,000
Stock	1,000	*Less* Drawings	300
			3,700
		Creditors	2,300
	$6,000		$6,000

Dec 1 Received a cheque from debtors, $200.
5 Took drawings in cash, $150.
10 Sold goods which cost $100 for cash, $300.
15 Purchased goods on credit for, $200.
19 Depreciated machinery by, $170.
21 Took a loan from the bank to buy machine costing, $2,000.
31 Paid $25 cash into bank.

(*Pitman Examinations Institute*)

21.6 A firm buys a fixed asset for $10,000. The firm estimates that the asset will be used for five years, and will then have no scrap valve. After exactly two and a half years, however, the asset is suddenly sold for $5,000. The firm always provides a full year's depreciation in the year of purchase and no depreciation in the year of disposal.

Required
(*a*) Write up the relevant accounts (including disposal account but not profit and loss account) for each of years 1, 2 and 3:
(i) using the straight-line depreciation method (assume 20% p.a.)
(ii) using the reducing balance depreciation method (assume 40% p.a.).
(*b*) (i) What is the purpose of depreciation? In what circumstances would each of the two methods you have used be preferable?
(ii) What is the meaning of the net figure for the fixed asset in the balance sheet at the end of year 2?

CHAPTER **22**

Bad Debts and Provisions for Bad Debts

Learning Objectives

- To understand how bad debts can be written off.
- To make provisions for possible bad debts.

22.1 Bad Debts

If a firm finds that it is impossible to collect a debt, then that debt should be written off as a **bad debt**. This can happen if the debtor simply cannot pay the debt. A bad debt is therefore an expense of the firm. An example of debts being written off as bad is given in Exhibit 22.1.

Exhibit 22.1

We sold $50 goods to C. Baptiste on 5 January 2005, but she became bankrupt. On 16 February 2005 we sold $240 goods to R. Shaw. He managed to pay $200 on 17 May 2005, but it became obvious that he would never be able to pay the final $40.

When drawing up our final accounts to 31 December 2005, we decided to write these off as bad debts. The accounts would appear as follows.

C. Baptiste

2005	$	2005	$
Jan 5 Sales	50	Dec 31 Bad debts expense	50

R. Shaw

2005	$	2005	$
Feb 16 Sales	240	May 17 Cash	200
		Dec 31 Bad debts expense	40
	240		240

(Cont'd)

Bad Debts Expense

2005	$	2005	$
Dec 31 C. Baptiste	50	Dec 31 Profit and loss a/c	90
Dec 31 R. Shaw	40		
	90		90

Profit and Loss Account for the year ended 31 December 2005

	$	
Bad debts expense	90	

22.2 Provisions for bad debts

Let us look at the accounts of K. Charles who started in business on 1 January 2000 and has just completed his first year of trading on 31 December 2000.

He has sold goods for $50,000 and they cost him $36,000, so his gross profit was $50,000 – $36,000 = $14,000. However, included in the $50,000 sales was a credit sale to C. Young for $250. C. Young has died, leaving no money, and he had not paid his account. The $250 debt is, therefore, a bad debt and should be charged in the profit and loss account as an expense.

Besides that debt, a credit sale of $550 on 1 December 2000 to L. Hall is unlikely to be paid. Charles cannot yet be certain about this, but he has been told by others that Hall has not paid his debts to other businesses. As Charles has given three months' credit to Hall, the debt is not repayable until 28 February 2001. However, the final accounts for the year 2000 are to be drawn up in January 2001, because the bank wants to see them. Charles cannot wait until after 28 February 2001 to see if the debt of $550 owing by Hall will be a bad debt.

What, therefore, can Charles do? When he shows the bank his final accounts, he wants to achieve the following objectives:

1 to charge as expenses in the profit and loss account for that year an amount representing sales of *that year* for which he will never be paid;
2 to show in the balance sheet as correct a figure as possible of the true value of debtors at the balance sheet date.

He can carry out (1) above by writing off Young's debt of $250 and then charging it as an expense in his profit and loss account.

For (2), he cannot yet write off Hall's debt of $550 as a bad debt, because he is not certain if it will be a bad debt or not. If he does nothing about it, then the debtors shown on the balance sheet will include a debt that is probably of no value. The debtors on 31 December 2000, after deducting Young's $250 bad debt, amounted to $10,000.

The answer to this dilemma is as follows:

K. Charles
Trading and Profit and Loss Account for the year ended 31 December 2000

	$	$
Sales		50,000
Less Cost of goods sold:		36,000
Gross profit		14,000

Less Expenses:		
Other expenses	5,000	
Bad debts	250	
Provision for bad debts	550	5,800
Net profit		8,200

K. Charles
Balance Sheet as at 31 December 2000 (extracts)

	$	$
Debtors	10,000	
Less Provision for bad debts	550	9,450

Exactly how we will do the double entry for this is explained in Section 22.4. What we have achieved so far is to show bad debts and provision for bad debts as an expense in the year when the sales were made. The debtors are also shown at probably what is their true value.

22.3 Provisions for bad debts: estimating provisions

The estimates of provisions for bad debts can be made:

- by looking into each debt, and estimating which ones will be bad debts
- by estimating, on the basis of experience, what percentage of the debts will result in bad debts.

It is well known that the longer a debt is owing, the more likely it will become a bad debt. Some firms draw up an ageing schedule, showing how long debts have been owing. Older debtors need higher percentage estimates of bad debts than newer debtors. Exhibit 22.2 gives an example of such an ageing schedule.

Exhibit 22.2

Ageing Schedule for Doubtful Debts

Period debt owing	*Amount*	*Estimated percentage doubtful*	*Provision for bad debts*
	$		$
Less than one month	5,000	1	50
1 month to 2 months	3,000	3	90
2 months to 3 months	800	5	40
3 months to 6 months	200	10	20
Over 6 months	160	50	80
	9,160		280

A provision may be a specific one, e.g. a $5,000 provision to cover the specified debts of W. Clarke $3,000 and T. Sangster $2,000. On the other hand it may be a general provision not linked to any specified debts, and usually calculated in a percentage fashion.

22.4 Accounting Entries for Provisions for Bad Debts

When the decision has been taken as to the amount of the provision to be made, then the accounting entries needed for the provision are as follows.

Year in which *provision first made*

1 **Debit** profit and loss account with amount of provision.
2 **Credit** provision for bad debts account.

Exhibit 22.3 shows the entries needed for a provision for bad debts.

Exhibit 22.3

At 31 December 2003 the debtors figure for J. Brown amounted to $10,000. It is estimated that 2% of debts (i.e. $200) will prove to be bad debts, and it is decided to make a provision for these. The accounts would appear as follows:

J. Brown
Profit and Loss Account for the year ended 31 December 2003

	$		
Provision for bad debts	200		

Provision for Bad Debts

		2003		$
		Dec 31	Profit and loss account	200

In the balance sheet the balance on the provision for bad debts will be deducted from the total debtors.

J. Brown
Balance Sheet (extracts) as on 31 December 2003

Current assets	$	$	
Debtors	10,000		
Less Provision for bad debts	200		
		9,800	

22.5 Increasing the Provision

Let us suppose that, for the same firm as in Exhibit 22.3, at the end of the following year, 31 December 2004, the bad debts provision needed to be increased. This was because the provision was kept at 2%, but the debtors had risen to $12,000. A provision of $200 had been brought forward from the *previous* year, but we now want a total provision of $240 (i.e. 2% of $12,000). All that is needed is a provision for an extra $40. The double entry will be the following.

1 **Debit**: Profit and loss account.
2 **Credit**: Provision for bad debts account.

J. Brown
Profit and Loss Account for the year ended 31 December 2004

	$		
Provision for bad debts	40		

Provision for Bad Debts

	$		$
2004		2004	
Dec 21 Balance c/d	240	Jan 1 Balance b/d	200
		Dec 31 Profit and loss account	40
	240		240
		2005	
		Jan 1 Balance b/d	240

The balance sheet as at 31 December 2004 will appear as set out below.

J. Brown
Balance Sheet (extract) as on 31 December 2004

Current assets	$	$
Debtors	12,000	
Less Provision for bad debts	240	
		11,760

22.6 Reducing the Provision

The provision is shown as a credit balance. Therefore to reduce it we would need a debit entry in the provision account. The credit would be in the profit and loss account. Let us assume that at 31 December 2005, in the firm already examined, the debtors figure had fallen to $10,500 but the provision remained at 2%, i.e. $210 (2% of $10,500). As the provision had previously been $240, it now needs a reduction of $30. The double entry is the following.

1 **Debit**: Provision for bad debts account.
2 **Credit**: Profit and loss account.

J. Brown
Profit and Loss Account for the year ended 31 December 2005

			$
		Provision for bad debts (reduction)	30

Provision for Bad Debts

		$			$
2005			2005		
Dec 31	Profit and loss account	30	Jan 1	Balance b/d	240
Dec 31	Balance c/d	210			
		240			240
			2006		
			Jan 1	Balance b/d	210

The balance sheet will appear as follows.

J. Brown
Balance Sheet (extracts) as on 31 December 2005

	$	$
Current assets		
Debtors	10,500	
Less Provision for bad debts	210	
		10,290

There are some things you have to remember about provisions for bad debts.

Year 1 Provision first made.

- Debit profit and loss account with full provision.
- Show in balance sheet as a deduction from debtors.

Later years Only the increase, or the decrease, in the provision is shown in the profit and loss account.

To increase debit the profit and loss account, credit the provision.

To decrease credit the profit and loss account, debit the provision.

The balance sheet will show the amended figure of the provision as a deduction from debtors.

Let us now look at a comprehensive example (Exhibit 22.4).

Exhibit 22.4

A business owned by J. Gupta starts on 1 January 2002 and its financial year end is 31 December annually. A table of the debtors, the bad debts written off and the estimated bad debts at the rate of 2% of debtors at the end of each year is now given. The double entry accounts, and the extracts from the final accounts follow.

Year to 31 December	*Debtors at end of year (after bad debts written off)*	*Bad debts written off during year*	*Debts thought at end of year to be impossible to collect: 2% of debtors*
	$	$	$
2002	6,000	423	120 (2% of $6,000)
2003	7,000	510	140 (2% of $7,000)
2004	7,750	604	155 (2% of $7,750)
2005	6,500	610	130 (2% of $6,500)

(Cont'd)

J. Gupta
Profit and Loss accounts for the year ended 31 December (extracts)

		$			$
2002	Bad debts expense	423			
	Provision for bad debts	120			
2003	Bad debts expense	510			
	Provision for bad debts (increase)	20			
2004	Bad debts expense	604			
	Provision for bad debts (increase)	15			
2005	Bad debts	610	2005	Provision for bad debts (reduction)	25

Provision for Bad Debts

		$			$
			2002		
			Dec 31	Profit and loss account	120
2003			2003		
Dec 31	Balance c/d	140	Dec 31	Profit and loss account	20
		140			140
2004			2004		
Dec 31	Balance c/d	155	Jan 1	Balance b/d	140
			Dec 31	Profit and loss account	15
		155			155
2005			2005		
Dec 31	Profit and loss account	25	Jan 1	Balance b/d	155
Dec 31	Balance c/d	130			
		155			155
			2006		
			Jan 1	Balance b/d	130

Bad Debts

		$			$
2002			2002		
Dec 31	Various debtors	423	Dec 31	Profit and loss account	423
2003			2003		
Dec 31	Various debtors	510	Dec 31	Profit and loss account	510
2004			2004		
Dec 31	Various debtors	604	Dec 31	Profit and loss account	604
2005			2005		
Dec 31	Various debtors	610	Dec 31	Profit and loss account	610

(Cont'd)

J. Gupta
Balance Sheets as at 31 December (extracts)

		$	$
2002	Debtors	6,000	
	Less Provision for bad debts	120	5,880
2003	Debtors	7,000	
	Less Provision for bad debts	140	6,860
2004	Debtors	7,750	
	Less Provision for bad debts	155	7,595
2005	Debtors	6,500	
	Less Provision for bad debts	130	6,370

You may see the term 'provision for doubtful debts'. This means exactly the same as 'provision for bad debts'; it is simply that some accountants prefer the other wording.

22.7 Diagram of Entries

Students often find it difficult to understand why there should be entries in the profit and loss account for bad debts expense and also a provision for bad debts. The following example should show why both of the items are needed.

T. Manley starts a business. Let us look at some of the figures from her first year's trading.

1. She has sold $50,000 goods on credit.
2. Debtors have paid her $39,600.
3. Two debtors owing her a total of $400 have been made bankrupt. No money will ever be received from them.
4. There was still another $10,000 owing to her at the year end (does not include (3).
5. Some of the $10,000 (4) will probably never be paid. Manley did not know exactly how much it would be. She estimates it at 1% of debtors; i.e. $10,000 × 1% = $100. She decides to make a provision for bad debts account, and extracts from the final accounts are now shown in Exhibit 22.5.

Exhibit 22.5

Bad Debts Expenses

	$		$
Balance b/d	400	Profit and loss account (3)	400

T. Manley
Trading and Profit and Loss Account for the year ended …

	$		$
		Sales (1)	50,000
Gross profit c/d			
Bad debts expense (3)	400	Gross profit b/d	
Provision for bad debts (5)	100		
Net profit			

Provision for Bad Debts

	$		$
Balance c/d	100	Profit and loss account (5)	100
		Balance b/d	100

For the balance sheet, the balances for debtors (4) and the provision for bad debts (5) have to be shown. There is no balance on the bad debts account, and therefore this will not appear.

T. Manley
Balance Sheet as at …

	$	$
Current assets		
Debtors (4)	10,000	
Less Provision for bad debts (5)	100	9,900

To summarize:

Sales $50,000: of this, the amount that would not be paid, $400 (definite) + further $100 (estimated) = $500.	Recorded in profit and loss account as	Bad debts $400, provision for bad debts $100 = $500 charged against profit.
Expected realizable value of debtors: debtors $10,000 *less* $100 estimated not receivable = $9,900	Shown in balance sheets as	Debtors $10,000 *Less* Provision for bad debts $100 $9,900

22.8 Provisions for discounts allowed on debtors

Some firms create provisions for discounts allowed to be allowed on the debtors outstanding at the balance sheet date. This, they maintain, is quite legitimate, as the amount of debtors less any doubtful debt provision is not the best estimate of collectable debts, owing to cash discounts which will be given to debtors if they pay within a given time. The cost of discounts, it is argued, should be charged in the period when the sales were made.

To do this, the procedure is similar to the doubtful debts provision. It must be borne in mind that the estimate of discounts to be allowed should be based on the net figure of debtors less bad debts provision, as it is obvious that discounts are not allowed on bad debts!

Exhibit 22.6

Year ended 31 December	*Debtors*	*Provision for bad debts*	*Provision for discounts allowed*
	$	$	%
2003	4,000	200	2
2004	5,000	350	2
2005	4,750	250	2

Profit and Loss Account for the year ended 31 December (extracts)

	$		$
2003 Provision for discounts on debtors ($3,800 × 2%)	76		
2004 Increase in provision for discounts on debtors ($4,650 × 2%) – $76	17		
		2005 Reduction in provision for discounts on debtors $93 – ($4,500 × 2%)	3

Provision for Discounts on Debtors

	$		$
2003		2003	
Dec 31 Balance c/d	76	Dec 31 Profit and loss account	76
2004		2004	
Dec 31 Balance c/d	93	Jan 1 Balance b/d	76
		Dec 31 Profit and loss account	17
	93		93
2005		2005	
Dec 31 Profit and loss account	3	Jan 1 Balance b/d	93
Dec 31 Balance c/d	90		
	93		93
		2006	
		Jan 1 Balance b/d	90

Balance Sheet as at 31 December (extracts)

		$	$	$
2003	Debtors		4,000	
	Less Provision for bad debts	200		
	Less Provision for discounts on debtors	76	276	3,724
2004	Debtors		5,000	
	Less Provision for bad debts	350		
	Less Provision for dicounts on debtors ($76 + $17)	93	443	4,557
2005	Debtors		4,750	
	Less Provision for bad debts	250		
	Less Provision for discounts on debtors ($76 + $17 – $3)	90	340	4,410

22.9 Multiple-choice Questions

Now answer Set no. 3, questions 41–60, beginning on p. 412.

New Terms

Bad debt (p. 180): A debt that we will not be able to collect.

Provision for bad debts (p. 181): An account showing the expected amounts of debtors at the balance sheet date who will not be able to pay their accounts.

Summary

1 Debts that we are unable to collect are credited to the customer's account (to cancel them) and debited to a bad debts account.

2 Provisions for bad debts are needed; otherwise the value of the debtors on the balance sheet will be showing too high a value, and could mislead anyone looking at the balance sheet. Also, this allows for more accurate calculation of profit or losses.

3 Provision for bad debts accounts are kept separate from the bad debts account. The amount of the provision is on the basis of the best guess that can be made taking all the facts into account.

4 An increase in a provision will have a debit in the profit and loss account.

5 A reduction in a provision will have a credit in the profit and loss account.

6 A provision for bad debts is shown as a deduction from the debtors in the balance sheet.

Exercises

22.1 On 1 January 2007 the balances below appeared in the sales ledger of S. Henry.

	$
D. Fung	200
C. Manley	120

During the year the following events took place.

Feb 1 After negotiation Henry agreed to accept $150 cash from D. Fung and regarded the outstanding balance as irrecoverable.
Mar 10 C. Manley was declared bankrupt. A payment of 30 cents in the $ was received in full settlement.

Show how these matters would be dealt with in Henry's ledger assuming that the financial year ends on 30 June.

22.2 On 30 September 2007 B. Fraser's debtors totalled $12,000. He decided to write off the following as bad debts.

	$
G. Green	60
H. Winston	80

He further decided to make a provision for bad debts of 10% on the remaining debtors.

Debtors on 30 September 2008 totalled $10,000 when Fraser decided to maintain the provision at 10%.

You are required to show, for each of the years ended 30 September 2007 and 2008:

(*a*) provision for bad debts account;
(*b*) the appropriate entries in the profit and loss account; and
(*c*) the necessary balance sheet entries on each of the above dates.

22.3X

Date: 31 Dec.	*Total debtors*	*Profit and loss*	*Dr./Cr*	*Final figure for balance sheet*
	$	$		$
2003	7,000			
2004	8,000			
2005	6,000			
2006	7,000			

The above table shows the figure for debtors appearing in a trader's books on 31 December of each year from 2003 to 2006. The Provision for Bad Debts is to be 1% of debtors from 31 December 2003. Complete the above table indicating the amount to be debited or credited to the profit and loss account for the year ended on each 31 December, and the amount for the final figure of debtors to appear in the balance sheet on each date.

22.4X A business started on 1 January 2005 and its financial year end is 31 December annually. A table of the debtors, the bad debts written off and the estimated bad debts at the end of the year is now given.

Year to 31 December	*Debtors at end of year (after bad debts written off)*	*Bad debts written off during the year*	*Debts thought at end of year to be impossible to collect*
	$	$	$
2005	12,000	298	100
2006	15,000	386	130
2007	14,000	344	115
2008	18,000	477	150

You are required to show the above in the double entry accounts, as well as the extracts from the profit and loss account for each year and the balance sheet extracts.

22.5X F. Grant maintained his accounting books from January to December. The debtors' balances and the rates for the provision for bad debts at the end of each of the following years were as follows.

Year	*Debtors' balance*	*Provision rate*
	$	%
2001	24,000	2½
2002	28,000	3
2003	26,000	4

(*a*) Write up the provision for bad debts account for the year ending 31 December 2000 to 31 December 2002.

(*b*) On 2 January 2003. J Brown, a debtor, was declared bankrupt and could pay only 25% of the $800 which he owed. Show the effect of this in the books of F. Grant.

(*c*) What is the reason for creating a provision for doubtful (bad) debts account?

(*CXC style*)

CHAPTER **23**

Other Adjustments for Final Accounts

Learning Objectives

- To adjust expense accounts for accruals and prepayments.
- To adjust revenue accounts for amounts owing.
- To show accruals, prepayments and revenue debtors in the balance sheet.
- To ascertain the amounts of expense and revenue items to be shown in the profit and loss account.
- To enter up necessary accounts for goods taken for private use.
- To know how to prepare final accounts for services-sector organizations.

23.1 Final Accounts So Far

The trading and profit and loss accounts you have looked at have taken the sales for a period and deducted all the expenses for that period, the result being a net profit (or a net loss).

Up to now, it has always been assumed that (except for bad debt provisions) the expenses belong exactly to the period for which the trading and profit and loss account is prepared. If the trading and profit and loss account for the year ended 31 December 2005 was being drawn up, then the rent paid as shown in the trial balance was exactly for 2005. There was no rent owing at the beginning of 2005 and none owing at the end of 2005; nor had any rent been paid in advance.

This was done to make your first meeting with final accounts much easier for you.

23.2 Adjustments Needed

Let us look now at two firms that pay rent for buildings. The rent for each building is $1,200 a year.

1 Firm A pays $1,000 in the year. At the year end it owes $200 for rent:
   - rent expense used up = $1,200
   - rent paid for = $1,000.

2 Firm B pays $1,300 in the year. This figure includes $100 in advance for the following year:
   - rent expense used up = $1,200
   - rent paid for = $1,300.

A profit and loss account for 12 months needs 12 months' rent as an expense = $1,200. This means that in both (1) and (2) the double entry accounts will have to be adjusted.

In all the examples following in this chapter, the trading and profit and loss accounts are for the year ended 31 December 2005.

23.3 Accrued Expenses

Assume that rent of $1,000 per year is payable at $250 at the end of every three months. The rent was not always paid on time. Details were as follows.

Amount	Rent due	Rent paid
$250	31 March 2005	31 March 2005
$250	30 June 2005	2 July 2005
$250	30 September 2005	4 October 2005
$250	31 December 2005	5 January 2006

The rent account to 31 December 2005 appeared as follows.

Rent

2005	$		
Mar 31 Bank	250		
Jul 2 Bank	250		
Oct 4 Bank	250		

The rent paid on 5 January 2006 will appear in the books of the year 2006 as part of the double entry.

The rent expense for 2005 is obviously $1,000, as that is the year's rent, and this is the amount needed to be transferred to the profit and loss account. But if $1,000 is put on the credit side of the rent account (the debit being in the profit and loss account), the account would not balance. We would have $1,000 on the credit side of the account and only $750 on the debit side. In this case, to make the account balance, the $250 rent owing for 2005, but paid in 2006, must be carried down to 2006 as a credit balance because it is a liability on 31 December 2005. Instead of rent owing, it could be called rent accrued or just simply an accrual. The completed account can now be shown (Exhibit 23.1). The balance c/d has been described as accrued c/d, rather than as a balance. This is to explain what the balance is for: it is for an **accrued expense**. It could have been described just as balance c/d, but stating what the balance represents makes it easier for someone looking at the books to understand why there is a balance.

Exhibit 23.1

Rent

2005	$	2005	$
Mar 31 Bank	250	Dec 31 Profit and loss	1,000
Jul 2 Bank	250		
Oct 4 Bank	250		
Dec 31 Accrued c/d	250		
	1,000		1,000
		2006	
		Jan 1 Accrued b/d	250

23.4 Prepaid Expenses

Insurance for a firm is at the rate of $840 a year, starting from 1 January 2005. The firm has agreed to pay this at the rate of $210 every three months. However, payments were not made at the correct times. Details were as follows.

Amount	Insurance due	Insurance paid
$210	31 March 2005	$210 28 February 2005
$210	30 June 2005	
$210	30 September 2005	$420 31 August 2005
$210	31 December 2005	$420 18 November 2005

The insurance account to the year end will be shown in the books as follows.

Insurance

2005	$		
Feb 28 Bank	210		
Aug 31 Bank	420		
Nov 18 Bank	420		

Now the last payment of $420 is not just for 2005: it can be split as $210 for the three months to 31 December 2005 and $210 for the three months ended 31 March 2006. For a period of 12 months, the total cost of insurance is $840 and this is threfore the figure needing to be transferred to the profit and loss account. If this is entered, the amount needed to balance the account will therefore be $210, and at 31 December 2005 this is a **prepaid expense** and needs carrying forward as such to 2006, i.e. as a debit balance.

The account for the year can now be completed (Exhibit 23.2).

Exhibit 23.2

Insurance

2005	$	2005	$
Feb 28 Bank	210	Dec 31 Profit and loss account	840
Aug 31 Bank	420		
Nov 18 Bank	420	Dec 31 Prepaid c/d	210
	1,050		1,050
2006			
Jan 1 Prepaid b/d	210		

Prepayment will also happen when items other than purchases are bought for use in the business and are not fully used up in the period.

For instance, stationery is normally not entirely used up over the period in which it is bought, there being a stock of stationery in hand at the end of the period. This stock is therefore a form of prepayment, and needs carrying down to the following period, as a debit entry.

This can be seen in the following example:

Year ended 31 December 2005:
Stationery bought in the year, $2,200.
Stock of stationery in hand as at 31 December 2005, $400.

Looking at the example, it can be seen that in 2005 the stationery used up will have been $2,200 – $400 = $1,800. We will still have a stock of $400 worth of stationery at 31 December 2005 to be carried forward to 2006. The $400 stock of stationery will be carried forward as an asset balance (debit balance) to 2006 (Exhibit 23.3). It is not added to the stock of unsold goods in hand in the balance sheet, but is added to the other prepayments of expenses.

Exhibit 23.3

Stationery

2005	$	2005	$
Dec 31 Bank	2,200	Dec 31 Profit and loss	1,800
		31 Stock c/d	400
	2,200		2,200
2006			
Jan 1 Stock b/d	400		

23.5 Revenue Owing at the End of Period

The **revenue** owing for sales is already shown in the books. These are the debit balances on our customers' accounts, i.e. debtors. There may be other kinds of revenue, all of which has not been received at the end of the period. An example now follows.

23.6 Worked Example

Our warehouse is larger than we need. We rent part of it to another firm for $800 per annum. Details for the year ended 31 December were as follows.

Amount	Rent due	Rent received
$200	31 March 2005	4 April 2005
$200	30 June 2005	6 July 2005
$200	30 September 2005	9 October 2005
$200	31 December 2005	7 January 2006

The account for 2005 will appear as follows.

Rent Income

		2005	$
		Apr 4 Bank	200
		Jul 6 Bank	200
		Oct 9 Bank	200

The rent received of $200 on 7 January 2006 will be entered in the books in 2006.

Any rent paid by the firm is charged as a debit to the profit and loss account. Any rent received, being the opposite, is transferred to the credit of the profit and loss account, as it is a revenue.

The amount to be transferred to the profit and loss account for 2005 is the revenue earned for the twelve months, i.e. $800. The rent income account is completed by carrying down the balance owing as a debit balance to 2006. The $200 owing is an asset on 31 December 2005.

The rent income account can now be completed (Exhibit 23.4).

Exhibit 23.4

Rent Income

2005	$	2005	$
Dec 31 Profit and loss a/c	800	Apr 4 Bank	200
		Jul 6 Bank	200
		Oct 9 Bank	200
		Dec 31 Accrued c/d	200
	800		800
2006			
Jan 1 Accrued b/d	200		

23.7 Expenses and Revenue Account Balances and the Balance Sheet

In all the cases listed dealing with adjustments in the final accounts, there will still be a balance on each account after the preparation of the trading and profit and loss accounts. All such balances remaining should appear in the balance sheet. The only question left is where and how they shall be shown.

The amounts owing for expenses are usually added together and shown as one figure. These could be called expense creditors, expenses owing, or accrued expenses. The items appear under current liabilities as they are expenses that have to be discharged in the near future.

The items prepaid are also added together and are called prepayments, prepaid expenses, or payments in advance. They are shown next under the debtors. Amounts owing for rents receivable or other revenue owing are usually added to debtors.

The balance sheet in respect of the accounts so far seen in this chapter would appear as follows.

Balance Sheet as at 31 December 2005

Current assets	$	*Current liabilities*	$
Stock		Trade creditors	
Debtors	200	Accrued expenses	250
Prepayments (400 + 210)	610		
Bank			
Cash			

23.8 Some More Examples

The following accounts for C. Holmes are shown entered up for transactions during the year ended 31 December 2005, before balancing off as at 31 December 2005.

Telephone

2005	$		
Apr 2 Bank	345		
Jul 3 Bank	420		
Oct 5 Bank	375		

Note: The telephone bill of $520 for the three months ended 31 December 2005 was not paid until 2006.

Rent

2005	$		
Jan 2 Bank	2,000		
Mar 31 Bank	2,000		
Jul 7 Bank	2,000		
Oct 2 Bank	2,000		
Dec 30 Bank	2,000		

Note: The payment for rent of $2,000 on 30 December 2005 covers the period 1 January 2006 to 31 March 2006.

Commission Income

		2005	$
		Apr 30 Bank	1,280
		Sept 2 Bank	1,400

Note: The commission income of $1,360 earned for the four months from 1 September to 31 December 2005 will be received in 2006.

The accounts now balanced off as at 31 December 2005 can be shown as follows.

Telephone

2005		$	2005		$
Apr 2	Bank	345	Dec 31	Profit and loss	1,660
Jul 3	Bank	420			
Oct 5	Bank	375			
Dec 31	Owing c/d	520			
		1,660			1,660
			2006		
			Jan 1	Owing b/d	520

Rent

2005		$	2005		$
Jan 2	Bank	2,000	Dec 31	Profit and loss	8,000
Mar 31	Bank	2,000	Dec 31	Prepayment c/d	2,000
Jul 7	Bank	2,000			
Oct 2	Bank	2,000			
Dec 30	Bank	2,000			
		10,000			10,000
2006					
Jan 1	Prepayment b/d	2,000			

Commission Income

2005		$	2005		$
Dec 31	Profit and loss	4,040	Apr 30	Bank	1,280
			Sept 2	Bank	1,400
			Dec 31	Accrued c/d	1,360
		4,040			4,040
2006					
Jan 1	Accrued b/d	1,360			

The items would appear in the profit and loss accounts as follows (extracts only).

C. Holmes
Profit and Loss Account for the year ended 31 December 2005

	$		$
Telephone	1,660	Commission receivable	4,040
Rent	8,000		

Balance sheet extracts will be as follows:

C. Holmes
Balance Sheet at 31 December 2005

Current assets	$	*Current liabilities*	$
Commission owing	1,360	Telephone bill owing	520
Rent prepaid	2,000		

23.9 Expenses and Revenue Accounts Covering More Than One Period

Students are often asked to draw up an expense or revenue account for a full year, and there are amounts owing or prepaid at *both* the beginning and end of the year. We can now see how this is done.

Example A

The following details are available.

1. On 31 December 2004 three months' rent of $3,000 was owing.
2. The rent chargeable per year was $12,000.
3. The following payments were made in the year 2005: 6 January $3,000: 4 April $3,000: 7 July $3,000: 18 October $3,000.
4. The final three months' rent for 2005 is still owing.

Now we can look at the completed rent account (Exhibit 23.5). The numbers (1)–(4) refer to the details above.

Exhibit 23.5

Rent

2005			$	2006			$
Jan 6	Bank	(3)	3,000	Jan 1	Owing b/f	(1)	3,000
Apr 4	Bank	(3)	3,000	Dec 31	Profit and loss account	(2)	12,000
Jul 7	Bank	(3)	3,000				
Oct 18	Bank	(3)	3,000				
Dec 31	Accrued c/d	(4)	3,000				
			15,000				15,000
				2006			
				Jan 1	Accrued b/d		3,000

Example B

The following details are available.

1. On 31 December 2004 stationery in hand amounted to $1,850
2. During the year to 31 December 2005 $27,480 was paid for stationery.

3 There were no stocks of stationery on 31 December 2005.

4 On 31 December 2005 we still owed $2,750 for stationery already received and used.

The stationery account will appear as shown in Exhibit 23.6. The figure of $32,080 is the difference on the account, and is transferred to the profit and loss account.

We can prove it is correct:

	$	$
Stock at start of year		1,850
Add: Bought and used:		
Paid for	27,480	
Still owed for	2,750	30,230
Cost of stationery used in the year		32,080

Exhibit 23.6

Stationery

2005		$	2005	$
Jan 1 Stock b/f	(1)	1,850	Dec 31 Profit and loss a/c	32,080
Dec 31 Bank	(2)	27,480		
Dec 31 Owing c/d	(4)	2,750		
		32,080		32,080
			2006	
			Jan 1 Owing b/d	2,750

Example C

Where different expenses are put together in one account, it can get even more confusing. Let us look at where rent and rates are joined together.

The details for the year ended 31 December 2005 are as follows.

1 Rent is payable of $6,000 per annum.

2 Rates of $4,000 per annum are payable by instalments.

3 At 1 January 2005 rent $1,000 had been prepaid in 2004.

4 On 1 January 2005 rates were owed of $400.

5 During 2005 rent was paid $4,500.

6 During 2005 rates were paid $5,000.

7 On 31 December 2005 rent $500 was owing.

8 On 31 December 2005 rates of $600 had been prepaid.

A combined rent and rates account is to be drawn up for the year 2005 showing the transfer to the profit and loss account, and balances are to be carried down in 2006 (Exhibit 23.7).

Exhibit 23.7

Rent and Rates

2005			$	2005			$
Jan 1	Rent prepaid b/f	(3)	1,000	Jan 1	Rates owing b/f	(4)	400
Dec 31	Bank: rent	(5)	4,500	Dec 31	Profit and loss account	(1) + (2)	10,000
Dec 31	Bank: rates	(6)	5,000	Dec 31	Rates prepaid c/d	(8)	600
Dec 31	Rent accrued c/d	(7)	500				
			11,000				11,000
2006				2006			
Jan 1	Rates prepaid b/d	(8)	600	Jan 1	Rent accrued b/d	(7)	500

23.10 Goods for Own Use

A trader will often take items out of the business stocks for his or her own use, without paying for them. There is nothing wrong about this, but an entry should be made to record the event along the following lines.

1 **Credit** the purchases account, to reduce cost of goods available for sale.
2 **Debit** the drawings account, to show that the proprietor has taken the goods for his or her private use.

Adjustments may also be needed for other private items. For instance, if a trader's private insurance had been incorrectly charged to the insurance account, then the correction would be as follows.

1 **Credit** the insurance account.
2 **Debit** the drawings account.

23.11 Final Accounts for Non-traders (Service Firms)

If the final accounts are for someone who is not trading in goods as such, for instance accountants, insurance agents, lawyers and the like, there will be no need for a trading account.

All of the revenue and expense items will be shown in a profit and loss account, disclosing a net profit (or net loss). Balance sheets for such providers of services (i.e. not goods) will be the same as for traders.

A simple example of the profit and loss account of a dentist might be shown in vertical form as Exhibit 23.8.

Exhibit 23.8

A Bailey, Dentist
Profit and Loss Account for the year ended 31 December 2005

		$	$
Fees earned			129,000
Less Expenses			
	Wages and salaries	31,000	
	Rent and rates	27,500	
	Dental materials	6,700	
	Stationery and postage	800	
	Light and power	1,200	
	Insurance	600	
	General expenses	900	
			68,700
Net profit			60,300

23.12 Vertical Forms of Final Accounts

Throughout this book we have often shown trading and profit and loss accounts and balance sheets using both the more old-fashioned horizontal style and the modern vertical style. We can see that the figures used are the same, whether it is for sales, purchases, expenses, assets, liabilities and capital. The only difference is in the ways they are displayed.

On quite a few occasions the horizontal style has been used to illustrate some aspect of double entry. It is easier to show double entry using the old horizontal method as the left-hand side of the trading and profit and loss account is the debit side, while the right-hand side is the credit side. This matches up with the debit and credit sides in all the other accounts such as sales, expenses, etc. When the final accounts are shown vertically it gets somewhat harder to see the double entry working out. For instance, expenses which are shown on the debit side of their accounts are shown as deductions in the profit and loss account, because a deduction there means that it is really a debit entry, but shown vertically instead of horizontally.

In the rest of this book, we will use the horizontal style where it is thought easier for a student to see what is happening. Other than that we will show final accounts in the vertical style. We will not normally show both methods for every example, except where it is of importance.

Unless your teacher tells you otherwise, you are to show the answers to exercises 23.10X–23.16 using the vertical style of final accounts.

New Terms

Accrued expense (p. 194): An expense that the firm has used, but which has not yet been paid for.

Prepaid expense (p. 195): An expense to be used up in a following period, but which has been paid for in advance.

Revenue (p. 196): Money earned by the firm.

Summary

1 Adjustments are needed so that the expenses and income shown in the final accounts will equal the expenses incurred in the period and the revenue that has accrued.
2 The balances caused by the adjustments will be shown on the balance sheet at the end of the period.
3 Goods taken for own use without anything being recorded in the books will necessitate a transfer from purchases to the drawings account.
4 Private expenses should not be charged as an expense in the trading and profit and loss accounts, but should instead be charged to the drawings account.

Exercises

23.1 K. Holding has just finished his first year of trading, which was for the year ended 31 December 2001. He wants you to complete the following expense accounts, showing the amounts transferred to the profit and loss account. Also show any balances of expenses owing or paid in advance carried down to the next year.

(*a*) Rent paid for the 11 months to 30 November 2001 $3,300. The rent for December 2001 of $300 was not paid until 2002.
(*b*) Telephone expenses paid in 2001 $589. The telephone bill for November and December 2001 of $107 was not paid until 2002.
(*c*) Staff pay during 2001 $14,690. The total pay of $330 for the last week of 2001 was not paid until 2002.
(*d*) Rates were $4,200 per year. During 2001 he paid $5,250, which included rates for the three months ended 31 March 2002.
(*e*) Insurance costs were $800 per year. During 2001 he had paid $1,200, which included insurance for the six months ended 30 June 2002.

23.2X J. Lloyd has just finished his first year of trading, which was for the year ended 31 December 2003. Write up the following expenses, show the amounts transferred to the profit and loss account and any balances to be carried down to the year 2004.

(*a*) Motor expenses paid in 2003 amounted to $4,971. A bill for motor repairs done in November 2003 for $410 was not paid until 2004.
(*b*) Sundry expenses paid in 2003 amounted to $115. A bill for a sundry expense of $12 was not paid until 2004.
(*c*) Electricity bills paid in 2003 totalled $885. The electricity bill for the months of November and December 2003 of $216 was not paid until 2004.
(*d*) Computer hire rental of $1,200 was paid in 2003. Of this figure, $300 was in respect of the first three months of 2004.
(*e*) Security expenses were $250 per month, but had to be paid three months in advance. In 2003, $3,750 had been paid, which included an amount for the first three months of 2004.

23.3 D. Weekes' first year of business ended 31 December 2006. Besides his main business he also earns extra money, which is treated as part of his business. Write up the following revenue accounts. Show the amount transferred to his profit and loss account for the year ended 31 December 2006 and show any balances carried down to the year 2007.

(*a*) Insurance commission received during 2006 $1,377. One item of $114, which should be been received in 2006, was not received until 2007.
(*b*) He sub-lets part of his premises for $4,800 per year. During 2006 he received payment for 14 months, which included January and February 2007.
(*c*) His store windows are also used for local advertising by his customers. During 2006 he received $248 for this, but was also owed $22 which was not received until 2007.
(*d*) He hires deckchairs to tourists who pay in advance for their use. During 2006, he received $3,122. Two tourists still owed $45 at 31 December 2006 and paid the amounts owing in 2007.

23.4X G. Hamilton's first year in business ended on 31 December 2005. Open revenue accounts for the following, showing the amounts transferred to the profit and loss account for the year 2005 and also the balances carried down to 2006. *(Cont'd)*

(*a*) Part of the building is sub-let to a tenant from 1 January 2005 for $4,200 per year. Rent for 15 months to 31 March 2006 was received in 2005.
(*b*) Commission is received of $3,820. Outstanding commission of $270 for December 2005 was not received until 2006.
(*c*) Bank interest is received on a business deposit account. $489 was received in 2005, but the interest for November and December 2005, a total of $114, was not received until 2006.
(*d*) Advertising revenue of $1,577 was received in 2005. Of this, $248 was in respect of an advertisement to be displayed in 2006.

23.5 The financial year of J. Thomas ended on 31 December 2006. Show the ledger accounts for the following items, including the balance transferred to the necessary part of the final accounts, as well as the balances carried down to 2007.
(*a*) Motor expenses: paid in 2006, $744; owing at 31 December 2006, $28.
(*b*) Insurance: paid in 2006, $420; prepaid as at 31 December 2006, $35.
(*c*) Rent: paid during 2006, $1,800; owing as at 31 December 2005, $250; owing as at 31 December 2006, $490.
(*d*) Rates: paid during 2006, $950; prepaid as at 31 December 2005, $220; prepaid as at 31 December 2006, $290.
(*e*) Thomas sub-lets part of the premises. He receives $550 during the year ended 31 December 2006. Tenant owed Thomas $180 on 31 December 2005 and $210 on 31 December 2006.

23.6X J. Persad's year ended on 30 June 2004. Write up the ledger accounts, showing the transfers to the final accounts and the balances carried down to the next year for the following.
(*a*) Stationery: paid for the year to 30 June 2004, $855; stocks of stationery at 30 June 2003, $290; at 30 June 2004, $345.
(*b*) General expenses: paid for the year to 30 June 2004, $590; owing at 30 June 2003, $64; owing at 30 June 2004, $90.
(*c*) Rent and rates (combined account): paid in the year to 30 June 2004, $3,890; rent owing at 30 June 2003, $160; rent paid in advance at 30 June 2004, $250; rates owing 30 June 2003, $205; rates owing 30 June 2004, $360.
(*d*) Motor expenses: paid in the year to 30 June 2004, $4,750; owing as at 30 June 2003, $180; owing as at 30 June 2004, $375.
(*e*) Persad earns commission from the sales of one item. Received for the year to 30 June 2004, $850; owing at 30 June 2003, $80; owing at 30 June 2004, $145.

23.7 On 1 January 2006, the following appear in M. Nelson's balance sheet: Rates in advance $150.

During the year, the following rates payments were made: 11 May 2006, $400; 23 November 2006, $400. The second $400 covers the period from 1 October 2006 to 31 March 2007.

Write up the account for the year ended 31 December 2006, showing clearly the amount to be charged to the profit and loss account for the year ended on that date.

Write down the amount that should appear in Nelson's balance sheet on 31 December 2006 and indicate whether the amount is an asset or a liability.

23.8X N. Roberts is a manufacturer who powers his boilers by oil.

On 1 January 2005, the stock of oil in hand was $35, and $50 was in hand on 31 December 2005. Roberts owed $60 to the oil suppliers on 1 January 2005 and there was an invoice for oil supplied during 2005, unpaid on 31 December 2005, of $145. During the year 2005, payments made to the oil suppliers amounted to $260.

Write up Roberts' fuel account for the year ending 31 December 2005, showing the appropriate transfer to profit and loss account and bringing down any remaining balanes.

23.9X From the following particulars, write up R. Brown's rates account for the year ended 31 October 2003 and show the amount transferred to profit and loss account:

1 November 2002. Rates owing for October 2002, $10.

Payment for rates in year to 31 October 2003.

4 November 2002 for half-year to 31 March 2003, $60.
11 April 2003 for half-year to 30 September 2003, $72.
26 October 2003 for half-year to 31 March 2004, $72.

23.10X Draw up the trading and profit and loss account of J. Lester for the year ended 31 December 2004 from the following information.

Balances

	$		$
Sales	152,000	Rent and rates	3,790
Purchases	81,500	Bad debts	570
Discounts received	3,100	Carriage outwards	510
Discounts allowed	1,650	Carriage inwards	360
Pay	21,470	Bank charges	230
Returns inwards	2,460	General expenses	2,490
Returns outwards	1,910	Commission received	820
Equipment	60,000	Stock 1 January 2004	21,600
Loan from J. Rogers	5,000		

The following information at 31 December 2004 is also available:

(*a*) Stock at 31 December 2004, $27,540.
(*b*) Rent in arrears, $320.
(*c*) Included in general expenses is a figure of $2,000 for equipment.
(*d*) Equipment to be depreciated by 20%.
(*e*) Carriage outwards, $70 owing.
(*f*) There was one year's loan interest of 8% owing to J. Rogers. *(CXC style)*

23.11 From the following trial balance of John Brown, grocery store owner, prepare a trading account and profit and loss account, for the year ended 31 December 2007, and a balance sheet as at 31 December 2007, taking into consideration the adjustments shown below.

Trial Balance as at 31 December 2007

	Dr. $	*Cr.* $
Sales		40,000
Purchases	35,000	
Sales returns	500	
Purchases returns		620
Opening stock at 1 January 2007	10,000	
Provision for bad debt		80
Pay	3,000	
Rates	600	
Telephone	100	
Shop fittings at cost	6,000	
Van at cost	4,000	
Provision for depreciation: fittings		2,000
Provision for depreciation: van		1,000
Debtors and creditors	980	700
Bad debts	20	
Capital		17,900
Bank balance	300	
Drawings	1,800	
	62,300	62,300

Adjustments:

(*a*) Closing stock at 31 December 2007, $12,000.
(*b*) Accrued pay, $500.
(*c*) Rates prepaid, $50.
(*d*) The provision for bad debts to be increased to 10% of debtors.
(*e*) Telephone account outstanding, $22.
(*f*) Depreciate shop fittings at 10% per annum, and van at 20% per annum, using the reducing balance method.

(Keep your answer. It will be used as a basis for work to be done in Chapter 24.)

23.12 J. Graham drew up the following trial balance as at 30 September 2008. You are to draft a trading and profit and loss account for the year to 30 September 2008 and a balance sheet as at that date.

	Dr.	*Cr.*
	$	$
Loan from P. Parkin		5,000
Capital		25,955
Drawings	8,420	
Cash at bank	3,115	
Cash in hand	295	
Debtors	12,300	
Creditors		9,370
Stock 30 September 2007	23,910	
Motor van	6,000	
Office equipment	8,000	
Provision for depreciation: motor van		1,900
Provision for depreciation: office equipment		1,750
Sales		130,900
Purchases	92,100	
Returns inwards	550	
Carriage inwards	215	
Returns outwards		307
Carriage outwards	309	
Motor expenses	1,630	
Rent and rates	2,970	
Telephone charges	405	
Pay	12,810	
Insurance	492	
Office expenses	1,377	
Sundry expenses	284	
	175,182	175,182

Notes: at 30 September 2008.

(*a*) Prepaid expenses: insurance, $105; rates, $405.
(*b*) Expenses owing: rent, $300; telephone, $85.
(*c*) Stock, $27,475.
(*d*) Depreciate motor van and office equipment at the rate of 20% on original cost.

23.13 The trial balance now shown was extraced from the books of J. Webster as at 31 December 2003.

	Dr.	*Cr.*
	$	$
Purchases	60,800	
Sales		91,400
Returns inwards	1,200	
Returns outwards		1,350
Carriage inwards	450	
Carriage outwards	310	
Motor expenses	1,864	
Pay	5,310	
Discounts allowed	309	
Discounts received		210
Rent and rates	810	
Insurance	204	
Bad debts written off	1,516	
Provision for bad debts, 1 January 2003		805
Stock-in-trade, 1 January 2003	31,630	
Debtors	22,460	
Creditors		11,960
Drawings	7,155	

(Cont'd)

Cash in hand	150	
Cash at bank	5,850	
Fixtures at cost	11,000	
Motor vans at cost	9,400	
Provision for depreciation as at 31 December 2002:		
Fixtures		4,400
Motor vans		2,360
Capital		47,933
	160,418	160,418

The following are to be taken into account as at 31 December 2003.
(*a*) Stock-in-trade, $36,530.
(*b*) Insurance prepaid, $44.
(*c*) Pay outstanding, $506.
(*d*) Provision for bad debts to be increased to $880.
(*e*) Provide for depreciation for the year: fixtures, $2,200; motor vans, $1,620.
You are required to prepare a trading and profit and loss account for the year ended 31 December 2003 and a balance sheet as at that date.

23.14X The following trial balance was extracted from the records of J. Jordan, a trader, as at 31 December 2001.

	Dr. $	*Cr.* $
Discounts allowed	410	
Discounts received		506
Carriage inwards	309	
Carriage outwards	218	
Returns inwards	1,384	
Returns outwards		810
Sales		120,320
Purchases	84,290	
Stock 31 December 2000	30,816	
Motor expenses	4,917	
Repairs to premises	1,383	
Pay	16,184	
Sundry expenses	807	
Rates and insurance	2,896	
Premises at cost	40,000	
Motor vehicles at cost	11,160	
Provision for depreciation motors as at 31 Dec 2000		3,860
Debtors and creditors	31,640	24,320
Cash at bank	4,956	
Cash in hand	48	
Drawings	8,736	
Capital		50,994
Loan from P. Holland		40,000
Bad debts	1,314	
Provision for bad debts at 31 December 2000		658
	241,468	241,468

The following matters are to be taken into account at 31 December 2001.
(*a*) Stock, $36,420.
(*b*) Expenses owing: sundry expenses, $62; motor expenses, $33.
(*c*) Prepayment: rates, $166.
(*d*) Provision for bad debts to be reduced to $580.
(*e*) Depreciation for motors to be $2,100 for the year.
(*f*) Part of the premises were let to a tenant who owed $250 at 31 December 2001.
(*g*) Loan interest owing to P. Holland, $4,000.
You are required to draw up a trading and profit and loss account for the year ended 31 December 2001 and a balance sheet as at that date.

23.15X Jane Jones is in business as a hairdresser. From the figures below prepare her profit and loss account for the year ended 31 December 2007 and a balance sheet on that date.

	Dr.	*Cr.*
	$	$
Capital 1 January 2007		9,740
Drawings	4,500	
Motor car	1,800	
Petty cash	40	
Cost of new hairdryer	120	
Equipment	1,000	
Freehold premises	6,000	
Advertising	230	
Cash at bank	5,400	
Motor car expenses	480	
Rates	140	
Telephone	110	
Revenue from hairdressing		10,400
Sundry expenses	1,200	
Provision for depreciation: car		480
Provision for depreciation: equipment		400
	21,020	21,020

The following should be taken into consideration.

(*a*) Rates prepaid 31 December 2007, $30.
(*b*) One-third of motor car expenses including depreciation for the year is to be regarded as private use.
(*c*) Provide for cleaning costs, $50.
(*d*) Depreciate all equipment on hand at 31 December 2007 by 10% of cost.
(*e*) Motor car is to be depreciated by 20% on reduced balance.

23.16 Harvey Brown is a retail trader. From the following information prepare a trading and profit and loss account for the year ended 31 December 2004 and a balance sheet on that date.

Trial Balance — 31 December 2004

	$	$
Capital 1 January 2004		6,400
Land and buildings	5,000	
Motor vehicles	1,200	
Provision for depreciation: motor vehicles		600
Drawings	1,400	
Stock	910	
Bank overdraft		96
Sales		14,260
Purchases	11,100	
Motor expenses	310	
Sundry expenses	106	
Pay	1,560	
Debtors	820	
Creditors		1,210
Rates and insurances	160	
	22,566	22,566

The following items should be taken into consideration.

(*a*) Stock at 31 December 2004, $1,820.
(*b*) A provision for doubtful debts of 5% on the debtors at 31 December 2004 is to be created.
(*c*) Depreciation is to be provided on motor vehicles at 20% on cost.
(*d*) Rates prepaid at 31 December 2004, $12.
(*e*) Motor expenses bill for December $26 is owing at 31 December 2004.
(*f*) Sundry expenses includes $15 for a private telephone bill of Harvey Brown.
(*g*) A cheque for $250 was paid to a creditor on 31 December 2004 but had not been entered in the books at the time of extracting the trial balance.

CHAPTER **24**

Work Sheets and Final Accounts

Learning Objectives

- To be able to draw up final accounts using work sheets.

24.1 Work sheets

Instead of drawing up a set of final accounts in the way already shown in this textbook, a work sheet could be drawn up instead. This may provide a useful aid where a large number of adjustments are needed. Work sheets are usually drawn up on specially preprinted types of stationery with suitable columns printed on them.

Exhibit 24.1 shows the work sheet drawn up for question 23.11. (You were asked to keep the traditional answer that has been drawn up.) The gross and net profits should be the same as those in your answer; it is simply the display that is different.

Stages of Preparation of the Work Sheet (see Exhibit 24.1)

1. Enter up details of the trial balance at the year ended in columns (1) and (2).
2. Find out the adjustments that are needed to the trial balance figures when drawing up the figures for transfer to the trading and profit and loss accounts, i.e. prepayments, accruals, payments in advance, depreciation expense, closing stock.
3. Enter the adjustments per (2) above in columns (3) and (4). In column (3) (Dr.) is entered the amounts of the adjustments needed on the debit side of the accounts. Column (4) (Cr.) should contain the amounts of the adjustments needed on the credit side of the accounts. Remember that each adjustment needs both a debit and a credit entry.
4. Enter in columns (5) and (6) the items that should be transferred to the trading account. These will consist of the appropriate items from columns (1) and (2), adjusted by the figures in columns (3) and (4). If you compare the balancing figure of $7,120, you will see that this is the same as the gross profit figure as per the normally displayed answer to question 23.11. In fact, the only adjustment that has been made is in respect of the closing stock as at 31 December 2007, as the closing stock (correctly so) was not shown in the original trial balance.

5 Enter in columns (7) and (8) the items that should be transferred to the profit and loss account. This will consist of the appropriate items from columns (1) and (2), adjusted by the figures in columns (3) and (4). For instance, the pay balance in column (1) $3,000 (debit) is added to by $500 (also a debit) from column (3); this gives a total of $3,500 (debit) for column (7). Rates from column (1) (debit) $600 are adjusted by $50 (credit) to give a net total of $550 (debit) for column (7). The balance on columns (7) and (8) is $1,910, which is the same as the net profit on the normally displayed answer to question 23.11.

6 In respect of all balances remaining, after the transfers to the trading and profit and loss accounts have been made, these are then shown in columns (9) and (10). These balance sheet figures agree with those in the answer to question 23.11, although they are not displayed in the normal way.

If you were an accountant working for John Brown, the final accounts given by you to John Brown, and to anyone else who was interested party, such as the Inspector of Taxes or the bank, would be the same as the conventional type. They would not be given the work sheets.

Exhibit 24.1

Final Accounts Work Sheet for John Brown for year ended 31 December 2007

John Brown: Exercise 23.11	*Trial Balance*		*Adjustments*		*Trading account*		*Profit and loss accountt*		*Balance sheet*	
Work sheet	(1) *Dr.*	(2) *Cr.*	(3) *Dr.*	(4) *Cr.*	(5) *Dr.*	(6) *Cr.*	(7) *Dr.*	(8) *Cr.*	(9) *Dr.*	(10) *Cr.*
Sales		40,000				40,000				
Purchases	35,000				35,000					
Sales returns	500				500					
Purchases returns		620				620				
Stock 1 Jan 2007	10,000				10,000					
Provision for bad debts		80		18 (iv)						98
Pay	3,000		500 (ii)				3,500			
Rates	600			50 (iii)			550			
Telephone	100		22 (v)				122			
Equipment	6,000								6,000	
Van	4,000								4,000	
Provision for depreciation: equipment		2,000		400 (vi)						2,400
Provision for depreciation: van		1,000		600 (vi)						1,600
Debtors	980								980	
Creditors		700								700
Bad debts	20						20			
Capital		17,900								17,900
Bank	300								300	
Drawings	1,800								1,800	
	62,300	62,300								

(Cont'd)

Stock 31.12 2007: Asset			12,000 (i)						12,000	
Stock 31.12 2007: Cost of goods sold				12,000 (i)		12,000				
Accrued pay expense				500 (ii)						500
Accrued telephone expense				22 (v)						22
Provision for bad debts			18 (iv)				18			
Prepaid rates expense			50 (iii)						50	
Depreciation expense: equipment			400 (vi)				400			
Depreciation expense: van			600 (vi)				600			
			13,590	13,590						
Gross profit (balancing figure)					7,120			7,120		
					52,620	52,620				
Net profit							1,910			1,910
(balancing figure)							7,120	7,120	25,130	25,130

This can also be called the extended trial balance.

CHAPTER **25**

Bank Reconciliation Statements

Learning Objectives

- To be able to reconcile cash book balances with bank statement balances.
- To understand how bank overdrafts affect the reconciliation process.
- To be able to make necessary entries for dishonoured cheques.

25.1 Completing Entries in the Cash Book

In our own books we will enter up the bank columns of our cash book, showing monies banked and paid out. Our bank will also record items paid into and out of our bank account with them.

If all the items entered in our cash book were the same as those entered in our account with the bank, then obviously the bank balance per our books and the bank balance per the bank's books would equal each other.

On the other hand, there may be items paid into and out of our account at the bank which have not been recorded by us in our cash book. To see what these are, if any, we will need a copy of our account as kept at the bank. They will give us such a copy, known as a bank statement. Let us look at an example of a cash book and a bank statement in Exhibit 25.1. We will tick off the items that are the same in both sets of records.

Exhibit 25.1

Cash Book
(Bank columns only, before balancing on 31 Dec. 2008)

2008			$	2008			$
Dec 1	Balance b/f	✔	250	Dec 5	J. Gordon	✔	65
Dec 20	P. Thomas	✔	100	Dec 27	K. Hughes	✔	175
Dec 28	D. Jones	✔	190				

(Cont'd)

Bank Statement

			Withdrawals	*Deposits*	*Balance*
2008			$	$	$
Dec 1	Balance b/f	✔			250
Dec 8	10625*	✔	65		185
Dec 21	Deposit	✔		100	285
Dec 28	Deposit	✔		190	475
Dec 29	10626*	✔	175		300
Dec 30	Bank Giro credit: P. Smith			70	370
Dec 31	Bank charges		50		320

*10625 and 10626 refer to the serial numbers on the cheques paid out.

It is now possible to see that the two items not shown in our cash book are:

Bank Giro credit: P. Smith	$70
Bank charges	$50

P. Smith had paid us $70, but instead of sending us a cheque he had paid the money direct into our bank account, using the bank's services. We did not know of this until we received the bank statement.

The other item was in respect of bank charges. The bank had charged us $50 for keeping our bank account and all the work connected with it. Instead of sending us an invoice they have simply taken the money out of our bank account.

As we have now identified the items missing from our cash book we can now complete writing it up as follows.

Cash Book

		$			$
2008		$	2008		$
Dec 1	Balance b/f	250	Dec 5	J. Gordon	65
Dec 20	P. Thomas	100	Dec 27	K. Hughes	175
Dec 28	D. Jones	190	Dec 31	Bank charges	50
Dec 30	P. Smith	70	Dec 31	Balance c/d	320
		610			610
2009					
Jun 1	Balance b/d	320			

Both closing balances are now shown as being $320.

25.2 Where Closing Balances Differ

Although a cash book may be written up to date by us, we obviously cannot alter the bank's own records. Even after writing up entries in our cash book there may still be a difference between our cash book balance and the bank statement balance. Exhibit 25.2 shows such a case.

Exhibit 25.2

Cash Book
(after being completed to date)

2009		$	2009		$
Jan 1	Balance b/d	320	Jan 10	C. Morgan	110
Jan 16	R. Lomas	160	Jan 20	M. McCarthy	90
Jan 24	V. Verity	140	Jan 28	Kingston PC rates	180
Jan 31	J. Soames (2)	470	Jan 30	M. Peck (1)	200
Jan 31	R. Johnson	90	Jan 31	Balance c/d	600
		1,180			1,180
Feb 1	Balance b/d	600			

Bank Statement

2009		Withdrawals $	Deposits $	Balance $
Jan 1	Balance b/f			320
Jan 12	10627	110		210
Jan 16	Deposit		160	370
Jan 23	10628	90		280
Jan 24	Deposit		140	420
Jan 28	Direct debit: Kingston PC	180		240
Jan 31	Bank Giro credit: R. Johnson		90	330

You can see that two items ((1) and (2)) are in the cash book but are not shown on the bank statement.

1 A cheque had been paid to M. Peck on January 30. He banked it at his bank on January 31 but it was not presented to our bank until February 2. This is known as an **unpresented cheque**.
2 Although we had received a cheque for $470 from J. Soames on January 31, we did not bank it until February 1. This will be known as a '*bank lodgement not yet credited*' to our bank's account.

The balance per our cash book on January 31 was $600, whereas our bank statement shows a balance of $330. To prove that although the balances are different they can be 'reconciled' with each other, a **bank reconciliation statement** will be drawn up. It is usual to start with the cash book balance and then reconcile it to the bank statement balance. In this case it would appear as follows.

Bank Reconciliation Statement as at 31 December 2008

		$
Balance as per cash book		600
Add Unpresented cheque	(1)	200
		800
Less Bank lodgement not credited	(2)	470
Balance per bank statement		330

If the two balances cannot be reconciled, then there will be an error somewhere. This will have to be located and then corrected.

25.3 The Bank Balance in the Balance Sheet

The balance to be shown in the balance sheet is that per the cash book after it has been written up to date. In Exhibit 25.2 the balance sheet figure would be $600.

25.4 Other Terms Used in Banking

1. **Standing orders** A firm can instruct its bank to pay regular amounts of money at stated dates to persons or firms. For instance, you may ask your bank to pay $200 a month to a building society to repay a mortgage.
2. **Direct debits** These are payments which have to be made, such as rates, insurance premiums and similiar items. Instead of asking the bank to pay the money, as with standing orders, you give permission to the creditor to obtain the money directly from your bank account. This is particularly useful if the amounts payable may vary from time to time, as it is the creditor who changes the payments, not you. With standing orders, if the amount is ever to be changed then you have to inform the bank. With direct debits it is the creditor who arranges that, not you.

Both of these items will be written up in your cash book before attempting a reconciliation.

25.5 Bank Overdrafts

The adjustment needed to reconcile the bank overdraft (shown by a credit balance in the cash book) according to the firm's books with that shown in the bank's books are the complete opposite of that needed when the account is not overdrawn.

Exhibit 25.3 is of a cash book and a bank statement showing an overdraft. Only the cheque for G. Cumberbatch (1) $106 and the cheque paid to J. Kelly (2) $63 need adjusting. Work through the reconciliation statement and then see the note after it.

Exhibit 25.3

Cash Book

2004			$	2004			$
Dec 5	I. Howe		308	Dec 1	Balance b/f		709
Dec 24	L. Mason		120	Dec 9	P. Davies		140
Dec 29	K. King		124	Dec 27	J. Kelly	(2)	63
Dec 31	G. Cumberbatch	(1)	106	Dec 29	United Trust		77
Dec 31	Balance c/f		380	Dec 31	Bank charges		49
			1,038				1,038

(Cont'd)

Bank Statement

		Dr.	*Cr.*	*Balance*
2004		$	$	$
Dec 1	Balance b/f			709 O/D
Dec 5	Cheque		308	401 O/D
Dec 14	P. Davies	140		541 O/D
Dec 24	Cheque		120	421 O/D
Dec 29	K. King: Credit transfer		124	297 O/D
Dec 29	United Trust: Standing order	77		374 O/D
Dec 31	Bank charges	49		423 O/D

Note: An overdraft is often shown with the letters O/D following the amount.

Bank Reconciliation Statement as on 31 December 2004

	$
Overdraft as per cash book	380
Add Bank lodgements not on bank statement	106
	486
Less Unpresented cheque	63
Overdraft per bank statement	423

Now compare the reconciliation statements in Exhibits 25.2 and 25.3. This shows the following.

	Balances	*Overdrafts*
Balance/overdraft per cash book	xxxx	xxxx
Adjustments		
Unpresented cheque	*Plus*	*Less*
Banking not entered	*Less*	*Plus*
Balance/overdraft per bank statement	xxxx	xxxx

Adjustments are, therefore, made in the opposite way when there is an overdraft.

25.6 Dishonoured Cheques

When a cheque is received from a customer and paid into the bank, it is recorded on the debit side of the cash book. It is also shown on the bank statement as a banking by the bank. However, at a later date it may be found that his bank will not pay us the amount due on the cheque. The bank has failed to honour the cheque. It is known as a **dishonoured cheque**.

There are several possible reasons for this. Let us suppose that K. King gave us a cheque for $5,000 on 20 May 2002. We bank it, but a few days later our bank returns the cheque to us. Typical reasons are:

1 King had put $5,000 in figures on the cheque, but had written it in words as five thousand five hundred pounds. You will have to give the cheque back to King for amendment.

2 Normally, cheques are considered *stale* six months after the date on the, cheque. In other words the banks will not pay cheques over six months old. If King had put the year 2001 on the cheque instead of 2002, then the cheque would be returned to us by our bank.

3 King simply did not have sufficient funds in his bank account. Suppose he had previously a balance of only $2,000 and yet he has given us a cheque for $5,000. His bank has not allowed him to have an overdraft. In such a case, the cheque would be dishonoured. The bank would write on the cheque '*refer to drawer*', and we would have to get in touch with King to see what he was going to do about it.

In all of these cases the bank would show the original banking as being cancelled by showing the cheque paid out of our bank account. As soon as this happens they will notify us. We will then also show the cheque as being cancelled by a credit in the cash book. We will then debit that amount to King's account.

When King originally paid his account, our records would have appeared as shown below.

K. King

2002	$	2002	$
May 1 Balance b/d	5,000	May 20 Bank	5,000

Bank Account

2002	$		
May 20 K. King	5,000		

After our recording the dishonour, the records will appear as follows.

K. King

2002	$	2002	$
May 1 Balance b/d	5,000	May 20 Bank	5,000
May 25 Bank: cheque dishonoured	5,000		

Bank Account

2002	$	2002	$
May 20 K. King	5,000	May 25 K. King: cheque dishonoured	5,000

In other words, King is once again shown as owing us $5,000.

New Terms

Bank Giro credit (p. 214): An amount paid by someone direct into our bank account.

Bank reconciliation statement (p. 215): A calculation comparing the cash book balance with the bank statement balance.

Direct debits (p. 216): Where we give permission for an organization to collect amounts owing direct from our account.

Dishonoured cheque (p. 217): A cheque which is found to be worth nothing.

Standing order (p. 216): Instructions to our bank to pay specified amounts at given dates.

Unpresented cheque (p. 215): A cheque which has been sent but has not yet gone through the bank account of the receiver of it.

Summary

1 A bank reconciliation statement should show whether or not errors have been made either in the bank columns of the cash book or on the bank statement.

2 It is best to update the cash book before attempting a bank reconciliation.

3 In the case of bank overdrafts, the reconciliation statements show adjustments that are the opposite to those shown with positive bank balances.

Exercises

25.1 The following are extracts from the cash book and the bank statement of J. Roche. You are required to:

(*a*) write the cash book up to date, and state the new balance as on 31 December 2005;
(*b*) draw up a bank reconciliation statement as on 31 December 2005.

Cash Book

2005	*Dr.*	$	2005	*Cr.*	$
Dec 1	Balance b/f	1,740	Dec 8	A. Dailey	349
Dec 7	T. J. Masters	88	Dec 15	R. Mason	33
Dec 22	J. Ellis	73	Dec 28	G. Small	115
Dec 31	K. Wood	249	Dec 31	Balance c/d	1,831
Dec 31	M. Barrett	178			
		2,328			2,328

Bank Statement

2005		*Dr.* $	*Cr.* $	*Balance* $
Dec 1	Balance b/f			1,740
Dec 7	Cheque		88	1,828
Dec 11	A. Dailey	349		1,479
Dec 20	R. Mason	33		1,446
Dec 22	Cheque		73	1,519
Dec 31	Credit transfer: J. Walters		54	1,573
Dec 31	Bank charges	22		1,551

25.2X William Kelly's cash book on 28 February 2006 showed a balance at bank of $456.48. On attempting a reconciliation with his bank statement, the following matters were discovered.

1 A payment from B. Green to W. Kelly of $40 by direct bank transfer had not been recorded in the cash book.
2 Cheques drawn but not presented to the bank were: A. Roe, $21.62; C. Mils, $36.55.
3 A paying-in slip dated 27 February 2006 totalling $372.31 was not credited by the bank until 1 March 2006.
4 A standing order for $21.58 payable on 20 February 2006 for fire insurance had been paid by the bank but not entered in the cash book.
5 Bank charges $15 had not been entered in the cash book.

(*a*) Open the cash book and make such additional entries as you consider necessary.
(*b*) Prepare a statement reconciling your *revised* cash book balance with the balance shown by the bank statement.

25.3 The bank columns in the cash book for June 2007 and the bank statement for that month for C. Grant are as follows.

Cash Book

2007	*Dr.*	$	2007	*Cr.*	$
Jun 1	Balance b/f	2,379	Jun 5	D. Blake	150
Jun 7	B. Green	158	Jun 12	J. Gray	433
Jun 16	A. Silver	93	Jun 16	B. Stephens	88
Jun 28	M. Brown	307	Jun 29	Orange Club	57
Jun 30	K. Black	624	Jun 30	Balance c/d	2,833
		3,561			3.561

Bank Statement

2007		*Dr.* $	*Cr.* $	*Balance* $
Jun 1	Balance b/f			2,379
Jun 7	Cheque		158	2,537
Jun 8	D. Blake	150		2,387
Jun 16	Cheque		93	2,480
Jun 17	J. Gray	433		2,047
Jun 18	B. Stephens	88		1,959
Jun 28	Cheque		307	2,266
Jun 29	U.D.T. standing order	44		2,222
Jun 30	Johnson: trader's credit		90	2,312
Jun 30	Bank charges	70		2,242

You are required to:
(*a*) write the cash book up to date to take the above into account;
(*b*) draw up a bank reconciliation statement as on 30 June 2007, reconciling the corrected cash book balance with bank statement balance.

25.4X On 31 October 2005 the cash book of N. Orange showed a balance at bank of $570. An examination of his records located the following errors.

1 Orange paid to R. Jones $175 by cheque on 15 October. This cheque was entered in the cash book as $195.
2 Bank charges not recorded in the cash book amounted to $25.
3 A cheque dated 19 October, value $150, payable to T. Jack was not paid by the bank until 5 November.
4 Orange on 23 October received from W. Green a cheque, value $125. This cheque was dishonoured on 29 October. No entry for the dishonour has been made in the cash book.

(Cont'd)

5 On 31 October a cheque, value $200, received from F. Brown was banked; however, the bank statement was not credited until 1 November.

You are required to:
(*a*) make the necessary entries in the cash book in order to show the revised cash book balance at 31 October 2005;
(*b*) prepare a statement reconciling the corrected cash book balance with the bank statement at 31 October 2005;
(*c*) state the balance at bank at 31 October 2005 as shown by the bank statement.

25.5 (*a*) You have the task of writing up B. Mills' cash book. From the following, write up the cash book for May 2001. All the details concern the bank columns only.

2001		$
May 1	Overdraft brought forward.	3,340
May 4	Bought motor van by cheque.	5,000
May 7	Cash sales banked immediately.	1,630
May 10	Mills introduced extra capital.	10,000
May 18	Paid D. Marple Ltd by cheque.	237
May 29	Cheque received from A. B. Ltd and banked.	555
May 30	Cashed a cheque to pay staff	470

(*b*) The bank statement of B. Mills on 31 May 2001 shows a balance of $1,995. The following information was discovered.

1 Bank charges of $110 have been entered in the bank statement but not in the cash book.
2 Dividends received from J. G. Ltd of $280 and banked in the month have not been recorded in the cash book.
3 The cheque banked on 29 May for $555 has not yet been entered on the bank statement.
4 Standing orders of $920 for insurance have been entered on the bank statement but not in the cash book.
5 A cheque of $75, received as cash sales on 7 May and banked, has been returned marked 'insufficient funds'. No entry has been made in the books.
6 The cheque paid to Marple $237 has not yet been presented by them.

You are required to:
(i) enter up all relevant information up to date in Mills' cash book for May 2001 and balance down;
(ii) draw up a bank reconciliation statement as on 31 May 2001, reconciling the corrected cash book balance with the bank statement balance.
(iii) explain why bank reconciliation statements are drawn up.

(*CXC style*)

25.6X The bank statement for G. Greene for the month of March 2006 is as follows.

2006		*Dr.* $	*Cr.* $	*Balance* $
Mar 1	Balance			5,197 O/D
Mar 8	L. Tulloch	122		5,319 O/D
Mar 16	Cheque		244	5,075 O/D
Mar 20	A. Bennett	208		5,283 O/D
Mar 21	Cheque		333	4,950 O/D
Mar 31	M. Turnbull: trader's credit		57	4,893 O/D
Mar 31	B.K.S.: standing order	49		4,942 O/D
Mar 31	Bank charges	28		4,970 O/D

(*Cont'd*)

The cash book for March 2006 is as follows

2006	*Dr.*	$	2006	*Cr.*	$
Mar 16	N. Marsh	244	Mar 1	Balance b/f	5,197
Mar 21	K. Alexander	333	Mar 6	L. Tulloch	122
Mar 31	U. Sinclair	160	Mar 30	A. Bennett	208
Mar 31	Balance c/d	5,280	Mar 30	J. Shaw	490
		6,017			6,017

You are to:
(*a*) write the cash book up to date;
(*b*) draw up a bank reconciliation statement as on 31 March 2006, reconciling the corrected cash book balance with the bank statement balance.

25.7X

(*a*) R. Rogers had a $3,470 balance in a bank current account. Show whether each of the following increases or reduces the balance.
(i) Bank charges $70.
(ii) Standing order paid of $250.
(iii) Dividends received and banked $400.
(iv) Payment to creditor $140.
(v) Item previously written off as bad debt, cheque received and banked $90.
(vi) Debtor paid direct into Rogers' bank account $470.
(vii) Drawings in form of cheque $150.
(viii) Cheque previously banked, $279, now dishonoured.

(*b*) A summary of D. Plant's bank account in his cash book for July 2004 was as follows.

	$		$
Balance b/f	6,272	Payments	7,140
Received	5,848	Balance c/d	4,980
	12,120		12,120

You are told the following.
(i) A cheque banked for $200 from K. Stevens has been treated as a payment in the cash book.
(ii) A cheque from T. Cooper for $180 banked in the month was dishonoured two days later, but no entry was made of the dishonour.
(iii) The unpresented cheques on 31 July 2004 were in the sums of $154 and $378.
(iv) Bank charges for July not yet entered, $10.
(v) $477 banked and entered in the cash book on 29 July had not been entered on the bank statement.
(vi) Standing order for rent $175 paid in July has not been entered.
(vii) A customer, R. Salt, deposited $760 direct into Plant's account on 29 July but this has not been entered in the cash book.

You are to:
(1) write up Plant's cash book to get it up to date, and balance down;
(2) by means of a bank reconciliation statement, calculate the balance per the bank statement as on 31 July 2004.

CHAPTER **26**

The Analytical Petty Cash Book and the Imprest System

Learning Objectives

- To be able to write up a petty cash book.
- To be able to post the petty cash items to ledger accounts.
- To understand the imprest system.

26.1 Division of the Cash Book

With the growth of the firm, it has been seen that it becomes necessary to have several books instead of just one ledger.

These ideas can be extended to the cash book. It is obvious that in almost any firm there will be many small cash payments to be made. It would be an advantage if the records of these payments could be kept separate from the main cash book. Where a separate book is kept, it is known as a **petty cash book**.

The advantages of such an action can be summarized as follows.

- The task of handling and recording the small cash payments could be given by the cashier to a junior member of staff. She would then be known as the 'petty cashier'. The cashier, who is a more highly paid member of staff, would be saved from routine work. This would then be done by the petty cashier, who is a junior member of staff.
- If small cash payments were entered into the main cash book, these items would then need posting one by one to the ledgers. If travelling expenses were paid to staff on a daily basis, this could mean over 250 postings to the staff travelling expenses account during the year, i.e. 5 days per week × 50 working weeks per year. However, if a special form of a petty cash book is kept, only the monthly totals for each period would need posting to the general ledger. If this is done, only 12 entries would be needed in the staff travelling expenses account instead of over 250.

When the petty cashier makes a payment to someone, that person has to fill in a voucher showing exactly what the payment was for. He usually has to attach bills – e.g. bills for petrol – to the petty cash voucher. He would sign the voucher to certify that his expenses had been paid to him by the petty cashier.

Two examples of petty cash vouchers are shown in Exhibit 26.1 – Petty cash vouchers 9 and 16.

Exhibit 26.1

No. 9

PETTY CASH VOUCHER

Date 15/9/2004

For what required	*Amount* $
Refund of overpayment: L. Waites Sales ledger 121	50
	50

Signature L. Waites

Passed by E. Charles

No. 16

PETTY CASH VOUCHER

Date 29/9/2004

For what required	*Amount* $
Parcel to Miami	22
	22

Signature K. Blake

Passed by E. Charles

26.2 The Imprest System

Under the **imprest system**, the cashier gives the petty cashier enough cash to meet her needs for the following period. At the end of the period the cashier finds out the amounts spent by the petty cashier, and gives her an amount equal to that spent. The petty cashier will produce the petty cash vouchers as evidence of the amount spent. The petty cash in hand should then be equal to the *original* amount with which the period was started. Exhibit 26.2 shows an example of this method.

Exhibit 26.2

		$
Period 1	The cashier gives the petty cashier:	100
	The petty cashier pays out in the period:	78
	Petty cash now in hand:	22
	The cashier now gives the petty cashier the amount spent:	78
	Petty cash in hand at the end of period:	100
Period 2	The petty cashier pays out in the period:	84
	Petty cash now in hand:	16
	The cashier now gives the petty cashier the amount spent:	84
	Petty cash in hand end of period 2	100

It may be necessary to increase the fixed sum, often called the cash 'float', that is to be held at the start of each period. In the above case, if we had wanted to increase the 'float' at the end of the second period to $120, then the cashier would have given the petty cashier an extra $20, i.e. $84 + 20 = 104.

26.3 A worked example of an analytical cash book

An analytical petty cash book is often used. One of these is shown as Exhibit 26.3 which records the following transactions.

2004			$
Sept	1	The cashier gave $600 as float to the petty cashier.	
		Payments out of petty cash during September:	
Sept	2	Petrol	63
Sept	3	K. Long – travelling expenses	32
Sept	3	Postage	24
Sept	4	D. Campbell – travelling expenses	21
Sept	7	Cleaning expenses	15
Sept	9	Petrol	19
Sept	12	K. Lee – travelling expenses	30
Sept	14	Petrol	35
Sept	15	L. Waites – refund: sales ledger account overpaid (see Exhibit 26.1)	50
Sept	16	Cleaning expenses	15
Sept	18	Petrol	24
Sept	20	Postage	28
Sept	22	Cleaning expenses	19
Sept	24	H. Wood – travelling expenses	75
Sept	27	Settlement of K. Young's account in the purchases ledger	33
Sept	29	Postage (see Exhibit 26.1)	22
Oct	1	The cashier reimbursed the petty cashier the amount spent in the month.	

The receipts column is on the debit side of the petty cash book. On giving $600 to the petty cashier on 1 September, the credit entry was made in the cash book while the debit entry was made in the petty cash book. A similar entry was made on 1 October for the $505 paid by the chief cashier to the petty cashier. This amount covers all expenses paid by the petty cashier.

On the credit side of the petty cash book the following happens.

1. Enter the dates and details of each payment. Put the amount in the total column.
2. For step 1 also put the amount in the column for the type of expense.
3. At the end of each period, add up the totals column.
4. Now add up each of the expense columns. The total of step 3 should equal the total of all the expense columns. In Exhibit 26.3 this is $505.
5. Then balance off the petty cash book, carrying down the petty cash in hand balance to the next period.

To complete double entry for petty cash expenses paid, take the following steps.

1. Total of each expense column is debited to the expense account in the general ledger.
2. Enter the folio number of each general ledger page under each of the expense columns in the petty cash book. This enables cross-reference to be made easily.
3. The last column in the petty cash book is a ledger column. In this column, items paid out of petty cash which need posting to the sales ledger and the purchases ledger are shown.

This would happen if a purchases ledger account was settled out of petty cash or if a refund was made out of petty cash to a customer who had overpaid his or her account.

The double entry for each of the items in Exhibit 26.3 appears in Exhibit 26.4.

Exhibit 26.3

Petty Cash Book *(p. 31)*

Receipts	*Folio*	*Date*	*Details*	*Voucher no.*	*Total*	*Motor expenses*	*Staff travelling expenses*	*Postages*	*Cleaning*	*Ledger folio*	*Ledger accounts*
$		2004			$	$	$	$	$		$
600	CB 19	Sept 1	Cash								
		Sept 2	Petrol	1	63	63					
		Sept 3	K. Long	2	32		32				
		Sept 3	Postage	3	24			24			
		Sept 4	D. Campbell	4	21		21				
		Sept 7	Cleaning	5	15				15		
		Sept 9	Petrol	6	19	19					
		Sept 12	K. Lee	7	30		30				
		Sept 14	Petrol	8	35	35					
		Sept 15	L. Waites	9	50					SL 121	50
		Sept 16	Cleaning	10	15				15		
		Sept 18	Petrol	11	24	24					
		Sept 20	Postage	12	28			28			
		Sept 22	Cleaning	13	19				19		
		Sept 24	H. Wood	14	75		75				
		Sept 27	K. Young	15	33					PL 18	33
		Sept 29	Postage	16	22			22			
					505	141	158	74	49		83
						GL 17	GL 29	GL 44	GL 64		
		Sept 30	Balance c/d		95						
600					600						
95		Oct 1	Balance b/d								
505	CB 22	Oct 1	Cash								

Reimbursement equals the total amount spent in September 2004.

Total amount spent in September 2004.

Exhibit 26.4

Cash Book (Bank column only) *(p. 19)*

		2004		$
		Sept 1	Petty cash PCB 31	600
		Oct 1	Petty cash PCB 31	505

General Ledger

Motor Expenses *(p. 17)*

2004			$	
Sept 30	Petty cash	PCB 31	141	

Staff Travelling Expenses *(p. 29)*

2004			$	
Sept 30	Petty cash	PCB 31	158	

(Cont'd)

Postage *(p. 44)*

2004		$		
Sept 30 Petty cash	PCB 31	74		

Cleaning *(p. 64)*

2004		$		
Sept 30 Petty cash	PCB 31	49		

Purchases Ledger
K. Young *(p. 18)*

2004		$	2004	$
Sept 27 Petty cash	PCB 31	33	Sept 1 Balance b/d	33

Sales Ledger
L. Waites *(p. 121)*

2004		$	2004	$
Sept 15 Petty cash	PCB 31	50	Sept 1 Balance b/d	50

In a firm with both a cash book and a petty cash book, the cash book is often known as a *bank cash book*. This means that all cash payments are entered in the petty cash book, and the bank cash book will contain only bank columns and discount columns. In this type of firm, any cash sales will be paid directly into the bank.

New Terms

Petty cash book (p. 223): A type of cash book kept especially for small payments.
Imprest system (p. 224): A system where a refund is made of the total paid out in a period.

Summary

1 The petty cash book saves the main cash book and the ledger accounts from containing a lot of trivial detail.
2 The use of the petty cash book enables the chief cashier to delegate this type of work to a much more junior member of staff.
3 The chief cashier should periodically check the work performed by the petty cashier.
4 All payments made by the petty cashier should have petty cash vouchers as proof of expense.

Exercises

26.1 Enter the following transactions in a petty cash book that has analysis columns for motor expenses, postage and stationery, cleaning, sundry expenses, and a ledger column. This is to be kept on the imprest system, the amount spent to be reimbursed on the last day of the month. The opening petty cash float is $1,000.

2006		$
May 1	Cleaning	36
May 3	Speedy Garage – petrol	24
May 4	Postage stamps	55
May 5	Envelopes	17
May 6	Poison licence	18
May 8	Unique Garage – petrol	57
May 9	Corner Garage – petrol	64
May 11	Postage stamps	58
May 12	F. Lee – ledger account (PL 121)	99
May 13	H. Norman – ledger account (PL 168)	44
May 15	Sweeping brush (cleaning)	23
May 16	Bends Garage – petrol	77
May 17	K. King – stationery	65
May 19	Driving licences	11
May 21	C. Hope – ledger account (PL 15)	72
May 25	Cleaning	68
May 27	Licence for guard dog	12
May 28	Guard dog – food	29
May 31	Corner Garage – petrol	54

26.2 Write up a petty cash book with analysis columns for office expenses, motor expenses, cleaning expenses and casual labour. The cash float brought down is $500 and the amount spent is reimbursed on 30 June. Show the balance carried down to 1 July.

2007		$
June 1	H. Sangster – casual labour	13
June 2	Letterheadings	22
June 2	Unique Motors – motor repairs	30
June 3	Cleaning materials	16
June 6	Envelopes	14
June 8	Petrol	28
June 11	J. Hogan – casual labour	15
June 12	Paper-clips	12
June 12	Mrs Bell – cleaner	27
June 14	Petrol	11
June 16	Typewriter ribbons	31
June 16	Petrol	29
June 21	Motor vehicle taxation	50
June 22	T. Cooke – casual labour	21
June 23	Mrs Bell – cleaner	10
June 24	P. King – casual labour	19
June 25	Copy paper	27
June 26	Flat Cars – motor repairs	21
June 29	Petrol	12
June 30	J. Young – casual labour	16

Also show how the items for motor expenses and office expenses would appear in the general ledger.

26.3X From the following details you are required to:

(*a*) record in a petty cash book, with headings for school bus expenses, staff travelling expenses, postage, cleaning and ledger accounts;

(*b*) balance down to 1 October 2004;

(*c*) show how the items would be entered in the general ledger.

(Cont'd)

2004		$
Sept 1	The headteacher gave $300 as float to the petty cashier	
	Payments out of petty cash during September:	
Sept 2	Petrol: school bus	16
Sept 3	T. Keats – travelling expenses of staff	23
Sept 3	Postage	12
Sept 4	D. Twist – travelling expenses of staff	32
Sept 7	Cleaning expenses	11
Sept 9	Petrol: school bus	21
Sept 12	K. Woods – travelling expenses of staff	13
Sept 14	Petrol: school bus	23
Sept 15	L. Blake – travelling expenses of staff	5
Sept 16	Cleaning expenses	11
Sept 18	Petrol: school bus	22
Sept 20	Postage	12
Sept 22	Cleaning expenses	11
Sept 24	H. Williams – travelling expenses of staff	7
Sept 27	Settlement of T. Clarke's account in the purchases ledger (PL 18)	13
Sept 29	Postage	12
Sept 30	The headteacher reimbursed the petty cashier the amount spent in the month	

26.4X C. Chester keeps a cash book with bank columns and discount columns only. All petty cash paid out is entered in a petty cash book. All payments above $50 are by cheque, below that figure by cash.

This is the information for August 2001.

2001		$
Aug 1	Bank balance	2,745
	Petty cash balance	29
Aug 2	Reimbursement to petty cashier by cheque which is cashed, restoring cash float	271
Aug 3	Petrol bought	19
Aug 5	Bank charges	77
Aug 6	Cheques received duly banked:	
	T. Grant (after cash discount $27)	513
	C. Riley (after cash discount $20)	380
Aug 9	Postage	48
Aug 11	Motor repairs	247
Aug 13	Motor spares	33
Aug 13	Paid the following:	
	F. Gordon (after cash discount $30)	1,170
	P. Clarke (after cash discount $16)	624
Aug 15	Envelopes bought	28
Aug 18	Drew cheque for pay	549
Aug 21	Received cheque from J. Franks to settle a debt of $2,947	2,820
Aug 22	Petrol bought	27
Aug 24	Postage	40
Aug 26	Copying paper bought	16
Aug 27	Paid V. Thomas to settle his account	39
Aug 28	Cleaning materials	21
Aug 29	Dog licence for guard dog	15
Aug 30	Paid rent	390

You are required to:

(*a*) write up and balance the cash book;

(*b*) write up the petty cash book, balancing down at the end of the month.

Analysis columns to be for: motor expenses; postage and stationery; general expenses; ledger accounts. The petty cash reimbursement takes place on 1 September.

(*CXC style*)

CHAPTER **27**

Errors Not Affecting Trial Balance Agreement

Learning Objectives

- To correct all errors which do not affect trial balance totals being equal.
- To distinguish between the different kinds of errors.

27.1 Trial Balance Agreement and Errors

There are two main classifications of errors.

Errors Not Affecting Trial Balance Agreement

These errors have resulted in the same amount of debits being entered as there were credits or in no entry being made on either the debit or credit side. This means that, if the trial balance had balanced before the error, then it would also have balanced after the error.

Examples of the different types of error that come under this heading are shown in Sections 27.3–27.8 below. You are also shown how to correct this type of error.

Errors Affecting Trial Balance Agreement

These errors mean that the total of the debit columns in the trial balance will not be the same as the total of the credit columns.

For instance, suppose we have made only one error in our books. We received cash $103 on 1 May 2005 from H. Leeds. We enter it as:

Cash Book

2005	*Cash*	*Bank*	
	$	$	
May 1 H. Leeds	103		

Sales Ledger

H. Leeds

	2005	$
	May 1 Cash	13

We have put $103 on the debit side of our books, and $13 on the credit side. When we draw up a trial balance its totals will be different by $90; i.e. $103 – $13 = $90.

This will be true in every case where a debit entry does not equal a credit entry for the item. The correction of these types of errors is shown in Chapter 28.

27.2 Correction of Errors

Most errors are found at a date later than the one on which they are first made. When we correct them we should not do so by crossing out items, tearing out accounts and throwing them away, or using chemicals to make the writing disappear.

We have to make corrections in double entry accounts by writing in the corrections in a double entry fashion. We should:

1 show the corrections by means of journal entries;
2 then show the corrections in the double entry set of accounts, by posting these journal entries to the ledger accounts affected.

27.3 Errors of Commission (Do Not Affect Trial Balance Agreement)

These are where the correct amounts are entered, but in the wrong person's account.

Example: T. Long paid us by cheque $50 on 18 May 2005. It is correctly entered in the cash book, but it is entered by mistake in the account for T. Lee. This means that there has been both a debit of $50 and a credit of $50. It has appeared in the personal account as:

T. Lee

			2005		$
			May 18	Bank	50

The error was found on 31 May 2005. We will now have to correct this. This needs two entries:

1 a debit of $50 in the account of T. Lee to cancel out the error on the credit side in that account;
2 a credit of $50 in the account of T. Long – this is where it should have been entered originally.

The accounts will now appear as follows.

T. Lee

2005		$	2005		$
May 31	T. Long: error corrected (1)	50	May 18	Bank	50

T. Long

2005		$	2005		$
May 1	Balance b/d	50	May 31	T. Lee: error corrected (2)	50

The Journal

The ways in which errors have been corrected should all be entered in the journal. The correction has already been shown above in double entry. In fact, the journal entries should be made before completing the double entry accounts for the transaction. For teaching purposes only, in this chapter the journal entries are shown last.

The journal entry will be:

The Journal

		Dr.	*Cr.*
2005			
May 31	T. Lee	50	
	T. Long		50
	Cash received … entered in wrong personal account, now corrected		

27.4 Errors of Principle (Do Not Affect Trial Balance Agreement)

This is where an item is entered in the wrong type of account.

For instance, the purchase of a fixed asset should be debited to a fixed asset account. If in error it is debited to an expense account, then it has been entered in the wrong type of account.

Example

The purchase of a motor lorry $5,500 by cheque on 14 May 2005 has been debited in error to the motor expenses account. In the cash book it is shown correctly. This means that there has been both a debit $5,500 and a credit of $5,500.

This will have appeared in the expense account as:

Motor Expenses

2005		$	
May 14	Bank	5,500	

The error is found on 31 May 2005. We will now correct it. Two entries are needed:

1 a debit in the motor lorry account of $5,500 to put it where it should have been entered;

2 a credit of $5,500 in the motor expenses account to cancel the error.

The accounts will now appear as follows.

Motor Lorry

2005		$	
May 31	Bank: entered originally in motor expenses (1)	5,500	

Motor Expenses

2005		$	2005		$
May 14	Bank	5,500	May 31	Motor lorry: error corrected (2)	5,500

The journal entries to correct the error will be shown as:

The Journal

		Dr.	*Cr.*
2005			
May 31	Motor lorry	5,500	
	Motor expenses		5,500
	Correction of error whereby purchase of motor lorry was debited to motor expenses account.		

27.5 Errors of Original Entry (Do Not Affect Trial Balance Agreement)

These occur where the original amount is incorrect.

This amount is then entered in double entry. For instance, if sales of $150 to T. Marley on 13 May 2005 had been entered as both a debit and a credit as $130, the accounts would appear:

T. Marley

2005		$			
May 13	Sales	130			

Sales

			2005		$
			May 31	Sales journal (part of total)	130

The error is found on 31 May 2005. The entries to correct it are now shown:

T. Marley

2005		$			
May 13	Sales	130			
May 31	Sales: error corrected	20			

Sales

			2005		$
			May 31	Sales journal	130
			May 31	T. Marley: error corrected	20

To correct the error, the journal entries will be:

The Journal

		Dr.	*Cr.*
2005			
May 31	T. Marley	20	
	Sales account		20
	Correction of error: sales of $150 had been incorrectly entered as $130.		

27.6 Errors of Omission (Do Not Affect Trial Balance Agreement)

These errors are where transactions are not entered into the books at all.

For instance, if we purchased goods from C. Richards for $250 but did not enter it in the accounts there would be nil debits and nil credits. We find the error on 31 May 2005. The entries to record it will be:

Purchases

2005		$			
May 31	C. Richards: error corrected	250			

C. Richards

			2005		$
			May 31	Purchases: error corrected	250

The journal entries to correct the error will be:

The Journal

		Dr.	*Cr.*
2005			
May 31	Purchases	250	
	C. Richards		250
	Correction of error: purchases omitted from books.		

27.7 Compensating Errors (Do Not Affect Trial Balance Agreement)

These are errors that cancel each other out.

Let us take a case where the sales journal is added up to be $100 too much. In the same period the purchases journal is also added up to be $100 too much.

If these were the only errors in our books, the trial balance totals would equal each other. Both totals would be wrong – they would both be $100 too much – but they would be equal.

If in fact the *incorrect* totals had purchases $7,900 and sales $9,900, the accounts would have appeared as:

Sales

			2005		$
			May 31	Sales journal	9,900

Purchases

2005		$			
May 31	Purchases journal	7,900			

When corrected, the accounts would appear as:

Sales

2005		$	2005		$
May 31	The journal: error corrected	100	May 31	Sales journal	9,900

Purchases

2005		$	2005		$
May 31	Purchases journal	7,900	May 31	The journal: error corrected	100

Journal entries to correct these two erros will be:

The Journal

2005		*Dr.*	*Cr.*
May 31	Sales account	100	
	Purchases account		100
	Correction of compensating errors: totals of both purchases and sales journals incorrectly added up $100 too much.		

27.8 Complete Reversal of Entries (Do Not Affect Trial Balance Agreement)

Here, the correct amounts are entered in the correct accounts, but each item is shown on the *wrong side* of each account. There has therefore been both a debit and a credit entry of equal amounts.

For instance, we pay a cheque for $200 on 28 May 2005 to D. Charles. We enter it as follows in accounts shown with the letter (A):

Cash Book (A)

		Cash	*Bank*		*Cash*	*Bank*
2005		$	$		$	$
May 28	D. Charles		200			

D. Charles (A)

		2005	$
		May 28 Bank	200

This is incorrect. It should have been as follows.

1 **Debit:** D. Charles $200.

2 **Credit:** Bank $200.

Both items have been entered in the correct accounts, but each is on the wrong side of its account.

Correction of such an error is more difficult to understand than for other errors. Let us look at how the items would have appeared if we had done it correctly in the first place. We will show the letter (B) behind the account names:

Cash Book (B)

	Cash	*Bank*		*Cash*	*Bank*
	$	$	2005	$	$
			May 28 D. Charles		200

D. Charles (B)

2005	$		
May 28 Bank	200		

We have found the error on 31 May. By using double entry we have to make the amounts shown to cancel the error be twice the amount of the error. This is because we need to do the following.

1 We have to cancel the error; this means entering the following amounts.

Debit: D. Charles $200.

Credit: Bank $200

2 We have to enter up the transaction.

Debit: D. Charles $200.

Credit: Bank $200

All together, then, the entries to correct the error are twice the amounts first entered.

When corrected, the accounts appear as follows, marked (C):

D. Charles (C)

2005	$	2005	$
May 31 Bank: error corrected	400	May 28 Bank	200

Cash Book (C)

	Cash	*Bank*		*Cash*	*Bank*
2005	$	$	2005	$	$
May 28 D. Charles		200	May 31 D. Charles: error corrected		400

You can see that accounts (C) give the same final answer as accounts (B):

	$	$
(B) **Debit:** D. Charles	200	
Credit: Bank		200
(C) **Debit:** D. Charles (400 – 200)	200	
Credit: Bank (400 – 200)		200

Journal entries would be shown as follows.

The Journal

		Dr.	*Cr.*
2005			
May 31	D. Charles	400	
	Bank		400
	Payment of $200 on 28 May 2005 to D. Charles incorrectly credited to his account, and debited to bank: error now corrected.		

27.9 Casting

You will often notice the use of the expression 'to cast', which means to add up. Overcasting means incorrectly adding up a column of figures to give an answer that is greater that it should be; undercasting means incorrectly adding up a column of figures to give an answer that is less than it should be.

New Terms

Error of commission (p. 231): Where a correct amount is entered, but in the wrong person's account.

Error of principle (p. 232): Where an item is entered in the wrong type of account, e.g. a fixed asset entered in an expense account.

Error of original entry (p. 233): Where an item is entered, but both debit and credit entries are of the same incorrect amount.

Error of omission (p. 234): Where a transaction is completely omitted from the books.

Compensating error (p. 234): Where two errors of equal amounts but on opposite sides of the accounts, cancel out each other.

Casting (p. 237): Adding up figures.

Summary

1 When errors are found, they should be amended by using proper double entry procedures.

2 All corrections of errors should take place via the journal, where entries are first recorded before being posted to the appropriate ledger accounts.

Exercises

27.1 Show the journal entries necessary to correct the following errors.

(*a*) A sale of goods $678 to J. Harris had been entered in J. Hart's account.

(*b*) The purchase of a machine on credit from L. Pyle for $4,390 had been completely omitted from our books.

(*c*) The purchase of a motor van $3,800 had been entered in error in the motor expenses account.

(*d*) A sale of $221 to E. Fitzwilliam had been entered in the books, both debit and credit, as $212.

(*e*) Commission received $257 had been entered in error in the sales account.

27.2X Show the journal entries needed to correct the following errors.

(*a*) Purchases of $699 on credit from K. Wong had been entered in H. Wood's account.

(*b*) A cheque of $189 paid for advertisements had been entered in the cash column of the cash book instead of in the bank column.

(*c*) Sale of goods $443 on credit to B. Ming entered in error in B. Gordon's account.

(*d*) Purchase of goods on credit K. Isaacs $89 entered in two places in error as $99.

(*e*) Cash paid to H. Marcano $89 entered on the debit side of the cash book and the credit side of H. Marcano's account.

27.3 Redraft the following balance sheet, correcting the errors in it. Ensure that it is shown in good style, with section headings and subtotals.

A. Smith
Balance sheet for the year ending 31 December 2006

	$		$
Drawings	20,000	Sundry debtors	43,200
Bank overdraft	9,000	Depreciation on furniture and equipment	5,000
Provision for bad debts	2,160		
Cash in hand	1,000	Net profit	30,000
Stock at 31 December 2006	38,500	Capital at 1 January 2006	310,000
Furniture and equipment	97,400	Goodwill	14,000
Stock at 1 January 2006	22,200	Rates prepaid	1,000
Creditors	39,680		
Premises	182,000		
Pay accrued	1,260		
	413,200		403,200

27.4X R. James drew up the following balance sheet on 31 December 2006.

Balance Sheet

	$	$		$	$
Fixed assets			*Capital*		
Furniture and fittings	1,540		1 January 2006	7,690	
Motor vehicles	2,980		Add Net profit	3,040	
		4,520		10,730	
Current assets			*Less* Drawings	2,860	
Stock	2,724				7,870
Sundry debtors	1,241		*Current liabilities*		
Cash at bank	1,235	5,200	Sundry creditors		1,850
		9,720			9,720

When checking the books, the following errors and omissions were found.

(Cont'd)

1 A purchase of fittings, $140, had been included in the purchases account.
2 Motor vehicles should have been depreciated by $280.
3 A debt of $41 included in sundry debtors was considered to be bad.
4 Closing stock had been overvalued by $124.

Required:

(*a*) show your calculation of the correct net profit;
(*b*) draw up a corrected balance sheet as at 31 December 2006.

27.5X When Daniel Martin prepared his final accounts, he calculated his net profit at $8,975. However, on more careful inspection of his accounts he found the following errors. Construct an adjustment of profit statement to show his true net profit.

(*a*) A bill for rates of $200 had not been recorded.
(*b*) Sales of $28 had not been recorded.
(*c*) Closing stock had been overvalued by $48.
(*d*) Depreciation of $200 had not been provided for.
(*e*) Rent receivable of $50 was outstanding.
(*f*) Sales returns of $22 had not been entered.
(*g*) Rent of $10 recorded in the profit and loss account related to the following year.
(*h*) A provision for bad debts of $20 should have been created.

(*Pitman Examination Institute*)

CHAPTER **28**

Suspense Accounts and Errors

Learning Objectives

- To correct errors using a suspense account.
- To recalculate profits after errors have been corrected.

28.1 Errors and the Trial Balance

In the last chapter we looked at errors which still left equal totals in the trial balance. However, many errors will lead to trial balance totals not being equal. These include:

- incorrect additions in any account;
- making an entry on only one side of the accounts e.g. a debit but no credit, a credit but no debit;
- entering a different amount on the debit side from the amount on the credit side.

28.2 Suspense Account

We should try very hard to find errors immediately when the trial balance totals are not equal. When they cannot be found, the trial balance totals should be made to agree with each other by inserting the amount of the difference between the two sides in a **suspense account**. This occurs in Exhibit 28.1, where there is a $40 difference in the trial balance of S. James. To make the two totals the same, a figure of $40 for the suspense account has been shown on the credit side. A suspense account is opened and the $40 difference is also shown there on the credit side.

Exhibit 28.1

S. James
Trial Balance as on 31 December 2005

	Dr.	*Cr.*
	$	$
Totals after all the accounts have been listed	100,000	99,960
Suspense account		40
	100,000	100,000

Suspense Account

	2005		$
	Dec 31	Difference per trial balance	40

28.3 The Suspense Account and the Balance Sheet

If the errors are not found before the final accounts are prepared, the suspense account balance will be included in the balance sheet. Where the balance is a credit balance, it should be included on the capital and liabilities side of the balance sheet. When the balance is a debit balance, it should be shown on the assets side of the balance sheet.

28.4 Correction of Errors

When the kinds of errors that make trial balance totals differ from each other are found, then they must be corrected. However, they may not be found until a later period. For example, you may have already done the final accounts for the year ended 31 December 2005, and it may not be until 30 September 2006 when the error is found. You cannot tear up the final accounts for the year 2005 an start again to do them. They may possibly have been given to the management, shown to the bank or the tax authorities and so on.

The correction, whenever found after a suspense account has been opened, must be corrected by using double entry. For these entries:

- one entry *must* be in the suspense account;
- one entry *must* be in the account where the error was made.

For all errors:

1. the double entry must be carried out, being a debit entry and a credit entry;
2. a journal entry must be made, otherwise, afterwards, it may not be possible to understand why the entries were made in the double entry records.

The first example is where only one error has been made, the $40 difference being shown as a credit balance in the trial balance, and a suspense account being opened with a credit balance of $40.

One Error Only

We will look at two examples.

Example 1

Assume that the error of $40 shown in Exhibit 28.1 is found in the following year on 31 March 2006. The error was that the sales account was undercast by $40. The action taken to correct this is as follows.

Debit suspense account to close it: $40.

Credit sales account to show item where it should have been: $40.

The accounts now appear as in Exhibit 28.2.

Exhibit 28.2

Suspense Account

2006		$	2006		$
			Jan 1	Balance b/d	
Mar 31	Sales	40		(difference in last year's trial balance)	40

Sales

			2006		$
			Mar 31	Suspense (error corrected)	40

Now that this error has been found, the suspense account can be closed. The journal entries are now shown as:

The Journal

		Dr.	*Cr.*
2006		$	$
Mar 31	Suspense	40	
	Sales		40
	(Narrative) Correction of undercasting of sales by $40 in last year's accounts.		

Example 2

In another business, the trial balance on 31 December 2006 had a difference of $168. It was a shortage on the debit side of the trial balance. A suspense account with $168 on the debit side was inserted into the trial balance to make the two totals agree.

On 31 May 2007 the error is found. We had made a payment of $168 to K. Small to close his account. It was correctly entered in the cash book, but it was not posted to K. Small's account.

First of all (A), the account of K. Small is debited with $168, as it should have been in 2006. Second (B), the suspense account is credited with $168 so that the account can be closed.

K. Small

2007			$	2007		$
May 31	Bank	(A)	168	Jan 1	Balance b/d	168

The account of K. Small is now correct.

Suspense Account

2006		$	2007			$
Dec 31	Difference per trial balance	168	May 31	K. Small	(B)	168

The journal entries are:

The Journal

		Dr.	Cr.
2007		$	$
Mar 31	K. Small	168	
	Suspense		168
	Correction of non-entry of payment last year in K. Small's account.		

More Than One Error

We can now look at Exhibit 28.3, where the suspense account difference was caused by more than one error.

Exhibit 28.3

> The trial balance at 31 December 2007 showed a difference of $77, being a shortage on the debit side. A suspense account is opened, and the difference of $77 is entered on the debit side of the account.
>
> On 28 February 2008 all the errors from the previous year are found:
>
> **1** a cheque of $150 paid to L. King had been correctly entered in the cash book, but had not been entered in King's account;
>
> **2** the purchase account had been undercast by $20;
>
> **3** a cheque of $93 received from K. Saunders had been correctly entered in the cash book, but had not been entered in Saunders' account.
>
> These three errors resulted in a net error of $77, shown by a debit of $77 on the debit side of the suspense account.

The journal entries should be made first, before posting the items to their respective accounts. To make it easier for the reader to understand the journal entries, however, the actual account entries will be shown first.

1 Make correcting entries in accounts for (1), (2) and (3).

2 Record double entry for these items in the suspense account.

L. King

			$	
2008			$	
Feb 28	Suspense	(1)	150	

Purchases

2008			$	
Feb 28	Suspense	(2)	20	

K. Saunders

			2008		$
			Feb 28 Suspense	(3)	93

Suspense Account

2008		$	2008		$
Jan 1 Balance b/d		77	Feb 28 L. King	(1)	150
Feb 28 K. Saunders	(3)	93	Feb 28 Purchases	(2)	20
		170			170

The Journal

		Dr.	Cr.
2008		$	$
Feb 28	L. King	150	
	Suspense		150
	Cheque paid omitted from King's account.		
Feb 28	Purchases	20	
	Suspense		20
	Undercasting of purchases by $20 in last year's accounts.		
Feb 29	Suspense	93	
	K. Saunders		93
	Cheque received omitted from Saunders's account.		

Only those errors which make the trial balance totals different from each other have to be corrected via the suspense account.

28.5 The Effect of Errors on Profits

Some of the errors will have meant that original profits calculated will be wrong. Other errors will have no effect upon profits. Exhibit 28.4 illustrates the different kinds of errors by showing a set of accounts in which such errors have been made.

In this chapter we are using the horizontal style for final accounts, as it is easier to follow the double entry records using this style.

Exhibit 28.4

K. Black
Trading and Profit and Loss Account for the year ended 31 December 2005

	$		$
Stock	500	Sales	8,000
Add Purchases	6,100		
	6,600		
Less Closing stock	700		
Cost of goods sold	5,900		
Gross profit c/d	2,100		
	8,000		8,000
Rent	200	Gross profit b/d	2,100
Insurance	120	Discounts received	250
Lighting	180		
Depreciation	250		
Net profit	1,600		
	2,350		2,350

K. Black
Balance Sheet as at 31 December 2005

	$	$		$	$
Fixed assets			*Capital*		
Fixtures at cost	2,200		Balance as at		
Less Depreciation			1 Jan 2005	1,800	
to date	800		*Add* Net profit	1,600	
		1,400		3,400	
Current assets			*Less* Drawings	900	
Stock	700				2,500
Debtors	600		*Current liabilities*		
Bank	340		Creditors		600
		1,640			
Suspense account		60			
		3,100			3,100

Errors That Do Not Affect Profit Calculations

If an error affects items only in the balance sheet, then the original calculated profit will not need altering. Exhibit 28.5 shows this.

Exhibit 28.5

Assume that in Exhibit 28.4 the $60 debit balance on the suspense account was because of the following error.

On 1 November 2005 we paid $60 to a creditor T. Monk. It was correctly entered in the cash book. It was not entered anywhere else. The error was found on 1 June 2006.

The journal entries to correct it will be as follows:

The Journal

		Dr.	*Cr.*
2006		$	$
Jun 1	T. Monk	60	
	Suspense account		60
	Payment to T. Monk on 1 November 2005 not entered in his account. Correction now made.		

Both of these accounts appeared in the balance sheet only, with T. Monk as part of creditors. The net profit of $1,600 does not have to be changed.

Errors That Do Affect Profit Calculations

If the error is in one of the figures shown in the trading and profit and loss account, then the original profit will need altering. Exhibit 28.6 shows this.

Exhibit 28.6

Assume that in Exhibit 28.4 the $60 debit balance was because the rent account was added up incorrectly; it should be shown as $260 instead of $200. The error was found on 1 June 2006. The journal entries required to correct this are:

The Journal

		Dr.	*Cr.*
2006		$	$
Jun 1	Rent	60	
	Suspense		60
	Correction of rent undercast last year		

Rent last year should have been increased by $60. This would have reduced net profit by $60. A statement of corrected profit for the year is now shown.

K. Black
Statement of Corrected Net Profit for the year ended 31 December 2005

	$
Net profit per the accounts	1,600
Less Rent understated	60
	1,540

Where There Have Been Several Errors

In Exhibit 28.4 assume there were four errors in the accounts of K. Black, found on 31 March 2006. Their correction can now be seen. Assume that the net difference had also been $60.

1	Sales overcast:	$70
2	Insurance undercast:	$40
3	Cash received from a debtor entered in the cash book only:	$50
4	A purchase of $59 entered in the books, debit and credit entries as:	$95

Note: Error (4) is known as an *error of transposition*, as the correct figures have been shown in the wrong order; i.e., they have been 'transposed'.

The entries in the suspense account and the journal entries will be as follows:

Suspense Account

2006		$	2006		$
Jan 1	Balance b/d	60	Mar 31	Sales	70
Mar 31	Debtor	50	Mar 31	Insurance	40
		110			110

The Journal

			Dr.	*Cr.*
2006			$	$
(1)	Mar 31	Sales	70	
		Suspense		70
		Sales overcast of $70 in 2005		
(2)	Mar 31	Insurance	40	
		Suspense		40
		Insurance expense undercast by $40 in 2005		
(3)	Mar 31	Suspense	50	
		Debtor's account		50
		Cash received omitted from debtor's account in 2005		
(4)	Mar 31	Creditor's account	36	
		Purchases		36
		Credit purchase of $59 entered both as debit and credit as $95 in 2005		

Note: In (4), the correction of the understatement of purchases does not pass through the suspense account, because it did not cause the trial balance totals to be unequal.

Now we can calculate the corrected net profit for the year 2005. Only items (1), (2) and (4) affect figures in the trading and profit and loss account. These are the only adjustments to be made to profit.

K. Black
Statement of corrected Net Profit for the year ended 31 December 2005

	$	$
Net profit per the accounts		1,600
Add Purchases overstated (4)		36
		1,636
Less Sales overcast (1)	70	
Rent undercast (2)	40	110
Corrected net profit for the year		1,526

Error (3), the cash not posted to a debtor's account, did not affect profit calculations.

28.6 Limitations of Trial Balances

In the last two chapters, you have seen various kinds of errors. Those in Chapter 27 were not revealed by trial balance totals being unequal, which is obviously a serious limitation depending completely on the trial balance being an absolute check on the accuracy of the entries in the books. To refresh your memory, the kinds of errors not disclosed by a trial balance were:

1 errors of commission;
2 errors of principle;
3 errors of original entry;
4 errors of omission;
5 compensating errors;
6 complete reversal of entries.

Even when a trial balance agrees, there can still be very large errors of various kinds which may mean that profits are wrongly calculated and that the balance sheet is incorrect.

With the errors you have looked at in the present chapter, the errors have resulted in a difference being put into a suspense account until the error or errors have been found. A very small amount in a suspense account could hide very large errors. For instance, $50 credit in a suspense account could eventually be found out to be either of the following.

7 Sales overcast $10,000, debtors total overcast $10,050. If the errors are not found, then both the gross and net profits will be overstated by $10,000 and the figure of debtors in the balance sheet overstated by $10,050.

8 Rent expense undercast by $2,000, total of creditors undercast by $1,950. In this case, the net profit will be shown at $2,000 more than it should be, while creditors in the balance sheet will be understated by $1,950.

This means that there is always a possibility of serious errors occurring without it being obvious at first sight.

28.7 Suspense Accounts: Businesses and Examinations

Businesses

Every attempt should be made to find errors. A suspense account should be opened only if all other efforts have failed.

Examinations

Unless it is part of a question, do not make your balance sheet totals agree by using a suspense account. The same applies to trial balances. If you do, the examiner will be very angry and you will lose marks.

New Terms

Suspense account (p. 240): Account showing balance equal to difference in trial balance.

Summary

1 Some of the errors made, but not all, will mean that the profits originally calculated were incorrect.

2 Errors that do not affect profit calculations will have an effect only on items in the balance sheet.

Exercises

28.1 On 31 March 2005 the following items are to be corrected via the journal. Show the corrections. Narratives are not required.

(*a*) T. Thomas, a customer, had paid us a cheque for $900 to settle his debt. The cheque has now been returned to us marked 'Dishonoured'.

(*b*) We had allowed C. Charles, a debtor, a cash discount of $35. Because of a dispute with her, we have now disallowed the cash discount.

(*c*) Office equipment bought for $6,000 has been debited to motor vehicles account.

(*d*) The copy sales invoice of sales to J. Graham $715 was lost, and therefore was completely omitted from our books.

(*e*) Cash drawings of $210 have been correctly entered in the cash book, but have been credited to the pay account.

(*CXC style*)

28.2 The following errors in the books of J. Holt have been found.

1 Equipment bought $2.500 by cheque has been debited to general expenses account.

2 $149 received from E. Grey has been correctly entered in the cash book but debited to Grey's account.

3 Goods sold $973 to J. Crook have been entered in error as $937.

4 A discount allowed to P. Paul of $44 has been debited to the discounts allowed account as $144.

5 $135 goods bought from D. D. Ltd have been credited to B. B. Ltd.

From the above you are to:

(*a*) state how *each* error affects the agreement of the trial balance totals;

(*b*) state which errors will affect net profits, and how;

(*c*) state which errors will affect gross profits, and how;

(*d*) state which of the above is:

(i) an error of principle?

(ii) an error of commission?

(iii) an error of original entry?

(*e*) show the journal entries needed to correct each error – narratives are not required.

28.3X At the close of business on 26 February 2007, John Blake, a sole trader, extracted a trial balance from his books. The trial balance did not agree, but Blake entered the difference in a suspense account. He then prepared his trading and profit and loss accounts for the year ending 26 February 2007 in the normal way. The profit and loss account so prepared showed a net profit amounting to $2,370.

During March 2007, Blake discovered the following errors in his books and these accounted for the entire difference in the trial balance.

1 The bad debts account had been debited with items of $62 and $54 in respect of bad debts, but the personal accounts of the individual debtors had not been credited.
2 The sales day book was overcast by $140.
3 Cash $72 received from Simon Johnson had been correctly entered in the cash book, but the double entry had been made on the wrong side of Johnson's personal account in Blake's ledger.
4 The discount allowed total in the cash book – $84 – had not been entered in the discount account.

Required:
(*a*) calculate the correct figure for net profit;
(*b*) show the journal entries necessary to correct the above;
(*c*) draw up the suspense account, showing the amount of the original balance on it.

28.4 The following is a trial balance which has been incorrectly drawn up:

Trial Balance as at 31 January 2009

	$	$
Capital 1 February 2008	5,500	
Drawings	2,800	
Stock 1 February 2008		2,597
Trade debtors		2,130
Furniture and fittings	1,750	
Cash in hand	1,020	
Trade creditors		2,735
Sales		7,430
Returns inwards		85
Discount received	46	
Business expenses	950	
Purchases	4,380	
	16,446	14,977

In addition to the mistakes evident above, the following errors were also discovered.

1 A payment of $75 made to a creditor had not been posted from the cash book into the purchases ledger.
2 A cheque for $56 received from a customer had been correctly entered in the cash book but posted to the customer's account as $50.
3 A purchase of fittings $120 had been included in the purchases account.
4 The total of the discounts allowed column in the cash book of $38 had not been posted into the general ledger.
5 A page of the sales day book was correctly totalled as $564 but carried forward as $456.

Show the trial balance as it would appear after all the errors had been corrected. You are required to show all workings.

28.5X Show how each of the following errors would affect trial balance agreement.

1 Equipment repairs $720 was debited to the equipment account.
2 $1,700 discounts allowed credited to discounts received account.
3 Stock at close overvalued by $2,000.
4 $750 commission received was debited to the sales account.
5 Drawings $305 credited to the capital account.

(Cont'd)

6 Cheque paying $170 to C. Charles entered in cash book but not in personal account.
7 Cheque $248 from L. Barnes credited to L. Barrett.

Format should be as follows:

Item	*If no effect state 'No'*	*Debit side exceeds credit side by amount shown*	*Credit side exceeds debit side by amount shown*
1			
2			
3			
4			
5			
6			
7			

(*CXC style*)

28.6X The final accounts for C. Taylor have quite a few errors.
You are required to:
(*a*) redraft the final accounts, correcting all errors;
(*b*) ensure that the redrafted accounts are shown in a good style.

Trading Account for the year ended 31 December 2003

	$		$
Stock at 31 Dec 2003	1,700	Sales	10,620
Purchases	7,750	Returns inwards	400
Returns outwards	300	Stock at 1 Jan 2003	1,590
Carriage outwards	50		
Net profit c/d	2,810		
	12,610		12,610
		Net profit b/d	2,810
Rent	250	Discounts allowed	120
General expenses	60	Stock at 1 Jan 2003	1,590
Depreciation: fixtures	80	Rent owing	50
Drawings	520		
Gross profit	3,660		
	4,570		4,570

Balance Sheet as at 31 December 2003

	$		$	$
Debtors	1,180	Fixtures		800
Bank	3,050	Cash		10
Creditors	650			
Stock	1,700	Capital		
		Opening balance	4,300	
		Add Gross profit	3,660	7,960
	6,580			8,770

(*CXC style*)

CHAPTER **29**

Introduction to Accounting Ratios

Learning Objectives

- To be able to calculate some basic accounting ratios.
- To be able to use accounting ratios to calculate missing or forecasted figures.
- To understand the reasons behind a change in the ratios.

29.1 Mark-up and Margin

The purchases and sale of goods may be shown as:

$$\text{Cost price} + \text{Profit} = \text{Selling price}$$

The profit when shown as a fraction, or percentage, of the cost price is known as the **mark-up**.

The profit when shown as a fraction, or percentage, of the selling price is known as the **margin**.

We can now calculate these using the following example:

$$\begin{array}{l} \text{Cost price} + \text{Profit} = \text{Selling price} \\ \quad \$4 \quad\ \ + \ \ \$1 \ \ = \$5 \end{array}$$

$$\text{Mark-up} = \frac{\text{Profit}}{\text{Cost price}}$$

as a fraction; if required as a percentage, multiply by 100:

$$\frac{\$1}{\$4} = \frac{1}{4}, \text{ or } \frac{1}{4} \times 100 = 25\%$$

$$\text{Margin} = \frac{\text{Profit}}{\text{Selling price}}$$

as a fraction; if required as a percentage, multiply by 100;

$$\frac{\$1}{\$5} = \frac{1}{5}, \text{ or } \frac{1}{5} \times 100 = 20\%$$

29.2 Calculating Missing Figures

Now we can use these ratios to complete trading accounts where some of the figures are missing.

All examples in this chapter:

- assume that all the goods in a firm have the same rate of mark-ups, and
- ignore wastages and theft of goods.

Example 1

The following figures are for the year 2005 for M. Smart:

	$
Stock 1 January 2005	400
Stock 31 December 2005	600
Purchases	5,200

A uniform rate of mark-up of 20% is applied. To find the gross profit and the sales figure, first of all, we enter the figures we already know in the trading account.

M. Smart
Trading Account for the year ended 31 December 2005

	$		$
Stock 1 January 2005	400	Sales	?
Add Purchases	5,200		
	5,600		
Less Stock 31 December 2005	600		
Cost of goods sold	5,000		
Gross profit	?		

Answer:

We know that: Cost of goods sold + Profit = Sales
and also that: Cost of goods sold + Percentage mark-up = Sales
We do know the following figures: $5,000 + 20% = Sales
After doing the arithmetic: $5,00 + $1,000 = $6,000

The trading account can be completed by inserting the gross profit $1,000 and $6,000 for sales.

Example 2

Another firm, J. MacDonald, has the following figures for 2006:

	$
Stock 1 January 2006	500
Stock 31 December 2006	800
Sales	6,400

A uniform rate of margin of 25% is in use. Find the gross profit and the figure of purchases.

First, enter these figures in the trading account.

J. MacDonald
Trading Account for the year ended 31 December 2006

	$		$
Stock 1 January 2006	500	Sales	6,400
Add Purchases	?		
	?		
Less Stock 31 December 2006	800		
Cost of goods sold	?		
Gross profit	?		
	6,400		6,400

Answer:

We know that: Cost of goods sold + Gross profit = Sales
and therefore: Sales – Gross profit = Cost of goods sold

As we can say margin instead of gross profit, we know therefore that:

Sales – 25% margin = Cost of goods sold

This becomes:

$6,400 – $1,600 = $4,800

We can now fill in the figure of $4,800 for cost of goods sold. This leaves just two missing figures, (1) and (2), as we can now see:

	$
Stock 1 January 2006	500
Add Purchases (1)	?
(2)	?
Less Stock 31 December 2006	800
Cost of goods sold	4,800

Figure (2) less $800 = $4,800; therefore (2) must be $5,600.

Now that we know this, $500 + (1), = (2), or $5,600. (1) is therefore $5,100.

In Exhibit 29.1 we can now show the completed trading account.

Exhibit 29.1

J. MacDonald
Trading Account for the year ended 31 December 2006

	$		$
Stock 1 January 2006	500	Sales	6,400
Add Purchases	5,100		
	5,600		
Less Stock 31 December 2006	800		
Cost of goods sold	4,800		
Gross profit	1,600		
	6,400		6,400

This method can be very useful to retail stores. They may want to increase their sales, and to do this they need to know the volume of purchases. They can also estimate stock levels or sales figures.

29.3 Other Accounting Ratios

There are some ratios that are often used to compare one period's results against those of a previous period. Three ratios in most common use are the ratio of gross profit to sales, the ratio of net profit to sales and the rate of turnover, or **stockturn**.

Gross Profit as Percentage of Sales

The basic formula is:

$$\frac{\text{Gross profit}}{\text{Sales}} \times 100 = \text{Gross profit as percentage of sales}$$

This is the amount of gross profit for every $100 of sales. If the answer turned out to be 15% this would mean that for every $100 of sales $15 gross profit was made before any expenses were paid.

This ratio is used as a test of the profitability of the sales. The fact that sales are increased may not mean that the gross profit will increase. The trading accounts in Exhibits 29.2 illustrate this.

Exhibit 29.2

D. Clive
Trading Accounts for the years ended 31 December

	2006	2007		2006	2007
	$	$		$	$
Stock	500	900	Sales	7,000	8,000
Purchases	6,000	7,200			
	6,500	8,100			
Less Stock	900	1,100			
Cost of goods sold	5,600	7,000			
Gross profit	1,400	1,000			
	7,000	8,000		7,000	8,000

In the year 2006 the gross profit as a percentage of sales was:

$$\frac{1,400}{7,000} \times 100 = 20\%$$

In the year 2007 it became:

$$\frac{1,000}{8,000} \times 100 = 12\tfrac{1}{2}\%$$

Sales had increased, but as the gross profit percentage had fallen by a relatively greater amount, the gross profit had fallen. There can be many reasons for such a fall in the gross profit percentage.

- Perhaps the goods being sold have cost more, but the selling price of the goods has not risen to the same extent.
- Perhaps, in order to increase sales, reductions have been made in the selling price of goods.
- There could be a difference in how much has been sold of each sort of goods, called the *sales mix*, between this year and last, with different kinds of goods carrying different rates of gross profit per $100 of sales.
- There may have been a greater wastage or theft of goods.

These are only some of the possible reasons for the decrease. The point of calculating the ratio is to show that the profitability per $100 of sales has changed. The firm would then try to find out why and how such a change has taken place.

Net Profit as Percentage of Sales

Here the formula is:

$$\frac{\text{Net profit}}{\text{Sales}} \times \frac{100}{1} = \text{Net profit as percentage of sales}$$

This calculation will show how much net profit has been made for every $100 of sales. It brings the expenses into the calculation, as opposed to the gross profit percentage, which ignores expenses.

Changes in the ratio will be due either to:

- the gross profit ratio changing; and/or
- the expenses per $100 of sales changing.

When changes are due to expenses, they will be examined to see if anything can be done in future to control expenses better.

Stockturn or Rate of Turnover

If we always kept just $100 of stock at cost, which when we sold it would sell for $125, then if we sold this amount eight times in a year we would make 8 × $25 = $200 gross profit. The quicker we sold our stock (we could say, the quicker we turned over our stock) the more the profit we would made, if our gross profit percentage stayed the same.

To check on how quickly we are turning over our stock, we can use the following formula:

$$\frac{\text{Cost of goods sold}}{\text{Average stock}} = \text{Number of times stock is turned over within the period}$$

It would be best if the average stock held could be calculated by valuing the stock quite a few times each year, then dividing the totals of the figures obtained by the number of valuations. For instance, monthly stock figures would be added up then divided by 12.

However, it is quite common, especially in examinations or in cases where no other information is available, to calculate the average stock as the opening stock plus the closing stock divided by two. Using the figures in Exhibit 29.2, we can calculate the **stockturn** for 2006 and 2007.

$$2006: \frac{5{,}600}{(500 + 900) \div 2} = \frac{5{,}600}{700} = 8 \text{ times per annum}$$

$$2007: \frac{7{,}000}{(900 + 1{,}100) \div 2} = \frac{7{,}000}{1{,}000} = 7 \text{ times per annum}$$

Instead of saying that the stockturn is so many times per annum, we could instead say on average how long we keep stock before we sell it. We do this by the following formula:

to express it in months: 12 ÷ Stockturn = x months
to express it in days: 365 ÷ Stockturn = x days

From Exhibit 29.2:

	2006	2007
in months:	$\frac{12}{8}$ = 1.5 months	$\frac{12}{7}$ = 1.7 months
in days:	$\frac{365}{8}$ = 45.6 days	$\frac{365}{7}$ = 52.1 days

All the above figures are rounded off to the nearest decimal point.

29.4 The Relationship Between Mark-up and Margin

As both of these figures refer to the same profit, but are expressed as a fraction or a percentage of different figures, there is a relationship between them. If one is known as a fraction, the other can soon be found.

If the mark-up is known, to find the margin take the same numerator to be the numerator of the margin. Then for the denominator of the margin take the total of the mark-up's denominator plus the numerator. For example:

Mark-up	**Margin**
$\frac{1}{4}$	$\frac{1}{4+1} = \frac{1}{5}$
$\frac{2}{11}$	$\frac{2}{11+2} = \frac{2}{13}$

If the margin is known, to find the mark-up take the same numerator to be the numerator of the mark-up. Then for the denominator of the mark-up take the figure of the margin's denominator less the numerator.

Margin	**Mark-up**
$\frac{1}{6}$	$\frac{1}{6-1} = \frac{1}{5}$
$\frac{3}{13}$	$\frac{3}{13-3} = \frac{3}{10}$

New Terms

Mark-up (p. 252): Profit shown as a percentage or fraction of cost price.
Margin (p. 252): Profit shown as a percentage or fraction of selling price.
Stockturn (p. 256): Number of times we sell our stock in an accounting period.

Summary

1 Accounting ratios can be used to deduce missing figures, given certain assumptions.
2 If the mark-up is known as a fraction, then the margin, as a fraction, can easily be calculated.
3 If the margin is known as a fraction, then the mark-up, as a fraction, can easily be calculated.

Exercises

29.1 J. Jackson is a trader who marks the selling price of his goods at 25% above cost. His books give the following information at 31 July 2003.

	$
Stock 1 August 2002	4,936
Stock 31 July 2003	6,310
Sales for year	30,000

You are required to:
(*a*) find 'cost of goods sold';
(*b*) show the value of purchases during the year;
(*c*) ascertain the gross profit Jackson made.
Note: Your answer should take the form of a trading account.

29.2 P.R. Masters produces from his trial balance at 31 August 2009 the following information.

	$
Stock 1 September 2008	2,000
Purchases	18,000

Masters has a 'mark-up' of 50% on 'cost of sales'. His average stock during the year was $4,000.

You are required to:
(*a*) calculate the closing stock for Masters at 31 August 2009;
(*b*) prepare his trading account for the year ended 31 August 2009;
(*c*) ascertain the total amount of profit and loss expenditure that Masters must not exceed if he is to maintain a net profit on sales of 10%.

29.3X A business has a rate of turnover of seven times. The average stock is $4,200. Trade discount allowed is 33⅓% of all selling prices. Expenses are given as 70% of gross profit. Calculate:
(*a*) cost of goods sold
(*b*) gross profit
(*c*) turnover
(*d*) total expenses
(*e*) net profit.

29.4X The following figures relate to the retail business of W. Watson for the month of May 2008. Goods that are on sale fall into two categories, A and B.

	Category A	*Category B*
Sales to the public at manufacturer's recommended list price	$3,000	$7,000
Trade discount allowed to retailers	20%	25%
Total expenses as a percentage of sales	10%	10%
Annual rate of stock turnover	12	20

Calculate for each category:

(*a*) cost of goods sold
(*b*) gross profit
(*c*) total expenses
(*d*) net profit
(*e*) average stock at cost, assuming that sales are distributed evenly over the year, and that there are 12 equal months in the year.

CHAPTER **30**

Single Entry and Incomplete Records

Learning Objectives

- To deduce the figure of profits where only the increase in capital and details of drawings are known.
- To draw up a trading and profit and loss account and balance sheet from records not kept on a double entry system.
- To deduce the figures of sales and purchases from incomplete records.

30.1 Why Double Entry is Not Used

It cannot be expected that every small storekeeper, market stallholder or other small business will keep its books using a full double entry system. A large number of the owners of such firms would not know how to write up double entry records, even if they wanted to.

It is more likely that they would enter details of a transaction once only, using a single entry system. Also, many of them would fail to record every transaction, resulting in incomplete records.

Somehow, however, the profits will have to be calculated, if only to work out the amount of income tax payable. How can profits be calculated if the bookkeeping records are inadequate or incomplete?

30.2 Profit as an Increase in Capital

Probably the way to start is to recall that, unless there has been an introduction of extra cash or resources into the firm, the only way that capital can be increased is by making profits. Therefore, profits can be found by comparing capital at the end of the last period with that at the end of this period.

Let us look at a firm where capital at the end of 2004 was \$2,000. During 2005 there have been no drawings, and no extra capital has been brought in by the owner. At the end of 2005 the capital was \$3,000.

		This year's capital		Last year's capital		
Net profit	=	\$3,000	–	\$2,000	=	\$1,000

If on the other hand the drawings had been $700, the profits must have been $1,700, calculated thus:

Last year's capital	+	Profits	–	Drawings	=	This year's capital
$2,000	+	?	–	$700	=	$3,000

Filling in the missing figure by normal arithmetical deduction, we can see that $1,700 profits is the figure needed to complete the formula:

$2,000	+	$1,700	–	$700	=	$3,000

Exhibit 30.1 shows the calculation of profit where insufficient information is available to draft a trading and profit and loss account, only information of assets and liabilities being known.

Exhibit 30.1

H. Williams has not kept proper bookkeeping records, but he has kept notes in diary form of the transactions of his business. He is able to give you details of his assets and liabilities as at 31 December 2005 and at 31 December 2006 as follows.

At 31 December 2005.
Assets: Motor van, $1,000; Fixtures, $700; Stock, $850; Debtors, $950; Bank, $1,100; Cash, $100.
Liabilities: Creditors, $200; Loan from J. Austin, $600.
At 31 December 2006.
Assets: Motor van (after depreciation), $800; Fixtures (after depreciation), $630; Stock, $990; Debtors, $1,240; Bank, $1,700; Cash, $200.
Liabilities: Creditors, $300; Loan from J. Austin $400; Drawings were $900.

First of all a **statement of affairs** is drawn up as at 31 December 2005. This is the name given to what would have been called a balance sheet if it had been drawn up from a set of records. The capital is the difference between the assets and liabilities.

H. Williams
Statement of Affairs as at 31 December 2005

	$	$
Fixed assets		
Motor van		1,000
Fixtures		700
		1,700
Current assets		
Stock	850	
Debtors	950	
Bank	1,100	
Cash	100	
	3,000	

(Cont'd)

Less Current liabilities		
Creditors	200	
Working capital		2,800
		4,500
Financed by:		
Capital (difference)		3,900
Long-term liability		
Loan from J. Austin		600
		4,500

A statement of affairs is now drafted up as at the end of 2006. The formula of Opening Capital + Profit – Drawings = Closing Capital is then used to deduce the figure of profit.

H. Williams
Statement of Affairs as at 31 December 2006

		$	$
Fixed assets			
Motor van			800
Fixtures			630
			1,430
Current assets			
Stock		990	
Debtors		1,240	
Bank		1,700	
Cash		200	
		4,130	
Less Current liabilities			
Creditors		300	3,830
			5,260
Financed by:			
Capital			
Balance at 1.1.2006		3,900	
Add Net profit	(C)	?	
	(B)	?	
Less Drawings		900 (A)	?
Long-term liability			
Loan from J. Austin			400

Deduction of net profit is achieved by:

Opening Capital + Net Profit – Drawings = Closing Capital

Finding the missing figures (A), (B) and (C) by deduction:

(A) is the figure needed to make the balance sheet totals equal, i.e. $4,860;
(B) is therefore $4,860 + $900 = $5,760;
(C) is therefore $5,760 – $3,900 = $1,860.

To check:

Capital		3,900	
Add Net profit	(C)	1,860	
	(B)	5,760	
Less Drawings		900	(A) 4,860

Obviously, this method of calculating profit is very unsatisfactory as it is much more informative when a trading and profit and loss account can be drawn up. Therefore, whenever possible the comparisons of capital method of ascertaining profit should be avoided and a full set of final accounts drawn up from the available records.

It is important to realize that a business would have exactly the same trading and profit and loss account and balance sheet whether they kept their books by single entry or double entry. However, as you will see, whereas the double entry system uses the trial balance in preparing the final accounts, the single entry system will have to arrive at the same answer by different means.

30.3 Drawing Up the Final Accounts

The following example shows the various stages of drawing up final accounts from a single entry set of records.

The accountant discerns the following details of transactions for J. Frank's retail store for the year ended 31 December 2005.

1 The sales are mostly on a credit basis. No record of sales has been made, but $10,000 has been received $9,500 by cheque and $500 by cash, from persons to whom goods have been sold.
2 Amount paid by cheque to suppliers during the year = $7,200.
3 Expenses paid during the year: by cheque, rent $200, general expenses $180; by cash, rent $50.
4 J. Frank took $10 cash per week (for 52 weeks) as drawings.
5 Other information available:

	At 31.12.2004	At 31.12.2005
	$	$
Debtors	1,100	1,320
Creditors for goods	400	650
Rent owing	—	50
Bank balance	1,130	3,050
Cash balance	80	10
Stock	1,590	1,700

6 The only fixed asset consists of fixtures which were valued at 31 December 2004 at $800. These are to be depreciated at 10 per cent per annum.

The following stages now need to be worked through.

Stage 1

Draw up a Statement of Affairs on the closing day of the last accounting period. This is now shown.

J. Frank
Statement of Affairs as at 31 December 2004

	$	$
Fixed assets		
Fixtures		800
Current assets		
Stock	1,590	
Debtors	1,100	
Bank	1,130	
Cash	80	
	3,900	
Less Current liabilities		
Creditors	400	
Working capital		3,500
		4,300
Financed by:		
Capital (difference)		4,300
		4,300

All of these opening figures are then taken into account when drawing up the final accounts for 2005.

Stage 2

Next, a cash and bank summary, showing the totals of each separate item, plus opening and closing balances, is drawn up.

	Cash	*Bank*		*Cash*	*Bank*
	$	$		$	$
Balances 31.12.2004	80	1,130	Suppliers		7,200
Receipts from debtors	500	9,500	Rent	50	200
			General Expenses		180
			Drawings	520	
			Balances 31.12.2005	10	3,050
	580	10,630		580	10,630

Stage 3

Calculate the figures for purchases and sales to be shown in the trading account. Remember that the figures needed are the same as those which would have been found if double entry records had been kept.

In double entry, purchases means the goods that have been bought in the period, irrespective of whether they have been paid for or not during that time. The figure of payments to suppliers must therefore be adjusted to find the figure for purchases.

	$
Paid during the year	7,200
Less payments made, but which were for goods which were purchased in a previous year (creditors 31.12.2004)	400
	6,800
Add purchases made in this year, but for which payment has not yet been made (creditors 31.12.2005)	650
Good bought in this year, i.e. purchases	7,450

The same answer could have been obtained if the information had been shown in the form of a total creditors account, the figure for purchases being the amount required to make the account totals agree. You can see that the total creditors account is very much like a purchases ledger control account.

Total Creditors

	$		$
Cash paid to suppliers	7,200	Balances b/f	400
Balances c/d	650	Purchases (missing figure)	7,450
	7,850		7,850

The sales figure will only equal receipts where all the sales are for cash. Therefore, the receipts figures need adjusting to find sales. This can only be done by constructing a total debtors account, the sales figure being the one needed to make the totals agree. Here the total debtors account is like a sales ledger control account.

Total Debtors

	$		$
Balances b/f	1,100	Receipts: Cash	500
		Cheque	9,500
Sales (missing figure)	10,220	Balances c/d	1,320
	11,320		11,320

Stage 4

Regarding expenses, where there are no accruals or prepayments, either at the beginning or end of the accounting period, then expenses paid will equal expenses used up during the period. These figures will be charged to the trading and profit and loss account.

On the other hand, where such prepayments or accruals exist, then an expense account should be drawn up for that particular item. When all known items are entered, the missing figure will be the expenses to be charged for the accounting period. In this case, only the rent account needs to be drawn up.

Rent Account

	$		$
Cheques	200	Rent (missing figure)	300
Cash	50		
Accrued c/d	50		
	300		300

Stage 5
Now, draw up the final accounts.

J. Frank
Trading and Profit and Loss Account for the year ended 31 December 2005

	$	$
Sales (Stage 3)		10,220
Less Cost of goods sold:		
Stock at 1.1.2005	1,590	
Add Purchases (Stage 3)	7,450	
	9,040	
Less Stock at 31.12.2005	1,700	7,340
Gross profit		2,880
Less expenses:		
Rent (stage 4)	300	
General expenses	180	
Depreciation: Fixtures	80	560
Net profit		2,320

Balance Sheet as at 31 December 2005

	$	$	$
Fixed assets			
Fixtures as at 1.1.2005		800	
Less Depreciation		80	720
Current assets			
Stock		1,700	
Debtors		1,320	
Bank		3,050	
Cash		10	
		6,080	

(Cont'd)

Less Current liabilities			
Creditors	650		
Rent owing	50	700	
Working capital			5,380
			6,100
Financed by:			
Capital			
Balance as at 1.1.2005			
(per Opening Statement of Affairs)			4,300
Add Net profit			2,320
			6,620
Less Drawings			520
			6,100

30.4 Disadvantages of Single Entry Recording

Someone without a double entry set of books will not be able to ascertain the following easily.

- **Debtors** They will not know who owes money, how much, and how long the money has been owed.
- **Creditors** They will not know to whom they owe money, how much, and how long it has been owed.
- **No proper checks on amounts paid** for fixed assets over the years.
- **No proper checks on amounts owing** for loans.

It will also make it easier for employees to defraud the business, e.g. by destroying sales invoices and getting money from the debtor for doing this.

30.5 Multiple-choice Questions

Now attempt Set No. 4, questions 61–80, p. 407.

New Terms

Statement of affairs (p. 261): A statement from which the capital of the owner is deduced by estimating assets and liabilities. Then Capital = Assets – Liabilities.

Summary

1. If the increase in capital over a period is known, and also details of drawings, then the net profit can be deduced without double entry records.
2. The figures needed for purchases and sales can be deduced from a total creditors' account and a total debtors' account.

Exercises

30.1 On 1 August 2006 S. Phillips started his business with $1,000 in his bank account. After the end of his first year of trading he realized that, because of his lack of bookkeeping knowledge, he was unable to prepare a balance sheet. He was, however, able to produce the following data for the year ended 31 July 2007.

	$
Furniture (cost $900)	800
Motor vehicles (cost $2,100)	1,600
Stock-in-trade	2,700
Creditors	3,300
Cash in hand	50
Balance at bank (overdrawn)	1,000
Debtors	1,600
Loan from B. Smith	200
Drawings	3,000

You are required to:

(*a*) ascertain his profit or loss for the year ended 31 July 2007;

(*b*) prepare his balance sheet as at 31 July 2007, showing clearly all the totals and sub-totals normally found in a balance sheet.

30.2 J. Marcano is a dealer who has not kept proper books of account. At 31 August 2006 her state of affairs was as follows.

	$
Cash	115
Bank balance	2,209
Fixtures	3,500
Stock	16,740
Debtors	11,890
Creditors	9,952
Motor van (at valuation)	3,500

During the year to 31 August 2007 her drawings amounted to $7,560. Winnings from a football pool $12,800 were put into the business. Extra fixtures were bought for $2,000.

At 31 August 2007 J. Marcano's assets and liabilities were: cash, $84; bank overdraft, $165; stock, $24,891; creditors for goods, $6,002; creditors for expenses, $236; fixtures to be depreciated, $300; motor van to be valued at $2,800; debtors, $15,821; prepaid expenses, $72.

Draw up a statement showing the profit or loss made by Marcano for the year ended 31 August 2007.

30.3X

G. Brown
Balance Sheet as at 31 May 2007

	$		$
Fixtures	5,000	Capital	14,000
Motor vans	4,000	Creditors	1,500
Stock	3,000		
Debtors	1,300		
Bank	2,000		
Cash	200		
	15,500		15,500

(Cont'd)

The following transactions took place on 1 June 2007.

	$
Purchases on credit	350
Sales on credit (cost $350)	500
Cash sales (cost $100)	150
A motor-van, book value $1,000, was sold for $950. A cheque was received in full settlement.	
Payment to creditors by cheque	800
Cheques received from debtors	700
A bad debt written off	100
Cash received from debtors	50
Stock taken by proprietor	150

Reconstruct the balance sheet as it would appear at close of business on 1 June 2007. You should neatly set out all your calculations.

30.4X On 1 July 2005 D. Lewis commenced business with $6,000 in his bank account. After trading for a full year, he ascertained that his position on 30 June 2006 was as follows.

	$		$
Plant	3,600	Fixtures	360
Creditors	720	Bank balance	600
Debtors	930	Stock-in-trade	1,350
Cash in hand	135	Drawings	1,600

You are required to:

(*a*) calculate D. Lewis' capital at 30 June 2006;

(*b*) prepare D. Lewis' balance sheet at 30 June 2006 (assuming a profit of $1,855), set out in such a manner as to show clearly the totals normally shown in a balance sheet.

30.5 A. Hernandez is a sole trader who, although keeping very good records, does not operate a full double entry system. The following figures have been taken from her records.

	31 March 2008	*31 March 2009*
	$	$
Cash at bank	1,460	1,740
Office furniture	600	500
Stock	2,320	2,620
Cash in hand	60	80

Debtors on 31 March 2008 amounted to $2,980 and sales for the year ended 31 March 2009 to $11,520. During the year ended 31 March 2009 cash received from debtors amounted to $10,820.

Creditors on 31 March 2008 amounted to $1,880 and purchases for the year ended 31 March 2009 to $8,120. During the year ended 31 March 2009 cash paid to creditors amounted to $7,780.

During the year to 31 March 2009 no bad debts were incurred. Also, during the same period there was neither discount allowed nor discount received.

Required:

(*a*) calculate debtors and creditors as at 31 March 2009;

(*b*) calculate Hernandez' capital as at 31 March 2008 and 31 March 2009;

(*c*) calculate her net profit for the year ended 31 March 2009, allowing for the fact that during that year her drawings amounted to $2,540.

Note: Calculations must be shown.

30.6X John Prince is a sole trader who does not keep his books on the double entry system. From his records, however, the following information is available.

	31 March 2006	*31 March 2007*
	$	$
Fixed assets	6,240	6,800
Current assets	7,980	8,520
Current liabilities	3,920	3,760

During the year ending 31 March 2007, Prince used his private banking account to purchase additional office furniture costing $720, and this was brought into his business. Also during the same period Prince made drawings of $2,560 in cash and $120 in goods (cost price).

Required:

(*a*) calculate the amount of Prince's capital as at 31 March 2006 and 31 March 2007;

(*b*) calculate his net profit for the year ending 31 March 2007;

(*c*) draw up his capital account for the year ending 31 March 2007, as it would appear under the double entry system.

Note: Calculations must be shown.

30.7 J. Evans has kept records of her business transactions in a single entry form. Her bank account for the year 2004 is as follows.

	$		$
Balance 1.1.2004	1,890	Cash withdrawn from bank	5,400
Receipts from debtors	44,656	Trade creditors	31,695
Loan from T. Hughes	2,000	Rent	2,750
		Rates	1,316
		Drawings	3,095
		Sundry expenses	1,642

Records of cash paid were: sundry expenses $122, trade creditors $642. Cash sales amounted to $698; cash drawings were $5,289.

The following information is also available.

	31.12.2003	*31.12.2004*
	$	$
Cash in hand	48	93
Trade creditors	4,896	5,091
Debtors	6,013	7,132
Rent owing	—	250
Rates in advance	282	312
Motor van (at valuation)	2,800	2,400
Stock	11,163	13,021

You are to prepare:

(*a*) calculation of capital as at 1 January 2004;

(*b*) a cash and bank summary for the year;

(*c*) a trading and profit and loss account for the year ended 31 December 2004.

(*CXC style*)

30.8X S. Agnew has lost his records of sales, and you will have to deduce the sales figure. The summary of his bank account for the year ended 31 December 2006 is as follows.

	$		$
Receipts from debtors	67,595	Balance 1 Jan 2006	2,059
Extra capital introduced	3,000	Suppliers for goods	49,382
		Motor expenses	4,624
		Rent and rates	3,728
		General expenses	846
		Fixtures bought	3,500
		Drawings	1,364
		Balance 31 Dec 2006	5,092
	70,595		70,595

A cash loan of $500 had been received on 1 July 2006. Interest is to be paid on this at the rate of 16% per annum. Cash payments were as follows.

	$
Drawings	6,070
Suppliers	406
General expenses	707

Cash received from debtors was $6,630.

Motor vans owned by the firm had cost $8,000 in January 2004, and depreciation should be written off at 25% using the reducing balance method. Fixtures costing $2,000 had been bought in January 2003 had depreciation is being written off at the rate of 10%, using the straight-line method.

The following information is also given.

	31.12.2005	*31.12.2006*
	$	$
Stock	10,500	11,370
Cash in hand	165	112
Creditors for goods	6,238	4,187
Debtors	16,840	19,385
Motor expenses owing	123	238
Rent paid in advance	115	—
Rent owing	—	230

You are required to:

(*a*) draw up total debtors' and total creditors' accounts;
(*b*) draw up the cash account summary for the year;
(*c*) calculate opening capital as on 1 January 2006;
(*d*) prepare the trading and profit and loss account for the year ended 31 December 2006.

(*CXC style*)

CHAPTER **31**

Capital and Revenue Expenditure

Learning Objectives

- To be able to distinguish between expenditure that is capital in nature and that which is revenue expenditure.
- To understand that some expenditure is part capital expenditure and part revenue expenditure.
- To realize the effect on the final accounts, and the profits shown there, if revenue expenditure is wrongly treated as being capital expenditure and vice versa.

31.1 Capital Expenditure

Capital expenditure is made when a firm spends money to either:

- buy fixed assets; or
- add to the value of an existing fixed asset.

Included in such amounts should be the costs of:

- acquiring fixed assets
- bringing them into the firm
- legal costs of buying buildings
- carriage inwards on machinery bought
- anything else needed to get the fixed asset ready for use.

31.2 Revenue Expenditure

Expenditure that is required not for increasing the value of fixed assets, but for running the business on a day-to-day basis, is known as **revenue expenditure**.

The difference can be seen clearly with the total cost of using a motor van for a firm. Buying a new motor van is capital expenditure. The motor van will be in use for several years and is, therefore, a fixed asset.

The cost of petrol to use in the motor van for the next few days is revenue expenditure. This is because the expenditure is used up in a few days and does not add to the value of fixed assets.

31.3 Differences between Capital and Revenue Expenditure

A few instances will demonstrate the difference. In Exhibit 31.1 you can see that revenue expenditure is that chargeable to the trading or profit and loss account, while capital expenditure will result in increased figures for fixed assets in the balance sheet.

Exhibit 31.1

	Expenditure	Type of expenditure
1	Buying motor van	Capital
2	Petrol costs for motor van	Revenue
3	Repairs to motor van	Revenue
4	Putting extra headlights on motor van	Capital
5	Buying machinery	Capital
6	Electricity costs of using machinery	Revenue
7	We spent $1,500 on machinery: $1,000 was for an item added to the machine, $500 for repairs	Capital $1,000 Revenue $500
8	Painting outside of new building	Capital
9	Three years later — repainting outside of building in (8)	Revenue

31.4 Joint Expenditure

Sometimes one item of expenditure will need dividing between capital and revenue expenditure.

A builder was engaged to tackle some work on our premises, the total bill being for $3,000. If one-third of this was for repair work and two-thirds for improvements, $1,000 should be charged in the profit and loss account as revenue expenditure, and $2,000 should be identified as capital expenditure and, therefore, added to the value of premises and shown as such in the balance sheet.

31.5 Incorrect Treatment of Expenditure

If either:

- capital expenditure is incorrectly treated as revenue expenditure; or
- revenue expenditure is incorrectly treated as capital expenditure

then both the balance sheet figures and trading and profit and loss account figures will be incorrect.

This means that the net profit figure will also be incorrect. If the expenditure affects items in the trading account, then the gross profit figure will also be incorrect.

31.6 Capital and Revenue Receipts

When an item of capital expenditure is sold, the receipt is called a **capital receipt**. Suppose a motor van is bought for $5,000, and sold five years later for $750. The $5,000 was treated as capital expenditure. The $750 received is treated as a capital receipt.

Revenue receipts are sales or other revenue items, such as rent receivable or commissions receivable.

New Terms

Capital expenditure (p. 272): Money spent by a firm to buy or add value to a fixed asset.

Revenue expenditure (p. 272): Expenses needed for the day-to-day running of the business.

Capital receipt (p. 273): Receipts from the sale of a fixed asset.

Revenue receipts (p. 273): All receipts that have not come from the sales of fixed assets, additional capital or loans.

Summary

1 Some items are part capital expenditure and part revenue expenditure, and need to be apportioned accordingly.

2 If capital expenditure or revenue expenditure is mistaken one for the other, then gross or net profit figures (or both) will be incorrectly stated, as will balance sheet figures.

3 If capital receipts or revenue receipts are mistaken one for the other, then gross or net profit figures (or both) will be incorrectly stated, as will balance sheet figures.

Exercises

31.1 For the business of J. James, wholesale chemist, classify the following between capital and revenue expenditure.

(*a*) Purchase of an extra motor van.
(*b*) Cost of rebuilding warehouse wall which had fallen down.
(*c*) Building extension to the warehouse.
(*d*) Painting extension to warehouse when it is first built.
(*e*) Repainting extension to warehouse three years after (*d*).
(*f*) Carriage costs on material for new warehouse extension.
(*g*) Carriage costs on purchases.
(*h*) Carriage costs on sales.
(*i*) Legal costs of collecting debts.
(*j*) Legal charges on acquiring new premises for office.
(*k*) Fire insurance premium.
(*l*) Costs of erecting new machine.

31.2X For the business of H. Paul, a food shop, classify the following between capital and revenue expenditure.

(*a*) Repairs to meat slicer.
(*b*) New tyre for van.
(*c*) Additional shop counter.
(*d*) Renewing signwriting on store.
(*e*) Fitting partitions in store.
(*f*) Roof repairs.
(*g*) Installing thief detection equipment.
(*h*) Store assistant's pay.
(*i*) Carriage on returns outwards.
(*j*) New cash register.
(*k*) Repairs to office safe.
(*l*) Installing extra toilet.

31.3 Explain clearly the difference between capital expenditure and revenue expenditure. State which of the following you would classify as capital expenditure, giving your reasons.

(*a*) Cost of building extension to factory.
(*b*) Purchases of filing cabinets for sales office.
(*c*) Cost of repairs to accounting machine.
(*d*) Cost of installing reconditioned engine in delivery van.
(*e*) Legal fees paid in connection with factory extension.

31.4X The following data were extracted from the book of account of H. E. Worth, a building contractor, on 31 March 2009, his financial year end.

	$
(*a*) Pay (includes the pay of two of Worth's employees who worked on improvements to Worth's premises, amount involved $1,500).	8,000
(*b*) Lighting (includes new wiring $500, part of premises improvement).	2,000
(*c*) Purchases of extra cement mixer (includes $200 for repair of old dumper).	2,500
(*d*) Rent.	400
(*e*) Carriage (includes $100 carriage on new cement mixer).	800
(*f*) Purchases of new lathe (extra).	4,000

Allocate each of the items listed above to either capital or revenue expenditure.

CHAPTER **32**

Receipts and Payments Accounts and Income and Expenditure Accounts

Learning Objectives

- To be able to draw up income and expenditure accounts and balance sheets for non-trading organizations.
- To be able to calculate profit and losses from special activities and incorporate them into the final accounts.
- To understand that various forms of revenue may need special treatment.

32.1 Non-trading Organizations

Clubs, associations and other non-profit-making organizations do not have trading and profit and loss accounts drawn up for them, as their main purpose is not trading or profit making. They are run so that their members can do things such as play football or cricket. The kind of final accounts prepared by these organizations are either **receipts and payments accounts** or **income and expenditure accounts**.

32.2 Receipts and Payments Accounts

Receipts and payments accounts are a summary of the cash book for the period. Exhibit 32.1 is an example.

Exhibit 32.1

The Homers Running Club
Receipts and Payments Account for the year ended 31 December 2005

Receipts	$	*Payments*	$
Bank balance 1.1.2005	236	Groundsman's pay	728
Subscriptions received for 2005	1,148	Sports stadium expenses	296
Rent received	116	Committee expenses	58
		Printing and stationery	33
		Bank balance 31.12.2005	385
	1,500		1,500

32.3 Income and Expenditure Accounts

When assets are owned, and there are liabilities, the receipts and payments account is not a good way of drawing up final accounts. Other than listing the cash received and paid out, it shows only the cash balances. The other assets and liabilities are not shown at all.

What is required is:

- a balance sheet
- an account showing whether the association's capital has increased.

In a profit-making firm, the latter would be a trading and profit and loss account. In a non-profit organization, it would be an income and expenditure account.

An income and expenditure account follows the same rules as trading and profit and loss accounts. The only differences are the terms used.

Profit-making firm	Non-profit organization
Trading and profit and loss account	Income and expenditure account
Net profit	Surplus of income over expenditure
Net loss	Excess of expenditure over income

32.4 Profit or Loss for a Special Purpose

Sometimes there are reasons for a non-profit-making organization wanting a profit and loss account.

This is when something is done to make a profit. The profit is not to be kept, but will be used to pay for the main purpose of the organization.

For instance, a football club may have discos or dances which people pay to go to. Any profit from these helps to pay football expenses. For these discos and dances a trading or profit and loss account may be drawn up. Any profit (or loss) would be transferred to the income and expenditure account.

32.5 Accumulated Fund

A sole trader or a partnership will have capital accounts. A non-profit-making organization will instead have an **accumulated fund**. It is in effect the same as a capital account, as it lists the difference between assets and liabilities.

In a sole trader or partnership.

$$\text{Capital} + \text{Liabilities} = \text{Assets}$$

In a non-profit-making organization:

$$\text{Accumulated fund} + \text{Liabilities} = \text{Assets}$$

32.6 Drawing Up Income and Expenditure Accounts

We can now look at the preparation of an income and expenditure account and a balance sheet of a club. This is drawn up on the basis of a trial balance (see Exhibit 32.2).

A separate trading account is to be prepared for a bar, where refreshments are sold to make a profit. The following information is also available: bar stocks at 31 December 2008, $2,362; provide for depreciation: sports equipment, $1,700: furniture and fittings, $1,315. Exhibits 32.3–32.5 show the resulting accounts.

As most members of clubs do not understand double entry, final accounts using the vertical style are easier for them to understand than when the horizontal style is used. This chapter therefore uses the vertical style for the final accounts.

Exhibit 32.2

Long Lane Football Club
Trial Balance as at 31 December 2008

	Dr.	*Cr.*
	$	$
Sports equipment	8,500	
Club premises	29,600	
Subscriptions received		6,490
Staff pay	4,750	
Furniture and fittings	5,260	
Rates and insurance	1,910	
General expenses	605	
Accumulated fund 1.1.2008		42,016
Donations received		360
Telephone and postage	448	
Bank	2,040	
Bar purchases	9,572	
Creditors for bar supplies		1,040
Bar sales		14,825
Bar stocks 1.1.2008	2,046	
	64,731	64,731

Exhibit 32.3

Long Lane Football Club Bar
Bar Trading Account for the year ended 31 December 2008

	$	$
Sales		14,825
Less Cost of goods sold		
Opening stock	2,046	
Add purchases	9,572	
	11,618	
Less Closing stock	2,362	
		9,256
Gross profit to income and expenditure account		5,569

Note:
The result of the club bar operation is calculated separately. The gross profit/loss will then be incorporated into the club's income and expenditure account for calculation of the overall result.

Exhibit 32.4

Long Lane Football Club
Income and Expenditure Account for the year ended 31 December 2008

	$	$
Income		
Gross profit from bar		5,569
Subscriptions		6,490
Donations received		360
		12,419
Less Expenditure		
Staff pay	4,750	
Rates and insurance	1,910	
Telephone and postage	448	
General expenses	605	
Depreciation: Furniture and fittings	1,315	
Sports equipment	1,700	
		10,728
Surplus of income over expenditure		1,691

Exhibit 32.5

Long Lane Football Club
Balance Sheet as at 31 December 2008

	$	$	$
Fixed assets	*Cost*	*Depreciation*	*Net book value*
Club premises	29,600	—	29,600
Furniture and fittings	5,260	1,315	3,945
Sports equipment	8,500	1,700	6,800
	43,360	3,015	40,345
Current assets			
Bar stocks		2,362	
Cash at bank		2,040	
		4,402	
Current liabilities			
Creditors for bar supplies		1,040	
Working capital			3,362
			43,707
Financed by:			
Accumulated fund			
Balance at 1 January 2008			42,016
Add Surplus of income over expenditure			1,691
			43,707

32.7 Subscriptions

Where there are no subscriptions owing, or paid in advance, at the beginning and end of a financial year, then the amount shown on the credit side of the subscriptions account can be transferred to the credit of the income and expenditure account, as follows.

Subscriptions Account

2003		$	2003		$
Dec 31	Income and expenditure account	3,598	Dec 31	Bank (total received)	3,598

Income and Expenditure Account for the year ended 31 December 2003

Income	$
Subscriptions	3,598

On the other hand, there may be subscriptions owing at both the start and end of the financial year. In a case where $325 was owing at the start of the year, a total of $5,668 was received during the year, and $554 was owing at the end of the year, then this would appear as:

Subscriptions Account

2005		$	2005		$
Jan 1	Owing b/d	325	Dec 31	Bank (total received)	5,668
Dec 31	Income and expenditure account (difference)	5,897	Dec 31	Balance c/d	554
		6,222			6,222

Income and Expenditure Account for the year ended 31 December 2005

Income	$
Subscriptions	5,897

In the third case, at the start of the year there are both subscriptions owing from the previous year and also paid in advance, then, also both subscriptions paid in the current year for next year (in advance) and also unpaid (owing) at the end of the current year.

An amateur theatre organization charges its members an annual subscription of $20 per member. It accrues for subscriptions owing at the end of each year and also adjusts for subscriptions received in advance.

1 On 1 January 2002, 18 members owed $360 for the year 2001.
2 In December 2001, 4 members paid $80 for the year 2002.
3 During the year 2002, we received cash for subscriptions $7,420.

For 2001	$360	
For 2002	$6,920	
For 2003	$140	$7,420

4 At close of 31 December 2002, 11 members had not paid their 2002 subscriptions.

Subscriptions Account

2002			$	2002			$
Jan 1	Owing b/d	(1)	360	Jan 1	Prepaid b/d	(2)	80
Dec 31	Income and expenditure		*7,220	Dec 31	Bank	(3)	7,420
Dec 31	Prepaid c/d	(3)	140	Dec 31	Owing c/d	(4)	220
			7,720				7,720
2003				2003			
Jan 1	Owing b/d	(4)	220	Jan 1	Prepaid b/d	(3)	140

*Difference between two sides of the account.

Income and Expenditure Account for the year ended 31 December 2002

Income	$
Subscriptions	7,220

In this case, in the balance sheet as at 31 December 2002, the amounts owing for subscriptions (4), $220, will be shown under current assets as a debtor. The subscriptions (3) paid in advance for 2003 will appear as an item under current liabilities as subscriptions received in advance, $140.

32.8 Donations

Any donations received are shown as income in the year in which they are received.

32.9 Entrance Fees

New members often have to pay an entrance fee in the year that they join, in addition to the membership fee for that year. Entrance fees are normally included as income in the year when they are received.

32.10 Life Membership

Sometimes members can pay one amount for membership, and they will never have to pay any more money. This membership will last for their lifetime.

In this case, all of the money received from life membership should not be credited to the income and expenditure account of that year. In a club where members joined at age 20 and would probably be members for 40 years, then one-fortieth (2½%) would be credited in the income and expenditure account each year. The balance not transferred to the income and expenditure account would appear in the balance sheet as a long-term liability. This is because it is the liability of the club to allow the members to use the club for the rest of their lives without paying any more for membership.

On the other hand, a club especially for old men over the age of 60 would transfer a much bigger share of the life membership fee paid to the income and expenditure account. This is because the number of years of future use of the club will be far less because people are old when they join. Let us say that 10 years' use, on average, might be expected. In this case, 10% per year would be transferred to the credit of the income and expenditure account.

New Terms

Receipts and payments account (p. 276): A summary of the cash book of a non-profit-making organization.

Income and expenditure account (p. 277): An account for a non-profit-making organization to find the surplus or deficit made during a period.

Accumulated fund (p. 277): A capital account for a non-profit organization.

Summary

1 A receipts and payments account does not show the full financial position of an organization, except for one where the only asset is cash.
2 Although the main object of the organization is non-profit-making, certain activities may be run at a profit (or may lose money) in order to help finance the main objects.
3 In an examination you should treat subscriptions owing at the end of a period in the same way as debtors, unless told otherwise.
4 Donations are usually treated as income of the period in which they are received.
5 Entrance fees are usually treated as income in the year in which they are received.
6 The treatment of life membership fees is purely at the discretion of the organization.

Exercises

32.1 The following trial balance was extracted from the books of the Marabella Town Sports Club at the close of business on 31 March 2008.

	Dr.	*Cr.*
	$	$
Club premises	13,500	
Sports equipment	5,100	
Bar purchases and sales	9,540	15,270
Bar stocks 1 April 2007	2,190	
Balance at bank	2,790	
Subscriptions received		8,640
Accumulated fund 1 April 2007		22,290
Secretary's pay	3,600	
Staff pay	5,280	
Postage and telephone	870	
Office furniture	1,200	
Rates and insurance	1,230	
Cash in hand	60	
Sundry expenses	840	
	46,200	46,200

Notes:

(*a*) All bar purchases and sales were on a cash basis. Bar stocks 31 March 2008 were $2,460.

(*b*) No subscriptions have been paid in advance but subscription in arrears at 31 March 2008 amounted to $90.

(*c*) Rates pre-paid at 31 March 2008: $60.

(*d*) Provide for depreciation as follows: sports equipment $600; office furniture $120.

(Cont'd)

Required:
Prepare the bar trading account and the income and expenditure account of the Club for the year ended 31 March 2008 together with a balance sheet as on that date. For this purpose, the pay of $5,280 should be shown in the income and expenditure account and not the bar trading account.

32.2 The East Point Social Club has 600 members, each paying an annual subscription of $50. Rent is payable of $500 per month. All money received is banked immediately. All payments are by cheque.

On 31 December 2004 the financial position of the club was as follows.

	$
Balance at bank (overdraft)	1,650
Equipment	16,100
Fixtures	2,100
Refreshment bar stocks	550

Twenty-four members did not pay their 2004 subscriptions until 2005.

During the year to 31 December 2005, the following transactions occurred.

	$
Refreshment bar purchases paid for	6,150
Refreshment bar takings	8,960
Subscription received	30,100
Rent paid	5,000
Refreshment bar staff pay	1,880
Purchases of equipment	8,900
Insurance paid	1,570
Affiliation fees paid	360
Donations received	4,240
Transport expenses	7,140
Ground staff pay	9,370

You are to draw up the following.

(*a*) A receipts and payments account.
(*b*) A refreshment bar trading account for 2005.
(*c*) An income and expenditure account for 2005, taking the following into account.
  (i) Bar stocks at 31 December 2005 were $940.
  (ii) Some subscriptions are owed by members at 31 December 2005.
  (iii) Equipment to be depreciated by 20%.
  (iv) Rent of $1,000 was owing at 31 December 2005.
  (v) Insurance paid in advance at 31 December 2005: $210.
(*d*) Calculation of accumulated fund at 31 December 2004.

(*CXC style*)

32.3X The following receipts and payments account for the year ending 31 May 2007 was prepared by the treasurer of the Port Maria Sports and Social Club.

Receipts	$	*Payments*	$
Balance at bank 1 June 2006	572	Purchases of new equipment	332
Subscriptions	270	Bar stocks purchased	794
Net proceeds of dance	426	Hire of rooms	128
Bar takings	1,086	Part-time staff pay	396
		Balance at bank 31 May 2007	704
	2,354		2,354

Notes:
(*a*) On 1 June 2006 the club's equipment was valued at $680.

(*Cont'd*)

(*b*) Bar stocks were valued as follows: 31 May 2006, $176; 31 May 2007 $202. There were no creditors for bar supplies on either of these dates.
(*c*) Allow $70 for depreciation of equipment during the year ended 31 May 2007.
(*d*) No subscriptions were outstanding at 31 May 2006, but on 31 May 2007 subscriptions due but unpaid amounted to $28.

Required:
Draw up the income and expenditure account of the Club for the year ended 31 May 2007, and a balance sheet as at 31 May 2007.

32.4X The treasurer of the City Domino Club has produced the following receipts and payments account for the year ended 31 December 2007.

Receipts	$	*Payments*	$
Balance at bank 1 June 2007	1,298	Coffee supplies bought	1,456
Subscriptions received	3,790	Attendants and cleaners' pay	1,776
Profits from dances	186	Rent of rooms	887
Profit on domino exhibition	112	New equipment bought	565
Coffee bar takings	2,798	Travelling expenses of domino teams	673
Sale of equipment	66		
		Balance at bank 31.12.2007	2,893
	8,250		8,250

Notes:
(i) Coffee bar stocks were valued: 31.12.2006, $59; 31.12.2007, $103. There was nothing owing for coffee bar stocks on either of these dates.
(ii) On 1.1.2007 the club's equipment was valued at $2,788. Included in this figure, valued at $77, was the equipment sold during the year for $66.
(iii) The amount to be charged for depreciation of equipment for the year is $279. This is in addition to the loss on equipment sold during the year.
(iv) Subscriptions owing by members: 31.12.2006, nil; 31.12.2007, $29.

You are required to do the following.
(*a*) draw up the coffee bar trading account for the year ended 31.12.2007. For this purpose, $650 of the pay is to be charged to this account; the remainder will be charged in the income and expenditure account.
(*b*) Calculate the accumulated fund as at 1.1.2007.
(*c*) Draw up the income and expenditure account for the year ended 31.12.2007, and a balance sheet as at 31.12.2007.

32.5X On 31 December 2002 the following information for the Sunny Bay Social Club is made available to you.

Balances on 1 January 2002	$
Bank	3,070
Subscriptions in arrears for 2001	290
Subscriptions received in advance for 2002	420
Equipment	1,800

In respect of the year to 31 December 2002, the following information is given to you.

	$
Subscriptions received (including 2001 arrears)	5,920
Equipment bought	700
Groundsman's pay	2,880
Sale of lottery tickets	1,090
Receipts from discos	7,510
Disco costs – including musicians	4,970

(Cont'd)

Teams' travelling expenses	1,220
Competition prizes bought	580
Rent of buildings	2,170
Receipts for ground hire	900
Committee expenses	690
Donations from well-wishers	1,500

Note that subscriptions due but unpaid at 31 December 2002 amounted to $370. Depreciate equipment 10%.

You are required to draw up the following:

(*a*) a subscription account for the year ended 31 December 2002;
(*b*) a receipts and payments account for the year 2002;
(*c*) an income and expenditure account for the year 2002.

(*CXC style*)

CHAPTER **33**

Accounting: Concepts and Conventions

Learning Objectives

- To appreciate the assumptions which are made when recording accounting data.
- To realize that one set of accounts is used for several different purposes.
- To understand what is meant by objectivity and subjectivity.
- To know the basic concepts of accounting.
- To see that the further overriding conventions of materiality, prudence and consistency affect the recording and adjustment of data.

33.1 Introduction

In this book we have been concerned with recording transactions in the books. While making such records, we have in fact been following certain *rules*. These rules under which we work are known as concepts and conventions.

The trading and profit and loss accounts and balance sheets shown in the previous chapters were drawn up for the owner of the business. As shown later in the book, businesses are often owned by more than just one person, and these accounting statements are for the use of all the owners.

An owner of a business may not be the only person to see the final accounts. He or she may have to show them to the bank manager when wanting to borrow money. The Inspector of Taxes will want to see them for the calculation of taxes. The owner may also need them to show to someone when trying to sell the business.

33.2 One Set of Final Accounts for All Purposes

If it had always been the custom to draft different kinds of final accounts for different purposes, so that one type was given to a banker, another type to someone wishing to buy the business, etc., then accounting would be different from what it is today. However, copies of the same set of final accounts are given to all of these different people.

This means that the banker, the prospective buyer of the business, the owner and the other people all see the same trading and profit and loss accounts and balance sheet. This is not always a very good idea, as the interests of each party are different, and different kinds of information are needed by each of them. For instance, the bank manager would really like to know how much the assets would sell for if the firm ceased trading; he or she could then see what the possibility would be of the bank obtaining repayment of its loan. Other people would also like to see the information in the way that is most useful to them. Yet normally only one sort of final accounts is available for all these different people.

This means that trading and profit and loss accounts and balance sheets have to be used for different purposes; and to be of any use, the different parties have to agree on the way in which they are drawn up.

Assume that you are in a class of students and that you have the problem of valuing your assets, which consist of 10 textbooks. The first value you decide is how much you could sell them for. Your own guess is $30, but the other members of the class may give figures ranging from $15 to $50.

Suppose that you now decide to put a value on their use to you. You may well think that the use of these books will enable you to pass your examinations and so enable you to get a good job. Another student may have the opposite idea concerning the use of the books. The use value placed on the books by still others in the class may be quite different again.

Finally, you decide to value the books by reference to cost. You take out of your pocket the bills for the books, which show that you paid a total of $60 for them. If the rest of the class do not think that you have altered the bills, then they can all agree that the value expressed as cost is $60. As this is the only value that you can all agree on, then each of you may decide to adopt the idea of showing the value of your books at their cost price.

33.3 Objectivity and Subjectivity

The use of a method that all can agree to, instead of everyone using a different method, is said to be an objective use. The cost of an asset is therefore an objective method of valuation.

When you are subjective, it means that you want to use your own method, even though no one else may agree to it.

Objectivity, or using methods that all people can agree to, is what financial accounting ensures. The rules that state how the transactions are recorded are usually known as concepts.

33.4 Basic Concepts

The Cost Concepts

The need for this has already been described. It means that assets are normally shown at cost price, and that this is the basis for valuation of the asset.

The Money Measurement Concept

Accounting is concerned only with those transactions covered by the following factors:

- they can be measured in money
- most people will agree to the money value of the transaction.

This means that accounting can never tell you everything about a business. For example, accounting does not show:

- whether the firm has good or bad managers
- that there are serious problems with the workforce
- that a rival product is about to take away a lot of the firm's best customers

- that the government is about to pass a law which will cost the business a lot of extra expense in future.

The reason these or similar items are not recorded is that it would be impossible to work out a money value for them which most people would agree to.

The Going Concern Concept

Normally we assume that a business will continue for a long time. Only if the business was going to be sold would we show how much the assets would sell for. This is because we use the cost concept. If businesses were not assumed to be going concerns, the cost concept could not be used. Should firms be treated as businesses to be sold immediately, then the saleable value of assets would be used instead of their cost.

The Business Entity Concept

The items recorded in a firm's books are limited to the transactions that affect the firm as a business entity. Suppose that a proprietor of a firm, from his personal monies outside the firm, buys a diamond necklace for his wife; as the money spent was not out of the firm's bank account or cash box, then this item will not be entered in the firm's books.

The only time that the personal resources of the proprietor affect the firm's accounting records is when he or she brings new capital into the firm, or takes drawings out of the firm.

The Realization Concept

Normally, profit is said to be earned at the time when:

- goods or services are passed to the customers
- the customer then incurs liability for them.

This concept of profit is known as the **realization concept**. Notice that profit is *not* said to be earned:

- when the order is received
- when the customer pays for the goods.

The Dual Aspect Concept

This states that there are two aspects of accounting, one represented by the assets of the business and the other by the claims against them. The concept states that these two aspect are always equal to each other. In other words,

$$\text{Assets} = \text{Capital} + \text{Liabilities}$$

'Double entry' is the name given to the method of recording the transactions for the **dual aspect concept**.

The Accrual Concept

The **accrual concept** says that net profit is the difference between revenues and expenses; i.e.:

$$\text{Revenues} - \text{Expenses} = \text{Net profit}$$

Determining the expenses used up to obtain the revenues is referred to as *matching* expenses against revenues.

A lot of people who have not studied accounting do not understand this concept. They think that receipts of a period, less payments of the period, equal net profit.

You know that expenses consist of the assets used up in a period. You also know that cash paid in a period and expenses of a period are usually different figures. This comes as a surprise to a lot of people.

You, however, know that we have to make adjustments for items such as expenses owing, payments in advance, depreciation and provisions for bad debts, etc. Only then can we calculate net profit.

33.5 The Assumption of the Stability of Monetary Measures

You do not have to be very old to remember that a few years ago many goods could be bought with less money than today. Your parents or grandparents can probably tell many stories of how little this item or the other used to cost many years ago. The currencies of the countries of the world change in terms of what each unit of currency can buy over the years.

Accounting, however, uses the cost concept, which states that an asset is normally shown at its cost price. This means that accounting statements can be misleading, because assets will be bought at different times at the prices then ruling, and the figures will be totalled up to show the value of the assets in terms of their original cost.

For instance, suppose that you bought a building 20 years ago for $20,000. You now decide to buy an identical additional building, but the price has risen to $40,000. You buy it, and the buildings account how shows buildings at a figure of $60,000. One building is in the currency of 20 years ago, while the other is at today's currency value. The figure of a total of $60,000 is historically correct, but it cannot be used for much else.

When we look at final accounts we must understand such problems. There are ways of adjusting accounts to make the figures more useful, but these are not in your syllabus. You will have to study them if you take accounting examinations at an advanced level.

33.6 The Conventions of Accounting

These concepts of accounting have become accepted in the business world. The concepts, however, could be interpreted in many ways if nothing had been done to standardize accounting methods.

Accounting therefore has tried to make certain that similar items are dealt with in similar ways. As a result we have the conventions of accounting.

The main conventions may be said to be: materiality, conservatism and consistency.

Materiality

This convention of **materiality** is adopted to try to stop you wasting time and effort doing completely unnecessary work. Accounting does not serve a useful purpose if the effort of recording a transaction in a certain way is not worthwhile. As an example, if a box of paper-clips is bought it will be used over a period of time, and some of this cost is used up every time someone uses a paper-clip. It is possible to record this as an expense every time it happens, but obviously, the price of a box of paper-clips is so low that it is not worth recording in this way.

The box of paper-clips is not a *material item*, and therefore would be charged as an expense in the period in which it was bought even thought it could last for more than one accounting period. You should not waste your time in the unnecessary recording of trivial items. Similarly, the purchase of a cheap metal ashtray would also be charged as an expense in the period in which it was bought because it is not a material item, even though it may last 20 years. It would not be worth calculating depreciation on it.

A motor lorry would be deemed to be a material item. We then calculate depreciation to charge each period, with the cost consumed in each period of its use.

You can see that small amounts are not material, while larger amounts are material. The question is, at what figure does an item become material? There is no fixed rule for this.

Firms make all sorts of rules to say what is material and what is not. There is no law that says what these should be. What is material and what is not depends upon judgement. A firm may decide that all items under $100 should be treated as expenses in the period in which they were bought, even though they may be in use in the firm for the following 10 years. Another firm, especially a large one, may put the limit at $1,000. Different limits may be set for different types of items.

The size and type of firm will affect the decisions as to what is material, and what is not.

Prudence (Alternatively Called Conservatism)

Very often an accountant has to use his or her judgement to decide which figure they will take for an item. Suppose a debt has been owing for quite a long time, and no one knows whether it will ever be paid. Should the accountant be an optimist in thinking that it will be paid or be more pessimistic?

It is the accountant's duty to see that people get the proper facts about a business. They should make certain that assets are not valued too highly. Similarly, liabilities should not be shown at values too low. Otherwise, people might inadvisedly lend money to a firm, which they would not do if they had the proper facts.

The accountant should always be on the side of safety, and this is known as **prudence**. The convention of prudence means that normally an accountant will take the figure which will understate rather than overstate the profit. Thus they should choose the figure which will cause the capital of the firm to be shown at a lower amount rather than at a higher one. They will also normally make sure that all losses are recorded in the books, but profits should not be anticipated by recording them before they should be.

It is only in the past ten years or so that the word 'prudence' has been used. It had been known as 'conservatism' for many years. This means that you may hear either term, but they both mean exactly the same.

Consistency

Even if we do everything already listed under concepts and conventions, there will still be quite a few different ways in which items can be recorded.

Each firm should try to choose the methods that give the most reliable picture of the business.

This cannot be done if one method is used in one year and another method the next year and so on. Constantly changing accounting methods will lead to misleading profits being calculated from the accounting records. Therefore the convention of **consistency** is used. This states that, when a firm has once fixed a method for the accounting treatment of an item, it will enter all similar items that follow in exactly the same way.

However, this does not mean that the firm has to follow the method until it closes down. A firm can change the method used, but such a change should not be taken without a lot of consideration. When such a change occurs and the profits calculated in that year are affected by a material amount, then the effect of the change should be stated, either in the profit and loss account itself or in one of the reports accompanying it.

For example, a company may decide to change from the straight line method of depreciating fixed assets to that of the reducing balance method. If this results in a change for depreciation for the year being $100,000 less under the new method, then this should be stated in the accounts.

33.7 Accounting Terminology

Unfortunately, many of the terms used in the description of accounting theory mean quite different things to different people. Things described as 'doctrines', 'concepts' and 'conventions' in this book may well be called 'principles' by someone else. They might be called 'concepts' without any attempt to distinguish between concepts and conventions. Provided that the reader realizes this, there is no problem.

Probably the most recent attempt to change a term involves the use of the word 'prudence' instead of 'conservatism', as described above. Both of these words can be taken to mean the same thing.

Quantifiability means the ability to make a proper measure of the transaction. This must take place if the transaction is to be measured in money.

33.8 Some Further Examples of Concepts and Conventions

In this section various examples are given. Consider which of the concepts and conventions cover the normal treatment of such an item and the advice you would give the owner(s) of the business. Sometimes more than one concept or convention may be applied. Write down your own answers before looking at Section 33.9 where the author's answers are shown. Do *not* simply look at the answers without attempting them yourself.

1 A sole trader wants to include the value of his own private house in the balance sheet, as he says that it is worth more than all the assets in the business. Should he do this?

2 The owner says that if the stock had to be sold very quickly, it would not sell for as much as it is shown on the balance sheet. Should he show the stock at this lower value on the balance sheet?

3 My cleverness, says the owner, is the main asset of the business. Why can't I show it as an asset on the balance sheet?

4 The business has had a poor trading year. The owner wants to change to the reducing balance method, instead of the straight line method, of depreciation so that his expenses will be less and his profit will increase. What is your advice?

5 The owner has bought some stock at a much lower price than usual. He wants to include it in the final accounts at the usual purchase price. Should he do this?

6 On the last day of the financial year 2001, the owner received a very large order. The goods will be delivered by him a month later in 2002. He wants to include this as a sale in 2001, as that is when he persuaded the other business to give him the order. Is this the correct way to do it?

7 As the owner says that a motor van cost him $20,000 in 2002, and he paid for it then why isn't it all an expense of 2002?

8 Twenty sales representatives working for T. Lee Ltd in 2004 have been given business identity cards which cost $10 per representative and will never wear out. The total cost of $200 has all been charged as an expense of the year 2004.

9 A change in the law means that two types of items held in stock will be affected. One type (stock type A) will now be able to be sold at a much higher price. The other type (stock type B) will have to be sold at less than cost. The accountant has valued type A at cost, and type B at net realizable value. Why has he done this?

10 The owner wants to value his machinery at a much higher figure than anyone else would expect. He says other people are stupid, and don't realize how valuable the machinery is. What is your advice and why?

11 A debtor owing a large amount cannot pay his account. The owner says that market conditions may change and the debtor will then be able to pay. Should you, as an accountant, agree with the owner, and if not, why?

12 The owner cannot understand why goods bought in 2003, but not actually paid for until 2004, should be treated as an expense in 2003. Explain why this is done.

33.9 Answers to Further Examples in Section 33.8

1 An owner's private assets are not shown as assets of his business. This is because of the business entity concept.

2 Businesses are assumed (unless there is other evidence) to continue for a fairly long time, i.e. the going concern concept. Stock is therefore not valued as though it has to be sold in an emergency. It is normally valued at the lower of cost or net realizable value. This is in accordance with the prudence concept.

3 The money measurement concept would not allow it. Cleverness cannot be measured in money, and most people would put different values on the owner's cleverness. It is also subjective, whereas accounting seeks objectivity. Lastly, as it has not cost anything, the cost concept cannot be used.

4 First, this goes against the convention of consistency. Second, the prudence concept, where profit should not be overstated, would also be ignored.

5 The prudence concept says that future profit should not be anticipated, therefore the stock should be shown at the actual cost. This also agrees with the cost concept.

6 The realization concept would not allow this. Profit cannot be said to be realized when an order is received and the goods have not yet been sent.

7 The accrual concept is concerned with expenses used up in an accounting period. The cost of the motor van will be used up over several accounting periods, and therefore cannot be charged wholly as an expense in one accounting period.

8 The convention of materiality allows small items of expenses to be shown as wholly an expense of one period, rather than be split and charged bit by bit over several periods.

9 Type A stock cannot be valued at more than cost because of the prudence concept which says that profit cannot be anticipated in advance. Type B stock can be value at lower than cost, because losses can be anticipated.

10 He cannot do this. The valuation is completely subjective, as only the owner thinks that this is its value. Accounting rests on the concept of objectivity, where other people can agree to the value. The valuation is also against the cost concept.

11 Here again the prudence concept looks at such items in a realistic way, and would make a provision for bad debt. Accounting does not look at the future as though everything will be better then, it tries to face facts as they really are.

12 The accrual concept is concerned with expenses when they are incurred, i.e. 2003, and not when they are paid for in 2004.

New Terms

Objectivity (p. 287): Using the method that everyone can agree to.

Subjectivity (p. 287): Using a method that other people may not agree to, derived from one's own personal preferences.

Cost concept (p. 287): Assets that are normally shown at cost price.

Money measurement concept (p. 287): The concept that accounting is concerned only with facts measurable in money, and for which measurements can obtain general agreement.

Going concern concept (p. 288): Assumption that a business is to continue for a long time.

Business entity concept (p. 288): Assumption that only transactions that affect the firm, and not the owner's private transactions, will be recorded.

Realization concept (p. 288): The concept of profit as being earned at a particular point.

Dual aspect concept (p. 288): The concept of dealing with both aspects of a transaction.

Accrual concept (p. 288): The concept that profit is the difference between revenues and expenses.

Materiality (p. 289): Recording something in a special way only if the amount is not a small one.

Prudence (p. 290): Ensuring that profit is not shown as being too high, or assets shown at too hight a value.

Consistency (p. 290): Keeping to the same method of recording transactions, except in special cases.

Quantifiability (p. 290): The ability to make a proper measure of the transaction.

Summary

1 Normally one set of final accounts has to serve many purposes.

2 The need for general agreement has given rise to the concepts and conventions that govern accounting records.

3 An assumption is made that monetary measures remain stable, i.e. that normally accounts are not adjusted for inflation or deflation.

4 The terms 'prudence' and 'conservatism' mean exactly the same thing.

Exercises

All the exercises shown are X questions, without answers. This is because sections 33.8 and 33.9 provided students with enough practice to test themselves.

33.1X Mr Wood is the sole owner of a trading company specializing in the sale of clocks. When he sees his first set of final accounts, prepared by his accountant, he asks the following questions.

(i) 'Why isn't something charged for my services against the profit. If I had to pay someone to do the duties I perform, then I would have to pay them at least $20,000 a year. Surely that should be charged as pay in the profit and loss account?'

(ii) 'I have kept our motor van in perfect condition. Why then should we have to charge something for depreciation?'

(iii) 'You have charged me for taking a clock for my personal use. If I did not have it, I might not be able to know when to go to the shop to start trading for the day. Surely it is a business expense?'

Required:
Explain to Mr Wood why you cannot agree to change the accounts because of the above statements.

33.2X Explain which accounting concept or convention is behind each of the following accounting entries in the books of Chan who has an accounting year end of 31 December.

(*a*) A smoke alarm costing $25 has been charged as sundry expenses even though it is expected to be in use for 5 years.

(*b*) A debt of $2,000 owing from Kong has been written off as a bad debt, even though his father is expected to die soon and leave him a fortune.

(*c*) Chan says that if he had to sell the stock very quickly he would be lucky if he got $10,000 for it, yet his accountant has shown it as an asset at cost $18,000.

(*d*) Chan wants to abolish his provision for bad debts account so as to show an increase in profits.

(*e*) Chan has been very lucky in buying some machinery at a bargain price of $75,000. Normally he would pay $140,000 for it. His accountant shows it in the balance sheet at the lower figure of $75,000, even though net realizeable value is $140,000.

33.3X John's accountant has drawn up the final accounts for the year ended 31 December 2004. John examines the accounts and asks the following questions. You answer them.

(*a*) I borrowed $100,000 from my uncle and he charges me 10% interest per annum. He allows me to add the interest to the outstanding loan and pay it all back in 10 years' time. Why then is the interest for 2004 charged as an expense in the profit and loss account?

(*b*) I maintain my machinery in perfect condition. Why then should it be depreciated in the accounts?

(*c*) Although everyone else disagrees with me, I think that my fixtures are worth three times as much as they are shown on the balance sheet. Why can't I show the increase in value?

(*d*) A man entering into business has to be an optimist, otherwise he would never do so. Why therefore should he be the opposite, a prudent person, when he draws up his accounts?

(*e*) Why do I have to charge carriage inwards in the trading account, whereas carriage outwards is charged in the profit and loss account? It's all concerned with carrying goods, so it's the same thing, surely?

33.4X Give examples of each of the following, *not* using the examples given in the textbook:

(*a*) materiality convention;

(*b*) business entity concept;

(*c*) prudence.

CHAPTER **34**

Partnership Accounts: An Introduction

Learning Objectives

- To understand exactly what a partnership is.
- To be able to distinguish between limited partners and the ones with unlimited liability.
- To know what the main features of a partnership agreement should be.
- To realize what will happen if no agreement has been made to share profits or losses.
- To be able to draw up the final accounts of a partnership.

34.1 The Need for Partnerships

So far we have considered mainly businesses owned by only one person. However, businesses that are set up to make a profit can often have more than one owner.

There are various reasons for multiple ownership:

- the capital required is more than one person can provide
- the experience or ability required to manage the business cannot be found in one person alone
- many people want to share management instead of doing everything on their own.

Very often, the partners will be members of the same family.

There are two types of multiple ownership: partnerships and limited companies. This chapter deals only with partnerships. Limited companies will be the subject of later chapters.

34.2 Nature of a Partnership

A **partnership** has the following characteristics.

- It is formed to make profits.
- It must obey the law as given in the Partnership Act of the Caribbean Commonwealth. The partnership laws in each of the Caribbean countries are very similar to one another. The differences are minor ones and may be ignored at this stage. The basic law from which the various countries' laws have evolved is the UK Partnership Act 1890.
- Normally there can be a minimum of 2 partners and a maximum of 20 partners.
- Exceptions are banks, where there cannot be more than 10 partners.

- Each partner (except for limited partners described below) must pay his or her share of any debts that the partnership cannot pay. If necessary, partners can be forced to sell all their private possessions to pay their share of the debts. This is what is meant by *unlimited liability*.

34.3 Limited Partners

Limited partners are not liable for the debts as described in Section 34.2 above. They have the following characteristics.

- Their liability for the debts of the partnership is limited to the capital they have put in. They can lose that capital, but they cannot be asked for any more money to pay the debts.
- They are not allowed to take part in the management of the partnership business. Not all the partners in a partnership can be limited partners: there must be at least one with unlimited liability.

34.4 Partnership Agreements

Agreements in writing are not necessary. However, it is better if a proper written agreement is drawn up by a lawyer or accountant. Where there is a proper written agreement there will be fewer problems between partners, and less confusion about what has been agreed.

34.5 Content of Partnership Agreements

The written agreement can contain as much, or as little, as the partners want. The law does not say what it must contain. The usual accounting contents are:

- the capital to be contributed by each partner
- the ratio in which profits (or losses) are to be shared
- the rate of interest, if any, to be paid on capital before the profits are shared
- the rate of interest, if any, to be charged on partners' drawings
- salaries to be paid to partners
- arrangements for the admission of new partners
- procedures to be carried out when a partner retires or dies.

The first five points are now examined in detail. The latter two will be taken up later.

Capital Contributions

Partners need not contribute equal amounts of capital. What matters is how much capital each partner *agrees* to contribute.

Profit- (or Loss)-sharing Ratios

Although partners can in fact agree to share profits/losses in any ratio that they desire, it is often thought by students that profits should be shared in the same ratio as that in which capital is contributed. For example, suppose the capitals were Allen $2,000 and Beet $1,000: many people would share the profits in the ratio of two-thirds to one-third, even though the work to be done by each partners is similar.

The division of the first few years' profits on such a basis is shown in Exhibit 34.1. It can be seen that in total Allen would receive $9,200, or $4,600 more than Beet. To treat each partner fairly, the difference between the two shares of profit when the duties of the partners are the same should be adequate to compensate Allen for putting extra capital into the firm. Some might feel that $4,600 extra profits is more than adequate for this purpose.

Consider too the capital ratio sharing of profits when one partner has put in $99,000 and the other $1,000 as capital. In this case, one partner would get 99/100ths of the profits, while the other would get only 1/100th!

To overcome the difficulty of compensating for the investment of extra capital, the concept of **interest on capital** was devised.

Exhibit 34.1

Years	*1*	*2*	*3*	*4*	*5*	*Total*
	$	$	$	$	$	$
Net profits	1,800	2,400	3,000	3,000	3,600	
Shared						
Allen ⅔	1,200	1,600	2,000	2,000	2,400	9,200
Beet ⅓	600	800	1,000	1,000	1,200	4,600

Interest on Capital

If the work to be done by each partner is of equal value but the capital contributed is unequal, it is reasonable to grant interest on the partners' capitals. This interest is treated as a deduction prior to the calculation of profits and their distribution according to the profit-sharing ratio.

The rate of interest is a matter of agreement between the partners, but it should equal the return they would have received if they had invested the capital elsewhere.

Taking Allen and Beet's firm again, but sharing the profits equally after charging 5% per annum interest on capital, the division of profits is shown in Exhibit 34.2. Here Allen has received $250 more than Beet, this being adequate return (in the partners' estimation) for her having invested an extra $1,000 in the firm for five years.

Exhibit 34.2

Years	*1*	*2*	*3*	*4*	*5*	*Total*
	$	$	$	$	$	$
Net profits	1,800	2,400	3,000	3,000	3,600	
Interest on capitals						
Allen	100	100	100	100	100 =	500
Beet	50	50	50	50	50 =	250
Remainder shared						
Allen ½	825	1,125	1,425	1,425	1,725 =	6,525
Beet ½	825	1,125	1,425	1,425	1,725 =	6,525

Summary	*Allen*	*Beet*
	$	$
Interest on capital	500	250
Balance of profits	6,525	6,525
	7,025	6,775

Interest on Drawings

It is obviously in the best interests of the firm if cash is withdrawn from the firm by the partners in accordance with the two basic principles of as little as possible and as late as possible. The more cash that is left in the firm, the more expansion can be financed, the greater the economies of having ample cash to take advantage of bargains and not missing out on cash discounts, and so on.

To deter the partners from taking out cash unnecessarily, the concept can be used of charging the partners interest on each withdrawal, calculated from the date of withdrawal to the end of the financial year. The amount charged to them helps to swell the profits divisible between the partners.

The rate of interest should be sufficient to achieve this without being too harsh.

Suppose that Allen and Beet have decided to charge interest on drawings at 5% per annum, and that their year end was 31 December. The drawings made are shown in Exhibit 34.3.

Exhibit 34.3

		Allen	
Drawings		*Interest*	
	$		$
1 January	100	$100 × 5% × 12 months	5
1 March	240	$240 × 5% × 10 months	10
1 May	120	$120 × 5% × 8 months	4
1 July	240	$240 × 5% × 6 months	6
1 October	80	$80 × 5% × 3 months	1
		Interest charged to Allen	26
		Beet	
Drawings		*Interest*	
	$		$
1 January	60	$60 × 5% × 12 months	3
1 August	480	$480 × 5% × 5 months	10
1 December	240	$240 × 5% × 1 month	1
		Interest charged to Beet	14

Salaries to Partners

One partner may have more responsibility or tasks than the others. As a reward for this, rather than change the profit and loss-sharing ratio, he or she may have their salary deducted before sharing the balance of profits.

34.6 An Example of the Distribution of Profits

Taylor and Clarke have been in partnership for one year, sharing profits and losses in the ratio of three-fifths to Taylor and two-fifths to Clarke. They are entitled to 5% per annum interest on capital, Taylor having $2,000 capital and Clarke $6,000. Clarke is to have a salary of $500. They charge interest on drawings, Taylor being charged $50 and Clarke $100. The net profit, before any distributions to the partners, amounted to $5,000 for the year ended 31 December 2007 (see Exhibit 34.4).

Exhibit 34.4

	$	$	$
Net profit			5,000
Add Charges for interest on drawings:			
Taylor		50	
Clarke		100	
			150
			5,150
Less Clarke's salary		500	
Interest on capital:			
Taylor	100		
Clarke	300		
		400	
			900
Balance of profits			4,250
Shared			
Taylor 3/5		2,550	
Clarke 2/5		1,700	
			4,250

The $5,000 net profits have therefore been shared as follows.

	Taylor $	*Clarke* $
Balance of profits	2,550	1,700
Interest on capital	100	300
Salary	—	500
	2,650	2,500
Less Interest on drawings	50	100
	2,600	2,400
	$5,000	

34.7 If There is No Partnership Agreement

A special section of the Partnership Act 1890 covers this situation. Quite simply, if there is no partnership agreement, written or otherwise, the following provisions will apply:

- profits and losses will be shared equally
- there is to be no interest on capital
- no interest is to be charged on drawings
- salaries are not allowed.

- If a partner puts a sum of money into a firm in excess of the capital he or she agreed to subscribe, that partner is entitled to interest at the rate of $x\%$ per annum on such an advance. (The percentage rate varies in different countries.)

34.8 The Final Accounts

If the sales, stock and expenses of partnership were exactly the same as those of a sole trader, then the trading and profit and loss accounts would be identical to those prepared for the sole trader. However, a partnership has an extra section shown under the profit and loss account. This section is called the *profit and loss appropriation account*, and it is in this account that the distribution of profits is shown. The heading to the trading and profit and loss accounts does not include the words 'appropriation account'. It is purely an accounting custom not to include it in the heading.

The trading and profit and loss accounts of Taylor and Clarke from the details given, plus revenue and expenses items, appear in Exhibit 34.5.

Exhibit 34.5

Taylor and Clarke
Trading and Profit and Loss Account for the year ended 31 December 2007

	$	$	$
Sales			48,500
Less Cost of goods sold:			
Purchases		41,500	
Less Closing stock		4,500	37,000
Gross profit			11,500
Less Expenses:			
Pay		2,400	
Rent and rates		3,200	
General expenses		900	6,500
Net profit			5,000
Add Interest on drawings			
Taylor		50	
Clarke		100	150
			5,150
Less Salary: Clarke		500	
Interest on capital			
Taylor	100		
Clarke	300	400	900
			4,250
Balance of profits shared			
Taylor $\frac{3}{5}$ths		2,550	
Clarke $\frac{2}{5}$ths		1,700	4,250

34.9 Capital Accounts

Each partner will want to know exactly the value of his or her holding in the firm. We can say that this consists of:

- the original capital put into the firm by the partner
- his or her share of the profits, interest on capital (if any), salary (if any), *less* interest on drawings (if any) and drawings themselves – in other words, this is really the amount of undrawn profits.

Now we could have an account for each partner which would contain both kinds of information. The balance on this account would fluctuate each year as drawings very rarely exactly equal profits. This is rather like a capital account in a sole trader's business. Because the balance fluctuates, these are called **fluctuating capital accounts**.

On the other hand, we could keep the original capital figure in an account for each partner. These we would keep at the same figure, and we would called these **fixed capital accounts**. We would show the share of the profits and interest on capital for each partner in separate accounts called *current accounts*.

Each of these methods can now be shown, using the example already seen of Taylor and Clarke. We can assume that the drawings for the year were $2,000 each.

Fixed Capital Accounts plus Current Accounts

Exhibit 34.6

Taylor: Capital

			2007		$
			Jan 1	Bank (Cash introduced)	2,000

Clarke: Capital

			2007		$
			Jan 1	Bank (Cash introduced)	6,000

Taylor: Current Account

2007		$	2007		$
Dec 31	Cash: drawings	2,000	Dec 31	Profit and loss	
Dec 31	Profit and loss			appropriation account:	
	appropriation account:			Interest on capital	100
	Interest on drawings	50		Share of profits	2,550
Dec 31	Balance c/d	600			
		2,650			2,650
			2008		
			Jan 1	Balance b/d	600

(Cont'd)

Clarke: Current Account

2007		$	2007		$
Dec 31	Cash: drawings	2,000	Dec 31	Profit and loss	
Dec 31	Profit and loss			appropriation account:	
	appropriation account:			Interest on capital	300
	Interest on drawings	100		Share of profits	1,700
Dec 31	Balance c/d	400		Salary	500
		2,500			2,500
			2008		
			Jan 1	Balance b/d	400

In Exhibit 34.6, notice that Clarke's salary was not given to him as such – it was merely credited to his account. If in fact it was paid in addition to his drawings, the $500 cash paid would have been debited to the current account, changing the $400 credit balance into a $100 debit balance.

Fluctuating capital accounts

The distribution of profits would be credited to the capital account, and the drawings and interest on drawings debited. Therefore the balance on the capital account will change each year; i.e. it will fluctuate.

If fluctuating capital accounts had been kept for Taylor and Clarke, they would have appeared as shown in Exhibit 34.7.

Exhibit 34.7

Taylor: Capital

2007		$	2007		$
Dec 31	Cash: drawings	2,000	Jan 1	Bank	2,000
Dec 31	Profit and loss		Dec 31	Profit and loss	
	appropriation account:			appropriation account:	
	Interest on drawings	50		Interest on capital	100
Dec 31	Balance c/d	2,600		Share of profits	2,550
		4,650			4,650
			2008		
			Jan 1	Balance b/d	2,600

(Cont'd)

Clarke: Capital

2007		$	2007		$
Dec 31	Cash: drawings	2,000	Jan 1	Bank	6,000
Dec 31	Profit and loss appropriation account:		Dec 31	Profit and loss appropriation account:	
	Interest on drawings	100		Interest on capital	300
Dec 31	Balance c/d	6,400		Salary	500
				Share of profits	1,700
		8,500			8,500
			2008		
			Jan 1	Balance b/d	6,400

These accounts, whether fixed or fluctuating, could have been shown in columnar fashion. This will be illustrated for fluctuating capital accounts (Exhibit 34.8). You can see that all that has happened when drawing up columnar capital accounts is that the accounts for each partner have the figures displayed in separate columns instead of using separate accounts. Examiners often ask for partnership capital accounts to be displayed in this way.

Exhibit 34.8

Capital Accounts

		Taylor	Clarke			Taylor	Clarke
2007		$	$	2007		$	$
Dec 31	Cash: drawings	2,000	2,000	Jan 1	Bank	2,000	6,000
Dec 31	Profit and loss appropriation account:			Dec 31	Profit and loss appropriation account:		
	Interest on drawings	50	100		Interest on capital	100	300
Dec 31	Balances c/d	2,600	6,400	Dec 31	Salary		500
				Dec 31	Share of profits	2,550	1,700
		4,650	8,500			4,650	8,500
				2008			
				Jan 1	Balances b/d	2,600	6,400

34.10 Fixed Capital Accounts Preferred

The keeping of fixed capital accounts plus current accounts is considered preferable to fluctuating capital accounts. When partners are taking out greater amounts than the share of the profits they are entitled to, this is shown up by a debit balance on the current account and so acts as a warning.

34.11 The Balance Sheet

We can look at the capital and liabilities sides only of the balance sheets for Taylor and Clarke, using both fixed and fluctuating capital accounts (Exhibit 34.9).

Exhibit 34.9

Fixed capital					$
Capital					
Taylor					2,000
Clarke					6,000
					8,000
Current accounts		*Taylor*		*Clarke*	
	$	$	$	$	
Interest on capital		100		300	
Salary				500	
Share of profits		2,550		1,700	
		2,650		2,500	
Less Drawings	2,000		2,000		
Less Interest on drawings	50	2,050	100	2,100	
		600		400	1,000
					9,000
Fluctuating capital					$
Capital		*Taylor*		*Clarke*	
	$	$	$	$	
Cash introduced		2,000		6,000	
Interest on capital		100		300	
Salary				500	
Share of profits		2,550		1,700	
		4,650		8,500	
Less Drawings	2,000		2,000		
Less Interest on drawings	50	2,050	100	2,100	
		2,600		6,400	9,000

If one of the current accounts had finished in debit, for instance if the current account of Clarke had finished up as $400 debit, the abbreviation Dr. would appear and the balances would appear net in the totals column:

	Taylor	*Clarke*	
	$	$	$
Closing balances	600	400 *Dr.*	200

If the net figure turned out to be a debit figure, then this would be deducted from the total of the capital accounts.

New Terms

Partnership (p. 295): A firm in which two or more people are working together as owners with a view to making profits.

Limited partner (p. 296): A partner whose liability is limited to the capital he or she has put into the firm.

Interest on capital (p. 297): An amount at an agreed rate of interest which is credited to a partner based on the amount of capital contributed by that partner.

Interest on drawings (p. 298): An amount at an agreed rate of interest based on the drawings taken out which is debited to the partners.

Partnership salary (p. 298): An agreed amount payable to a partner in respect of duties undertaken by that partner.

Fluctuating capital accounts (p. 301): Capital accounts whose balances change from one period to the next.

Fixed capital accounts (p. 301): Capital accounts that consist only of the amounts of capital actually paid into the firm.

Summary

1. There is no limited liability in partnerships except for 'limited partners'.
2. The contents of a partnership agreement will override anything written in this chapter. Partners can agree to anything they want to, in as much or as little detail as they wish.
3. If there is no partnership agreement, then the provisions of the Partnership Act, (details shown in Section 34.7) will apply.
4. Partners can agree to show their capital accounts using either the fixed capital or fluctuating capital methods.
5. If more than 20 owners of an organization are needed, then a partnership would not be suitable; instead, a limited company would be preferable.

Exercises

34.1 Stephens, Owen and Jones are partners. They share profits and losses in the ratios of ⅖, ⅖ and ⅕ respectively.

For the year ended 31 December 2006, their capital accounts remained fixed at the following amounts:

	$
Stephens	6,000
Owen	4,000
Jones	2,000

They have agreed to give each other 10% interest per annum on their capital accounts.

In addition to the above, partnership salaries of $3,000 for Owen and $1,000 for Jones are to be charged.

The net profit of the partnership, before taking any of the above into account, was $25,200.

You are required to draw up the appropriation account of the partnership for the year ended 31 December 2006.

34.2 Draw up a profit and loss appropriation account for the year ended 31 December 2007 and balance sheet extracts at that date, from the following.

1 Net profit $30,350.
2 Interest to be charged on capitals: Williams, $2,000; Powell, $1,500; Howe, $900.
3 Interest to be charged on drawings: Williams, $240; Powell, $180; Howe, $130.
4 Salaries to be credited: Powell, $2,000; Howe, $3,500.
5 Profits to be shared: Williams, 50%; Powell, 30%; Howe, 20%.
6 Current accounts: Williams, $1,860; Powell, $946; Howe, $717.
7 Capital accounts: Williams, $40,000; Powell, $30,000; Howe, $18,000.
8 Drawings: Williams, $9,200; Powell, $7,100; Howe, $6,900.

34.3X Dent, Bishop and White are in partnership. They share profits and losses in the ratio 3:2:1 respectively. Interest is charged on drawings at the rate of 10% per annum and credited at the same rate in respect of the balances on the partners' capital accounts.
Bishop is to be credited with a salary of $2,000 per annum.

In the year to 31 December 2004 the net profit of the firm was $50,400. The partners' drawings of Dent $8,000, Bishop $7,200 and White $4,800 were taken in two equal instalments by the partners on 1 April 2004 and 1 October 2004.

The balances of the partner's accounts 31 December 2003 were as follows (all credit balances):

	Capital accounts	*Current accounts*
	$	$
Dent	30,000	750
Bishop	28,000	1,340
White	16,000	220

You are required to:

(*a*) prepare the firm's profit and loss appropriation account for the year ended 31 December 2004;
(*b*) show how the partners' capital and current accounts are recorded in the balance sheet as at 31 December 2004.

34.4 Mendez and Marshall are in partnership, sharing profits and losses equally. The following is their trial balance as at 30 June 2006.

	Dr.	*Cr.*
	$	$
Buildings at cost	50,000	
Fixtures at cost	11,000	
Provision for depreciation: fixtures		3,300
Debtors	16,243	
Creditors		11,150
Cash at bank	677	
Stock at 30 June 2005	41,979	
Sales		123,650
Purchases	85,416	
Carriage outwards	1,288	
Discounts allowed	115	
Loan interest: Khan	4,000	
Office expenses	2,416	
Pay	18,917	
Bad debts	503	
Provision for bad debts		400
Loan from J. Khan		40,000

(Cont'd)

Capital:		
Mendez		35,000
Marshall		29,500
Current accounts:		
Mendez		1,306
Marshall		298
Drawings:		
Mendez	6,400	
Marshall	5,650	
	244,604	244,604

Prepare a trading and profit and loss appropriation account for the year ended 30 June 2006, and a balance sheet as at that date.

1 Stock, 30 June 2006: $56,340
2 Expenses to be accrued: office expenses, $96; pay, $200.
3 Depreciate fixtures 10% on reducing balance basis. Depreciate buildings $1,000.
4 Reduce provision for bad debts to $320.
5 Partnership salary: $800 to Mendez. Not yet entered.
6 Interest on drawings: Mendez, $180, Marshall, $120.
7 Interest on capital account balances at 10%.

34.5X Oscar and Felix are in partnership. They share profits in the ratio, Oscar 60%, Felix 40%. The following trial balance was extracted as at 31 March 2006.

	Dr. $	*Cr.* $
Office equipment at cost	6,500	
Motor vehicles at cost	9,200	
Provision for depreciation at 31 March 2005:		
Motor vehicles		3,680
Office equipment		1,950
Stock 31 March 2005	24,970	
Debtors and creditors	20,960	16,275
Cash at bank	615	
Cash in hand	140	
Sales		90,370
Purchases	71,630	
Pay	8,417	
Office expenses	1,370	
Discounts allowed	563	
Current accounts at 31 March 2005:		
Oscar		1,379
Felix		1,211
Capital accounts:		
Oscar		27,000
Felix		12,000
Drawings:		
Oscar	5,500	
Felix	4,000	
	153,865	153,865

Draw up a set of final accounts for the year ended 31 March 2006 for the partnership. The following notes are applicable at 31 March 2006.

1 Stock 31 March 2006: $27,340.
2 Office expenses owing, $110.
3 Provide for depreciation: motors, 20% of cost, office equipment, 10% of cost.

(Cont'd)

4 Charge interest on capital at 10%.
5 Charge interest on drawings: Oscar, $180, Felix, $210.

34.6 Q and P have similar businesses and decide to amalgamate and form a partnership. On 1 January 2005 they had the following assets and liabilities:

	Q	*P*
	$	$
Equipment	7,000	8,500
Debtors	2,100	3,900
Stock	12,000	9,000
Premises	15,000	—
Motor van	—	7,200
Creditors	1,970	2,040
Prepaid expenses	300	230
Expenses owing	430	790

From 1 January 2005, they agreed that:
1 profits and losses would be shared equally;
2 interest on capital at 10% would be allowed;
3 P was to get a salary of $2,000 per annum;
4 Interest on drawings at 10% per annum would be charged; for 2005 this amounted to $120 for Q and $200 for P.

For the year to 31 December 2005, a net profit of $23,680 was made. Q's drawings were $5,200 and P's, $8,400.

You are required to:
(*a*) ascertain opening capitals;
(*b*) draw up a profit and loss appropriation account for the year ended 31 December 2005;
(*c*) draw up capital accounts as they would be shown in the balance sheet as at 31 December 2005, assuming fluctuating capital accounts are to be used.

(CXC style)

34.7X Steve and Jane are in partnership. The terms of the partnership are:
1 profit and losses to be shared in the ratios Steve ⅔, Jane ⅓;
2 10% interest is allowable on fixed capitals;
3 10% interest is to be charged on drawings, whenever taken;
4 Jane is to have a salary of $6,000.

The following profit and loss account for the year ended 31 December 2003 is:

Steve and Jane
Profit and Loss Account for the year ended 31 December 2003

	$	$		$
Pay		17,560	Net profit b/d	56,000
Interest on loan from T. Briggs		2,000		
Interest on capital:				
Steve	4,000			
Jane	6,000	10,000		
Drawings:				
Steve	6,000			
Jane	9,000	15,000		
Rent and rates		4,440		
Net profit		7,000		
		56,000		56,000

Steve and Jane are surprised at the above accounts.

(Cont'd)

The following is also made available:

(i) pay includes Jane's salary of $6,000;

(ii) as yet, no interest has been charged on drawings;

(iii) other balances include the following as at 31 December 2003:

	$
Capital:	
Steve	40,000
Jane	60,000
Current accounts:	
Steve	500 *Dr.*
Jane	3,700 *Cr.*

Using what has been given already:

(*a*) redraft the profit and loss account;

(*b*) draw up the profit and loss appropriation account;

(*c*) write up the current accounts of the partners;

(*d*) what do the balances on the current accounts signify?

(*CXC style*)

CHAPTER **35**

New Partners: Entries on Admission, Goodwill and Premiums

Learning Objectives

- To understand why new partners may be needed.
- To understand the meaning of goodwill.
- To be able to make adjustments for goodwill in partnership accounts.

35.1 Reasons for Admission of a New Partner

New partners may be admitted to a partnership, usually for one of three reasons:

1. as an additional partner, either because the firm has grown or because someone is needed who has different skills to those of the existing partners;
2. to replace a partner who is leaving the firm: this might be because of the retirement or death of a partner;
3. to bring in additional capital.

35.2 Capital to be Contributed

As we have seen in the last chapter, the amount of capital to be brought into a business by a new partner is dependent on the agreement drawn up between the old partners and the new partner.

35.3 The Nature of Goodwill

Suppose you have been in business for some years and you want to sell up. How much would you ask as the total sale price of the business? You decide to list how much you could get for each asset if sold separately. This list might be as follows.

	$
Buildings	225,000
Machinery	75,000
Debtors	60,000
Stock	40,000
	400,000

Instead, however, you sell the whole of the business as a going concern to Ms Lee for $450,000. She has therefore paid $50,000 more than the total for all the assets. This extra payment of $50,000 is for what is called **goodwill**.

Ms Lee has paid this because she wanted to take over the business as a going concern. Thus,

Purchased goodwill = Total price – Value of identifiable assets

35.4 Reasons for Payment of Goodwill

In buying an existing business which has been established for some time, there may be quite a few possible advantages. For example:

- there is a large number of regular customers who will continue to deal with the business under a new owner
- the business has a good reputation
- it has efficient and reliable employees
- it is in a good location
- it has good contacts with suppliers.

Few of those advantages are available to a completely new business. For this reason, many people will decide to buy an existing business and pay an extra amount for goodwill.

35.5 Existence of Goodwill

Goodwill does not necessarily exist in a business, even if it is a going concern. If the business has a bad reputation, an inefficient workforce or other negative factors, the owners may be unlikely to be paid for goodwill on selling the business.

35.6 Methods of Calculating Goodwill

There is no single way of calculating goodwill on which everyone can agree. The seller will probably want more for the goodwill than the buyer will want to pay. All that is certain is that, when an agreement is reached between buyer and seller, the selling price includes the amount of goodwill. Various methods are used to help buyer and seller come to an agreed figure. The calculations give buyer and seller a figure with which to begin discussions of the value of the business.

Very often, each industry or occupation has its own customary way of calculating goodwill.

Average Sales Method

In many retail businesses the average yearly sales for the past few years are multiplied by an agreed figure.

For instance, suppose that it is agreed that the goodwill should be three times the average yearly sales for the last two years. Exhibit 35.1 shows such a calculation.

Exhibit 35.1

Year	*Sales*
	$
2005	140,000
2006	160,000
Total	300,000

Average annual sales = $300,000 ÷ 2 = $150,000
Goodwill = 3 × $150,000 = $450,000

Annual Fees Method

Professional firms, such as accountants or lawyers, often use a method based on gross annual income from fees, before charging expenses. Exhibit 35.2 shows such a calculation.

Exhibit 35.2

A firm of accountants is selling its business. It is asking a figure for goodwill that is two and a half times the average annual fees received for the last two years.

Year	*Sales*
	$
2005	180,000
2006	220,000
Total	400,000

Average annual fees = $400,000 ÷ 2 = $200,000
Goodwill = 2.5 × $200,000 = $500,000

Average Net Annual Profits Method

Using this method, the average net profits for a number of years is multiplied by a stated amount. An illustration is given in Exhibit 35.3.

Exhibit 35.3

Suppose goodwill is taken to be four times the average net annual profits for the past three years.

Year	*Net profits*
	$
2004	62,000
2005	69,000
2006	79,000
Total	210,000

Average net annual profits = $210,000 ÷ 3 = $70,000
Goodwill = 4 × $70,000 = $280,000

Super Profits Method

It may be argued, as in the case of a sole trader, for example, that the net profits are not 'true' profits. This is because the sole trader has not charged for the following expenses.

- The services of the proprietor. The proprietor has worked in the business, but has not charged for such services. Any drawings that he or she makes are charged to a capital account, not to the profit and loss account.
- The use of the money the proprietor has invested in the business. If this money had been invested elsewhere it would have earned interest or dividends.

Super profits are what is left of the net profits after allowances have been made for the services of the proprietor and the use of his or her capital.

It is usually calculated as follows.

	$	$
Annual net profits		80,000
Less Remuneration proprietor would have earned for similar work elsewhere	20,000	
Interest that would have been earned if capital had been invested elsewhere	10,000	30,000
Annual super profits		50,000

The annual super profits are then multiplied by a number agreed by the seller and purchaser of the business.

35.7 Goodwill on Admission of New Partners

The new partner will be entitled to a share in the profits, and normally, will also be entitled to the same share of the value of goodwill. It is correct to charge a new partner for taking over that share of the goodwill.

35.8 Calculation of Goodwill Adjustments

This calculation is carried out in three stages.

1. Show the value of goodwill divided between the original partners in the old profit- and loss-sharing ratios.
2. Then show the value of goodwill divided between the partners in the new partnership in the new profit- and loss-sharing ratio.
3. Goodwill *gain* shown: charge partners for the gain.
   Goodwill *loss* shown: give partners an allowance for their losses.

This is illustrated in Exhibits 35.4 and 35.5. We will see that the method in Exhibit 35.5 is the same as that in 35.4 even when old partners take a different share of the profit from each other than before the change.

Exhibit 35.4

A and B are in partnership, sharing profits and losses equally. C is admitted as a new partner. The three partners will share profits and losses one-third each. Total goodwill is valued at $60,000.

Stage 1			**Stage 2**		**Stage 3**		
Partners	*Old profit shares*	*Share of goodwill*	*New profit shares*	*Share of goodwill*	*Gained or lost*	*To compensate for lost*	*To charge for gain*
		$		$	$		
A	½	30,000	⅓	20,000	10,000 lost	*Cr.* A Capital	
B	½	30,000	⅓	20,000	10,000 lost	*Cr.* B Capital	
C		—	⅓	20,000	20,000 gained		*Dr.* C Capital
		60,000		60,000			

This means that A and B need to have their capitals increased by $10,000 each. C needs his capital reducing by $20,000. You may well wonder why A and B should have their capitals increased by $10,000 each, i.e. receive a credit of $10,000 in each of their capital accounts. They have each given up part of their ownership of an asset, in this case goodwill, to the new partner, C. C should be charged for this, which is done by debiting his capital account by $20,000. As it is A and B that have passed over to him part of their ownership, the corresponding credits should be made in their capital accounts for $10,000 each. If this were not done, they would have given up their shares of the goodwill for nothing.

Note that A and B have kept their profits in the same ratio to each other. While they used to have one-half each, now they have one-third each.

Exhibit 35.5

D and E are in partnership sharing profits one-half each. A new partner F is admitted. Profits will now be shared D one-fifth, and E and F two-fifths each. D and E have therefore not kept their shares equal to each other.

Goodwill is valued at $60,000. It can be seen that D needs her capital increased by $18,000; E's capital is to be increased by $6,000; and F needs his capital reduced by $24,000.

(Cont'd)

Stage 1			Stage 2		Stage 3		
Partners	*Old profit shares*	*Share of goodwill*	*New profit shares*	*Share of goodwill*	*Gained or lost*	*To compensate for lost*	*To charge for gain*
		$		$	$		
D	½	30,000	⅕	12,000	18,000 lost	*Cr.* D Capital	
E	½	30,000	⅖	24,000	6,000 lost	*Cr.* E Capital	
F			⅖	24,000	24,000 gained		*Dr.* F Capital
		60,000		60,000			

35.9 Accounting Entries for Goodwill Adjustments

These depend on how the partners wish to arrange the adjustment. Three methods are usually used.

1 Cash is paid by the new partner privately to the old partners for his or her share of the goodwill. No goodwill account is opened. In Exhibit 35.5, F would therefore give $24,000 in cash: $18,000 to D and $6,000 to E. D and E would bank these amounts in their private bank accounts. No entry would be made for this in the accounts of the partnership.

2 Cash is paid by the new partner into the business bank account for his or her share of the goodwill. No goodwill account is opened. Assume that the capital balances before F was admitted were D $50,000 and E $50,000, and F was to paid in $50,000 as capital plus $24,000 for goodwill. In Exhibit 35.5 the entries would be shown in the capital accounts as seen in Exhibit 35.6.

Exhibit 35.6

Capital Accounts							
	D	*E*	*F*		*D*	*E*	*F*
	$	$	$		$	$	$
Adjustments for gain of goodwill			24,000	Balances b/f	50,000	50,000	
Balances c/d	68,000	56,000	50,000	Cash for capital			50,000
				Adjustments for loss of goodwill	18,000	6,000	
				Cash for goodwill			24,000
	68,000	56,000	74,000		68,000	56,000	74,000

3 A goodwill account is to be opened. No extra cash is to be paid in by the new partner for goodwill. The opening capitals were D $50,000, E. $50,000; F paid in $50,000 as capital.
Here the action required is as follows.
   (i) **Debit** goodwill account with total value of goodwill. **Credit** capitals of old partners with their shares of goodwill in old profit ratios.
   (ii) **Debit** adjustments gains to partners' capitals. **Credit** adjustment losses to partners' capitals.

For Exhibit 35.5, the entries would appear as shown in Exhibit 35.7.

Exhibit 35.7

Goodwill

	$		$
Value divided:			
D capital	30,000	Balance c/d	60,000
E capital	30,000		
	60,000		60,000

Capital Accounts

	D $	*E* $	*F* $		*D* $	*E* $	*F* $
Adjustments for gain of goodwill			24,000	Balances b/f	50,000	50,000	
Balances c/d	98,000	86,000	26,000	Cash for capital			50,000
				Goodwill	30,000	30,000	
				Adjustments for loss of goodwill	18,000	6,000	
	98,000	86,000	50,000		98,000	86,000	50,000

35.10 Premiums for Goodwill

The amounts paid in by the new partners, or charged to them, for goodwill is often known as a **premium**.

Sometimes all that is known is that a partner has paid a certain amount for his or her share of the goodwill, but you are not told the total value of goodwill. A little arithmetic will help you find the total value. Thus, $10,000 for a one-third share means that goodwill is valued at $30,000, while $10,000 for a one-fourth share means that goodwill is valued at $40,000.

New Terms

Goodwill (p. 311): The excess amount that has to be paid to acquire a part or the whole of a business as a going concern over and above the value of the net assets owned by the business.

Super profits (p. 313): Net profits less allowance for alternative earnings and alternative return on capital invested.

Premium (p. 316): The amounts paid in by, or charged to, new partners for goodwill.

Summary

1 The true value of goodwill can be established only when the business is sold, but for various reasons of fairness between partners it is valued the best way possible when there is no imminent sale of a business.
2 If the old partners agree, a new partner can be admitted without paying anything in as capital.
3 Goodwill is usually owned by the partners in the ratio in which they share profits.
4 If there is a change in partnership without adjustments for goodwill, then some partners will make an unfair gain while others will quite unfairly lose money.
5 If a new partner pays a specific amount for his or her share of the goodwill, then that payment is said to be a 'premium'.

Exercises

35.1 June Graves and Cyril Regis want you to value the goodwill of their business, which they are going to sell. You advise them that for their kind of business the 'average sales method' is appropriate.

They say that they would agree to a valuation of four times the average yearly sales for the last three years. The sales for the last three years have been: 2001, $240,000; 2002, $280,000; 2003, $275,000.

Show your calculation of the value of goodwill.

35.2X Hill and Dale are selling their business. They are asking for a value for goodwill of one and a half times the average yearly sales for the last four years.

Sales have been: 2002, $160,000; 2003, $192,000; 2004, $188,000; 2005, $208,000.

Calculate the value placed on the goodwill by the partners.

35.3 Scott and Simpson are selling their dental practice. They are asking a figure for goodwill which is five times the average annual fees received for the last four years. The fees received were as follows.

	$
2001	163,500
2002	181,000
2003	178,500
2004	201,000

You are required to calculated the value of goodwill in accordance with the above figures.

35.4X Rivers and Nelson, a firm of patent agents, are selling their firm. For goodwill they are asking for a figure that is three times the average annual fees received for the last five years. The fees received amounted to the totals listed below.

	$
2001	250,000
2002	295,000
2003	275,000
2004	370,000
2005	425,000

You are to calculate the figure they are asking for goodwill.

35.5 James Barnes is selling his business. He has worked full-time in the business. Drawings, as they should be, have been charged up to his capital account, not to the profit and loss account.

The cash that Barnes has invested in the business amounts to $200,000. If he had invested it elsewhere he would have been able to get interest on it of 12%.

Barnes is a qualified engineer. If he had not been working in his own business he could have been employed elsewhere for $60,000 a year.

His accountant advises him to value his goodwill at a figure equalling five years of 'super profits'.

Required:
Calculate the value of goodwill at the figure stipulated by the accountant, given the above information and the fact that his annual net profits amount to $110,000.

35.6X Rita Worrall wants to sell her business. For goodwill, she is going to ask for a figure equalling eight years of 'super profits'.

Worrall has invested $60,000 in her business. If she had invested it elsewhere with similar risk, she would have earned 9% on her money.

If she had worked elsewhere, rather than in her own business, she could have earned $35,000 a year.

Her annual net profits from the business have been $55,000 a year.

From the above, you are required to calculate the figure that she should be asking for goodwill.

35.7 Marshall and Russell are in partnership sharing profits and losses in the ratio of Marshall two-thirds, Russell one-third. A new partner, Sangster, is introduced. Profits will be shared in the ratio: Marshall one-half, Russell one-quarter, Sangster one-quarter. Just before the introduction of Sangster, the balance sheet had been as set out below.

Balance Sheet as at 31 December 2004

	$	$
Fixed assets		
Buildings		11,000
Current assets		
Stock	6,000	
Debtors	2,000	
Bank	1,000	
	9,000	
Less Current liabilities		
Creditors	2,000	
Working capital		7,000
		18,000
Capital:		
Marshall	10,000	
Russell	8,000	18,000

(Cont'd)

Show the different balance sheets given the different situations below after Sangster is introduced on 1 January 2005.

(*a*) Sangster pays in a $8,000 cheque for capital, plus another $3,000 for his share of the goodwill; or instead

(*b*) Sangster pays in an $8,000 cheque for capital; the $3,000 for goodwill is paid privately by him to Marshall & Russell; or instead

(*c*) a goodwill account is to be opened of total estimated value $12,000. Sangster pays into the business a cheque for $8,000 only in respect of capital.

35.8X Lee and Henry are in partnership, sharing profits and losses in the ratios Lee 3: Henry 2. A new partner, Nunez, is introduced. Profit will be shared in the ratios Lee 3: Henry 2: Nunez 1. Before the introduction of Nunez, the balance sheet had been as follows.

Balance Sheet as at 31 March 2005

	$	$	$
Fixed assets			
Fixtures			3,000
Motor vehicles			7,000
			10,000
Current assets			
Stock		3,500	
Debtors		1,500	
		5,000	
Less Current liabilities			
Creditors	3,000		
Bank overdraft	2,000	5,000	
Working capital:			—
			10,000
Capital:			
Lee		5,000	
Henry		5,000	10,000

Show the different balance sheets under the following different proposals.

(*a*) Nunez paid in $4,000 cheque as capital and $3,000 cheque for his share of the goodwill.

(*b*) Nunez paid in $4,000 cheque for capital; the $3,000 for goodwill was paid privately by him to Lee and Henry.

(*c*) A goodwill account was opened for $18,000; Nunez paid in a cheque for $4,000 only in respect of capital.

CHAPTER **36**

Sales and Purchases Analysis Books

Learning Objectives

- To decide which basis is to be used for the selection of analysis columns for columnar day books.
- To write up analysis books for sales, purchases or for any other aspect of an organization.

36.1 Introduction

In many cases, just knowing the total of the credit sales or credit purchases of a business is not enough. We may wish to know more than that. There are a number of reasons why we would want more information.

36.2 Departmental Use

Our firm may have various departments. We may want to know how much of our sales and purchases were for each department. There would be a 'Total' column, in which the totals of each invoice would be entered; then there would be extra columns, one for each department. Such a book could be called either a **sales analysis book** or a columnar book. Exhibit 36.1 is an example.

Exhibit 36.1

Sales Analysis Book

Date	Name of firm	Total	Sports Dept	Household Dept	Electrical Dept
2005		$	$	$	$
May 1	N. Coward	190		190	
May 5	L. Olivier	200	200		
May 8	R. Colman and Co.	307	102		205
May 16	A. Smith	480			480
May 27	H. Marshall	222	110	45	67
May 31	W. Pratt	1,800		800	1,000
		3,199	412	1,035	1,752

In this exhibit the sales to N. Coward were all goods from the Household Department. The sales to R. Colman & Co were $102 of goods from the Sports Department and $205 goods from the Electrical Department. When added up at the end of the month we can find the total of sales for each department. The total of the total column should equal the sum of all the other totals; i.e., $412 + $1,035 + $1,752 = $3,199. A columnar **purchases analysis book** would be similarly drawn up.

36.3 Control Accounts Use

If we have control accounts (see Chapter 19), we may have more than one sales ledger or more than one purchases ledger. In this case we need to know the amount of sales or purchases and other items entered in each ledger.

If we had three purchases ledgers, containing accounts for customers with name initials A to F, G to O and P to Z, the purchases analysis or columnar book might be as in Exhibit 36.2. We now know that the purchases entered during February 2006 in the A–F purchases ledger amounted to $396, $1,635 in the G–O ledger and $130 in the P–Z ledger.

Exhibit 36.2

Purchases Analysis Book

Date	**Details**	**Total**	**Ledgers**		
			A–F	G–O	P–Z
2006		$	$	$	$
Feb 1	J. Archer	58	58		
Feb 3	G. Gaunt	103		103	
Feb 4	T. Brown	116	116		
Feb 8	C. Dunn	205	205		
Feb 10	A. Smith	16			16
Feb 12	P. Smith	114			114
Feb 15	D. Owen	88		88	
Feb 18	B. Blake	17	17		
Feb 22	T. Green	1,396		1,396	
Feb 27	C. Males	48		48	
		2,161	396	1,635	130

36.4 Other Uses

Another way of keeping a columnar sales book would be to find the sales in each geographical area. For instance, we may sell goods to customers in Jamaica. West Africa and France. The sales book might be as shown in Exhibit 36.3.

Exhibit 36.3

Sales Analysis Book					
Date	**Details**	**Total**	**Jamaica**	**West Africa**	**France**
2006		$	$	$	$
May 1	R. Smith	407	407		
May 5	T. Ogunlade	116		116	
May 8	P. Mitterand	210			210
May 12	T. Sangster	1,165	1,165		
May 18	K. Distel	180			180
May 22	J. Onifade	307		307	
May 31	L. Nwosu	416		416	
		2,801	1,572	839	390

The examples shown in this chapter do not cover all the possibilities, as we can use the analysis columns to obtain desirable information in any way that we may wish.

36.5 Advantages of Analysis Books

The advantages of analysis books are that we are provided with exactly the information we need, at the time when we want it. Different firms have different needs, and therefore analyse their books in different ways.

Analysis books will enable us to do such things as:

- calculate the profit or loss made by each part of a business
- draw up control accounts for the sales and purchases ledgers
- keep a check on the sales of each type of goods
- keep a check on goods sold in the Caribbean and those sold overseas
- find the purchase of each type of goods.

New Terms

Sales analysis book (p. 320): The addition of extra columns to a sales journal to enable the transactions to be analysed in a desirable manner (also called a *columnar sales analysis book*).

Purchases analysis book (p. 321): The addition of extra columns to a purchases journal to enable the transactions to be analysed for a particular purpose (also called a *columnar purchases analysis book*).

Summary

1 Where there is more than one sales ledger, or more than one purchases ledger, it is often the case that analysis books will have provided the figures for sales or purchases for each control account.
2 Computers make the analysis of transactions much easier than with manual methods.
3 The extra information obtained via sales and purchases analysis books enables the profit or loss for each section of the business to be calculated.

Exercises

36.1 J. Goode subdivides her purchases ledger into three alphabetical sections: A–G, H–M and N–Z, the creditors' accounts being entered according to their surnames.

Draw up a purchases analysis book (or journal) with appropriate analysis columns and enter the following invoices. Rule and total for the period 1–6 February 2009.

Date	Supplier	Invoice no	Invoice total
2009			$
Feb 1	F. Archer	21	960
Feb 2	J. Potter	22	360
Feb 3	J. Harris	23	575
Feb 4	C. Cooper	24	106
Feb 5	B. Singh	25	91
Feb 6	F. Lewis	26	450

36.2X D. Johnson, a hardware merchant, divides his business into three departments: glass, china and miscellaneous. During October 2006 Johnson made the following sales.

2006		
Oct 4	To John Davis:	
	100 buckets	@ $6 per ten
	48 pans	@ $2 each
	10 jugs (china)	@ $10 each
	50 teapots (china)	@ $15 each
Oct 17	To D. Brown:	
	150 glasses	@ $50 per hundred
Oct 20	To F. James:	
	6 teapots (china)	@ $14 each
	25 buckets	@ $8 per ten
	18 glass flower bowls	@ $4 each

You are required to:
(*a*) prepare D. Johnson's tabular sales journal and enter the above listed items therein;
(*b*) post from the sales journal to the nominal and the personal ledgers.

36.3 T. York has three sales ledgers, each one representing a particular geographical area. These are Britain, the Far East and the United States.

Draw up a sales journal, with appropriate analysis columns, in respect of the following sales for May 2006.

(Cont'd)

2006		$
May 1	Hiram K. Hiram, New York	119
May 3	P. Osaki, Tokyo	288
May 5	B. Hardcastle, London	249
May 10	A. Smith, London	44
May 15	T. Roosevelt, Washington	387
May 17	L. Nakamura, Tokyo	84
May 19	C. Rockefeller, Los Angeles	219
May 28	I. Aoki, Singapore	188
May 31	S. Chang, Hong Kong	572

36.4X M. Lyle has a sports store with four departments: Golf, Cricket, Football and Tennis. The following are the details of sales for the month of September 2005. You are to write up a sales journal with appropriate analysis columns.

2005		$
Sept 1	T. Holt, golf clubs	388
Sept 3	M. Nunez, cricket gear $165, footballs $99	264
Sept 5	P. Moores, tennis nets	65
Sept 8	N. Good, golf balls, $67; football posts, $432	499
Sept 11	H. Hart, tennis balls, $44; golf clubs, $66	110
Sept 12	T. Holt, tennis racquets	70
Sept 18	P. O'Hara, cricket bats	55
Sept 21	P. Chester, footballs, $123; cricket balls, $66	189
Sept 30	H. Patterson, football kits	111

CHAPTER **37**

Manufacturing Accounts

Learning Objectives

- To be able to calculate prime cost and production cost of goods manufactured.
- To be able to draw up manufacturing accounts.
- To be able to adjust the accounts in respect of work-in-progress.

37.1 Manufacturing: Not Retailing

We now have to deal with firms that are manufacturers. For these firms a **manufacturing account** is prepared in addition to the trading and profit and loss accounts.

37.2 Divisions of Costs

In a manufacturing firm the costs are divided into different types. These may be summarized as follows.

Direct materials Direct labour Direct expenses	**Prime cost**		
plus			
Factory or works overhead expenses		**Production cost** (Prime cost + Factory overhead expenses)	
plus			
Administrative expenses Selling and distribution expenses			**Total cost** (Production cost + Administrative and Selling and distribution expenses)

37.3 Direct and Indirect Costs

When you see the words **direct costs**, you know that the costs of making an item can be traced to the item being manufactured. If a cost cannot easily be traced to the item being manufactured then it is an *indirect* expense, and will be included under factory overhead costs.

For example, the pay of a machine operator making a particular item will be direct labour; the pay of a foreman in charge of many men on different jobs will be indirect labour, and will be part of factory overhead expenses.

Other instances of costs being direct costs include:

- the cost of direct materials, including carriage inwards on raw materials;
- the hire of special machinery for a job.

37.4 Factory Overhead Expenses

Factory overhead costs are all those costs that occur in the factory where production is being done, but which cannot easily be traced to the specific items being manufactured. Examples are:

- cleaners' pay
- crane drivers' pay
- rent and rates of the factory
- depreciation of plant and machinery
- costs of operating fork-lift trucks
- factory power
- factory lighting.

37.5 Administration Expenses

Administration expenses consist of such items as managers' pay, legal and accountancy charges, the depreciation of accounting machinery and secretarial pay.

37.6 Selling and Distribution Expenses

Selling and distribution expenses are items such as the salesforce's pay and commission, carriage outwards, depreciation of delivery vans, advertising and display expenses.

37.7 Format of Final Accounts

Manufacturing Account

This account is debited with the production cost of goods completed during the accounting period. It contains costs of:

- direct materials
- direct labour
- direct expenses
- factory overhead expenses.

When completed, the manufacturing account will show the total of all production costs. This figure will then be transferred down to the trading account.

Trading Account

This account includes:

- production cost brought down from the manufacturing account
- opening and closing stocks of finished goods
- sales.

When completed, the trading account will disclose the gross profit. This will then be carried down to the profit and loss account part.

The manufacturing account and the trading account can be shown in the form of a diagram. See Exhibit 37.1.

Exhibit 37.1

Manufacturing Account

			$
Production costs for the period:			
Direct materials			xxx
Direct labour			xxx
Direct expenses			xxx
Factory overhead expenses			xxx
Production cost of goods completed c/d to trading account			xxx

Trading Account

		$	$
Sales			xxx
Less Production cost of goods sold:			
Opening stock of finished goods	(1)	xxx	
Add Production costs of goods completed b/d		xxx	
		xxx	
Less Closing stock of finished goods	(2)	xxx	xxx
Gross profit			xxx

(1) is the production costs of goods unsold in the previous period.
(2) is the production costs of goods unsold at the end of the period.

Profit and Loss Account

This account includes:

- gross profit brought down from the trading account
- all administration expenses
- All selling and distribution expenses.

When completed, the profit and loss account will show the net profit.

37.8 A Worked Example of a Manufacturing Account

Exhibit 37.2 shows the necessary details for a manufacturing account for C. Clarke. It has been assumed that there were no partly completed units (known as **work-in-progress**) either at the beginning or at the end of the period.

Exhibit 37.2

Details of production cost for the year ended 31 December 2007	
	$
1.1.2007: Stock of raw materials	500
31.12.2007: Stock of raw materials	700
Raw materials purchased	8,000
Manufacturing (direct) pay	21,150
Indirect pay	9,000
Rent of factory buildings excluding administration and selling and distribution	440
Depreciation of plant and machinery in factory	400
General indirect expenses	310

The production cost of goods completed, when calculated, is carried down to the trading account, to the place where normally purchases are shown (see Exhibit 37.3).

Exhibit 37.3

C. Clarke
Manufacturing Account for the year ended 31 December 2007

	$	$
Stock of raw materials 1.1.2007		500
Add Purchases		8,000
		8,500
Less Stock of raw materials 31.12.2007		700
Cost of raw materials consumed		7,800
Manufacturing pay		21,150
Prime cost		28,950
Add Factory Overhead Expenses		
Rent	440	
Indirect pay	9,000	
General indirect expenses	310	
Depreciation of plant and machinery	400	10,150
Production cost of goods completed c/d		39,100

37.9 Work-in-progress

The production cost to be carried down to the trading account is the production cost of goods completed during the period. If items have not been completed they cannot be sold; therefore they should not appear in the trading account.

For instance, if we have the following information, we can calculate the transfer to the trading account.

	$
Total production costs expended during the year	5,000
Production costs last year on goods not completed last year, but completed in this year (work-in-progress)	300
Production costs this year on goods that were not completed by the year end (work-in-progress)	440

The calculation is:

	$
Total production costs expended this year	5,000
Add Costs from last year, in respect of goods completed in this year (work-in-progress)	300
	5,300
Less Costs in this year, for goods to be completed next year (work-in-progress)	440
Production costs expended on goods completed this year	4,860

37.10 Another Worked Example

The following information is available for the business of T. Hawkins.

	$
1 January 2007: Stock of raw materials	800
31 December 2007: Stock of raw materials	1,050
1 January 2007: Work-in-progress	350
31 December 2007: Work-in-progress	420
Pay to 31 December 2007:	
Direct	3,960
Indirect	2,550
Purchase of raw materials	8,700
Fuel and power	990
Direct expenses	140
Lubricants	300
Carriage inwards on raw materials	200
Rent of factory	720
Depreciation of factory plant and machinery	420
Internal transport expenses	180
Insurance of factory buildings and plant	150
General factory expenses	330

T. Hawkins
Manufacturing Account for the year ended 31 December 2007

		$	$
	Stock of raw materials 1.1.2007		800
	Add Purchases		8,700
	Carriage inwards		200
			9,700
	Less Stock of raw materials 31.12.2007		1,050
Costs which are directly related to production are shown here as part of the prime cost.	Cost of raw materials consumed		8,650
	Direct pay		3,960
	Direct expenses		140
	Prime cost		12,750
	Add Factory overhead expenses		
Costs which are indirectly related to production are shown under factory overhead expenses.	Fuel and power	990	
	Indirect pay	2,550	
	Lubricants	300	
	Rent	720	
	Depreciation of plant and machinery	420	
	Internal transport expenses	180	
	Insurance	150	
	General factory expenses	330	5,640
			18,390
	Add Work-in-progress 1.1.2007		350
			18,740
	Less Work-in-progress 31.12.2007		420
	Production cost of goods completed c/d		18,320

The trading account is concerned with finished goods. If in the foregoing example there had been $3,500 stock of finished goods on 1 January 2007 and $4,400 on 31 December 2007, and the sales of finished goods amounted to $25,000, then the trading account would appear as.

T. Hawkins
Trading Account for the year ended 31 December 2007

	$	$
Sales		25,000
Less Cost of goods sold		
Stock of finished goods 1.1.2007	3,500	
Add Production cost of goods completed b/d	18,320	
	21,820	
Less Stock of finished goods 31.12.2007	4,400	17,420
Gross profit c/d		7,580

The profit and loss account is then constructed in the normal way.

A complete worked example is now given in the following section. Note that in the profit and loss account the expenses have been separated so as to show whether they are administration expenses, selling and distribution expenses or financial charges.

37.11 A Full Set of Final Accounts

The trial balance that follows has been extracted from the books of R. James, toy manufacturer, as on 31 December 2008. The manufacturing, trading and profit and loss accounts and the balance sheet are then drawn up from the trial balance details.

Notes at 31 December 2008

1. Stock of raw materials \$2,400, stock of finished goods \$4,000, work-in-progress \$1,500.
2. Lighting, and rent and insurance are to be apportioned: factory ⅚, administration ⅙.
3. Depreciation on productive and accounting machinery at 10% per annum on cost.

R. James
Trial balance as on 31 December 2008

	Dr.	*Cr.*
	\$	\$
Stock of raw materials 1.1.2008	2,100	
Stock of finished goods 1.1.2008	3,890	
Work-in-progress 1.1.2008	1,350	
Pay (direct, \$18,700: factory indirect, \$14,500)	33,200	
Carriage inwards (on raw materials)	350	
Purchases of raw materials	37,000	
Productive machinery (cost \$28,000)	23,000	
Accounting machinery (cost \$2,000)	1,200	
General factory expenses	3,100	
Lighting	750	
Factory power	1,370	
Administrative staff pay	4,400	
Sales force's pay	3,000	
Commission on sales	1,150	
Rent	1,200	
Insurance	420	
General administration expenses	1,340	
Bank charges	230	
Discounts allowed	480	
Carriage outwards	590	
Sales		100,000
Debtors and creditors	14,230	12,500
Bank	5,680	
Cash	150	
Drawings	2,000	
Capital as at 1.1.2008		29,680
	142,180	142,180

R. James
Manufacturing, Trading and Profit and Loss Account for the year ended 31 December 2008

	$	$	$
Stock of raw materials 1.1.2008			2,100
Add Purchases			37,000
Carriage inwards			350
			39,450
Less Stock of raw materials 31.12.2008			2,400
Cost of raw materials consumed			37,050
Direct labour			18,700
Prime cost			55,750
Add Factory Overhead Expenses			
General factory expenses		3,100	
Lighting ⅚ths		625	
Power		1,370	
Rent ⅚ths		1,000	
Insurance ⅚ths		350	
Depreciation of productive machinery		2,800	
Indirect labour		14,500	23,745
			79,495
Add Work-in-progress 1.1.2008			1,350
			80,845
Less Work-in-progress 31.12.2008			1,500
Production cost of goods completed c/d			79,345
Sales			100,000
Less Cost of goods sold			
Stock of finished goods 1.1.2008		3,890	
Add Production cost of goods completed b/d		79,345	
		83,235	
Less Stock of finished goods 31.12.2008		4,000	79,235
Gross profit			20,765
Less Administration Expenses			
Administrative staff pay	4,400		
Rent ⅙th	200		
Insurance ⅙th	70		
General expenses	1,340		
Lighting ⅙th	125		
Depreciation of accounting machinery	200	6,335	

(Cont'd)

Selling and Distribution Expenses			
Sales force's pay	3,000		
Commission on sales	1,150		
Carriage outwards	590	4,740	
Financial charges			
Bank charges	230		
Discounts allowed	480	710	11,785
Net profit			8,980

R. James
Balance Sheet as at 31 December 2008

	$	$
Fixed assets		
Productive machinery at cost	28,000	
Less Aggregate depreciation		
$(28,000 – 23,000 + 28,000 × 10%)	7,800	20,200
Accounting machinery at cost	2,000	
Less Aggregate depreciation		
$(2,000 – 1,2000 + 2,000 × 10%)	1,000	1,000
		21,200
Current assets		
Stock:		
Raw materials	2,400	
Finished goods	4,000	
Work-in-progress	1,500	
Debtors	14,230	
Bank	5,680	
Cash	150	
	27,960	
Less Current liabilities		
Creditors	12,500	
Working capital		15,460
		36,660
Financed by:		
Capital		
Balance as at 1.1.2008		29,680
Add Net profit		8,980
		38,660
Less Drawings		2,000
		36,660

In the accounting records of a manufacturing business, stock is shown by classifying raw materials, finished goods and work-in-progress.

New Terms

Manufacturing account (p. 325): An account in which production cost is calculated.
Prime cost (p. 325): Direct materials plus direct labour plus direct expenses.
Production cost (p. 325): Prime cost plus factory overhead costs.
Total cost (p. 325): Production cost plus administration, selling and distribution expenses.
Direct cost (p. 325): Costs that can be traced to the item being manufactured.
Factory overhead costs (p. 326): Production costs in the factory which cannot be traced to the item being manufactured.
Work-in-progress (p. 328): Items not completed at the end of a period.

Summary

1 The trading account is used for calculating the gross profit made by selling the goods manufactured.
2 The profit and loss account shows as net profit what is left of gross profit after all administration, selling and distribution costs incurred have been deducted.
3 Work-in-progress, both at the start and the close of a period, must be adjusted to ascertain the production costs of goods completed in the period.

Exercises

37.1 Super Shoes makes ladies shoes. The following details relate to May 2005.

1 Stocks of leather and accessories:
    1 May 2005 $7,800
    31 May 2005 $4,950
2 Purchases of leather and accessories, $10,100.
3 Factory manager's pay was $2,460.
4 Machine operators earned $16,340.
5 Light and power cost, $880; 75% of this relates to the factory.
6 Rental of factory space was $770.
7 The factory machinery had cost $24,000. It is being depreciated on a straight line basis over five years.
8 Sales force's pay comes to $4,620.
9 Bookkeeper's pay was $1,950.
10 General expenses were $390.
11 All shoes produced in the month were sold for $52,000.

Draw up manufacturing, trading and profit and loss accounts for the month of May 2005. The following should be clearly marked:
(i) cost of raw materials used
(ii) prime costs
(iii) factory overheads
(iv) production cost
(v) gross profit
(vi) net profit.

(CXC style)

37.2X CCC Ltd makes ornaments which it sells in wooden cases. The following information is made available to you in respect of the year ended 31 December 2003.

	1 Jan 2003	31 Dec 2003
	$	$
Raw materials	4,500	5,800
Wooden cases	2,250	1,920
Work-in-progress	1,250	1,900

The activities for the year ended 31 December 2003 were as follows.

Raw materials purchase	8,800
Purchase of wooden cases	2,250
Carriage outwards	210
Carriage inwards on raw materials	390
Pay	22,500
Factory manager's pay	1,650
Factory power	1,820
Factory rates	910
Lighting	600
Administration expenses	2,400
Sales force's pay	5,950

The firm completely finished the manufacture of 1,000 ornaments. All ornaments were sold immediately on completion for $80 each.

Notes:

1 Factory plant was valued at $100,000 on 1 January 2003. It depreciates by 20% for 2003.
2 80% of the pay is for production workers, and 20% for factory overheads.
3 50% of the lighting is for the factory.

You are required to:

(*a*) draw up a manufacturing account to disclose the:
  (i) cost of raw materials used;
  (ii) cost of wooden cases used;
  (iii) prime costs;
  (iv) factory overheads;
  (v) cost of production;

(*b*) draft the trading and profit and loss account for the year ended 31 December 2003;

(*c*) ascertain the production cost of each boxed ornament;

(*d*) calculate the gross profit on each boxed ornament sold. *(CXC style)*

37.3 From the following ledger balances of G. C. & Co., prepare manufacturing, trading and profit and loss account for the year ended 31 December 2004.

Stocks at 1 January 2004	$
Raw materials	12,600
Partly manufactured goods	16,000
Finished goods	12,000
Stocks at 31 December 2004	
Raw materials	10,160
Partly manufactured goods	36,000
Finished goods	10,000
Other balances	
Purchases of raw materials	44,000
Freight and carriage on raw materials	1,760
Production workers' pay	44,000
Rent and rates	2,000
Gas and fuel	3,600
Office workers' pay	4,600
Depreciation of productive machinery and plant	3,600
Sales	147,200

(Cont'd)

Rent and rates, and gas and fuel must be apportioned as to Factory ¾, Office ¼. Clearly indicate prime cost in your answer.

37.4 The R. B. Manufacturing Co. have the following information in respect of the year ended 31 December 2006.

	$
Stocks: 1 January 2006	
Raw materials	3,777
Work-in-progress	5,500
Purchases of raw materials	48,917
Factory workers' pay (all direct)	39,600
Factory maintenance paid	3,950
Factory maintenance owing on 31 December 2006	220
Stocks: 31 December 2006	
Raw materials	4,394
Work-in-progress	7,500
Factory power	1,694
Plant and machinery depreciation	3,490
Factory workers' pay (indirect)	7,146
Factory rent	4,800
Carriage on raw materials	2,800

You are required to:

(*a*) Draw up the manufacturing account for the year ended 31 December 2006 to disclose:
- (i) cost of raw materials used;
- (ii) prime cost;
- (iii) factory overheads;
- (iv) cost of production for goods completed.

(*b*) If R. B. Manufacturing had produced 1,000 units during the year, calculate the unit cost of production.

(*c*) If the goods produced by R. B. Manufacturing could be bought elsewhere at $120 per unit, should R. B. Manufacturing carry on production? Give your reasons.

(CXC style)

37.5X

(*a*) Ideal Products deals in only one item. The following is in respect of the year ended 31 December 2002.

Stocks	*1.1.2002*	*31.12.2002*
	$	$
Raw materials	12,400	13,800
Finished goods	37,500	39,600
Work-in-progress	6,200	7,000

Also available is the following information for 2002.

	$
Raw materials purchased	84,500
Carriage inwards on raw materials	4,900
Lighting in factory	12,700
Depreciation of factory equipment	5,600
Production staff pay	59,200
Repairs in the factory	11,500
Factory indirect expenses	6,100
Factory rent	2,000
Factory indirect pay	5,700
Finished goods purchased	6,800
Sales	300,000

(Cont'd)

Draw up a manufacturing and trading account showing:

(i) cost of raw materials consumed;
(ii) prime costs;
(iii) factory overhead expenses;
(iv) total cost of production;
(v) cost of goods completed;
(vi) cost of goods sold;
(vii) gross profit.

(*b*) Another manufacturer, Other Things Ltd, makes similar items. During 2002 the following figures obtained.

	$
Cost of raw materials consumed	78,000
Production staff pay	65,000
Factory overhead expenses	55,000

There was no work-in-progress,

The number of items produced was as follows: Ideal Products 10,000 items; Other Things Ltd, 11,000 items.

(i) Calculate the average cost per unit for each factory.
(ii) Which factory is more productive? Give reasons.

CHAPTER **38**

The Payroll

Learning Objectives

- to know the difference between payment on a time basis and payment by piece-work.
- To be able to calculate gross pay and deductions therefrom.
- To enter up time cards and time sheets.
- To calculate net pay payable.

38.1 Payrolls

The word *pay* is generally used as an all-inclusive term rather than the traditional division of wages and salaries.

Wages are usually taken to be earnings paid on a weekly basis. Salaries are earnings paid monthly or four-weekly. Wages can be paid on a time basis or on a piece-work basis.

The term **payroll** means the list of employees specifying the pay given to each, but it is often used to mean the cash required to pay this total list of employees.

38.2 Payment on a Time Basis

This means being paid a given amount per hour for every hour worked. Usually a flat rate is paid per hour up to a given number of hours (normal time). Above that number of hours, any extra time worked is called *overtime*. Overtime hours are paid at a higher rate than normal hours. The higher rates are usually stated as 'time and a quarter', 'time and a half' or 'double time'.

If normal time is $4 per hour, then;

- time and a quarter is $\$4 \times 1\frac{1}{4} = \$5$
- time and a half is $\$4 \times 1\frac{1}{2} = \$6$
- double time is $\$4 \times 2 = \$8$.

We can look at the earnings of two workers. They are paid $4 per hour for a 40-hour week, time and a quarter for the next 10 hours, and time and a half for any hours in excess of that.

- Campbell worked 48 hours:

		$
40 hours × $4 (normal time)	=	160
8 hours × $5 (time and a quarter)	=	40
Gross pay		200

- Lee worked 55 hours:

		$
40 hours × $4 (normal time)	=	160
10 hours × $5 (time and a quarter)	=	50
5 hours × $6 (time and a half)	=	30
Gross pay		240

38.3 Payment by Piece-work

This relates payment to the amount of work performed. The fixing of piece-work rates is usually based on an expected time in which 1 unit can be made or an expected time in which 1 unit of work can be performed. Based on this, an amount payable is agreed between the firm and the employee for each unit of work completed.

This means that, if the agreed rate is $2 per unit and Harris completes 96 units in the week, then his gross pay will be $192. Lopez, on the other hand, will get $170 for completing 85 units.

38.4 Deductions from Gross Pay

Naturally, throughout the various countries in which students take the examinations of the Caribbean Examinations Council, there are differences in such deductions. Jamaica, for instance, has deductions for contributions to the National Housing Trust; this is not found in Trinidad and Barbados; and so on.

The main structure of deductions is, however, very similar in each country. This chapter is concerned with general principles, not with matters of exact detail for each island. All of the rates of income tax and of social security deductions are for purposes of illustration *only*; it must *not* be thought that these are the exact rates for your country.

Income Tax

The pay of all employees is liable to have income tax deducted from it. This does not mean that everyone will pay income tax, but if income tax is found to be payable, then the employer will deduct tax from the employee's pay.

Each person is allowed to subtract various amounts from their earnings, after which they are liable to pay income tax on the balance. The amounts given for each person depend on his or her personal circumstances. An extra amount can be deducted by a man who is married, as compared with a single man; further amounts will be given for circumstances such as having children, and so on. This means that, for instance, a single man earning a given amount might pay income tax, whereas a married man who is eligible for extra allowances might have the same earnings but pay no income tax at all. The amounts to be deducted are changed from time to time by the government of each country.

Once the amounts to be deducted (called 'reliefs') have been taken from the earnings, also the amount of earnings that are allowed free of tax, any earnings above that figure are subject to income tax. As the rates of income tax change from time to time, all that can be given here are the basic principles; the rates given are for purposes of illustration only. A further complication arises because the rate of tax increases in steps when the excess of the earnings exceeds certain figures.

In most countries the first few thousand dollars are not taxable. Let us suppose that the tax rates are as follows:

Annual income	*Income tax rate*
On the first $10,000	No tax
On the next $2,000	30%
On the next $5,000	40%
On the remaining income above this	50%

Miss Jones earns $11,500 per annum. Her personal relief amounts to $2,000. This leaves $9,500, but as the first $10,000 is free of tax she pays nothing.

Mr Blake earns $13,300 per annum. His personal relief amounts to $2,000, leaving $11,300. After deducting $10,000 free of tax, he will pay tax of 30% on $1,300 = $390.

Mr Hernandez earns $16,200 per annum. His personal relief amounts to $3,000. The calculation of his tax payable is as follows.

	$	$
Earnings		16,200
Less Personal relief	3,000	
Amount free of tax	10,000	13,000
Income tax payable on:		3,200
Income tax calculated:		$
on the first $2,000 at 30%		600
on the next $1,200 at 40%		480
Income tax payable for the year		1,080

Mrs Prendergast earns $25,000 per annum. Her personal relief amounts to $3,600. The calculation of tax payable is as follows.

	$	$
Earnings		25,000
Less Personal relief	3,600	
Amount free of tax	10,000	13,600
Income tax payable on:		11,400
Income tax calculated:		$
on the first $2,000 at 30%		600
on the next $5,000 at 40%		2,000
on the remaining $4,400 at 50%		2,200
		4,800

The actual deduction of the income tax from the earnings of the employee is made by the employer. The tax is commonly called PAYE tax, which represents the initial letters for Pay As You Earn.

For every employee, the Inland Revenue Department sends the firm a Notice of Coding, and on this there is a code number. The code numbers are based on the amount of 'relief' for that particular employee. By comparing the code number with the earnings and a set of tax tables, the amount of PAYE for each employee, for that week or that month, can be calculated.

So far the amount of tax payable by anyone has been looked at on an annual basis. However, PAYE means precisely that – it involves paying the tax as the earnings are calculated on each pay date, i.e. weekly or monthly, and not waiting until after the end of the year to pay the bill. The code numbers and the tax tables supplied to the employer by the Inland Revenue Department are so worked out that this is possible.

It is outside the scope of this book to examine in detail how this is done. However, in the case of the three people already listed who will have to pay tax, if we assume that Mr Blake is paid weekly, then from each week's pay he will have to pay one week's tax, in his case $\$390 \div 52 = \$7.50$ per week. If Mr Hernandez and Mrs Prendergast are paid on a monthly basis, then Mr Hernandez will pay $\$1,080 \div 12 = \$90$ per month, and Mrs Prendergast $\$4,800 \div 12 = \$400$ per month.

Social Security Contributions

Employees are also liable to pay social security contributions. These are usually allowed as deductions for income tax, such tax being paid only on the balance.

The payment of such contributions is to ensure that the payer will be able to claim benefits from the State, if and when he or she is in a position to claim, e.g. retirement and unemployment benefits.

Superannuation Contributions

Many firms have superannuation schemes towards which employees make payments. These are schemes whereby the employee will receive a pension on retiring from the firm, plus, very often, a lump sum payment in cash. They also usually include benefits that will be paid to an employee's wife or husband if the employee dies before reaching retirement age.

These contributions are usually allowed as deductions for income tax, such tax being paid on the balance.

38.5 Calculation of Net Pay Payable

Two illustrations of the calculation of the net pay to be made to various employees can now be looked at. The percentages used for national insurance and superannuation are for illustration purposes only.

G. Jones

	$
Gross earnings for week ended 8 May 2004	240
Income tax: found by consulting tax tables and employee's code number	8
National insurance: 5% of gross pay	

G. Jones: Payslip for week ended 8 May 2004

	$	$
Gross pay for the week		240
Less Income tax	8	
National insurance: 5% of 240	12	20
Net pay		220

H. Russell:

	$
Gross earnings for the month of May 2004	2,000
Income tax (from tax tables)	360
Superannuation: 6% of gross pay	
National insurance: 5% of gross pay	

H. Russell: Payslip for month ended 31 May 2004

	$	$
Gross pay for the month		2,000
Less Income tax	360	
Superannuation: 6% of 2,000	120	
National insurance: 5% of 2,000	100	580
Net pay		1,420

38.6 Time Cards and Time Sheets

In many businesses employees will have a time card that must be 'punched' in a special machine when they arrive at work, and again when they leave work. The machine contains a clock and a printing device that prints the times on to the time card when it is inserted (punched) into the machine. It is from such time cards that time sheets are made out.

The type of business where this is particularly important is where employees are paid on a time basis; obviously, the firm then needs accurate measures of the time worked per employee so as to correctly calculate their pay.

In other establishments staff may sign in, by recording their names in a book and adding the times of arrival and departure. It all depends on the nature of the business and the firm's attitude towards timekeeping. In the case of fixed annual pay, irrespective of the number of hours worked, there is no need for exact timekeeping for the purposes of earnings calculations.

Where a time card system or something similar is used, then time sheets can be made out. Exhibit 38.1 shows a typical time sheet. In this case, if overtime is paid at the rate of time and a half, then Hamilton will be paid for $40 + (3 \times 1\frac{1}{2} = 4\frac{1}{2}) = 44\frac{1}{2}$ hours.

Exhibit 38.1

Time Sheet								
Name of company: Atlantic Enterprises Ltd					*Week commencing*: 17 May 2005			
Name of employee: Hamilton, Joseph					*Works no.* 567	*Department*: Packing		
Day	*a.m.*		*p.m.*		*Normal hours*	*Overtime hours*	*Total hours*	
	In	*Out*	*In*	*Out*				
Mon	0800	1200	1300	1700	8		8	
Tues	0800	1200	1300	1900	8	2	10	
Wed	0800	1200	1300	1700	8		8	
Thur	0800	1200	1300	1800	8	1	9	
Fri	0800	1200	1300	1700	8		8	
Sat								
Sun								
Total					40	3	43	

38.7 Payroll

For each payment date the firm will prepare a payroll register. This will show the earnings for all the employees. Exhibit 38.2 shows an uncompleted payroll register. Each of the columns has a number in brackets. If there were any other type of deductions, an extra column could be added, which would become column (11) with the total column then being renumbered (12) and net pay (13).

We can now look at what needs to be entered in each column:

1 the name of the employee;
2 the total hours worked by the employee during the period;
3 the number of hours worked at the regular rate of pay × pay per hour;
4 the hours worked at overtime rates × pay per hour;
5 the gross pay – i.e. before deductions – earned during the period;
6 the gross earnings of the employee from the start of the accounting year until the end of this payroll period; i.e., if 15 weeks' earnings have been paid, then this column shows the total of all the 15 weeks *before* any deductions have been made;
7 the amount of national insurance to be deducted for the period;
8 the amount of income tax to be deducted for the period;
9 the amount of life insurance to be deducted for the period;
10 the amount to be deducted in respect of amount due to the credit union;
11 the total amount of all the deductions;
12 the gross pay column (5) *less* the total deductions column (11): i.e. the net pay for the period.

Exhibit 38.2

Payroll Register

(1) *Employee*	(2) *Total hours*	(3) *Regular* $	(4) *Over-time* $	(5) *Gross* $	(6) *Accumulated or year-to-date earnings* $	(7) *Nat. ins.* $	(8) *Income tax* $	(9) *Life ins.* $	(10) *Credit union* $	(11) *Total* $	(12) *Net pay* $

Now let us look at the completion of the payroll register for week 10 of the accounting year in Exhibit 38.2. Taking a firm with only three employees (to make the illustration easy for you to follow), we are given the following details regarding the employees.

1	Names	*J. Blake*	*R. Marley*	*D. Scott*
2	Total of hours worked	48	40	60
3	Total of hours worked at regular rate of pay	40	40	40
4	Hours worked at overtime rate	8		20
5	Gross pay for week 10	?	?	?
6	Accumulated earnings to end of previous week 9	$2,100	$2,400	$780
7	National insurance on gross pay	5%	5%	5%
8	Income tax	$65	$60	$105
9	Life insurance	$10	$10	$10
10	Credit union	$15	$20	$25
11	Net pay	?	?	?

Note: D. Scott joined the firm at the start of week 7 of the accounting year.

Hourly pay rates are: regular rates J. Blake, $5; R. Marley, $6; D. Scott, $6. All overtime rates are at time and a half.

Completing the payroll register for week 10, we arrive at the figures in Exhibit 38.3.

Exhibit 38.3

Payroll Register

(1) *Employee*	(2) *Total hours*	(3) *Regular* $	(4) *Over-time* $	(5) *Gross* $	(6) *Accumulated or year-to-date earnings* $	(7) *Nat. ins.* $	(8) *Income tax* $	(9) *Life ins.* $	(10) *Credit union* $	(11) *Total* $	(12) *Net pay* $
J. Blake	48	200	60	260	2,360	13	65	10	15	103	157
R. Marley	40	240	–	240	2,640	12	60	10	20	102	138
D. Scott	60	240	180	420	1,200	21	105	10	25	161	259

Let us see how the figures have been calculated for J. Blake.

- Column (3): 40 × \$5 = \$200
- (4): 8 × \$5 × 1½ = \$60
- (6): Previous week's total \$2,100 + column (5) \$260 = \$2,360
- (7): 5% × column (5) = \$13
- (11): columns (7) + (8) + (9) + (10) = \$103
- (12): columns (5) – (11) = \$157.

38.8 Employee's Earnings Record

For each employee, there will be an employee earnings record, showing the full details of the employee's earnings for the accounting year on a week-by-week basis. This will be similar to the payroll register, except that each sheet will be for a separate employee.

Exhibit 38.4 shows such a record for J. Blake for weeks 10 and 11.

Exhibit 38.4

Employees Earnings Record: J. Blake

Period ended		*Accumulated or year-to-date earnings*	*Regular*	*Overtime*	*Gross*	*Nat. ins.*	*Income tax*	*Life ins.*	*Credit union*	*Total*	*Net pay*
		\$	\$	\$	\$	\$	\$	\$	\$	\$	\$
Week	10	2,360	200	60	260	13	65	10	15	103	157
Week	11	2,640	200	80	280	14	70	10	15	109	171

New Terms

Payroll (p. 338): The list of employees specifying the pay due to each, or the total cash required to pay this list.

Wages (p. 338): Traditional term for payment made on a time basis: a flat rate paid for every hour worked.

Overtime (p. 338) a higher rate than the flat rate, paid for hours worked over an agreed number.

Piece-work (p. 339) payment related to the number of units of work performed.

Summary

1 Each country in the Caribbean will have certain differences in its legislation concerning deductions from earnings. In particular, income tax rates will vary.

2 Each employee should be given full details of earnings and deductions on his or her payslip which should accompany the cash, cheque or bank credit used for payment.

3 The actual net pay received is often known as 'take-home pay'.

Exercises

38.1 The following hours have been worked by the employees of Engineering Associates for the week commencing 15 May 2005.

		Mon	*Tues*	*Wed*	*Thurs*	*Fri*	*Works no.*
Jones. S.	a.m.	8.00–12.00	8.00–12.00	8.00–12.00	8.00–12.00	8.00–12.00	15
(Works)	p.m.	13.00–17.00	13.00–18.00	13.00–18.30	13.00–19.30	13.00–17.00	
Thomas, R.	a.m.	8.00–12.00	8.00–12.00	8.00–12.00	8.00–12.00	8.00–12.00	17
(Works)	p.m.	13.00–18.00	13.00–18.00	13.00–17.00	13.00–19.00	13.00–17.00	
Wallace, V.	a.m.	8.30–12.00	8.30–12.00	8.30–12.00	8.30–12.00	8.30–12.00	22
(Design)	p.m.	13.00–19.00	13.00–19.00	13.00–19.00	13.00–17.00	13.00–17.00	
Worrall, W.	a.m.	8.30–12.00	8.30–12.00	8.30–12.00	8.30–12.00	8.30–12.00	24
(Office)	p.m.	13.00–17.00	13.00–18.00	13.00–17.00	13.00–18.00	13.00–19.00	

The Works employees work a basic week of 40 hours; anything above that is paid at the rate of time and a half. The Design employee works a basic week of 37½ hours, with anything above that at time and a third. The Office employee works a basic week of 37½ hours, all overtime being paid at a rate of time and a quarter.

From the above you are to draft a time sheet for the week for each employee. Keep your answer; you will need it when attempting question 38.2.

38.2 Using the information given about the employees in 38.1 draw up the payroll register for Engineering Associates for the week commencing 15 May 2005, taking into account the following information also.

1 Basic pay rates: Works, $6 per hour, Design, $8 per hour; Office, $6 per hour.
2 Income tax deductions for the week: Jones, $48; Thomas, $59; Wallace, $85; Worrall, $37.
3 National insurance for the week: Jones, $17; Thomas, $16; Wallace, $26; Worrall, $14.
4 Life insurance: $15 per employee.
5 Credit union: Jones and Thomas, $20 each; Worrall and Wallace, $28 each.
6 Accumulated earnings up to the end of the previous week (week 5); Jones, $1,387; Thomas, $1,488; Wallace, $1,932; Worrall, $1,312.

You are required to:

(*a*) draw up the payroll register for the week commencing 15 May 2005;
(*b*) given the following details for R. Thomas for the succeeding week, commencing 22 May 2005, complete the employee's earnings record for R. Thomas in respect of the two weeks shown:
regular earnings, $240; overtime earnings, $18; national insurance, $15; income tax, $55; life insurance, $15; credit union, $20;
(*c*) show the completed payslip for V. Wallace for the week commencing 15 May 2005.

38.3X The following hours have been worked by the employees of Chemical Laboratories Ltd for the week commencing 1 February 2004.

							Works no.
L. Richards	a.m.	8.00–12.00	8.00–12.00	8.00–12.00	8.00–12.00	8.00–12.00	7
(Processing)	p.m.	13.00–18.00	13.00–18.00	13.00–19.00	13.00–19.00	13.00–17.00	
D. Garner	a.m.	8.00–12.00	8.00–12.00	8.00–12.00	8.00–12.00	8.00–12.00	11
(Processing)	p.m.	13.00–17.00	13.00–17.00	13.00–19.00	13.00–18.00	13.00–18.00	
C. Weekes	a.m.	9.00–12.00	9.00–12.00	9.00–12.00	9.00–12.00	9.00–12.00	14
(Chemist)	p.m.	13.30–16.30	13.30–16.30	13.30–16.30	13.30–16.30	13.30–16.30	
R. Walcott	a.m.	9.00–12.00	9.00–12.00	9.00–12.00	9.00–12.00	9.00–12.00	16
(Office)	p.m.	13.00–17.30	13.00–18.00	13.00–18.00	13.00–18.00	13.00–19.00	

(Cont'd)

The Processing employees work a basic week of 40 hours; anything above that is paid at the rate of time and a quarter. The Chemist is paid a fixed amount for a week of 30 hours; if he works more than that he is entitled to double time. The Office worker works a basic week of 37½ hours, anything above that being at the rate of time and a half.

Draft a time sheet for the week for each employee from the above information. Keep your answer; it will be used when tackling question 38.4X.

38.4X Using the information given about the employees in 38.3X, draw up the payroll register for the week commencing 1 February 2004, taking the following extra information into account too.

1 Basic pay rates: Processing, $10 per hour; Chemist: $600 per week, but overtime at $30 per hour; Office worker, $12 per hour.
2 Income tax deductions: the workers are allowed to have the following earnings free of tax each week; on the excess the rate of tax is 25%; Richards, $75; Garner, $90; Weekes, $100; Walcott, $80.
3 National insurance: Richards, $29; Garner, $27; Weekes, $40; Walcott, $32,
4 Life insurance: $30 each for Processing workers; $25 for other workers.
5 Credit union: Richards and Garner, $40 each; Weekes, $50; Walcott, $35.
6 Their accumulated earnings up to the end of the previous week were: Richards, $1,990; Garner, $2,050; Weekes, $2,400; Walcott, $2,280.

You are required to:

(*a*) draw up the payroll register for the week commencing 1 February 2004 (week 5);
(*b*) given the following details for L. Richards for the week commencing 8 February 2004, complete the employee's earnings record for him in respect of the two weeks shown:
regular earnings, $400; overtime earnings, $115; income tax and national insurance at same rates as previous week; life insurance and credit union at same amounts as previous week;
(*c*) show the completed payslips for Garner and Walcott for the week commencing 1 February 2004.

38.5 H. Smith is employed by a firm of carpenters at a rate of $6 per hour. During the week to 18 May 2005, he worked his basic week of 40 hours. The income tax due on his pay was $10, and he is also liable to pay social security contributions of 5%. Calculate his net pay.

38.6 B. Charles is employed as an undertaker's assistant. Her basic working week consists of 40 hours, paid at the rate of $4 per hour. For hours worked in excess of this she is paid at the rate of 1½ times her basic earnings. In the week ended 12 March 2006 she worked 60 hours. Up to $240 a week she pays no income tax, but she pays it at the rate of 30% for all earnings above that figure. She is liable to pay social security at the rate of 5% on gross earnings. Calculate her net pay.

38.7X R. Kennedy is a security van driver. His pay is $220 per week, and danger money of $10 per hour in addition for every hour he spends transporting gold bullion to Piarco Airport. During the week, 20 of the hours worked by him are spent in taking gold bullion to the airport. He pays income tax at the rate of 30% on all his earnings above $280 per week. He pays social security at the rate of 5% on gross earnings. Calculate his net pay for the week.

38.8X A firm employs Jane Jones at a standard rate of $6 per hour. Time and a half is paid for all hours worked in excess of 40. All employees pay a superannuation contribution of 5% of all pay earned in a normal working week (40 hours). Time worked in excess of 40 hours is not subject to superannuation. Social security contributions are 5% of gross pay. In the week ending 7 June, Jane Jones has worked 50 hours. She pays income tax at 30% on all she earns over $200 per week after superannuation has been deducted.

You are required to:

(*a*) calculate her gross pay;
(*b*) show the value of each deduction and calculate her net pay.

CHAPTER **39**

An Introduction to the Final Accounts of Limited Liability Companies

Learning Objectives

- To understand how limited companies differ from other organizations.
- To be able to calculate how distributable profits available for dividends are divided between the different classes of shares.
- To realize the differences between shares and debentures.
- To be able to draw up the trading and profit and loss accounts for a limited company.
- To be able to draw up a balance sheet for a limited company.

39.1 The Need for Limited Companies

Limited companies are needed because of the disadvantages from which partnerships suffer.

A partnership can have no more than 20 owners, not counting limited partners. The amount of capital needed to operate a very large organization is often more than 20 people can provide. In contrast, a public limited company can have as many owners as it wants.

In addition, if a partnership business fails, a partner can lose part or all of his or her private assets as well as the business assets: except for limited partners, a partner's liability is not limited to the business assets. Limited companies enable larger businesses to be formed, and help the owners safeguard their private assets.

39.2 Limited Liability

The capital of a limited company is divided into **shares**. Shares can be priced at $1, $5, $10 or any other amount. To become a member of a limited company, i.e. a shareholder, a person must buy one or more of the shares.

If the shareholders have paid in full for their shares, their liability is limited to those shares. If a company loses all its assets, all the shareholders can lose is their shares. They cannot be forced to pay anything out of their private money in respect of the company's losses.

Shareholders who have only partly paid for their shares can be forced to pay the balance owing on the shares. Apart from that, they cannot be forced to pay out of their private money for company losses.

This is known as *limited liability*, and the company is known as a limited company. You can see that it meets the need of organizations requiring limited liability for their owners and a large amount of capital.

39.3 Private and Public Companies

The two classes of limited company are the private company and the public company. There are a lot more private companies than public companies.

A **private company**:

- has a minimum membership of 2
- does not have more than 50 members (in Jamaica not more than 20), although there also can be extra members who are working or have worked for the company
- must ask people to buy company shares *privately*: it cannot do so in public, e.g. by advertising the shares in a newspaper.

Any company that does not follow the above is a **public company**. It must have at least 7 members, and can have as many members as it wants.

39.4 Company Directors

A shareholder normally has the right to attend the general meetings of a company, and can vote at such meetings. Shareholders use their votes to appoint **directors**, who manage the business on behalf of the shareholders.

At each annual general meeting, the final accounts for the year are given to the shareholders. The directors at the meeting have to give a report on the progress made by the company.

39.5 Legal Status of a Limited Company

A limited company is said to possess a 'separate legal entity' from that of its shareholders. Put simply, this means that a company is not seen as being exactly the same as its shareholders. For instance, a company can sue one or more of its shareholders, and similarly, a shareholder can sue the company. This would not be the case if the company and its shareholders were exactly the same thing, as no one can sue oneself.

39.6 Share Capital

A shareholder will receive a share of the profits, known as a **dividend**. Not all the net profits will be paid out as dividends. The directors calculate the net profit and decide how much to hold back as reserves. Then they decide on the amount of dividend to be paid.

The dividend is usually shown as a percentage. A dividend of 10% in firm A on 500,000 ordinary shares of $1 each will amount to $50,000. A dividend of 6% in firm B on 200,000 ordinary shares of $2 each will amount to $24,000. A shareholder having 100 shares in each firm would receive $10 from firm A and $12 from firm B.

There are two main types of share:

- **preference shares** these get an agreed percentage rate of dividend before the ordinary shareholders receive anything
- **ordinary shares** these receive the remainder of the total profits available for dividends – there is no upper limit to the amounts of dividends they can receive.

For example, if a company had 10,000 5% preference shares of $1 each and 20,000 ordinary shares of $1 each, then the dividends payable would be as shown in Exhibit 39.1.

Exhibit 39.1

Year	**1**	**2**	**3**	**4**	**5**
	$	$	$	$	$
Profits appropriated for dividends	900	1,300	1,600	3,100	2,000
Preference dividends	(5%) 500	500	500	500	500
Ordinary dividends	(2%) 400	(4%) 800	(5½%) 1,100	(13%) 2,600	(7½%) 1,500

There are two main types of preference shares.

- **Non-cumulative preference shares** These can receive a dividend up to an agreed percentage each year. If the amount paid is less than the maximum agreed amount, the shortage is lost by the shareholders. They cannot carry forward that shortage and get it in a future year.
- **Cumulative preference shares** These also have an agreed maximum percentage dividend. However, any shortage of dividend paid in a year can be carried forward. These arrears of preference dividends will have to be paid before the ordinary shareholders receive anything.

Exhibit 39.2 illustrates the two types of shares. A company has 5,000 $1 ordinary shares and 2,000 5% non-cumulative preference shares of $1 each. The profits available for dividends are: year 1 $150, year 2 $80, year 3 $250, year 4 $60, year 5 $500.

Exhibit 39.2

Year	**1**	**2**	**3**	**4**	**5**
	$	$	$	$	$
Profits	150	80	250	60	500
Non-cumulative preference dividend (limited in years 2 and 4)	100	80	100	60	100
Dividends on ordinary shares	50	–	150	–	400

If instead the preference shares in Exhibit 39.2 had been cumulative, the dividends would be as shown in Exhibit 39.3.

Exhibit 39.3

Year	1	2	3	4	5
	$	$	$	$	$
Profits	150	80	250	60	500
Cumulative preference dividend	100	80	120*	60	140*
Dividends on ordinary shares	50	–	130	–	360

*Including arrears.

39.7 Share Capital: Different Meanings

The term 'share capital' can have any of the following meanings.

- **Authorized share capital** Sometimes known as registered capital or nominal capital. This is the total of the share capital which the company is allowed to issue to shareholders.
- **Issued share capital** This is the total of the share capital actually issued to shareholders. If all of the authorized share capital has been issued, then both authorized and issued share capital would be the same amount.
- **Called-up capital** Where only part of the amounts payable on each share has been asked for, the total amount asked for on all the shares is known as the called-up capital.
- **Uncalled capital** This is the total amount that is to be received in future, but which has not yet been asked for.
- **Calls in arrears** The total amount for which payments has been asked for (i.e. called for), but has not yet been paid by shareholders.
- **Paid-up capital** This is the total of the amount of share capital that has been paid for by shareholders.

Exhibit 39.4 illustrates these different meanings.

Exhibit 39.4

- Better Enterprise Ltd was formed with the legal right to issue 100,000 shares of $1 each.
- They have actually issued 75,000 shares.
- None of the shares has yet been fully paid up. So far the company has made calls of 80 cents ($0.80) per share.
- All the calls have been paid by shareholders except for $200 owing from one shareholder.
  - Authorized or nominal share capital is $100,000.
  - Issued share capital is $75,000.
  - Called up capital is 75,000 × $0.80 = $60,000.
  - Uncalled capital is issued share capital *less* called-up capital – $75,000 – $60,000 = $15,000.
  - Calls in arrears amounted to $200.
  - Paid-up capital is called-up capital *less* uncalled capital – $60,000 – $200 = $59.800.

39.8 Trading and Profit and Loss Accounts

The trading and profit and loss accounts for both private and public companies are drawn up in exactly the same way.

The trading account of a limited company is no different from that of a sole trader or a partnership. There are, however, some differences in the profit and loss account. There are two main expenses that would be found only in company accounts.

- **Directors' remuneration** As directors exist only in companies, this type of expense is found only in company accounts. Directors are legally employees of the company, appointed by the shareholders. Their remuneration is charged to the main profit and loss account.
- **Debenture interest** The term **debenture** refers to money received by the company as a loan from someone. A special written agreement shows all the agreed terms for the debenture. For this loan, the lender is paid interest at an agreed percentage. This is known as debenture interest. It must be paid even if the company is making a loss. In contrast, dividends are payable only if profits have been made. Debenture interest is an expense to be charged in the main profit and loss account.

39.9 The Appropriation Account

Next under the profit and loss account is a section called the profit and loss appropriation account. The appropriation account shows how the net profits are to be *appropriated*, i.e. used.

We may find any of the following in the appropriation account.

Credit Side

- **Net profit for the year** This is the net profit brought down from the main profit and loss account.
- **Balance brought forward from last year** As you will see, not all the profit may be appropriated during a period. This then will be the balance on the appropriation account, as brought forward from the previous year.

Debit Side

- **Transfers to reserves** The directors may decide that some of the profits should not be included in the calculation of how much should be paid out as dividends. These profits are transferred to **reserve accounts**. There may be a specific reason for the transfer, such as a need to replace fixed assets; in this case an amount would be transferred to a fixed assets replacement reserve. Or the reason may not be specific; in this case an amount would be transferred to a general reserve account.
- **Amounts written off as goodwill** Goodwill in a company may have amounts written off it from time to time. When this is done the amount written off should be shown in the appropriation account and not in the main profit and loss account.
- **Amounts written off as preliminary expenses** When a company is formed, there are many kinds of expenses concerned with its formation, e.g. legal expenses and various government taxes. The amount of **preliminary expenses** can be written off and charged in the appropriation account.

- **Taxation payable on profits** Although this is not on your syllabus, taxation in fact is an appropriation of profits and would be shown as a debit in the appropriation account.
- **Dividends** Out of the remainder of the profits, the directors propose the amount of dividends to be paid.
- **Balance carried forward to next year** After the dividends have been proposed, there will probably be some profits that have not been appropriated. These profits will be carried forward to the following year. These are usually known as retained profits.

We now show the profit and loss appropriation accounts of a new business for its first three years of trading (see Exhibit 39.5).

IDO Ltd has a share capital of 40,000 ordinary shares of $1 each and 20,000 5% preference shares of $1 each.

The net profits for the first three years of business ended 31 December are: 2004, $5,967; 2005, $7,864, and 2006, $8,822.

Transfers to reserves are made as follows: 2004, nil; 2005, general reserve, $1,000; 2006, fixed assets replacement reserve, $1,500.

In 2006, $500 was written off as goodwill and $250 was written off preliminary expenses.

Dividends were proposed for each year on the preference shares at 5%, and on the ordinary shares at: 2004, 10%, 2005, 12½%; 2006, 15%.

Exhibit 39.5

IDO Ltd
Profit and Loss Appropriation Accounts

(1) For the year ended 31 December 2004

	$	$
Net profit b/d		5,967
Less Proposed dividends:		
Preference dividend of 5%	1,000	
Ordinary dividend of 10%	4,000	5,000
Retained profits carried forward to next year		967

(2) For the year ended 31 December 2005

	$	$
Net profit b/d		7,864
Add Retained profits from last year		967
		8,831
Less Transfer to general reserve	1,000	
Proposed dividends:		
Preference dividend of 5%	1,000	
Ordinary dividend of 12½%	5,000	7,000
Retained profits carried forward to next year		1,831

(Cont'd)

(3) For the year ended 31 December 2006

	$	$
Net profit b/d		8,822
Add Retained profits from last year		1,831
		10,653
Less Transfer to fixed assets replacements reserve	1,500	
Preliminary expenses written off	250	
Goodwill written off	500	
Proposed dividends:		
Preference dividend of 5%	1,000	
Ordinary dividend of 15%	6,000	9,250
Retained profits carried forward to next year		1,403

39.10 The Balance Sheet

The appropriate Companies Act sets out what should be shown in the balance sheet. An example of a balance sheet is given in Exhibit 39.6.

Exhibit 39.6

JPC Ltd
Balance Sheet as at 31 December 2007

	Cost	*Depreciation to date*	*Net*
	$	*$*	*$*
Fixed assets			
Buildings	15,000	6,000	9,000
Machinery	8,000	2,400	5,600
Motor vehicles	4,000	1,600	2,400
	27,000	10,000	17,000
Current assets			
Stock		6,000	
Debtors		3,000	
Bank		2,000	
		11,000	
Less Current liabilities			
Proposed dividends	1,000		
Creditors	3,000	4,000	
Working capital			7,000
			24,000

(Cont'd)

Less Long-term liabilities		
6% debentures		6,000
		18,000
Financed by:		
Share capital		
Authorized: 20,000 ordinary shares $1 each	20,000	
Issued: 12,000 ordinary shares $1 each		12,000
Reserves:		
General reserve	5,000	
Retained profits per profit and loss account	1,000	6,000
		18,000

The balance sheet must conform to the regulations specified in the Companies Act. The following notes are applicable

Notes:

1 Fixed assets should normally be shown either at cost or at some other valuation. In either case, the method chosen should be clearly stated.

2 The total depreciation from date of purchase to the date of the balance sheet should be shown.

3 The authorized share capital, when it is different from the issued share capital, is shown as a note as in Exhibit 39.6. It is not added into the balance sheet totals.

4 When shares are only partly called up, it is the amount actually called up that appears in the balance sheet and not the full amount.

5 A total for share capital plus reserves should be shown, i.e. $18,000 in Exhibit 39.6.

Reserves consist of those unused profits either remaining in the appropriation account, or transferred to a reserve account appropriately titled, e.g. general reserve, fixed assets replacement reserve, etc. At this juncture, all that needs to be said is that any account labelled as a reserve has originated by being charged as a debit in the appropriation account and credited to a reserve account with an appropriation title. These reserves are shown in the balance sheet after share capital under the heading 'Reserves'.

One reserve that is in fact not labelled with the word 'reserve' in its title is the share premium account. As you will see in section 39.11, shares can be issued for more than their face or nominal value. The excess of the price at which they are issued over the nominal value of the shares is credited to a share premium account. This is then shown with the other reserves in the balance sheet.

39.11 Accounting for an Issue of Shares

When a company is first formed, it raises its capital by issuing shares. Thus, if it needs $100,000 to finance its business, it may issue 100,000 ordinary shares at $1 each to provide the money.

The company first asks people to apply for the shares. If the full amount is to be paid on application, then the would-be shareholders send in $1 for each share they have applied for. If people send in more money than the number of shares to be allotted, then refunds will have to be made for excess applications.

Let us look at the accounting needed in two exhibits. In Exhibit 39.7 exactly the correct number of shares have been applied for; in Exhibit 39.8 people have applied for more shares than are available.

The double entry is as follows.

1 Cash received as applications for shares.
   Debit bank.
   Credit share applicants.
2 Any excess money received, when refunded.
   Debit share applicants.
   Credit bank.
3 Shares allotted.
   Debit share applicants.
   Credit share capital account.

These three points are to show the double entry needed. As no refunds were made in Exhibit 39.7, no entries regarding the second point are needed.

Exhibit 39.7

The company has 10,000 ordinary shares of $1 each to issue. Exactly 10,000 shares are applied for with the applicants paying $1 per share. The shares are then allotted.

Bank

		$			
Ordinary share applicants	(1)	10,000			

Ordinary Share Applicants

		$			$
Ordinary share capital	(3)	10,000	Bank	(1)	10,000

Ordinary Share Capital

					$
			Ordinary share applicants	(3)	10,000

Exhibit 39.8

The company has 20,000 ordinary shares of $2 each to issue. Applications, with the money, are received for 23,000 shares. Refund is made of the excess money received.

Bank

		$			$
Ordinary share applicants	(1)	46,000	Ordinary share applicants (refunds)	(2)	6,000

Ordinary Share Applicants

		$			$
Bank (refunds)	(2)	6,000	Bank	(1)	46,000
Ordinary share capital	(3)	40,000			

Ordinary Share Capital

					$
			Ordinary share applicants	(3)	40,000

When a company first starts up in business, any shares that are issued to shareholders will be at *par*. The 'par value' means that, for instance, a $1 share will be issued for $1. So a shareholder buying 50 of such shares will pay $50.

After a year or two the company may have prospered, and the 50 shares originally bought by the shareholder may be worth quite a lot more money. If the company now issued 50 new $1 shares to someone else, then that person would own as big a share as the first shareholder. Obviously, the company would not issue new shares for $1 each if they were worth much more than that. For instance, $1 shares may then be issued at $1.50 each, $0.50 more than par value. This extra amount is the *share premium*.

Similarly, if the company had made some losses, then shares originally issued for $1 each might be worth less than that. Any more shares may then be issued at less than par value. If, for instance a $1 share is issued for $0.75, then the $0.25 difference is known as the *discount on shares*.

However, the accounting requirement of your syllabus is limited to looking at recording the issue of shares at par value.

39.12 Accounting for an Issue of Debentures

Another way of raising the necessary finance for a firm is to issue debentures. By this method people lend money to the company, and are given a debenture deed which shows the rate of interest that is to be paid on the debenture each year.

The accounting for a debenture issue follows a similar pattern to that of shares. Thus, if we had 10 debentures of $1,000 each to issue and exactly this amount was applied for, then the accounts would appear as Exhibit 39.9.

Exhibit 39.9

Bank

		$			
Debenture applicants	(1)	10,000			

Debenture Applicants

		$			$
Debentures	(3)	10,000	Bank	(1)	10,000

Debentures

					$
			Debenture applicants	(3)	10,000

39.13 Bonds and Treasury Bills

Treasury bills and bonds are sold to the public to finance governments' budgetary requirements and special development projects. When investors purchase these marketable securities they are lending their money to the government. Treasury bills and bonds can usually be purchased at auctions directly from the country's Central Bank and the Ministry of Finance and Planning, respectively. These marketable securities may also be bought and sold after the auction through licensed financial institutions, stock brokers and primary dealers. They are called marketable securities because after their original issue they can be bought or sold in the secondary (commercial) market at prevailing market prices.

Treasury bills are short-time obligations with a term of twelve months or less and are usually accepted as liquid assets. Treasury bills are bearer notes and must be transferred 'under cover', that is, a cover letter is given to the purchaser by the seller effecting the transfer. No interim interest is paid on treasury bills before maturity.

Treasury bills are usually sold below par value (face value). The difference between the purchase price of the bill and the amount that is paid at maturity (par) is the interest earned on the bill.

Treasury bill rates may be determined in two ways: (1) noncompetitive bid — this is where the investor agrees to accept a rate determined by the auction; (2) competitive bid — the investor submits a tender specifying a discount rate. If the bid falls within the range accepted at the auction, the investor will be awarded the security. Where the bid is at the high rate of yield, the investor may not be awarded the full amount bid. Competitive bidders may be at a disadvantage as there is the possibility that their bids might be rejected, and in multiple-price auctions they may pay a higher price for the security than the noncompetitive bidder.

The major types of bonds usually available are debentures and local registered stocks (LRS). Debentures and LRS are not regarded as liquid assets. LRS only become liquid assets less than nine months prior to maturity.

The interest rates in the beginning for debentures and LRS are usually fixed for the first three to six months (depending on the terms of issue). Thereafter interest can, for example, be paid every three to six months at a variable rate between 2–2.75 percentage points above the weighted average yield rate applicable to the six month Treasury Bill Tender held immediately prior to the commencement of each half-yearly interest period.

Treasury bills, debentures and local registered stocks cannot be redeemed before maturity, unless by the terms of their issue they are callable. Generally, bonds are long-term instruments. However, in the Caribbean this is not so. Exceptional cases exist in Trinidad and Barbados where bonds have been issued, in recent times, for 25 years and 12 years, respectively.

New Terms

Limited company (p. 348): An organization owned by its shareholders, whose liability is limited to their share capital.

Shares (p. 348): The division of the capital of a limited company into parts.

Private company (p. 349): A limited company that must issue its shares privately.

Public company (p. 349): A company that can issue its shares publicly, and for which there is no maximum number of shareholders.

Directors (p. 349): Officials appointed by shareholders to manage the company for them.

Dividends (p. 349): The amount given to shareholders as their share of the profits of the company.

Preference shares (p. 350): Shares that are entitled to an agreed rate of dividend before the ordinary shareholders received anything.

Ordinary shares (p. 350): Shares entitled to dividends after the preference shareholders have been paid their dividends.

Debenture (p. 352): Loan to a company.

Reserve accounts (p. 352): The transfer of appropriated profits to accounts for use in future years.

Preliminary expenses (p. 352): All the costs that are incurred when a company is formed.

Summary

1 Limited companies exist because of the disadvantages and constraints arising from partnerships.
2 A fully paid-up shareholder's liability is limited to the shares he or she holds in the company. Shareholders cannot then be asked to pay any other company debt from their private resources.
3 There are far more private companies than public companies.
4 A limited company has a 'separate legal entity' from that of its members.
5 Directors' remuneration is charged to the main part of the profit and loss account.
6 Debenture interest is charged to the main part of the profit and loss account.
7 Transfers to reserves, dividends and taxation are charged to the appropriation part of the profit and loss account.
8 Any balance of profits unappropriated at the end of a period is carried forward as a balance to the next period.
9 Companies are governed by the country's Companies Act.

Exercises

39.1 Draw up a balance sheet for a limited company R. O. Ltd from the following as at 31 December 2004.

	$
Premises at cost	45,000
Machinery at cost	24,000
Fixtures at cost	12,000
Stock	18,000
Bank	6,000
Debtors	9,000
Depreciation to date:	
Premises	18,000
Machinery	7,200
Fixtures	4,800
Authorized share capital: ordinary shares $1	60,000
Issued share capital: fully paid	36,000
Debentures: 10%	18,000
Proposed dividend owing	3,000
Creditors	9,000
General reserve	15,000
Profit and loss account (balancing figure, for you to ascertain)	?

39.2X C. Blake Ltd has an authorized share capital of 90,000 ordinary shares of $1 each and 10,000 10% preference shares of $1 each. The company's trial balance extracted after one year of trading was as follows on 31 December 2004.

	$
Net profit for year to 31 Dec 2004	11,340
Debentures	30,000
Issued ordinary share capital, fully paid	60,000
Issued preference share capital, fully paid	10,000
Creditors	3,550
Debtors	4,120
Cash	2,160
Stock	8,800
Provision for bad debts	350
Provision for depreciation: equipment	4,500
Equipment at cost	45,000
Premises at cost	50,000
Bank (use the balancing figure)	?

The directors decide to transfer $1,500 to the general reserve and to recommend a dividend of 12½% on the ordinary shares. The preference dividend was not paid until after January 2005.

You are required to:

(*a*) draw up the appropriation account for the year ended 31 December 2004;
(*b*) draft a balance sheet as at 31 December 2004. *(CXC style)*

39.3 C. A. Company Ltd, manufacturing agricultural implements, made a net profit after taxation of $210,000 for the year to 31 December 2002. Retained profits at 31 December 2001 amounted to $17,000. At the directors' meeting the following appropriations were agreed.

	$
To be transferred to general reserve	30,000
To be transferred to foreign exchange reserve	5,000
Goodwill to be written off	11,000

(Cont'd)

It has also been agreed that a dividend of 10% be proposed on the ordinary share capital. This amounted to 500,000 shares of $2 each.

Preference share dividends of 10% had been paid during the year on 250,000 preference shares of $1 each.

You are required to draw up the company's profit and loss appropriation account for the year ended 31 December 2002.

(CXC style)

39.4X Baker Ltd was authorized to issue a total of $200,000 share capital, divided into 150,000 ordinary shares of $1 and 50,000 8% preference shares. All ordinary shares were issued and fully paid up. Of the preference shares, 20,000 only were issued and fully paid. 100 10% debentures of $100 each were issued at par. These were all taken up and paid in full.

From the above, answer the following.

(*a*) How much was received from the issue of preference shares?

(*b*) Assuming there are sufficient profits, how much would be received in total by preference shareholders as annual dividends?

(*c*) How much was received from the issue of debentures?

(*d*) How much will be paid annually as debenture interest?

(*e*) If net profits before charging debenture interest were $35,000 and it was all distributed, what was the rate of dividend paid to ordinary shareholders?

(CXC style)

39.5 The following is the trial balance of BBC Ltd as on 31 December 2003.

	Dr.	*Cr.*
	$	$
Share capital issued: ordinary shares $1		75,000
Debtors and creditors	28,560	22,472
Stock 31 December 2002	41,415	
Bank	16,255	
Machinery at cost	45,000	
Motor vehicles at cost	28,000	
Depreciation provisions at 31 Dec 2002		
Machinery		18,000
Motor vehicles		12,600
Sales		97,500
Purchases	51,380	
Motor expenses	8,144	
Repairs to machinery	2,308	
Sundry expenses	1,076	
Pay	11,372	
Directors' remuneration	6,200	
Profit and loss account as at 31 Dec 2002		6,138
General reserve		8,000
	239,710	239,710

Given the following information, you are to draw up trading and profit and loss accounts for the year ended 31 December 2003, and a balance sheet as at that date.

1 Authorized share capital: $100,000 in ordinary shares $1.
2 Stock at 31 Dec 2003, $54,300.
3 Motor expenses owing, $445.
4 Ordinary dividend proposed of 20%.
5 Transfer $2,000 to general reserve.
6 Provide for depreciation of all fixed assets at 20% reducing balance method.
7 Ignore taxation.

39.6X You are to draw up trading and profit and loss accounts for the year ended 31 December 2004, and a balance sheet as at that date, from the following trial balance and details of B. Tyler Ltd.

	Dr.	*Cr.*
	$	$
Bank	6,723	
Debtors	18,910	
Creditors		12,304
Stock 31 Dec 2003	40,360	
Buildings at cost	100,000	
Equipment at cost	45,000	
Profit and loss account as at 31 Dec 2003		15,286
General reserve		8,000
Foreign exchange reserve		4,200
Authorized and issued share capital		100,000
Purchases	72,360	
Sales		135,486
Carriage inwards	1,570	
Carriage outwards	1,390	
Pay	18,310	
Rates and occupancy expenses	4,235	
Office expenses	3,022	
Sundry expenses	1,896	
Provisions for depreciation at 31 Dec 2003:		
Buildings		32,000
Equipment		16,000
Directors' remuneration	9,500	
	323,276	323,276

Notes: at 31 Dec 2004

1 Stock at 31 Dec 2004, $52,360.
2 Rates owing, $280; office expenses owing, $190.
3 Ordinary dividend of 10% proposed.
4 Transfer to reserves: general, $1,000; foreign exchange, $800.
5 Depreciation on cost: buildings, 5%; equipment, 20%.
6 Ignore taxation.

CHAPTER **40**

Methods of Processing Data: From Bound Books to Computers

Learning Objectives

- To understand the development of methods of processing double entry data, from bound books to computers.
- To understand the difference between hardware and software.
- To appreciate why different businesses need different bookkeeping programs.
- To be able to code information.

40.1 Introduction

Probably one of the best ways to understand modern accounting methods is to trace their development from the conventional double entry system. The firm at which you are employed, or will be employed, will be at some stage along this span of development. You should then be able to relate the firm's bookkeeping methods to what used to be done, and also to what may be done in your firm in the future.

It must always be borne in mind that, barring the legal needs that accounts fulfil, the costs of running the system should not exceed the benefits. To take an exaggerated example, a, very small shop could hardly be expected to use an expensive computer, as the costs of running it would far exceed any benefits the firm might receive. This test should always be applied before advocating a more advanced system of bookkeeping.

We will now take a look at how modern methods have developed.

40.2 Bound Books

Up to the advent of the typewriter in 1866, bound volumes were universally used for bookkeeping records. The accounts took the basic double entry form described in this book, but there was a lot of manual copying of items that has been eliminated from the present basic system. As carbon paper had not been invented, the sales invoices, debit and credit notes were copied into the sales and returns books before they were dispatched to customers and suppliers.

40.3 Loose-leaf Ledgers and Carbon Paper

The typewriter and the consequent development of carbon paper led to the transition away from bound books to loose-leaf ledgers.

Typewriters could obviously be used more easily with loose sheets of paper and, with the use of carbon paper, could give several copies of such things as invoices and debit and credit notes. Typed ledger accounts were also neater than handwritten records.

At first, the loose-leaf ledgers were kept in covers that could be opened and closed by operating a key. The loose sheets therefore had to be extracted and placed into the typewriter, then removed from the typewriter and replaced in the covers. Soon it was seen, that continually extracting them from and replacing them in the covers was a waste of time. The loose leaves, especially if they were somewhat sturdier and in the form of cards, could easily be kept in trays.

40.4 From the Typewriter and the Adding Machine to the Accounting Machines

Adding machines were in existence in the latter part of the nineteenth century. In 1901, an accounting machine was constructed in the United States which was a combination of the adding machine and the typewriter. Other machines were developed, some being based primarily on the adding machine while others were developed from the typewritter.

40.5 Punched Card Accounting Machines

A class of accounting machine that worked in an entirely different way was also developed. This was the punched card machine developed in the United States by Dr Hollerith in 1884. This method of accounting was based on information that was recorded by the means of holes punched into cards.

Since the advent of the electronic computer, the punched card accounting machine has fallen into disuse.

40.6 Computers: Introduction

For accounting work, computers followed on logically from punched cards. Computers were first used for business purposes around 1952. The first **computers** were quite large machines. As a rough comparison, a machine that would have filled up the whole of the space in a room then could, today, have its work performed quicker and more efficiently by a machine that would easily fit on a space no bigger than two sheets of paper on top of your desk.

A computer has five basic types of components:

- input devices – e.g. a keyboard, mouse, scanner
- storage devices – e.g. hard disc, floppy disc
- a central processing unit (CPU) – this contains its main memory, arithmetic unit, and control unit
- output devices – e.g. a monitor, printer
- communications devices – e.g. modem.

Whatever could be written about the use of computers in business would be out of date by the time this book is printed and on sale. It is therefore pointless in a general textbook to be too specific about particular makes of computers. We shall therefore instead consider the general principles involved.

The larger computers, used by bigger firms, have very substantial memories and are called 'mainframe computers'. A 'minicomputer' has all the characteristics of a mainframe computer, but it is on a much smaller scale and will cost less than a mainframe computer. A 'microcomputer' is the smallest in the range of computers, and is based on *microchips*, which are small electronic devices that enable the computer to be small in size. There is no clear dividing line between mainframe and minicomputers. In addition, there is very little practical difference between the smaller of the minicomputers and the larger of the microcomputers.

Mainframe computers cost a lot of money and take up a fair amount of space. This is not true of microcomputers, which are relatively cheap and take up very little space. The time has now come when the production of microcomputers means that any business, even the very smallest, can afford to have a computer.

As the microcomputer is almost certainly the type of computer that most students will meet, whether at college or at home, it is that type of computer with which this book will be concerned.

This brings us to the view expressed by some students that, if computers can perform bookkeeping extremely well, then why should they bother to learn about it? After all, if they can be taught to press a few buttons, then that is all they need know. However, if something goes wrong and you do not understand bookkeeping properly, then you are going to believe the bookkeeping records produced on the computer. We all know the student who multiples 25 by 14 on a pocket calculator and gets an answer of 13,360 and believes it. Basic knowledge of arithmetic should have told the student that the answer cannot be more than a few hundred. Similar conditions apply when using computers.

40.7 Computer Hardware

For small firms, the typical microcomputer system will consist of four main types of equipment, or **hardware**, as it is called.

- **The microcomputer** This resembles a small typewritter with a keyboard, on which you can type instructions and data. It will also have 'memory', in which it can store data and information, and a processing unit, in which calculations are performed.
- **A monitor** Still sometimes called a VDU (visual display unit), this is rather like a television set. In fact, many readers will know that early personal computers often used ordinary television sets, enabling the user to keep costs down. Nowadays, virtually all microcomputers are sold with a monitor. Any information that is held inside the computer can be displayed on the monitor.
- **A printer** This will produce printed copies of the ledger accounts, journals, trial balance, etc.
- **Disk drives** Only a limited amount of information can be held in a computer's memory; and this information is wiped out when the machine is switched off. For business use, a computer must keep a copy of everything that is input. In microcomputers this information is usually kept stored on magnetic disks. Most microcomputers now have a hard disk permanently located inside them where software and data is stored and a floppy disk drive which can read from and write to floppy disks (sometimes called 'diskettes') that are stored separately from the microcomputer. More recent microcomputers also have compact disk (CD) drives. CD-ROMs can store far more than floppy disks and are now the most common way in which new programs are installed on microcomputers.

40.8 Computer Software

The computer has to be given instructions as to exactly what the user wants it to do. These instructions are called programs. The collective name given to computer programs is **software**.

The programs will vary, depending on exactly what it is that you want the computer to do. They may also vary with different makes of computers. If you were sufficiently expert, and had enough time, you could write your own sets of programs for your computer. However, most software is written by computer experts and should have been exhaustively tested before being put on to the market for sale.

The software is normally supplied on disks or CD-ROMs. Exactly how much information can be supplied will depend on the type of disk drive in use.

40.9 Bookkeeping Programs

There are, in fact, a large number of bookkeeping programs available on the market. There are two main types of microcomputers – personal computers (PCs) and Apple Macintosh computers (MaCs). Unfortunately, it is not always possible or straightforward to use programs written for one type on the other. As a result, different programs are needed for each type of microcomputer.

Even if you have the same type of microcomputer as other firms, you may well use a different program for the same bookkeeping function. A firm with several branches would probably want a different program from that of a firm without branches. A firm that had only cash sales would want a different program from a firm that had only credit sales. A firm that supplied services only would want a different program from a firm that supplied goods only.

To start off, the program is installed onto the hard disk of the computer. Once this is done, the program can be started either from a menu or, for those computers with a graphics-based operating environment (e.g. Microsoft's Windows) by using a mouse to click on an *icon* (a small picture) on the monitor screen. The program that then appears on the screen will allow you to feed in data that are to be processed, e.g. entering credit sales. It would be impossible here to state how this should be done, for every program is different.

In an ordinary manual system of bookkeeping, the entering of credit sales would be in the sales journal and in the sales ledger accounts. Similarly, credit purchases would be entered in the purchases journal and the purchases ledger. That would completely finish the bookkeeping entries. With most bookkeeping programs run on a computer, it is possible to get automatic by-products of the data fed in for other reasons. If sales are known in detail, i.e. exactly which items have been sold, and how many of each item, and purchases are known, and how many of each item has been bought, then it is possible for the computer automatically to produce stock records, for every single item of stock.

In a firm dealing in quite a few types of goods, a simple bookkeeping system could not have shown how many of a particular item should be in stock at any time. The only way this could have been found out would have been for someone to actually go and count the items. In a computerized system, the entering of items sold will not only be entered in the figures in the sales journal, but will be entered automatically in the stock records as well. Similarly with items bought. Given the opening stock of every individual item, if the sales and purchases of each item is put into the stock records then the closing stock of each item on a particular day can automatically be produced by the computer. There will be actual physical stock checks from time to time to ensure that the computer system is working properly.

40.10 Computer Inputs

Where computers are used in the accounting process, the basic information, instead of being handwritten into the system, needs to be entered by a means that the computer can accept. This can be by a number of methods, such as keyboard, scanner or direct download over a network.

For most accounting transactions the information will be entered through a keyboard, the keys of which are laid out in a way that is similar in many ways to that of a typewritter. The computer screen shows what has been entered on the keyboard in the same way as paper placed in a typewriter shows what has been typed. The operator can, therefore, check visually that the entry made on the keyboard is correct.

40.11 Problems of Data Collection

Whatever method of data collection is used, its accuracy and completeness is vital if a computer system is to work properly. There is a standard saying for computers, 'Garbage In Garbage Out' (GIGO), which means that if you do not put the correct data into the computer you cannot possibly get the correct output when required. Great care has therefore to be taken to check the accuracy of the input. This may for example involve having two independent operators prepare input from the original data. These will be compared automatically and used only if they agree. This is only one of a whole range of checks to make sure a system is accurate.

Mistakes are just as important in a manual system, but they can usually be traced more easily since a written record can be looked at directly. Once information is recorded on disk it is much less visible, and errors become harder to spot.

40.12 Coding Information

One special requirement when entering data into a computer system is to describe the input in a way that enables the computer to work efficiently. In a manual system, words as well as numbers are used to describe the data being entered. A customer will be entered by name and the products that the customer is ordering will be described in words, in addition to the quantities involved.

A computer system works much better if the information is transformed into numerical terms. Thus, instead of describing the customer as Mr Jones, the computer will require a code number for Mr Jones, say customer number 3562. Similarly, it is necessary to have code numbers for the products rather than simply to use a name. To help people using information from the computer, the printout usually shows the customer name in addition to the number; but for working purposes the computer is interested only in the number.

Code numbers are often made easier to understand. Take the following example from a clothes shop. The first digit describes the nature of the product:

1 hats	2 socks
3 gloves	4 trousers.

The second digit describes the material from which the item is made:

1 wool	2 cotton
3 nylon	4 felt.

The third digit may describe the colour of the product:

1 blue	2 grey
3 black	4 white.

Thus, a product with number 142 would be a grey felt hat.

As people remember words more easily than numbers, it is sometimes useful to combine words or letters with the numbers. A good example is the coding of flights from airports that include an abbreviated description of the airline with a specific flight number, e.g. WIA 192: West Indian Airways flight number 192. People find this easier to remember and check than a six-number code.

40.13 Checks and Errors

It is beyond the scope of this book to describe exactly how checks are built into a computerized accounting system, but a couple of examples will give you a general idea of how they work. Suppose that a payroll is put on to the computer and, in error, one employee is shown as working 250 hours in a week–obviously quite impossible. Included in the automatic check that will be thrown up by the computer is the restriction that no one can work more than (say) 80 hours per week. Also, if a sales invoice works out as minus $280 then that will be shown up automatically by the check, as minus figures are impossible for sales.

When feeding numerical data into a computer, the following types of error can be made.

Error	*Example*		
Transcription	12345	becomes	12545
Transposition	12345	becomes	12435
Double Transposition	12345	becomes	12543
Omission	12345	becomes	1345
Addition	12345	becomes	123745
Random	A combination of two or more of the above or any other error.		

40.14 Data Processing

As there is an enormous difference between firms, in terms of both the work that they do and their size and organization, there is correspondingly a very wide variety of methods of data processing for accounting purposes. Each organization must decide how it wants to keep its information, with regard to both cost and effectiveness. A very small firm may find that a simple manual recording system is adequate, whereas a large firm will need to handle a much higher volume of data and therefore may require a computerized system.

New Terms

Computer (p. 364): an electronic machine consisting of five basic units: input, storage, CPU, output, and communications.

Hardware (p. 365): a term used to describe the mechanical and electrical equipment comprising a computer.

Software (p. 366): a term used to describe the instructions that control the operation of a computer. Individually, these are called 'programs'.

Summary

1 Both computers and manual methods should provide the same basic information from a given set of accounting data. What will be different is the speed at which the computer handles the data, and it may also be easily made to produce other desirable information which would be very time-consuming in a manual set-up.

2 There are a lot of bookkeeping programs specially written for use with computers. Whether they will suit a particular organization's needs can be ascertained only after full investigation. Quite often, the organization will have a special program devised just for its own use.

3 No computer system is foolproof, no matter what the computer expert may tell you. This is why you should understand accounting without computers in order to be able to check, whether or not the computer is providing you with the correct information.

Exercises

40.1 The sports shop of the Sky Hotel also sells sports shoes for squash or tennis which are made by ABC Ltd. The manufacturer produces shoes in half-sizes as follows.

	Size ranges
Mens	6½ to 9½
Boys	2 to 6
Ladies	3 to 8
Girls	1 to 6

An eight-digit code is used to identify shoes. Reading from left to right, it is made up as follows.

- Digit one shows whether the shoes are men's, boys', ladies' or girls'. The numbers in use are men's 1, boys' 2, ladies' 3, girls' 4.
- Digit two shows the situation concerning laces. No laces is given number 0, short black laces 1, long black laces 2, short brown laces 3, long brown laces 4, short white laces 5, long white laces 6.
- Digit three shows the colour: black 1, dark brown 2, tan 3, white 4, blue 5, green 6, yellow 7.
- Digit four shows the material of the upper part of the shoes: leather 1, synthetic 2, canvas 3, suede 4.
- Digit five shows the material of the sole: leather 1, rubber 2, synthetic 3.
- Digit six shows whether any guarantee is given to the purchaser as to period of use during which shoes can be returned if worn out: no guarantee 0, three months 1, six months 2, one year 3.
- Digits seven and eight show size: size 1 is shown as 10, size 1½ as 15, size 2 as 20, size 2½ as 25, and so on.

Examples of codes are:

1 code 10433085 is a pair of men's shoes with no laces, white canvas, synthetic sole, no guarantee given, size 8½.

2 code 43211240 is a pair of girl's shoes with short brown laces, dark brown leather uppers with leather soles, six months' guarantee, size 4.

(*a*) You are required to give the code numbers that would apply to:

(i) boy's shoes, with long black laces, black in colour, synthetic uppers, leather soles, six months' guarantee, size 5;

(ii) ladies' shoes, no laces, yellow, leather uppers and soles, no guarantee, size 6½;

(iii) men's tan shoes, leather sole, synthetic uppers, short brown laces, three months guarantee, size 9½;

(iv) girls' blue shoes, size 3½, no laces, suede uppers and leather sole, no guarantee.

(Cont'd)

(*b*) State exactly what kinds of shoes are denoted by the following code numbers:
(i) 31123045
(ii) 26432060
(iii) 10223085
(iv) 40612320.

(*c*) If red shoes were added to the product range, what do you think would happen to the code?

(*d*) What would you suggest should happen to the code numbers if the range of footwear was extended to boots for men and for boys?

(*e*) What other information do you think would be desirable for ladies' shoes that is not already given in the code?

(*f*) If the exact system of coding was adhered to, and the company extended its men's shoe range up to size 12, what problems would result?

40.2 What kinds of errors are these:

(*a*) 56789 shown in error as 5679?
(*b*) 56789 shown in error as 56987?
(*c*) 56789 shown in error as 56879?
(*d*) 56789 shown in error as 567899?
(*e*) 56789 shown in error as 56779?
(*f*) 56789 shown in error as 658976?

CHAPTER **41**

Stock Records and Stock Valuation

Learning Objectives

- To understand that there can be more than one way of valuing stocks.
- To be able to calculate the value of stock using the different methods.
- To be able to adjust stock valuations, where necessary, by a reduction to net realizable values.
- To be able to adjust stock valuations in respect of goods on sale or return.
- To enter up quantities of items in stock records.

41.1 Different Valuations of Stock

Most people would think that there can be only one figure for the valuation of stock. This is not true. In this chapter we will examine how different figures for stock can be calculated.

Assume that a firm has just completed its first financial year and is about to value stock at cost price. It has dealt in only one type of goods. A record of the transactions is now shown in Exhibit 41.1. Still in stock on 31 December were 8 units. The total figure of purchases is $1,440 and that of sales is $1,840. The trading account for the first year of trading can now be completed if the closing stock is brought into the calculations.

Exhibit 41.1

Bought			**Sold**		
2005		$	2005		$
January	10 at $30 each	300	May	8 for $50 each	400
April	10 at $34 each	340	November	24 for $60 each	1,440
October	20 at $40 each	800			
	40	1,440		32	1,840

But what value do we put on each of the 8 units left in stock at the end of the year? If all of the units bought during the year had cost $30 each, then the closing stock would be 8 × $30 = $240. However, we have bought goods at different prices. This means that the valuation depends on which goods are taken for this calculation – the units at $30, $34, or at $40.

Many firms do not know exactly whether they have sold all the oldest units before they sell the newer units. For instance, a firm selling spanners may not know if the oldest spanners had been sold before the newest spanners.

The stock valuation will therefore be based on accounting custom, and not on the facts of exactly which units were still in stock at the year end. The three main methods of doing this are described in Sections 41.2, 41.3 and 41.4.

41.2 First In, First Out Method

This is usually known as **FIFO**, from the first letters of each word.

This method assumes that the first goods to be received are the first to be issued. Using the figures in Exhibit 41.1, we can now calculate the closing figure of stock as shown in Exhibit 41.2. It can be seen that the closing stock at 31 December 2005 is thereby valued at $320.

Exhibit 41.2

	Received	Issued	Stock after each transaction	$	$
2005				$	$
January	10 at $30 each		10 at $30 each		300
April	10 at $34 each		10 at $30 each	300	
			10 at $34 each	340	640
May		8 at $30 each	2 at $30 each	60	
			10 at $34 each	340	400
October	20 at $40 each		2 at $30 each	60	
			10 at $34 each	340	
			20 at $40 each	800	1,200
November		2 at $30 each			
		10 at $34 each			
		12 at $40 each			
		24	8 at $40 each		320

41.3 Last In, First Out Method

This is usually known as **LIFO**. As each issue of goods is made they are said to be from the last lot of goods received before that date. Where there is not enough left of the last lot of goods, then the balance of goods needed is said to come from the previous lot still unsold.

From the information shown in Exhibit 41.1, the calculation can now be worked as in Exhibit 41.3. It can be seen that the closing stock at 31 December 2005 is thereby valued at $240.

Exhibit 41.3

	Received	Issued	Stock after each transaction		
2005				$	$
January	10 at $30 each		10 at $30 each		300
April	10 at $34 each		10 at $30 each	300	
			10 at $34 each	340	640
May		8 at $34 each	10 at $30 each	300	
			2 at $34 each	68	368
October	20 at $40 each		10 at $30 each	300	
			2 at $34 each	68	
			20 at $40 each	800	1,168
November		20 at $40 each			
		2 at $34 each			
		2 at $30 each	8 at $30 each		240
		24			

41.4 Average Cost Method (AVCO)

Using the **AVCO** method, with each receipt of goods the average cost for each item of stock is recalculated. Further issues of goods are then priced at that figure, until another receipt of goods means that another recalculation is needed.

From the information in Exhibit 41.1, the calculation can be shown in Exhibit 41.4. It can be seen that the closing stock at 31 December 2005 is thereby valued at $296.

Exhibit 41.4

Received		Issued	Average cost per unit of stock held	Number of units in stock	Total value of stock
2005			$		$
January	10 at $30		30	10	300
April	10 at $34		32*	20	640
May		8 at $32	32	12	384
October	20 at $40		37*	32	1,184
November		24 at $37	37	8	296

*In April, this is calculated as follows; stock 10 × $30 = $300 + stock received (10 × $34 = $340) = total $640. There are 20 units in stock, so the average is $640 ÷ 20 = $32. In October this is calculated as follows: stock 12 × $32 = $384 + stock received (20 × $40 = $800) = $1,184. There are 32 units in stock, so the average is $1,184 ÷ 32 = $37.

41.5 Stock Valuation and the Calculation of Profits

Using the figures from Exhibit 41.1 with stock valuation shown by the three methods of FIFO, LIFO and AVCO, the trading accounts would appear as shown in Exhibit 41.5. As you can see, different methods of stock valuation mean that different profits are shown.

The choice of stock valuation method depends on many factors, involving many complicated economic factors, so it is not dealt with here. Students taking professional examinations later in their lives will deal with such matters.

Exhibit 41.5

Trading Account for the year ended 31 December 2005

	FIFO	*LIFO*	*AVCO*		*FIFO*	*LIFO*	*AVCO*
	$	$	$		$	$	$
Purchases	1,440	1,440	1,440	Sales	1,840	1,840	1,840
Less Closing stock	320	240	296				
Cost of goods sold	1,120	1,200	1,144				
Gross profit	720	640	696				
	1,840	1,840	1,840		1,840	1,840	1,840

41.6 Reduction to Net Realizeable Value

The **net realizeable value** of stock is calculated as follows:

Saleable value – Expenses needed before completion of sale = Net realizable value

If saleable value is $300 and expenses needed is $20, the net realizable value would be $280. Now if the net realizable value of stock is lower than the valuation at cost, the figure to be taken for the final accounts will be the net realizable value. If stock at cost valuation is $500 and net realizable value is $400, then the figure of $400 will be used in the trading account and the balance sheet.

41.7 Goods on Sale or Return

Goods Received on Sale or Return

Sometimes we may receive goods from one of our suppliers on a **sale or return** basis. What this means is that we do not have to pay for the goods until we sell them. If we do not sell them we have to return them to our supplier.

This means that the goods do not belong to us. If we have some goods on sale or return at the stocktaking date, they should not be included in our stock valuation.

Goods Sent to our Customers on Sale or Return

We may send goods on a sale or return basis to our customers. The stock will belong to us until it is sold. At our stocktaking date any goods held by our customers on sale or return should be included in our stock valuation.

41.8 Stock Records: Quantities

In a small retail shop such as grocer's, we would not expect the shop assistant to record the exact nature of each sale. If there were a queue of people waiting it would be more than annoying if they had to wait while we recorded that we had just sold a jar of jam or a tin of soup. What the shop assistant would do would be to record only the cash received, without identifying the exact nature of the sale.

On the other hand, a second-hand car sales firm *would* record each sale in detail. Otherwise, if there were no check on sales, any of the employees would be able to steal a car quite easily, as the firm would not know which cars they should still have in stock. In addition, it would also be made quite easy for a member of the public to take a car without paying for it.

The type of firm will therefore indicate whether or not it is desirable to keep an exact record of all goods received and all goods disposed of. Sometimes, of course, an inefficient firm will not keep records when it would be in its interest to do so; also, some firms will keep detailed records when it is rather ridiculous for them so to do.

Let us look at a typical example. A firm that makes its products out of a metal that is very valuable wants to ensure that there are no stock losses. Exhibit 41.6 presents the records of two items, component FG and component JK. As each item is bought, the reference number of the purchases invoice is given. As each item is issued from the stores to the employees, a voucher has to be filled in and signed by the employee before the item is handed over by the shopkeeper, and each voucher is given a number. Any items returned by employees will also be given a separate number.

Exhibit 41.6

Component FG	*No. of items*	*Component JK*	*No. of items*
2006		2006	
Jan 1 Stock b/fwd	86	Jan 1 Stock b/fwd	28
Jan 2 Received (invoice 5543)	20	Jan 2 Received (invoice 5549)	300
Jan 4 Issue P67	16	Jan 3 Issue R323	44
Jan 6 Issue P68	29	Jan 5 Issue R324	23
Jan 10 Issue P132	19	Jan 9 Issue R129	107
Jan 21 Received (invoice 5874)	70	Jan 11 Issue R325	79
Jan 25 Issue P69	33	Jan 13 Return in RA229	18
Jan 31 Issue P243	18	Jan 19 Received (invoice 5799)	200
		Jan 22 Issue R354	96
		Jan 29 Issue R130	64
		Jan 31 Return in RA230	5

From these stock records, we should be able to work out exactly how many of component FG and of component JK are in stock on 31 January 2006. We also do a physical stockcheck (i.e., we actually look at and count the items in the store) and find that we have 61 of FG and 134 of JK on that date.

We can now draft up a stock record card for each of these components. As each item is issued or received, we alter the balance of stock in hand. With component FG (Exhibit 41.7), the actual stock equals the stock as per the stock card, verifying that there have been no stock losses. With component JK, we can see in Exhibit 41.8 that the stock card records disclose a stock loss of four items.

Exhibit 41.7

Stock Record Card

Component FG

Date	*Ref.*	*In*	*Out*	*Balance*
2006				
Jan 1	Opening balance			86
Jan 2	5543	20		106
Jan 4	P67		16	90
Jan 6	P68		29	61
Jan 10	P132		19	42
Jan 21	5874	70		112
Jan 25	P69		33	79
Jan 31	P243		18	61

Exhibit 41.8

Stock Record Card

Component JK

Date	*Ref.*	*In*	*Out*	*Balance*
2006				
Jan 1	Opening balance			28
Jan 2	5549	300		328
Jan 3	R323		44	284
Jan 5	R324		23	261
Jan 9	R129		107	154
Jan 11	R325		79	75
Jan 13	RA229	18		93
Jan 19	5799	200		293
Jan 22	R354		96	197
Jan 29	R130		64	133
Jan 31	RA230	5		138
Jan 31	Stock loss		4	134

The stock loss of four items of component JK will now have to be investigated. There may be a satisfactory explanation, or it may be a case of theft, with the police being called in to investigate. It is up to the individual firm to decide what course of action is to be taken, but the stock loss should be looked into to establish the reasons for the deficiency.

New Terms

FIFO(p. 372): the units of stock that are bought first are assumed to be the first units to be used or sold; hence First In First Out prices at the cost of the earliest units bought.

LIFO (p. 372): the units of stock that are bought last are assumed to be the first units used or sold; hence Last In First Out prices at the cost of the latest units bought.

AVCO (p. 373): the cost of units are averaged over the period and units used are priced at average cost.

Net realizable value (p. 374): the sale price of units of stock in the market less any expenses needed before completion of sale.

Summary

1 The methods of pricing out stocks, e.g. FIFO or LIFO, are methods of pricing out stocks only. It does not mean that goods are physically handed out on a FIFO or LIFO basis.

2 Different stock valuing methods mean that different amounts of profit will be shown for a particular period.

3 Using the net realizable value when this is lower than cost is an example of the convention of prudence in accounting so that profits are not overstated.

4 Without stock records of quantities of items, it would be very difficult to track down theft or losses or to detect wastages of goods.

Exercises

41.1 Rule up a card suitable for the recording of the quantity of an item in stock. The card should show receipts, issues and balance. The names of suppliers should be shown against receipts, and the requisition number against issues.

Item number 24		
1 May 2009 Balance in stock		500
Receipts		
2 May 2009 Starlight Co Ltd		300
8 May 2009 Moonbeam & Sons		200
24 May 2009 Starlight Co Ltd		350
Issues		
8 May 2009 Requisition number	740	173
10 May 2009	810	294
14 May 2009	976	104
28 May 2009	981	206

41.2 Henriques is a sole trader whose year end is 31 January each year. Owing to pressure of business, he is unable to value his stock in trade at the close of business on 31 January 2004 but he does so on 7 February 2004 when the value, *at cost price*, is calculated at $2,830.

For the period 1–7 February his purchases were $296, of which goods costing $54 were in transit at the time of stocktaking.

Sales for the period 1–7 February amounted to $460, all of which had left the warehouse at the time of stocktaking. His gross profit is 20% of sales.

Also during the period 1–7 February, Henriques took goods costing $38 for his personal use.

Included in the valuation figure of $2,830 given above were goods that cost $120, but which had a *market price* of $97 only at the date of the year end, i.e. 31 January 2004.

Required:
Calculate the figure that should be shown as 'Stock at 31 January 2004' in Henrique's trading account for the year ended 31 January 2004.
Note: Calculations must be shown.

41.3X C. Jones, a builders' merchant, has no reliable method of recording his stock receipts and issues. At the present time he has no means of obtaining a valuation for his stock-in-trade (without undertaking a lengthy and costly stocktaking).

Jones has produced the following data from the month ended 30 September 2009.

Marble chippings stock	1 Sept	2 tonnes
Purchased from J. Brown	4 Sept	8 tonnes
Sold to T. Williams	10 Sept	6 tonnes
Purchased from B. Green	14 Sept	9 tonnes
Sold to W. Thomas	20 Sept	2 tonnes
Sold to B. Dunstan	25 Sept	7 tonnes

All stock and purchases are priced at $50 per tonne. All issues of stock are priced at $65 per tonne.

You are required to show Jones' trading account for the month ended 30 September 2009.

41.4X You are valuing stock at your business as it was at 31 December 2007. The actual date on which the stock was taken was 7 January 2008. The stock sheets show a total of $85,980 at cost as on that date. You are to adjust this figure to find out the stock as at 31 December 2007.

The rate of gross profit was 25% on selling price.

On further scrutiny you find:

(*a*) goods received after 1 January and for which invoices bear the date of January amounted to $3,987;
(*b*) one of the stock sheets has been added up to give a total of $4,897 instead of $4,798;
(*c*) goods selling at $480 had been sent to a customer on 'sale or return' during December; – these had not been sold by the customer, and they had been omitted from the stock figures;
(*d*) an item of 360 items priced at $1.60 each had been extended on the stock sheets as $420;
(*e*) goods had been returned to suppliers amounting to $98 during the first week of January.

41.5 Receipts and issues of a good are as follows.

	Receipts		*Sales*
Jan	20 at $30 each	June	6 for $45 each
May	10 at $33 each	Aug	22 for $46 each
July	16 at $38.5 each	Dec	10 for $48 each
Oct	12 at $39 each		

There was no opening stock-in-hand.

(*a*) You are required to calculate the closing stock-in-trade using (i) FIFO; (ii) LIFO; (iii) AVCO.

(Cont'd)

(*b*) Draw up the trading account showing the different reported gross profits from the figures given in (*a*)

41.6X

(*a*) From the following figures, calculate the closing stock-in-trade that would be shown using (i) FIFO; (ii) LIFO; (iii) AVCO methods on a perpetual inventory basis.

	Bought		*Sold*
Jan	24 at $10 each	June	30 at $16 each
April	16 at $12.50 each	Nov	34 at $18 each
Oct	30 at $13 each		

There was no opening stock-in-hand.

(*b*) Draw up trading accounts using each of the three methods.

41.7X JCD Ltd, which deals in radios, has the following purchases for May 2002.

Date	*Details* (no. of radios)	*Price per radio* $	*Total* $
May 1	15	20	300
May 7	20	24	480
May 24	16	26	416
May 30	6	30	180
			1,376

(*a*) JCD Ltd sold 15 radios at $40 each on 16 May, and 10 radios $45 each on 28 May. Use the FIFO method of valuation to work out the value of closing stock at 31 May; also calculate gross profit.

(*b*) Use the LIFO method to calculate the following:
(i) value of closing stock;
(ii) gross profit.

(CXC style)

CHAPTER **42**

An Introduction to the Analysis and Interpretation of Accounting Statements

Learning Objectives

- To be able to understand how the use of ratios can help to analyse the effectiveness of businesses.
- To be able to calculate the main accounting ratios.

In Chapter 29 we took a brief look at accounting ratios. These will be useful to you when considering the interpretation of accounting statements. Before doing this, however, some other points will be dealt with. We will not limit our examination of accounts to those of limited companies.

42.1 Rate of Return of Net Profit on Capital Employed

The term 'capital employed' is often not defined properly, and people can easily misunderstand what is meant by it. Usually it is taken to mean Assets – Liabilities. You can see that this will be the same figure for a sole trader as the balance on his or her capital account. For a company it will be the same figure as Share capital + Reserves.

When calculating ratios, we could base them on the capital employed at the end of the year, or we could instead use the average amount, calculated by taking the opening figure for the year, adding the closing figure for the year and then dividing the total figure by two. In this chapter the average of the capital account will be used; i.e.: (Opening balance + Closing balance) ÷ 2.

The formula used is:

$$\frac{\text{Net profit}}{\text{Capital employed}} \times \frac{100}{1} = \text{Rate of return on capital employed}$$

The answer will show how much net profit has been made for every $100 of capital employed during the period.

In businesses C and D in Exhibit 42.1 the same amount of net profits have been made, but capitals employed are different. **Returns on capital employed** are:

(C) $$\frac{3{,}600}{(8{,}000 + 10{,}000) \div 2} \times \frac{100}{1} = 40\%$$

(D) $$\frac{3{,}600}{(14{,}000 + 16{,}000) \div 2} \times \frac{100}{1} = 24\%$$

Exhibit 42.1

Balance Sheets

	C	*D*
	$	$
Fixed + Current assets – Current liabilities	10,000	16,000
Capital accounts:		
Opening balance	8,000	14,000
Add Net profits	3,600	3,600
	11,600	17,600
Less Drawings	1,600	1,600
	10,000	16,000

The ratio illustrates that what is important is not simply how much profit has been made but how well the capital has been employed. Business C has made far better use of its capital, achieving a return of $40 net profit for every $100 invested, whereas D has received a net profit of only $24 per $100.

42.2 Profitability and Liquidity

The return of profit on capital employed gives an overall picture of profitability. It cannot always be assumed, however, that profitability is everything that is desirable. It has been stressed earlier in our studies that accounting is needed not just to calculate profitability, but also to know whether or not the business will be able to meet its commitments as they fall due.

42.3 Liquidity Ratios

The two most important factors in the running of a business are, first, to ensure that it operates at a profit, and, second, to organize matters so that a business can pay its creditors and expenses at the correct times. Failure to ensure that both of these points are covered effectively could mean that the business will have to be closed down. Being able to pay one's debts as they fall due is known as being 'liquid'.

Several of the ratios that show up various aspects of liquidity are now defined. From a management point of view, this is equivalent to the management of working capital (Current assets – Current liabilities), since these are the most liquid of the business assets and liabilities.

The Current Ratio

This ratio measures current assets: current liabilities. In general terms, we are comparing assets that will be turned into cash within the next 12 months with liabilities that will have to be paid within the same period. If, therefore, the current assets are \$125,000 and the current liabilities are \$50,000, then the **current ratio** will be:

$$\frac{\$125{,}000}{\$50{,}000} = 2.5 : 1$$

Alternatively, this may be said to be 2.5 times. This is sometimes known as the working capital ratio.

The Acid Test Ratio

In order to bring about a further aspect of liquidity, this ratio is used; it takes only those current assets that are cash or will convert very quickly into cash. This will normally mean Cash + Bank + Debtors. You can see that this means exactly the same as Current assets – Stock. The **acid test ratio** may, therefore, be stated as:

Current assets – Stock: Current liabilities

If, therefore, the total of current assets is \$40,0000 and stock is \$10,000, and the total of current liabilities is \$20,000, then the ratio will be:

$$\frac{\$30{,}000}{\$20{,}000} = 1.5 : 1$$

Alternatively, this may be said to be 1.5 times.
The acid test ratio is also known as the quick ratio.

Debtor: Creditor Ratio

This ratio measures the relationship between how much credit is granted by the business to its customers, i.e. debtors, and how much credit has been received by the business from its suppliers, i.e. creditors.

Debtors: Sales Ratio

This ratio assesses how long it takes for our debtors to pay us. The calculation is made as follows:

$$\frac{\text{Debtors}}{\text{Sales for the year}} \times 12 = \text{Number of months debtors (on average) take to pay us}$$

For example:

	Firm A	*Firm B*
Sales for the year	\$240,000	\$180,000
Debtors per balance sheet	\$60,000	\$30,000

In firm A, therefore, debtors take three months on average to pay their accounts; i.e.,

$$\frac{60{,}000}{240{,}000} \times 12 = 3 \text{ months}$$

In firm B debtors take two months on average to pay their accounts; i.e.,

$$\frac{30{,}000}{180{,}000} \times 12 = 2 \text{ months}$$

The longer customers take to pay their accounts, the greater the likelihood of bad debts. Also, it means that we have more money tied up in overdue accounts than necessary, money that could otherwise have been invested elsewhere and some more profit made with it.

Creditors: Purchases Ratio

This ratio assesses how long it takes a firm on average to pay its suppliers. The calculation is made as follows:

$$\frac{\text{Creditors}}{\text{Purchases for the year}} \times 12 = \text{Number of months it takes (on average) to pay its suppliers}$$

For example:

	Firm A	*Firm B*
Purchases for the year	\$120,000	\$90,000
Creditors per balance sheet	\$40,000	\$22,500

Firm A therefore takes four months' credit on average from its suppliers; i.e.,

$$\frac{40{,}000}{120{,}000} \times 12 = 4 \text{ months}$$

Firm B takes on average three months to pay its suppliers; i.e.,

$$\frac{22{,}500}{90{,}000} \times 12 = 3 \text{ months}$$

Taking longer to pay suppliers could be a good thing or a bad thing, depending upon circumstances. If so long is taken to pay that possible discounts received are lost, or that suppliers refuse to supply us again, it is a bad thing to do. On the other hand, paying before it is necessary simply takes money out of the firm early without deriving any benefit from so doing.

42.4 Overall View of Liquidity

Each of the liquidity ratios already stated can be compared period by period to see if that particular aspect of liquidity is getting better or worse. Although in the past it was often thought that there was a 'correct' figure for each liquidity ratio, it used to be said that the current ratio should be about 2 : 1. However, in recent years it has become recognized that such a 'rule of thumb' figure cannot possibly apply to every business, as the types and circumstances of businesses vary widely.

Exhibit 42.2 shows how two businesses may have a similar profitability, yet their liquidity positions may be quite different.

Exhibit 42.2

		E		*F*
	$	$	$	$
Fixed assets		40,000		70,000
Current assets				
Stocks	30,000		50,000	
Debtors	45,000		9,000	
Bank	15,000		1,000	
	90,000		60,000	
Less Current liabilities	30,000	60,000	30,000	30,000
		100,000		100,000
Capital				
Opening capital		80,000		80,000
Add Net profit		36,000		36,000
		116,000		116,000
Less Drawings		16,000		16,000
		100,000		100,000

(*Note*: Sales for both E and F amounted to $144,000.)

Profitability is the same for both businesses:

$$\text{Net profit as a percentage of sales} = \frac{36{,}000}{144{,}000} \times \frac{100}{1} = 25\%$$

$$\text{Net profit as a percentage of capital employed} = \frac{36{,}000}{(80{,}000 + 100{,}000) \div 2} \times \frac{100}{1} = 40\%$$

However, there is a vast difference in the liquidity of the two businesses:

$$\text{Current ratios: E} = \frac{90{,}000}{30{,}000} = 3;\ \text{F} = \frac{60{,}000}{30{,}000} = 2$$

This looks adequate on the face of it, but the acid test ratio reveals that firm F is in distress, as it will probably find it difficult to pay its current liabilities on time.

$$\text{Acid test ratios: E} = \frac{60{,}000}{30{,}000} = 2;\ \text{F} = \frac{10{,}000}{30{,}000} = 0.33$$

Therefore, it is not enough for a business to be profitable: it should be adequately liquid as well.

New Terms

Return on capital employed (p. 380): Net profit as a percentage of capital employed; often abbreviated as ROCE.

Liquidity ratios (p. 381): Those ratios that relate to the cash position in an organization and hence its ability to pay liabilities when due.

Current ratio (p. 381): A ratio comparing current assets with current liabilities.

Acid test ratio (p. 382): A ratio comparing current assets *less* stock with current liabilities.

Debtor: creditor ratio (p. 382): A ratio comparing how much credit is allowed to and by the business.

Debtor: sales ratio (p. 382): A ratio assessing how long it takes our debtors to pay us.

Creditors: purchases ratio (p. 383): A ratio assessing how long we take to pay creditors.

Summary

1 A business must be both profitable *and* sufficiently liquid to be successful. One factor without the other can lead to serious trouble.

2 Careful credit control to ensure that the debtors: sales ratio is not too high is usually essential to the wellbeing of any business.

3 Comparing the trends to see if the ratios are getting better or worse as each period passes is essential for proper control. Prompt action needs to be taken where a trend in a ratio becomes worse than previously.

Exercises

42.1 You are to study the following financial statements for two similar types of retail stores and then answer the questions that follow.

Summary of Financial Statement

	A		*B*	
	$	$	$	$
Sales		80,000		120,000
Less Cost of goods sold				
Opening stock	25,000		22,500	
Add Purchases	50,000		91,000	
	75,000		113,500	
Less Closing stock	15,000	60,000	17,500	96,000
Gross profit		20,000		24,000
Less Depreciation	1,000		3,000	
Other expenses	9,000	10,000	6,000	9,000
Net profit		10,000		15,000

Balance sheets	*A*		*B*	
Fixed assets	$	$	$	$
Equipment at cost	10,000		20,000	
Less Depreciation to date	8,000	2,000	6,000	14,000

(Cont'd)

Current assets				
Stock	15,000		17,500	
Debtors	25,000		20,000	
Bank	5,000		2,500	
	45,000		40,000	
Less Current liabilities				
Creditors	5,000	40,000	10,000	30,000
		42,000		44,000
Financed by:				
Capital				
Balance at start of year		38,000		36,000
Add Net profit		10,000		15,000
		48,000		51,000
Less Drawings		6,000		7,000
		42,000		44,000

(*a*) Calculate the following ratios:
- (i) gross profit as percentage of sales;
- (ii) net profit as percentage of sales;
- (iii) expenses as percentage of sales;
- (iv) stockturn;
- (v) rate of return of net profit on capital employed (use the average of the capital account for this purpose);
- (vi) current ratio;
- (vii) acid test ratio;
- (viii) debtor: sales ratio;
- (ix) creditor: purchases ratio.

(*b*) Comment on the differences, and similarities, of the accounting ratios for A and B. Which business seems to be the most efficient? Give possible reasons.

42.2X Study the following final accounts of two companies and then answer the questions that follow. Both companies are shops selling textile goods.

Trading and profit and loss accounts

	R. Ltd		*T. Ltd*	
	$	$	$	$
Sales		250,000		160,000
Less Cost of goods sold				
Opening stock	90,000		30,000	
Add Purchases	210,000		120,000	
	300,000		150,000	
Less Closing stock	110,000	190,000	50,000	100,000
Gross profit		60,000		60,000
Less Expenses				
Pay	14,000		10,000	
Directors' remuneration	10,000		10,000	
Other expenses	11,000	35,000	8,000	28,000
Net profit		25,000		32,000
Add Balance from last year		15,000		8,000
		40,000		40,000

(Cont'd)

Less Appropriations				
General reserve	2,000		2,000	
Dividend	25,000	27,000	20,000	22,000
Balance carried to next year		13,000		18,000
Balance sheets				
Fixed assets	$	$	$	$
Equipment at cost	20,000		5,000	
Less Depreciation to date	8,000	12,000	2,000	3,000
Motor lorries	30,000		20,000	
Less Depreciation to date	12,000	18,000	7,000	13,000
		30,000		16,000
Current assets				
Stock	110,000		50,000	
Debtors	62,500		20,000	
Bank	7,500		10,000	
	180,000		80,000	
Less Current liabilities				
Creditors	90,000		16,000	
		90,000		64,000
		120,000		80,000
Financed by:				
Issued share capital		100,000		50,000
Reserves				
General reserve	7,000		12,000	
Profit and loss	13,000	20,000	18,000	30,000
		120,000		80,000

(*a*) Calculate the following ratios for each of R. Ltd and T. Ltd:
- (i) gross profit as percentage of sales;
- (ii) net profit as percentage of sales;
- (iii) expenses as percentage of sales;
- (iv) stockturn;
- (v) rate of return of net profit on capital employed (for the purpose of this question only, take 'capital' as being total of share capital + reserves at the balance sheet date);
- (vi) current ratio;
- (vii) acid test ratio;
- (viii) debtor: sales ratio;
- (ix) creditor: purchases ratio

(*b*) Comment briefly on what you notice when you compare the ratios of the two companies. State which company appears to be the most efficient, giving what you consider to be possible reasons.

42.3X

(*a*) Draw up a balance sheet for Rio Grande Ltd as at 31 December 2005 using the balances now shown. You will have to deduce whether the bank balance shows an overdraft or otherwise, and also what the figure will be.

	$
Authorized and issued share capital	120,000
Cash in hand	470
Debtors	15,430
General reserve	25,000

(Cont'd)

Profit and loss account	3,700
Land and buildings at cost	190,000
Equipment at cost	35,000
Insurance prepaid	800
10% debentures	20,000
Provision for depreciation on equipment	17,800
Proposed ordinary dividend	17,000
Creditors	86,000
Stock 31 Dec 2005	37,500
Debentures interest owing (6 months)	1,000
Bank balance (or overdraft): use balancing figure	?

(*b*) Is Rio Grande in a good position financially? Give a reason in support of your answer.

(*CXC style*)

CHAPTER **43**

Cooperative Societies: Basic Features and Accounting Procedures

Learning Objectives

- To be able to define the term **cooperative society**.
- To be able to define the legal status and types of cooperative societies.
- To know the six cooperative principles.
- To realize who controls cooperative societies.
- To be able to define the different ways of raising capital.
- To understand how to apply accounting procedures in cooperatives for:
  - recording contributions/loans;
  - distribution of surplus;
  - drawing up the balance sheet and income and expenditure statement of a cooperative society.

43.1 What is a Cooperative Society?

A cooperative society is a legally constituted business entity formed for the explicit purpose of furthering the economic welfare of its members and that of the wider society by providing them with goods and services. It should be noted that a cooperative society is not a charitable organization funded by donations or government grants. The income is largely earned by rendering services to its members. A cooperative society may offer a variety of services to its members, such as insurance, credit, housing, agricultural supplies or consumer goods. Cooperative societies are tax exempted, that is, they do not pay tax on surplus income, or stamp duty on instruments executed by or on behalf of a registered society.

43.2 The Legal Status of Cooperative Societies

All cooperative societies are required to be registered under the Cooperative Societies Act. This registration makes them bodies corporate by the names under which they are registered. Cooperative societies have perpetual (everlasting) succession, power to hold property and enter into contracts, and to institute and defend legal action taken against them and other legal proceedings.

43.3 Who controls a Cooperative Society?

A cooperative society is owned and controlled by its members. In Jamaica and the other Caribbean territories, cooperatives are governed by various Cooperative Societies Acts and Regulations. Despite the varied Acts, all cooperative societies are voluntarily formed and democratically operated with the common purpose of meeting their members' needs economically and efficiently.

43.4 Types of Cooperatives

The business ventures that cooperatives can operate are unlimited. A cooperative may decide to embark on any number of business ventures depending on the needs of its members. Cooperatives fall into two main categories, namely service cooperatives and production or worker cooperatives.

Service Cooperatives

These cooperatives are owned by their members. Their members trade with them, that is they buy from them and sell to them. Generally, service cooperatives provide marketing opportunities, credit facilities, supplies, equipment and other such services to their members. The success of this type of cooperative depends largely on the extent to which members use it. Examples of service cooperatives include the following.

- **Suppliers cooperatives** These consist of groups of people who come together to provide for themselves any necessities, such as farm or fishing equipment and raw materials for industrial operations.
- **Thrift or credit cooperatives** These cooperatives provide their members with savings as well as loan facilities, the loans being available at an interest rate lower than the rates charged by ordinary banks, etc. The credit unions belong to this category of cooperatives. Credit unions are the strongest sector of the cooperative movement in the Caribbean and the rest of the world. A credit union may be defined as a financial cooperative made up of groups of people who join together to make certain financial services available to themselves, the members of the credit union. Apart from providing savings and loans facilities, credit unions offer other financial services, such as educating their members on thrift, regular savings and the wise use of credit.
- **Transport and tillage cooperatives** In these types of cooperatives farmers may pool their resources to provide needed transport facilities for their produce from the farm to the markets. Also, equipment may be provided to till the soil, for example the purchase of a tractor.
- **Consumer cooperatives** These are formed out of the need to always provide a variety of goods and services at the lowest possible cost. Consumer cooperatives may range in size from large, wholesale distributors to small retail outlets. These cooperatives have not been successful in the Caribbean as a whole.
- **Housing cooperatives** These cooperatives provide housing solutions for their members, either by purchasing the houses, providing loans to purchase the houses or having the houses built for the members.

- **Insurance cooperatives** These cooperatives provide a variety of insurance services to their members. For example, The Jamaica Agricultural Society Cattle Insurance Cooperative insures cattle for its members. The CUNA Mutual Insurance Society provides loan protection and life savings insurance for credit union members worldwide.
- **Marketing cooperatives** The members of these cooperatives organize themselves to market their products, such as farming and handicrafts. Examples of these cooperatives are the coffee and cocoa growers cooperative societies in Jamaica.
- **Multipurpose cooperatives** These cooperatives provide a wide range of services for their members, such as credit, marketing, farm supplies, field technology services, acquisition and development of land for residential, recreational and commercial purposes. Examples of these cooperatives may be found in Jamaica and the Bahamas.

Production or Worker Cooperatives

These cooperatives are also known as industrial cooperatives or workshop, cooperatives. The members of these cooperatives not only provide goods and services to the public, but also employment for themselves. Cooperatives that fall under this heading include the following types.

- **Agricultural cooperatives** In the Caribbean, agricultural cooperatives are categorized according to the functions they perform for their members. The two categories are:
  - **service cooperatives** which provide their members with different kinds of assistance, such as distribution of farm supplies, marketing of produce, provision of credit, adequate irrigation, agricultural technology, insurance, farming equipment and transport services;
  - **collective production cooperatives** which involve members uniting and farming collectively, thus providing themselves with employment and producing marketable products.
- **Communal production cooperatives** These exist where members live together in a community owned by the cooperative and share common dining and other facilities. Both collective production and collective consumption is carried on.
- **Entertainment service cooperatives** These cooperatives are formed by people in the entertainment sector, with the aims of maintaining a high standard of performance and establishing a single bargaining agency. One such cooperative was formed in Jamaica by a group of entertainers providing entertainment for hotels on the north coast.
- **Junior cooperatives societies** These societies belong only to the Caribbean territories of St Vincent and Trinidad and Tobago. They are organized to educate students in thrift and the principles and practices of cooperation.
- **Transport service cooperatives** The objective of these cooperatives is to provide means of transport for the general public. The cooperative management controls all contracts, despite the fact that the units are owned by the members. Transport cooperatives are found in Jamaica and Barbados. Presently, this system of providing public transport is being altered to make it more efficient by the government of Jamaica, with a view to providing a modern and reliable means of transport.

43.5 The Principles of Cooperatives

These are certain principles and practices which cooperatives are required to follow. These distinguish cooperatives from the normal commercial business organizations. The following six basic cooperative principles, which are considered 'essential to genuine and effective cooperative practice', were adopted at the International Co-operative Alliance (ICA) 23rd Congress in 1966.

- **Open membership** Membership should be open to all those who wish to join and use the services provided, as long as they are prepared to accept the responsibilities of membership. There should be no restriction to membership based on social, political, racial or religious grounds. The members carry out their responsibilities by:
  - conducting business with the society;
  - attending and participating in membership meetings;
  - ensuring that they understand and are kept informed of the business operations of their society;
  - being available for election to office;
  - assisting in financing their cooperative.
- **Democratic control** Cooperative societies are formed voluntarily by a group of people, are controlled by its members and democratically operated by them. The affairs of cooperative societies are administered by those who are elected or appointed in a manner agreed to by the members. These people are accountable to the members. Each member has only one vote, irrespective of the size of their investment. Whereas in a public company a stockholder may appoint a proxy (someone else) to vote on his or her behalf, this is not allowed by cooperative societies.
- **Limited interest on capital** The focus of investing in a cooperative society is not on the return on investment, but on the use of services provided. Therefore, share capital should only receive a modest dividend. However, there are cooperatives that pay no dividend on share capital.
- **Patronage refund** The returns from the operations of a cooperative society belong to the members, and therefore should be distributed to them in such a manner that no member gains at the expense of the others. To prevent any unfairness in the distribution of any surplus, the members may decide to:
  - provide for the development of the business of the cooperative;
  - make available to all members common services;
  - distribute (the surplus) among the members in proportion to the amount of business that they have conducted with the society over the accounting period.

  Before distributing the surplus to members, a mandatory (i.e. compulsory) transfer of 20% must be made to a statutory reserve fund. (Currently this rate is under review in Jamaica.) If a member did no business with the society, even if he or she had a large investment, that member might receive only a small dividend.

- **Continuous education** It is the responsibility of all cooperative societies to make provision for the continuous education of their members, officers, employees and the public about the general operations of cooperatives as well as on cooperative principles and techniques. This continuous education process is designed to make members better able to guide their cooperatives in a dynamic business environment.
- **Cooperation among cooperatives** It is felt that cooperative organizations can best serve the interests of their members and communities if they work together at local, national and international levels. The degree of cooperation is sometimes documented in the by-laws of the societies, particularly in the case of credit unions. In the Caribbean, there is a well-established network which links cooperatives regionally, nationally and to the world body.

43.6 Ways of Raising Capital

A cooperative society's primary source of capital is its members, who purchase goods and services from the society, and from the net earnings on successful operations with reinvestment of part or all of the savings.

43.7 Members' Deposits

Cooperative societies offer to their members the facility of opening deposit accounts. Deposit accounts are a convenient means of short-term savings and payment of standing commitments through the standing order payment facility associated with the account. These deposit accounts attract varying rates of interest depending on the minimum balance held and the period of time the deposits remain in the cooperative.

43.8 Affiliation Fees

Cooperative societies that are members of local, regional and international cooperative societies are required to pay membership fees – known as affiliation fees – to these societies.

43.9 Accounts of Cooperative Societies

Cooperative societies prepare income and expenditure accounts, cash flow statements and balance sheets, accompanied by the appropriate notes to these financial statements. The accounts of the societies must be audited and distributed to their members. There are no requirements for these accounts to be made available to the public at large as is the case for public companies.

The excess of income over expenditure is called a *surplus*, while the excess of expenditure over income is referred to as a *deficit*.

The following example (Exhibit 43.1) is a typical set of accounts for a cooperative society. The horizontal style of final accounts will be used in this chapter, as it is the style in which these accounts are generally drawn up.

Exhibit 43.1

Carib Cooperative Society
Income and Expenditure Account for the year ended 31 December 2000

	$		$
Expenditure		*Income*	
Telephone	14,000	Membership dues	180,000
Stationery and office supplies	32,000	Interest and dividends	500,000
Office expenses	3,000	Other	47,000
Travelling by messenger	500		
Provision for depreciation	30,000		
Auditor's remuneration	60,000		
Repairs and maintenance	10,000		
Annual general meeting expenses	80,000		
Committee meetings	10,000		
Motor vehicle expenses	6,000		
Bank charges and interest	4,000		
Interest on members' deposits	10,000		
Application: subscriptions and dues	30,000		
Surplus for year c/d	437,500		
	727,000		727,000
Transfers to reserves:		Surplus for the year b/d	437,500
Statutory reserve	30,500	Undistributed surplus at	
Special reserve	30,000	beginning of year b/f	200,000
Honoraria	10,000		
Proposed dividend	36,000		
Undistributed surplus carried forward to next year	531,000		
	637,500		637,500

Notes:

1 By the law of the country, i.e. on 'statute', a minimum percentage of any net income should be transferred to a 'statutory reserve'.

2 The special reserve is for any specific named purpose.

3 The **honoraria** (voluntary payments as an appreciation for services performed) paid to members of the committee of management are treated as an appropriation of profit, not an expense. As such they will be shown in the appropriation account instead of in the income and expense account.

4 The dividends will be fixed at the annual general meeting. The balance sheet might appear as below.

Carib Cooperative Society
Balance Sheet as at 31 December 2000

	$	$		$
Employment of capital:			*Capital employed:*	
Fixed assets			Share capital	2,172,500
Leasehold premises		1,000,000	Statutory reserve	30,500
Equipment at cost	980,000		Special reserve	30,000
Less Depreciation			Undistributed surplus income	531,000
to date	450,000	530,000		2,764,000
Motor vehicles	370,000			
Less Depreciation				
to date	40,000	330,000		
		1,860,000		
Current assets			*Current liabilities*	
Stock	120,000		Proposed dividends	36,000
Receivables:				
Membership dues	600,000			
Cash and bank				
balances	200,000			
Prepayments	20,000	940,000		
		2,800,000		2,800,000

43.10 The Accounting Cycle in Relation to Various Organizations

You have seen the accounting cycle for profit-making organizations shown as a diagram (Exhibit 18.3). We can now look at the cycle as it affects the various types of organization.

Sole Traders

The completion of the cycle for each period is by the trader using the final accounts for various purposes, e.g. to show to the bank and to the inspector of taxes, to take decisions about the future of the business and his or her part in it, etc.

Partnerships

Partnerships will complete the cycle in the same way as a sole trader, but in addition, as there is more than one owner, the various partners will jointly have to assess the future of the business, and their part in it. Some, on the basis of the final accounts, might decide to leave the partnership, as it is not profitable enough for their needs. Others may want to buy a bigger share in the partnership and be willing to buy out some of the other partners.

Limited Companies

These firms will complete the cycle by sending copies of the final accounts to all of their owners, i.e. their shareholders. From their view of how the business has progressed, and what their personal financial states are like, the shareholders will each have to decide whether to keep their shares in the company, to buy more shares or to sell some or all of their shares. The Registrar of Companies will also need a copy of these final accounts.

Cooperatives

The cycle for the period will come to an end with the sending of copies of the income and expenditure account, the appropriation account and the balance sheet to all of the cooperative's members, and also to the government official whose job it is to oversee the regulation of cooperatives.

Members will then decide whether they want to retain their membership or give it up. Similarly, the government official will keep the accounts and scrutinize them, to see if the government's regulations are being kept to properly.

Governments

Governmental accounts are unlike accounts for a profit-making concern or for a cooperative. The accounts simply show the amount of cash received from taxes and other sources and also how this money has been spent during the accounting period. Copies of the accounts will be placed before all the members elected to the central seat of government, be it called parliament or something else.

These will be used as a basis in making future decisions about the amounts or taxes to be levied on the people of the country and other revenues. The amount to be spent by government in respect of its many services will also be considered in the light of the accounts.

Other Specialized Bodies

All that can be said here is that the accounting cycle will be used to serve the purposes of the various bodies. Each has its own specialized requirements and accounting cycle.

43.11 Multiple-choice Questions

You can now attempt Set No. 5, questions MC81–MC100 inclusive, to be found on p. 417 onwards.

New Terms

Co-operative society (p. 389): Business entity formed to further the economic welfare of its members by providing them with goods and services.

Affiliation fees (p. 393): Membership fees paid to local, regional or international cooperative societies.

Honoraria (p. 394): Voluntary payment to members of committees that run cooperatives as a form of thanks for their help.

Summary

1 Cooperatives are owned and controlled by their members.
2 The different types of cooperative societies can be divided between service co-operatives and production or worker cooperatives.
3 There are six basic principles and practices that cooperatives have to follow.
4 A cooperative society's primary source of capital is from its members.

Exercises

43.1 Prepare the appropriation account of Farmers' Cooperative Ltd for the year ended 31 December 2003 from the information given below.

	$
Surplus before adjustments for reserves	80,000
Proposed dividends: 5% (share capital is $400,000)	
Undistributed surplus brought forward from last year	11,170
Transfer to statutory reserve 30% of this year's surplus	
Transfer to special reserve 10% of surplus (after deducting statutory reserve)	

43.2 The Teachers' Cooperative Credit Union Ltd prepares annual accounts on 31 December. From the following information, prepare the appropriation account and balance sheet for the year ended 31 December 2002.

	$
Undistributed surplus from last year (i.e. as at 31 December 2001)	50,000
Surplus for the year to 31 December 2002, before adjustments for any reserves	150,000
Statutory reserve: balance at 31 December 2001	72,000
This year's transfer to statutory reserve: 20% of surplus for the year	?
This year's transfer to special reserve: 10% of surplus after adjustment for statutory reserve	?
Honorarium paid to retiring secretary	20,000
Proposed dividends	70,000
Share capital	250,000
Fixed assets *less* depreciation	150,000
Investments	50,000
Loans to members	199,500
Interest owing by members	15,000
Cash and bank balances	22,500
Members' deposits (repayable at short notice)	7,000
Accrued expenses	5,000
Long-term liability: mortgage with building society	23,000

43.3X Prepare the final accounts of the Printers' Cooperative Credit Union Ltd for the year ended 31 December 2005 from the following trial balance as at 31 December 2005.

	Dr. $	*Cr.* $
Accounting expenses	8,400	
Auditor's remuneration	1,950	
Advertising and publicity	3,060	
Repairs and maintenance	2,100	
General expenses	4,630	
Affiliation fees	2,000	
Mortgage with building society (repayable over period 5–15 years)		115,500
Loans to members	271,600	
Buildings at cost	220,000	
Motor vehicles at cost	30,000	
Provision for depreciation: buildings		60,000
Provision for depreciation: motor vehicles		10,000
Cash and bank balances	52,770	

(Cont'd)

Interest income:		
Interest on members' loans		34,600
Interest on investments		11,180
Interest on members' deposits	6,220	
Members' deposits (repayable at short notice)		61,400
Undistributed surplus from last year		7,650
Statutory reserve		40,000
Share capital		430,000
Investments	167,600	
	770,330	770,330

The following must be taken into consideration as on 31 December 2005:

(*a*) accrued affiliation fees of $500: honorarium to retiring secretary of $1,500;
(*b*) advertising prepaid, $480;
(*c*) provide for depreciation:
  buildings at 2% of cost;
  motor vehicle at 10% of cost;
(*d*) transfer to statutory reserve 10% of year's surplus;
(*e*) proposed dividends: 2% of share capital.

CHAPTER **44**

School-based Assessment – Project

Learning Objectives

- To understand the requirements of the school-based assessment in its structure and layout.
- To know how to identify a suitable topic for the school-based assessment and the various stages you will need to deal with.
- To assist the student in comparing their school accountancy studies with the accounting practices used in the business world.

44.1 Introduction

The CXC Secondary Education Certificate at both Basic and General Proficiency is assessed by means of two written papers and a school-based assessment. Paper 1 is a multiple choice paper and Paper 2 is a problem-solving paper. The school-based assessment allows you to gain a proportion of your marks before taking the final examination papers. The marks can be up to 25% of the total in the Basic Proficiency Certificate and up to 20% of the total in the General Certificate. It gives you the opportunity of gaining practical experience of a realistic accounting situation. The work you undertake will aid your preparation for the final examination papers.

44.2 The School-based Assessment – Project

The school-based assessment is essentially an accounting project which is carried out over a period of time with the support and guidance of your teacher. Your project will be marked by your teacher using a structured marking scheme which allocates marks for very specific aspects and so it is important to take note of your teacher's guidance.

44.3 Basic Proficiency Project

The requirements of the CXC state that 'each candidate must participate in a project which involves the simulation or actual operation of a business entity'. The project should centre on entities which buy and sell tangible goods only, i.e. sole traders. It is anticipated that the project as a whole will take about 10 hours. It is permitted for the project to be done by a group, but when this happens each individual must submit a project report.

The project syllabus specifies that the requirements of Units II, III and IV are addressed in undertaking the project. Thus, the various components of a sole trader's activities to be addressed include:

- **Unit II** the balance sheet;
- **Unit III** books of Original Entry (i.e. sales and purchases day books, the returns inwards and outwards day books, cash book, petty cash book, journal, etc.);
- **Unit IV** the ledger (making entries from the above books of original entry and the journal into the ledger).

44.4 General Proficiency Project

The requirements of the CXC are similar to the basic proficiency project in that 'each candidate must participate in a project which involves the simulation or actual operation of a small business entity'. However, candidates may also visit business enterprises in their neighbourhood to observe and report on accounting procedures used.

The choice of entities is wider and, as well as sole traders, it may include:

- school cafeteria
- school club
- saving society/thrift in the school
- sole trader/farmer
- household or other organization to which students will have access.

The project should be capable of being completed in about 15 hours. It may be done on an individual basis or by a group. Where group work is involved, each candidate in the group must submit a separate report. The CXC suggests that the project could involve writing up the cash book, accounts receivable and payable, stock account and preparation of trial balance, payroll, balance sheet and income statements.

44.5 The Teacher's Role

Teachers have a crucial role to play in assisting candidates with their projects. They will provide instructions for doing each project, help in the selection of a suitable topic or subject and give guidance during the project when a simulation or actual operation is being done.

The CXC states that the project should start in term 3 of form 4 and be completed by mid-March of the year of the examination.

44.6 The Sequence of Activities for Those Undertaking the Project

The following points show a suggested sequence for tackling the project.

Review, Visit and Explain

Review businesses that could be possible sources for the project. These could include sole traders with whom someone in your family is familiar or does business with, i.e. builder, garage, local shop, and who might allow you access to their financial information.

As this is a sensitive area, there may be reluctance by these people to permit investigation of their books. Alternatively, it may be possible to investigate your family's finances or use a simulated situation provided by the teacher.

Having selected a possible business, arrange a visit and make sure you have a letter of introduction to show on your initial approach to the business. Explain the aims of the project to the owner, that is, 'to compare the accounting procedures learnt in the classroom to those that are actually practised in the business world'.

Agree a Subject

Agree with your teacher that you have selected a suitable business and chosen an area for investigation within the business.

For example, if your initial visit is to a local locksmith, you may find that there is little evidence of proper stock records. From your school studies you would know that inaccurate stock records affect both the trading and profit and loss account and the balance sheet.

Define a Topic for Study

As stated previously, the CXC syllabus permits the project to be centred on either a simulated or actual entity. This section assumes that an actual business entity is to be used as the basis for the project and deals with the visits that may be made to business enterprises at general proficiency level.

When you visit a particular business, you should take care to stress that you wish to observe and report on the accounting procedures used by the business, and that you will then compare these to your school accountancy studies.

Using the example of stock records, mentioned in the step described above, you might take this further and observe the methods of stock control and stock valuation. You could then compare these methods to those covered in your school studies where you would have learned about accepted accounting methods for valuations.

You might also look at stock levels and comment as to whether or not these are too high or too low relative to the activity of the business.

Investigate

The investigation into the topic that has been chosen requires careful thought and will be influenced by the availability of information within the business. This information may be in the form of documents and records, but where there is lack of documentation it could be necessary to gain the required information from the owner or employees.

It is possible that some or all of the following methods may be needed to collect data.

- **Documents and records** Collect relevant documents and records and review these. Make notes on the aspects of them that are relevant to the project.
- **Questionnaires** These are normally used when information and opinions need to be collected from a number of people. They would not be used unless there were more

than six people as the time required to construct a questionnaire would not be justified for fewer people than this. In designing a questionnaire, two main points need consideration:

- posing the right questions to gain the relevant information;
- structuring the questions in such a way that provides for a choice of answers, say 4 or 5, and then allows easy analysis of these answers.

Example:

In general, how good or poor would you say the standard of stock control is in the business?

Very good	Fairly good	Poor	Very poor	Don't know
☐	☐	☐	☐	☐

If you think it is poor, please give details of why you think this is.

The question in the example above gives a choice of answers, allows easy analysis but also asks for additional information when the 'Poor, or Very poor' responses have been chosen. Limit the number of questions to about 10 to 12, making sure that those that give the opportunity for opinions to be recorded do not exceed more than 20% of the questions as otherwise analysis will be difficult. This is due to the variety of opinions that could be offered, which can cause problems in how to present these in the findings.

- **Interviews** These provide face-to-face contact with the person from whom you wish to gain information and allow flexibility in the questioning. However, each interview should be structured by preparing the questions beforehand. This will ensure that the person being questioned doesn't deviate from the theme of the interview. Interviews can be time-consuming and so a time limit should be estimated before undertaking these. Aim to ask about 10 questions. Make notes of the interviewees' answers for analysis later.
- **Observations** These are a very valuable source of data, but it should be clear before commencing the observation that it is going to provide information relevant to the project. It is also essential to have some knowledge of the activity to be observed. If you are unfamiliar with the activities, it can be confusing to watch them. Again, observations can be time-consuming, but there is the opportunity during the activity to ask questions of the person being observed. Ensure good records are made of the observation for later analysis.

Analyse

Having collected the data, it will now be necessary to analyse the information. In the case of questionnaires, this will involve looking at the answers to see if any trends emerge with each question. Notes taken during interviews need to be examined and the main points from the answers need to be assessed and recorded.

When observations have been used, you should have good notes from the observed activity – possibly more than will eventually be needed. Review these notes and extract the relevant points for inclusion in your findings.

Report the Findings

At this stage it will be necessary to report your findings in a clear and factual manner. You should present the information in the most appropriate way relative to the method of investigation. For example, the results of a questionnaire could be set out in a table, showing the various responses to individual questions.

When an interview has been carried out, the answers to the questions asked should be stated. You might have been given quite lengthy answers in some instances and these should be edited so that only the relevant points are stated.

Do not make any comments on the findings at this stage.

Conclusion

Here you should use your findings to come to some conclusion. Ask yourself 'What did I set out to find, and how does what I really found compare to that?'

Recommendations

This is where you make some proposal or suggestion to improve the situation you found. Aim to discuss two ways in which to improve the accounting procedures used. For example, in the case of the stock control problem referred to earlier, you might be able to compare previous trading and profit and loss accounts and balance sheets with recent financial statements where more realistic stock figures had been used. You might also be able to recommend the importance of keeping to a consistent method of valuing stock as required by the accounting concepts.

44.7 The Completed Project

The sequence referred to above will have given a good indication as to how the stages of the project should be dealt with. The CXC syllabus is specific regarding how the report is to be presented at both basic and general levels.

Basic Proficiency Level

The project report should comprise:

- table of contents
- aims of the project
- information about entity operated or simulated in the classroom:
  - name of entity and description of activities;
  - actual accounting procedures used and records kept;
  - trial balances;
  - actual accounts kept showing result, i.e., balances c/d, balances transferred, profits/losses, etc.;
  - financial statements, balance sheet
- appendices: source documents, questionnaires, diagrams, charts, statistical data, etc.

General Proficiency Level

The project report should comprise:

- table of contents
- aims of the project
- information about the entity operated and/or simulated in the classroom, i.e.:
  - name of the entity and a description of the activity;
  - actual accounting procedures used and records kept;
  - performance of the business;
  - interpretation of results, using simple ratios, comparisons, etc.;
  - conclusion
- Appendices: source documents, questionnaires, diagrams, charts, statistical data, etc.

44.8 Sample School-based Project

This sample gives an indication of the kind of scenario that you may find and an appropriate topic. It has been shown in a very brief form only – to comply with the requirements of the CXC it would need to be presented much more formally.

Example of a School-based Project

J. Lopez is a locksmith who has a shop selling high-security locks and safes. As a friend of your father, he is aware of your need to undertake an accounting project and has asked you to look at the issue of stock valuation and control. He hands you his draft trading account for the year to 31 December 2001.

J. Lopez
Draft Trading Account for the year ended 31 December 2001

	$	$
Sales		33,500
Less Cost of sales		
Opening stock	1,500	
Add Purchases	21,300	
	22,800	
Less Closing stock	3,000	19,000
Gross profit		13,700

The figures that are of particular interest to you in terms of stock valuation are opening stock of $1,500 and closing stock of $3,000.

You decide to interview Mr Lopez and find that:

- he employed a bookkeeper to do the stocktaking at the end of December 2000 who valued the stock at cost price
- he carried out the stocktake at the end of December 2001
- his records of the December 2001 stocktake were not fully detailed
- he used the list of selling prices to value his stock
- he could not show you any formal stock records
- he re-orders stock when he runs out
- his profit margin is 33⅓%.

As a result of the interview, you decide to do a detailed stocktake with Mr Lopez, valuing the stock on the same basis as previously, i.e. cost price. On completion of the task, the closing stock is now found to be valued at $2,000 (cost price) and you then produce an amended trading account.

J. Lopez
Amended Trading Account for the year ended 31 December 2001

	$	$
Sales		33,500
Less Cost of sales		
Opening stock	1,500	
Add Purchases	21,300	
	22,800	
Less Closing stock	2,000	20,800
Gross profit		12,700

In concluding the project you could state that:

- the stock was not properly counted and was incorrectly valued at 31 December 2001
- as a result of this, the profit was overstated.

Your recommendations could now be presented:

- proper stock records should be maintained:
  - to help with stocktaking
  - to set minimum and maximum stock levels
  - to establish re-order levels to ensure stock does not run out
  - to monitor financial value of stock
- a consistent and proper basis of stock valuation should be adhered to, as required by the accounting concept – in this example, 'consistency' – so you propose cost price as a proper basis.

44.9 Some Project Ideas for School-based Assessment

Some ideas are suggested below. The left-hand states the topic and the right-hand side a possible way of dealing with the issue.

Topic	*Approach*
Idea 1: An analysis of profitability A retail business has two main ranges of products but no analysis is done of the profitability. A system is needed to identify the profitability on an ongoing basis for each product.	Investigate the present system of recording purchases and sales. Decide on action required to introduce some form of analysis of purchases and sales, i.e. analytical day books and cash books with some means of reporting weekly profit.
Idea 2: Petty cash A business operates a petty cash system using the imprest system with a weekly float of $40. The owner is concerned at the increase in petty cash expenses, sometimes up to $100 per week.	Examine petty cash records and interview the petty cashier. This reveals that no one is directly responsible for the system – some receipts exceed the amount of float and no formal checks are made. Propose the action required to correct the situation.
Idea 3: Credit control A business finds that the amounts owed by debtors are increasing and the cash float is being affected by late payments.	On reviewing the invoicing system, it is found that late and incorrect invoices are being sent out due to the accounts clerk not getting timely and proper information from other departments. Decide on a system that will help the clerk.
Idea 4: Payment of invoices The manager finds that, after paying invoices for goods purchased, there have been instances of goods being defective or incorrect quantities being received.	On examination, it is found that invoices are taken at face value and paid. No one is approving the payment of invoices. The person responsible for receiving and checking goods doesn't always see the goods. Propose a system to introduce proper controls.
Idea 5: Recording and collecting information A restaurant is finding that the sale of drinks does not tally with the weekly stockcheck, indicating that either some drinks are not being charged for or there is pilfering of stock.	It is found that clients eating at the restaurant sometimes go to the bar for drinks and ask for them to be charged to their table. Records of these purchases are, in some instances, not being passed to the cash desk and, thus, not charged. A waiter service for drinks does exist, but the owner does not want clients to use this exclusively. Propose a system of ensuring that all drinks are charged.

Multiple-choice questions

Each multiple-choice question has four suggested answers, (A), (B), (C) or (D). Read each question and then decide which choice is best. On a separate piece of paper, write down your choice. Unless the textbook you are reading belongs to you, it is best not to make a mark against your choice in the textbook.

Set No. 1: 20 questions

(*Answers on p. 420*)

MC1 Which of the following statements is incorrect?

(A) Assets + Capital = Liabilities.
(B) Capital = Assets – Liabilities.
(C) Liabilities + Capital = Assets.
(D) Liabilities = Assets – Capital.

MC2 Which of the following is not an asset?

(A) Cash at the bank.
(B) Premises.
(C) Stock.
(D) Creditors.

MC3 Which of the following is a liability?

(A) Buildings.
(B) Debtors.
(C) Loan from J. Henry.
(D) Equipment.

MC4 Which of the following is incorrect?

	Assets	*Liabilities*	*Capital*
	$	$	$
(A)	18,270	5,290	12,980
(B)	9,340	3,120	6,220
(C)	15,160	6,380	7,780
(D)	12,230	1,390	10,840

MC5 Which of the following statements is correct?

		Effect upon	
		Assets	*Liabilities*
(A)	Sold goods on credit.	– Stock	+ Creditors
(B)	J. Charles lends us $1,000 in cash.	+ Cash	+ Loan from Charles
(C)	We paid a creditor by cheque.	– Bank	– Debtors
(D)	Bought goods paying by cheque.	– Bank	– Creditors

MC6 Which of the following are incorrect?

	Accounts	*To record*	*Entry in the account*
(i)	Liabilities	an increase	Debit
		a decrease	Credit
(ii)	Assets	an increase	Debit
		a decrease	Credit
(iii)	Capital	an increase	Debit
		a decrease	Credit

(A) (i) and (ii).
(B) (ii) and (iii).
(C) (i) and (iii).
(D) None of them.

MC7 Which of the following are incorrect?

		Account to be debited	*Account to be credited*
(i)	Bought equipment on credit from C. Lee.	Equipment	C. Lee
(ii)	Introduced extra capital in cash.	Capital	Cash
(iii)	Paid a creditor, C. Brown, by cheque.	C. Brown	Bank
(iv)	F. Grant lent us $1,000 in cash.	F. Grant: Loan	Cash

(A) (ii) and (iv) only.
(B) (i), (ii) and (iii) only.
(C) (ii) and (iii) only.
(D) (iii) and (iv) only.

MC8 Which of the following are correct?

		Account to be debited	*Account to be credited*
(i)	Returned some equipment to C. Lee.	Equipment	C. Lee
(ii)	Sold office fixtures for cash.	Cash	Office fixtures
(iii)	Repaid part of loan from F. Grant by cheque.	Bank	F. Grant: Loan
(iv)	Bought office fixtures on credit from shopfitters.	Office fixtures	Shopfitters Ltd

(A) (i) and (iv) only.
(B) (ii) and (iii) only.
(C) (ii) and (iv) only.
(D) (i) and (iii) only.

MC9 Which of the following *best* describes the meaning of 'Sales'?
(A) Items sold for cash or on credit.
(B) Assets sold on credit.
(C) The sale of items bought previously.
(D) Sale of items previously included in 'Purchases'.

MC10 Which of the following should not be called 'Purchases'?
(A) Purchases of a motor van for use by firm.
(B) Goods bought on credit.
(C) Goods bought for cash.
(D) Items bought for the prime purpose of resale.

MC11 Which of the following are incorrect?

		Account to be debited	*Account to be credited*
(i)	Goods returned by us to D. Williams.	D. Williams	Returns outwards
(ii)	Fixtures found to be faulty returned to C. Hammond.	C. Hammond	Purchases
(iii)	A. Holmes, a creditor, paid by proprietor from his private account.	Capital	A. Holmes
(iv)	Motor vehicle sold for cash.	Cash	Motor vehicles

(A) (ii) and (iii).
(B) (i) and (ii).
(C) (iii) and (iv).
(D) (ii) and (iv).

MC12 Which of the following are correct?

		Account to be debited	Account to be credited
(i)	Machinery bought on credit form K. Hill.	Machinery	K. Hill
(ii)	Goods returned to us by A. Chin.	A. Chin	Returns inwards
(iii)	Goods sold for cash.	Cash	Sales
(iv)	Motor vehicle bought by cheque.	Motor vehicle	Bank

(A) (i), (iii) and (iv) only.
(B) (i), (ii) and (iii) only.
(C) All of them.
(D) (i), (ii) and (iv) only.

MC13 Given the following, what is the amount of capital? Premises, $55,000, motor vehicles, $17,800, stock, $6,450, debtors, $3,720, bank, $1,110, creditors, $4,000, loan from D. Allen, $10,000.
(A) $60,080.
(B) $65,580.
(C) $70.080.
(D) None of the above.

MC14 Which of the following is correct?
(A) Capital is reduced by a loss.
(B) Profit does not affect capital.
(C) If there is no profit there is no capital.
(D) A loan received will reduce capital.

MC15 Of the following, which are incorrect?

		Account to be debited	Account to be credited
(i)	Sold motor van to T. Hall on credit.	T. Hall	Motor van
(ii)	Received cheque as refund of telephone bill paid twice.	Telephone	Bank
(iii)	Cash drawings taken by proprietor.	Drawings	Cash
(iv)	Surplus stationery sold for cash.	Stationery	Cash

(A) (ii) and (iv) only.
(B) (i), and (iv) only.
(C) (i) and (iii) only.
(D) (ii) and (iii) only.

MC16 Which of the following are correct?

		Account to be debited	Account to be credited
(i)	Received refund of rent in cash.	Rent	Cash
(ii)	Paid rates by cheque.	Rates	Bank
(iii)	Stationery bought on credit from Egan Reid.	Stationery	Egan Reid
(iv)	Paid general expenses by cash.	General expenses	Bank

(A) (i), (ii) and (iv) only.
(B) (i), and (ii) only.
(C) (i), (ii) and (iii) only.
(D) (ii) and (iii) only.

MC17 What is the balance on the following account on 30 June 2009?

P. Norman

2009	$	2009	$
June 16 Bank	505	June 4 Purchases	505
June 20 Returns outwards	96	June 26 Purchases	420
		June 29 Purchases	204

(A) A debit balance of $601.
(B) A credit balance of $1,129.
(C) A credit balance of $528.
(D) Nil.

MC18 What was the balance on the account of P. Norman in MC17 on 23 June 2009?
(A) A credit balance of $96.
(B) A debit balance of $96.
(C) A credit balance of $528.
(D) A debit balance of $528.

MC19 Which of the following *best* describes a trial balance?
(A) Is the final account in the books.
(B) Shows all the asset balances.
(C) Is a list of balances on the books.
(D) Discloses the financial position of a business.

MC20 When should the trial balance totals differ?
(A) Only when it is drawn up by the accountant.
(B) When drawn up before the profit and loss account is prepared.
(C) If drawn up halfway through the financial year.
(D) Never.

Set No. 2: 20 questions

(*Answers on p. 420*)

MC21 Gross profit is calculated in the:
(A) profit and loss account;
(B) balance sheet;
(C) trading account;
(D) trial balance.

MC22 Net profit is:
(A) sales *less* purchases *add* opening stock *less* closing stock;
(B) gross profit *add* expenses of the period;
(C) capital plus all expenses;
(D) gross profit *less* expenses of the period.

MC23 The debit entry for net loss is on the debit side of:
(A) the capital account;
(B) the trading account;
(C) the balance sheet;
(D) the profit and loss account.

MC24 We calculate the value of closing stock at the end of a period by:
(A) looking at the balance in the stock account;
(B) deducting opening stock from purchases;
(C) deducting purchases and opening stock from sales;
(D) conducting a stocktaking.

MC25 Using the 'permanency' method, the descending order in which current assets should be shown in a balance sheet is:
(A) cash, bank, debtors, stock;
(B) stock, debtors, bank, cash;
(C) stock, bank, cash, debtors;
(D) debtors, stock, bank, cash.

MC26 Which is the *best* definition of a balance sheet?
(A) A double entry account.
(B) A list of balances after the profit and loss account has been drawn up.
(C) A statement of all the assets.
(D) An account proving the books balance.

MC27 Which of the following are *not* part of the double entry system?
(i) Trading account.
(ii) Balance sheet.

(Cont'd)

(iii) Trial balance.
(iv) Profit and loss account.

(A) (i) and (ii).
(B) (i) and (iii).
(C) (ii) and (iii).
(D) (ii) and (iv).

MC28 Carriage inwards is charged to the trading account because:
(A) it is not a balance sheet item;
(B) it is not part of our motor expenses;
(C) returns inwards also goes in the trading account;
(D) it is basically part of the cost of buying goods.

MC29 Given figures showing: sales of $28,500, opening stock of $4,690, closing stock of $7,240, carriage inwards of $570 and purchases of $21,360, the cost of goods sold figure is:
(A) $19,830;
(B) $19,380;
(C) $18,810;
(D) another figure.

MC30 In the trading account the returns inwards should be:
(A) added to cost of goods sold;
(B) deducted from purchases;
(C) deducted from sales;
(D) added to sales.

MC31 The purchases journal is *best* described as:
(A) a list of purchases bought on credit;
(B) containing suppliers' accounts;
(C) a list of purchases bought for cash;
(D) part of the double entry system.

MC32 Customers' personal accounts are found in the:
(A) private ledger;
(B) general ledger;
(C) purchases ledger;
(D) sales ledger.

MC33 Which of the following are *not* personal accounts:
(i) Debtors.
(ii) Drawings.
(iii) Rent.
(iv) Creditors.

(A) (iii) only.
(B) (i) and (ii) only.
(C) (i) and (iv) only.
(D) (ii) and (iii) only.

MC34 The total of the sales journal is entered on:
(A) the debit side of the sales day book;
(B) the credit side of the sales account in the general ledger;
(C) the debit side of the sales account in the general ledger;
(D) the debit side of the profit and loss account.

MC35 A trade discount is *best* described as:
(A) a discount given if the invoice is paid;
(B) a discount given for cash payment;
(C) a discount given to suppliers;
(D) a discount given to traders.

MC36 The sales journal does not contain:
(A) credit sales made without deduction of trade discount;
(B) credit sales made to overseas customers;
(C) cash sales;
(D) credit sales which eventually turn out to be bad debts.

MC37 The purchases journal consists of:
(A) cash purchases;
(B) suppliers' ledger accounts;
(C) a list of purchase invoices;
(D) payment for goods.

MC38 The total of the purchases journal is transferred to the:
(A) debit side of the purchases account;
(B) credit side of the purchases journal;
(C) debit side of the purchases day book;
(D) debit side of the purchases ledger.

MC39 The balances in the purchases ledger are usually:
(A) credit balances;
(B) contras;
(C) nominal account balances;
(D) debit balances.

MC40 Debit notes sent out by us are entered in our:
(A) returns outwards journal;
(B) returns inwards journal;
(C) purchases account;
(D) returns outwards account.

Set No. 3: 20 questions

(*Answers on p. 420*)

MC41 When Fisher makes out a cheque for $100 and sends it to Hamilton, then Hamilton is known as:
(A) the payee;
(B) the drawer;
(C) the debtor;
(D) the banker.

MC42 A cheque crossed 'A/c Payee only, Not Negotiable':
(A) can be cashed at the bank where the drawer's account is based;
(B) can be paid into any bank account;
(C) can only be banked in the account of the payee;
(D) cannot be banked immediately on receipt.

MC43 Accounts used for regular bankings and withdrawals by cheque are known as:
(A) deposit accounts;
(B) savings accounts;
(C) current accounts;
(D) revolving accounts.

MC44 A credit balance of $500 in the cash columns of the cash book would mean:
(A) the bookkeeper has made a mistake;
(B) we have $500 cash in hand;
(C) we have spent $500 cash more than we have received;
(D) someone has stolen $500 cash.

MC45 $200 withdrawn from the bank and placed in the cash till is entered:
(A) debit bank column $200, credit bank column $200;
(B) debit cash column $200, credit bank column $200;
(C) debit bank column $200, credit cash column $200;
(D) debit cash column $400, credit cash column $400.

MC46 A contra item is where:
(A) cash is banked before it has been paid out;
(B) double entry is completed within the cash book;
(C) the proprietor has repaid his capital in cash;
(D) sales have been paid by cash.

MC47 An invoice shows a total of $3,200 less 2½% cash discount. If this was paid in time, the amount of the cheque paid would be for:
(A) $2,960;
(B) $3,040;
(C) $3,120;
(D) $2,800.

MC48 The total of the discount received column in the cash book is posted to the:
(A) credit of the discounts received account;
(B) credit of the discounts allowed account;
(C) debit of the discounts allowed account;
(D) debit of the discounts received account.

MC49 A bank overdraft is *best* described as:
(A) a firm wasting its money;
(B) having more receipts than payments;
(C) a firm having bought too many goods;
(D) a firm having paid more out of its bank account than it has put in it.

MC50 A cash discount is *best* described as a reduction in the sum to be paid:
(A) if goods are bought on credit and not for cash;
(B) if either cheque or cash payment is made within an agreed period;
(C) if cash is paid instead of cheques;
(D) if trade discount is also deducted.

MC51 If a sales invoice shows 12 items of $250 each, less trade discount of 20% and cash discount of 5%, then the amount to be paid, if the payment is made within the credit period, will be for:
(A) $2,440;
(B) $2,360;
(C) $2,280;
(D) $2,500.

MC52 A statement of account:
(A) is used instead of an invoice;
(B) means that our customers need not keep accounts;
(C) saves us sending out invoices;
(D) acts as a reminder to the purchaser of the amount owed.

MC53 Originally we bought 80 items at $60 each, less trade discount of 25%. We now return 5 items, so we will issue a debit note amounting to:
(A) $270;
(B) $240;
(C) $225;
(D) $220.

MC54 The straight line method of depreciation consists of:
(A) unequal amounts of depreciation each year;
(B) increasing amounts of depreciation each year;
(C) reducing amounts of depreciation each year;
(D) equal amounts of depreciation each year.

MC55 Depreciation is:
(A) the cost of a current asset wearing away;
(B) the cost of a replacement for a fixed asset;
(C) the salvage value of a fixed asset plus its original cost;
(D) the part of the cost of the fixed asset consumed during its period of use by the firm.

MC56 A firm bought a machine for $50,000. It is expected to be used for 6 years then sold for $5,000. What is the annual amount of depreciation if the straight line method is used?
(A) $7,000.
(B) $8,000.
(C) $7,500.
(D) $6,750.

MC57 When a separate provision for depreciation account is in use, then bookkeeping entries for the year's depreciation are:
(A) debit profit and loss, credit the balance sheet;
(B) debit profit and loss, credit asset account;
(C) debit asset account, credit provision for depreciation account;
(D) debit profit and loss, credit provision for depreciation account.

MC58 In the trial balance, the balance on the provision for depreciation account is:
(A) shown as a credit item;
(B) not shown, as it is part of depreciation;
(C) shown as a debit item;
(D) sometimes shown as a credit, sometimes as a debit.

MC59 If a provision for depreciation account is in use, then the entries for the year's depreciation would be:
(A) debit asset account, credit profit and loss account;
(B) credit asset account, debit provision for depreciation account;
(C) credit profit and loss account, debit provision for depreciation account;
(D) none of the above.

MC60 A reduction in a provision for bad debts is recorded by:
(A) *Dr*. profit and loss, *Cr*. bad debts;
(B) *Cr*. profit and loss, *Dr*. provision for bad debts;
(C) *Cr*. profit and loss, *Dr*, balance sheet;
(D) *Dr*. profit and loss, *Cr*. provision for bad debts.

Set No. 4: 20 questions

(*Answers on p. 420*)

MC61 A debit balance brought down on an insurance account means that:
(A) we owe that insurance on that date;
(B) we have paid too little insurance;
(C) we have paid that insurance in advance on that date;
(D) we have paid too much insurance.

MC62 Stock of packing material at the end of the period is:
(A) carried forward as a debit balance;
(B) carried forward as a credit balance;
(C) transferred to the debit of the profit and loss account;
(D) deducted from carriage outwards.

MC63 A regular payment made by your bank, for which you have given authority, is:
(A) a credit transfer;
(B) a standing order;
(C) an unpresented cheque;
(D) a dishonoured cheque.

MC64 A bank reconciliation statement is:
(A) drawn up by the bank regularly and kept by them;
(B) sent by the bank to us monthly;
(C) drawn up by us to verify our cash book balance with the bank statement balance;
(D) sent to the bank when we have made an error.

MC65 Which of the following are not true? A bank reconciliation statement is:
(i) part of the double entry system;
(ii) not part of the double entry system;
(iii) sent by the firm to the bank;
(iv) posted to the ledger accounts.

(A) (i), (iii) and (iv).
(B) (i) and (ii).
(C) (i), (ii) and (iv).
(D) (ii), (iii) and (iv).

MC66 Of the following, which should *not* be entered in the journal?
(i) Cash payments for pay.
(ii) Bad debts written off.
(iii) Credit purchases of goods.
(iv) Sale of fixed assets.

(A) (i) and (ii).
(B) (i) and (iii).
(C) (ii) and (iii).
(D) (iii) and (iv).

MC67 The journal is:
(A) part of the double entry system;
(B) a form of sales day book;
(C) a form of diary;
(D) a supplement to the balance sheet.

MC68 Given a desired cash float of $700, if $541 is spent in the period, and the opening cash float has been $700, how much will be reimbursed at the end of the period?
(A) $541.
(B) $700.
(C) $159.
(D) None of the above.

MC69 A petty cash book:
(A) is used only in limited companies;
(B) is used when we have a bank overdraft;
(C) is used for small cheque payments;
(D) will keep down the number of entries in the general ledger.

MC70 Which of the following do *not* affect trial balance agreement?
(i) Purchases of $585 from C. Owens completely omitted from the books.
(ii) Sales of $99 to R. Morgan entered in account as $90.
(iii) Rent account added up to be $100 too much.
(iv) Error on sales invoice of $14 being entered in the books.

(A) (i) and (iv).
(B) (i) and (ii).
(C) (i) and (iii).
(D) (iii) and (iv).

MC71 Which of the following *are* errors of principle?
(i) Rent entered in buildings account.
(ii) Purchases of $150 completely omitted from the books.
(iii) Sale of machinery of $500 entered in sales account.
(iv) Cheque payment to R. Kago entered only in the cash book.

(A) (ii) and (iii).
(B) (iii) and (iv).
(C) (i) and (ii).
(D) (i) and (iii).

MC72 When the trial balance totals do not agree, the difference is entered in:
(A) the balance account;
(B) a suspense account;
(C) an errors account;
(D) the profit and loss account.

MC73 Which of these errors would be disclosed by the trial balance?
(A) An error on a purchase invoice.
(B) Purchases from T. Morgan entered in C. Morgan's account.
(C) Carriage outwards debited to the sales account.
(D) Overcast of total on the sales account.

MC74 In a purchase ledger control account, the discounts received should be shown:
(A) as a debit;
(B) as a credit;
(C) sometimes as a debit, sometimes as a credit;
(D) as a balance carried down.

MC75 Given closing debtors of $65,220, sales of $50,000 and receipts from debtors of $44,000, the *opening* debtors should have been:
(A) $60,220;
(B) $65,220;
(C) $109,220;
(D) none of the above.

MC76 If the cost price is $120 and the selling price is $150, then the:
(i) margin is 25%;
(ii) mark-up is 20%;
(iii) mark-up is 25%;
(iv) margin is 20%.

(A) (i) and (ii).
(B) (i) and (iii).
(C) (iii) and (iv).
(D) (ii) and (iv).

MC77 If sales are $60,000 opening stock $4,500, closing stock $7,500 and margin 20%, then stockturn is:
(A) 8 times;
(B) 7 times;
(C) 6 times;
(D) 5 times.

MC78 If last year's capital is $57,500, this year's capital is $64,300 and drawings are $11,800, then profit must have been:
(A) $18,600;
(B) $18,100;
(C) $16,600;
(D) $19,600.

MC79 If last year's capital was $74,500, closing capital was $46,200 and drawings were $13,400, then the:
(A) profit for the year was $14,900;
(B) loss for the year was $14,900;
(C) loss for the year was $15,900;
(D) profit for the year was $16,800.

MC80 If this year's closing capital is $29,360, the year's net profit is $8,460 and drawings are $5,320, what was the capital at the beginning of the year?
(A) $29,360.
(B) $26,220.
(C) $34,680.
(D) None of the above.

Set No. 5: 20 questions

(*Answers on p. 420*)

MC81 In a commercial firm an 'accumulated fund' would be known as:
(A) fixed assets;
(B) total assets;
(C) net current assets;
(D) capital.

MC82 A receipts and payments account does not show:
(A) cheques paid out during the year;
(B) the accumulated fund;
(C) receipts from sales of assets;
(D) bank balances.

MC83 Does a partnership have to ensure that each partner receives a salary?
(A) Only when profits are split equally.
(B) Only when profits are split unequally.
(C) Only when there is agreement between partners.
(D) Only when interest is charged on capital.

MC84 With fluctuating capital accounts, interest on drawings must be:
(A) credited to partners' current accounts;
(B) credited to partners' capital accounts;
(C) debited to partners' current accounts;
(D) debited to partners' capital accounts.

MC85 You agree to buy an existing business for $190,000. Buildings are valued at $85,000, fixtures at $17,000, stock at $30,000 and debtors at $38,000. This means that:
(A) you have made a mistake;
(B) you are paying too much for the assets;
(C) you are paying $20,000 for goodwill;
(D) you should not have bought an existing business.

MC86 Goodwill is normally owned by partners:
(A) equally;
(B) in the same ratio as capital accounts;
(C) in the same ratio as capital accounts + current accounts;
(D) in the same ratio as profits shared.

MC87 Which of these are good reasons for keeping sales and purchase analysis books?
(i) Wanting to know sales and purchases for each department.
(ii) Wanting to know the totals of sales and purchases.
(iii) To ascertain sales and purchases in given geographical areas.
(iv) To calculate gross profit for the firm.

(A) (i) and (iii).
(B) (i) and (iv).
(C) (ii) and (iv).
(D) (iii) and (iv).

MC88 Which of the following should be charged to the manufacturing account?
(A) Office rent.
(B) Carriage on sales.
(C) Managing director's pay.
(D) Carriage on raw materials.

MC89 The production cost is the total of:
(A) prime cost + works overhead expenses;
(B) direct labour + direct materials + direct expenses;
(C) administrative expenses + selling expenses;
(D) none of the above.

MC90 Work-in-progress is the:
(A) sales less cost of goods sold;
(B) sales plus cost of goods sold;
(C) value of finished goods on hand;
(D) value of partly finished goods.

MC91 If someone owns a food store, which of the following are *not* capital expenditure?
(i) Rent.
(ii) Motor van.
(iii) Fixtures.
(iv) Fire insurance.

(A) (ii) and (iii).
(B) (i) and (ii).
(C) (i) and (iii).
(D) (i) and (iv).

MC92 If $750 was added to the rent instead of being added to a fixed asset:
(A) gross profit would not be affected;
(B) gross profit would be affected;
(C) both gross and net profits would be affected;
(D) just the balance sheet items would be affected.

MC93 Superannuation contributions and income tax should be:
(A) added to the gross pay to give net pay;
(B) deducted from gross pay to give the amount payable to an employee;
(C) deducted from net pay;
(D) added to net pay to give the amount payable to an employee.

MC94 Pay for piece-work is related to:
(A) the amount of work performed;
(B) net pay;
(C) the time taken;
(D) holiday pay.

MC95 In a limited company, which of the following are *not* shown in the appropriation account?
(i) Pay.
(ii) Proposed dividends.
(iii) Transfers to reserves.
(iv) Debenture interest.

(A) (i) and (ii).
(B) (ii) and (iii).
(C) (ii) and (iv).
(D) (i) and (iv).

MC96 Paid-up capital is:
(A) authorized capital – calls in arrears;
(B) called-up capital – calls in arrears;
(C) issued capital + called-up capital;
(D) authorized capital – issued capital.

MC97 The issued capital of a company is:
(A) always the same as the authorized capital;
(B) the same as preference share capital;
(C) equal to the reserves of the company;
(D) none of the above.

MC98 A company wishes to pay out all available profits as dividends. Net profit is £26,000. There are 20,000 8% preference shares of £1 each, and 50,000 ordinary shares of £1 each. £5,000 is to be transferred to the general reserve. What ordinary dividends are to be paid, in percentage terms?

(A) 20%.
(B) 40%.
(C) 10%.
(D) 60%.

MC99 What is missing in this formula of the acid test ratio?

$$\frac{?}{\text{Current liabilites}}$$

(A) Total of fixed + current assets.
(B) Current assets.
(C) Current assets – stock.
(D) Stock + debtors.

MC100 Net realizeable value is:

(A) what stock can be sold for;
(B) what stock can be replaced for;
(C) estimated saleable value of stock less its cost;
(D) saleable value – expenses needed before completion of the sale.

Answers to Sets of Multiple-choice Questions

Set No. 1

1 (A)	2 (D)	3 (C)	4 (C)	5 (B)
6 (C)	7 (A)	8 (C)	9 (D)	10 (A)
11 (A)	12 (A)	13 (C)	14 (A)	15 (A)
16 (D)	17 (C)	18 (B)	19 (C)	20 (D)

Set No. 2

21 (C)	22 (D)	23 (A)	24 (D)	25 (B)
26 (B)	27 (C)	28 (D)	29 (B)	30 (C)
31 (A)	32 (D)	33 (D)	34 (B)	35 (D)
36 (C)	37 (C)	38 (A)	39 (A)	40 (A)

Set No. 3

41 (A)	42 (C)	43 (C)	44 (A)	45 (B)
46 (B)	47 (C)	48 (A)	49 (D)	50 (B)
51 (C)	52 (D)	53 (C)	54 (D)	55 (D)
56 (C)	57 (D)	58 (A)	59 (D)	60 (B)

Set No. 4

61 (C)	62 (A)	63 (B)	64 (C)	65 (A)
66 (B)	67 (C)	68 (A)	69 (D)	70 (A)
71 (D)	72 (B)	73 (D)	74 (A)	75 (D)
76 (C)	77 (A)	78 (A)	79 (B)	80 (B)

Set No. 5

81 (D)	82 (B)	83 (C)	84 (D)	85 (C)
86 (D)	87 (A)	88 (D)	89 (A)	90 (D)
91 (D)	92 (A)	93 (B)	94 (A)	95 (D)
96 (B)	97 (D)	98 (B)	99 (C)	100 (D)

Appendix

The next few pages contain specimen examination papers set to cater for the general proficiency level. These papers have been devised by the authors of this book. They are *not* copies of any papers set by the Caribbean Examination Council.

Principles of Accounts
Specimen Paper 1 (General Proficiency)
(Your teacher will give you full instructions before you start to attempt this paper.)
Time allowed: 1½ hours

1 Which of the following statements is incorrect?
(A) Capital = Assets – Liabilities.
(B) Assets + Liabilities = Capital.
(C) Liabilities = Assets – Capital.
(D) Capital + Liabilities = Assets.

2 Of the following, which are nominal accounts?
(i) Fixtures account.
(ii) Machinery account.
(iii) Pay account.
(iv) Rent account.

(A) (i) and (iii) only. (B) (ii) and (iii) only.
(C) (iii) and (iv) only. (D) (i) and (iii) only.

3 A bank item posted to the credit of an insurance account, could mean that:
(A) we owe for insurance;
(B) we have paid for some insurance;
(C) we have received the refund of insurance already paid;
(D) some of the insurance was for private use.

Questions 4–7 are based on the following information.

C. Henry
Balance Sheet as at 31 December 2005

	$	$		$	$
Machinery		2,000	Cash introduced	11,000	
Fixtures		5,000	*Add* Net profit	6,800	
Motor vehicles		2,400			
				17,800	
		9,400	*Less* Drawings	5,200	12,600
Stock	4,000				
Debtors	1,700		Creditors	2,900	
Bank	600		Expenses owing	300	3,200
Cash	100	6,400			
		15,800			15,800

4 The current ratio is:
(A) 1.5: 1;
(B) 2.5: 1;
(C) 2:1;
(D) 3:1.

5 The closing capital is:
(A) \$12,600;
(B) \$11,000;
(C) \$17,800;
(D) \$15,800.

6 The liquid assets total:
(A) \$6,400;
(B) \$4,000;
(C) \$2,500;
(D) \$2,400.

7 The current liabilities total:
(A) \$2,900;
(B) \$300;
(C) \$2,000;
(D) \$3,200.

8 Which of the following are capital expenditure?
(i) Repairs to a machine.
(ii) An additional cash register.
(iii) Legal charges on buying additional premises.
(iv) Carriage inwards on purchases.
(v) A new motor van.

(A) (ii), (iii) and (v) only.
(B) (ii), (iii) and (iv) only.
(C) (i), (iv) and (v) only.
(D) (i), (ii) and (iii) only.

9 Do cooperatives draw up profit and loss accounts?
(A) No.
(B) Only when they incur losses.
(C) Only when they make profits.
(D) When the cooperative is owned by a limited company.

10 We buy goods from J. Lee at a list price of \$900. Given that there will be trade discount of 33⅓% and cash discount of 5%, how much will we have to pay, assuming we pay promptly?
(A) \$600.
(B) \$540.
(C) \$570.
(D) \$575.

11 In a partnership, in the absence of any agreement, profits should be:
(A) shared in the ratio of the capital contributed;
(B) after interest on capital, shared equally;
(C) shared equally;
(D) shared in accordance with the amount of work performed.

12 A trader had capital at 1 January 2005 of \$18,400, and it had risen to \$24,700 by 31 December 2005. During that year she had paid an extra \$600 into the business and had made drawings of \$3,000. Her net profit was:
(A) \$8,700;
(B) \$7,800;
(C) \$9,400;
(D) \$10,200.

13 Which of the following are factory overheads?
(i) Prime cost.
(ii) Raw materials consumed.
(iii) Factory rent.
(iv) Pay of crane drivers in the factory.
(v) Salesforce's commission.

(A) (iii) and (v) only. (B) (iii) and (iv) only.
(C) (i) and (iv) only. (D) (iv) and (v) only.

14 Two items found only in the profit and loss accounts of companies are:
(A) loan interest and dividends;
(B) dividends and debenture interest;
(C) transfer to reserves and dividends;
(D) directors' remuneration and debenture interest.

15 A receipts and payments account can be compared with:
(A) a cash and bank account;
(B) an income and expenditure account;
(C) a bar trading account;
(D) a profit and loss account.

16 A trial balance is drawn up to:
(A) check the accuracy of the books of original entry;
(B) ensure that nothing has been omitted from the journal;
(C) make certain that all transactions have been entered in the books;
(D) help check the arithmetical accuracy of the double entry records.

Look at the following and then answer questions 17–19.

	$
Stocks of raw materials 1 January 2005	3,000
31 December 2005	5,000
For the year 2005:	
Direct pay	10,000
Raw materials purchased	20,000
Factory overhead expenses	15,000
Selling and distribution expenses	7,000
Administrative expenses	9,000

17 The cost of raw materials consumed is:
(A) $18,000;
(B) $22,000;
(C) $20,000;
(D) $19,000.

18 The prime cost is:
(A) $24,000;
(B) $26,000;
(C) $32,000;
(D) $28,000.

19 The production cost is:
(A) $36,000;
(B) $39,000;
(C) $43,000;
(D) $38,000.

20 In a limited company, the day-to-day control of the business is entrusted to:
(A) stewards;
(B) shareholders;
(C) directors;
(D) debenture holders.

21 The journal is *best* described as:
(A) a supplement to the sales and purchases journals;
(B) a supplement to the cash book;
(C) used instead of the cash book;
(D) a form of diary for certain transactions.

22 If it is desired to keep fixed capitals, any share of profits must be:
(A) credited to partners' current accounts;
(B) credited to capital accounts;
(C) debited to capital accounts;
(D) debited to partners' current accounts.

23 Given net profit of \$24,000; interest on capital: Johnson, \$2,000, Thompson, \$3,000; interest on drawings, \$2,000, and profits shared: Johnson, ⅔, Thompson, ⅓, then balance of profits is shared:
(A) Johnson, \$14,000 : Thompson, \$7,000;
(B) Johnson, \$15,000 : Thompson, \$9,000;
(C) Johnson, \$18,000 : Thompson, \$9,000;
(D) Johnson, \$16,000 : Thompson, \$8,000.

24 Assuming a company has ordinary shares only, and given authorized capital of \$100,000 and issued capital of \$80,000, a dividend of \$8,000 represents a dividend of:
(A) 10%;
(B) 8%;
(C) 12½%;
(D) none of these.

25 Can a cooperative operate any kind of legal business venture?
(A) No.
(B) Yes.
(C) Only if it is a service cooperative.
(D) When 75% of members vote in favour.

26 The documents from which the returns inwards journal is written up are:
(A) sales invoices;
(B) debit notes;
(C) credit notes;
(D) purchases invoices.

27 When we discount a bill of exchange with our bank, we should:
(A) debit bank account, credit debtor's account;
(B) debit bank account, credit bills payable account;
(C) debit bank account, credit bills receivable account;
(D) debit bad debts account, credit debtor's account.

28 In a cooperative, honoraria are charged to:
(A) reserve accounts;
(B) appropriation account;
(C) income and expenditure account;
(D) balance sheet.

29 Given a quotation for an item with a list price of \$750, trade discount of 20%, cash discount of 5%, how much would you pay?
(A) \$540;
(B) \$585;
(C) \$570;
(D) \$560.

30 To 'post' an item means:
(A) to use the services of the Post Office;
(B) to use one of the books of original entry as a medium for entering items in the correct accounts;
(C) to balance off debtors' and creditors' accounts at the end of each month;
(D) to ensure that all trial balance items are accounted for.

31 A credit balance of $200 on the cash columns of the cash book means that:
(A) our bookkeeper has made a mistake;
(B) we have $200 cash in hand;
(C) we have overspent cash by $200;
(D) someone has stolen $200 cash.

32 If building materials totalling $3,000 bought for an extension to the office were debited to the purchases account, any profits calculated would be:
(A) gross profit overstated $3,000; net profit overstated $3,000;
(B) gross profit overstated $3,000; no effect on net profit;
(C) no effect on gross profit; net profit understated $3,000;
(D) gross profit understated $3,000; net profit understated $3,000.

33 Discounts received are:
(A) discounts given when we receive money;
(B) discount received when we pay accounts;
(C) trade discounts received by us;
(D) an allowance given for faulty items.

34 A credit balance of $1,610 carried down on the bank columns of our cash book means:
(A) we have a bank balance of $1,610;
(B) we have a bank overdraft of $1,610;
(C) we are owed $1,610 by the bank;
(D) our bookkeeper has made a mistake.

35 Stock is normally valued for the accounts at:
(A) selling price;
(B) cost price plus an addition for profit;
(C) cost price;
(D) selling price less expected selling expenses.

36 A cumulative preference share is one which:
(A) has a higher rate of dividend;
(B) does not carry arrears of dividend forward;
(C) carries forward arrears of dividend;
(D) is paid a dividend before other preference shares.

37 Before distributing any surplus to its members, a cooperative must transfer a percentage of such surplus to a:
(A) statutory reserve fund;
(B) accumulated reserve account;
(C) contingency plan reserve;
(D) share capital account.

38 What journal entries would be needed to correct the purchases of machinery $2,000 being debited to the purchases account?
(A) *Dr*. Purchases account $2,000; *Cr*. Machinery account $2,000.
(B) *Dr*. Capital account $2,000; *Cr*. Machinery account $2,000.
(C) *Dr*. Machinery account $2,000; *Cr*. Suspense account $2,000.
(D) *Cr*. Purchases account $2,000; *Dr*. Machinery account $2,000.

39 L. Hamilton is paid $2 per hour for a basic 40-hour week, plus time-and-a-half on all hours above that. During the week he worked 60 hours. He pays 25% income tax on all earnings above $100 and social security of $8. His net pay for the week was:
(A) $105;
(B) $122;
(C) $125;
(D) $115.

40 Real accounts consist of:
(i) fixtures account;
(ii) debtors' accounts;
(iii) motor vehicles account;
(iv) bad debts account.

(A) (i) and (iii) only.
(B) (ii) and (iii) only.
(C) (i) and (iv) only.
(D) (iii) and (iv) only.

Questions 41–43 are based on the following information.

Trading Account for the year ended 31 December 2006

	$	$		$
Opening stock		4,000	Sales	15,000
Purchases	9,700			
Carriage inwards	300	10,000		
		14,000		
Less Closing stock		2,000		
		12,000		
Gross profit		3,000		
		15,000		15,000

41 The gross profit percentage on cost is:
(A) 20%;
(B) 33⅓%;
(C) 25%;
(D) 30%.

42 The rate of turnover is:
(A) 3;
(B) 4;
(C) 5;
(D) 6.

43 The cost of goods sold is:
(A) $14,000;
(B) $13,700;
(C) $11,700;
(D) $12,000.

44 If machinery had been bought on credit, the following changes would take place in the balance sheet:
(A) + Machinery, + Debtors;
(B) – Machinery, – Bank;
(C) + Machinery, – Creditors;
(D) + Creditors, + Machinery.

45 At the end of a trading period, to find the value of stock, the proprietor:
(A) adds opening stock to purchases, then deducts cost of goods sold;
(B) deducts purchases from cost of goods sold;
(C) deducts cost of goods sold from sales;
(D) conducts a stocktake.

46 Working capital can be defined as:
(A) current assets *less* current liabilities;
(B) capital introduced by the proprietor;
(C) the capital put to use in the business;
(D) capital created by work done.

47 Which of the following cannot be found in the accounting records?
(i) The profitability of the firm.
(ii) The cost of buying fixed assets.
(iii) The value of good morale in the firm.
(iv) The fact that a strike is about to take place.

(A) (i) and (iii).
(B) (ii) and (iii).
(C) (iii) and (iv).
(D) (i) and (ii).

48 On admission of a new partner, and the raising of a goodwill account, the goodwill should be:
(A) credited to all new partners' capital accounts;
(B) debited to all new partners' capital accounts;
(C) credited to only old partners' capital accounts;
(D) debited to only old partners' capital accounts.

49 If an error had been made in the previous year, and a suspense account opened, then the error of sales undercast $400 should be corrected where?
(A) *Dr*. Suspense account $400, *Cr*. Sales account $400.
(B) *Dr*. Sales account $400, *Cr*. Suspense account $400.
(C) *Cr*. Sales account $400, *Dr*. Profit and loss account $400.
(D) *Dr*. Suspense account $800, *Cr*. Sales account $800.

50 The amount of members' subscriptions paid in advance will be shown in a club's balance sheet as:
(A) a prepaid expense;
(B) an asset;
(C) a liability;
(D) an addition to accumulated fund.

51 Authorized capital is:
(A) the amount of share capital issued;
(B) the amount of share capital paid up;
(C) the amount of share capital on which dividends are paid;
(D) the amount of share capital which the company is allowed to issue.

52 A cheque from J. Mills for $150 and duly banked is later found to be dishonoured. On being informed of the dishonour by our bank, we should:
(A) debit the cash book bank columns, credit J. Mills account;
(B) credit the cash book bank columns, debit dishonoured cheques account;
(C) debit J. Mills account, credit dishonoured cheques account;
(D) credit cash book bank columns, debit J. Mills account.

53 Given opening debtors of $3,150, closing debtors of $2,850 and cash received from debtors of $8,200, the sales for the period must amount to:
(A) $8,100;
(B) $7,900;
(C) $8,200;
(D) $8,000.

54 To compensate one partner for performing some extra tasks not undertaken by the other partners:
(A) the partner could receive a salary;
(B) interest on capital should be paid;
(C) interest on drawings should be charged;
(D) the other partners could pay in more capital.

55 What is the correct order for current assets in the balance sheet?
(A) Stock, bank, cash, debtors.
(B) Cash, bank, stock, debtors.
(C) Debtors, stock, bank, cash.
(D) Stock, debtors, bank, cash.

56 J. Nelson is on piece-work. She is paid \$2 per complete item. During the week she completed 40 items. Income tax is at the rate of 25% on all earnings over \$60 per week. She also pays social security at 5% on gross pay. Her net pay for the week was:
(A) \$69;
(B) \$73;
(C) \$71;
(D) \$67.

57 'Being concerned with the work of entering information into accounting records, and afterwards maintaining such records properly' is a definition of:
(A) accounting;
(B) business management;
(C) office organization;
(D) bookkeeping.

58 If the proprietor had paid a creditor from his private monies outside the firm, the following changes would take in balance sheet items:
(A) – Capital, – Bank;
(B) + Capital, – Creditors;
(C) + Drawings, – Debtors;
(D) – Creditors, – Capital.

59 The total of the discount received column in the cash book is posted to:
(A) the debit side of the discounts received account;
(B) the credit side of the discounts received account;
(C) the debit side of the purchases account;
(D) the credit side of the purchases journal.

60 The entry for a transfer to a general reserve account is:
(A) *Dr.* Profit and loss appropriation account, *Cr.* General reserve;
(B) *Dr.* General reserve account, *Cr.* Profit and loss appropriation account;
(C) *Cr.* General reserve, *Dr.* Bank;
(D) *Dr.* General reserve account, *Cr.* Bank.

The next few pages contain a specimen examination paper set by the authors. The questions are not copies of any of the CXC past questions, although they are of a comparable standard. The answers are not given in this textbook, but your teachers should possess copies of the suggested answers.

Principles of Accounts
Specimen Paper 2 (General Proficiency)
Time allowed: 2 hours
Answer *all* the questions in Section I and *any two* questions from Section II.

Section I
Answer *all* the questions in this section

1 The following trial balance was extracted by K. King from his books as at 30 June 2008. He is unable to get the totals to agree.

Trial Balance as at 30 June 2008

	Dr.	*Cr.*
	\$	\$
Sales		87,050
Purchases	62,400	
Discounts allowed and received	305	410
Pay	3,168	
General expenses	595	
Fixtures	10,000	
Stock at 1 July 2007	12,490	

(Cont'd)

Debtors and creditors	8,120	5,045
Bank	6,790	
Drawings	4,520	
Capital		17,017
Suspense	1,134	
	109,522	109,522

The following errors are found:
1 sales journal overcast by $350;
2 discounts allowed undercast by $100;
3 fixtures, bought for $850, have been entered in the cash book but not in the fixtures account;
4 credit purchase of $166 was entered in the purchases journal only, but not in the creditor's account;
5 cheque payment to a creditor of $490 had been debited to the drawings account in error.

You are required to:
(*a*) draw up the suspense account to record the corrections;
(*b*) redraft the trial balance after all corrections have been made;
(*c*) calculate the corrected net profit if the original net profit from the above figures would have been $19,000 – assume a depreciation rate of 10% on fixtures.

(20 marks)

2 We are given the following figures from a trading and profit and loss account.

	$		$
Opening stock	(A)	Sales	480,000
Add Purchases	380,000		
	(B)		
Less Closing stock	70,000		
Cost of goods sold	(C)		
Gross profit c/d	(D)		
	480,000		480,000
Commission paid	(G)	Gross profit b/d	(E)
General expenses	(H)		
Net profit	61,300		
	(I)		(F)

The following additional information is given to you:
1 mark-up is 33⅓%;
2 employees are paid on the basis of a commission of 7.5% of sales.

You are required to:
(*a*) complete the trading and profit and loss account in respect of the figures (A) to (I);
(*b*) calculate the rate of stockturn;
(*c*) calculate the gross profit percentage on sales;
(*d*) calculate the net profit percentage on sales (to one decimal place);
(*e*) if the gross profit percentage is 5% less than last year, give two reasons why this might have happened.

(20 marks)

3 Following is a summary of Kelly's bank account for the year ended 31 December 2007.

	$		$
Balance 1.1.2007	405	Payments to creditors	
Receipts from debtors	37,936	for goods	29,487
Balance 31.12.2007	602	Rent	1,650
		Rates	890
		Sundry expenses	375
		Drawings	6,541
	38,943		38,943

All of the business takings have been paid into the bank, with the exception of £9,630. Out of this, Kelly has paid staff £5,472, taken drawings of £1,164 and purchased goods of £2,994.

The following additional information is available.

	31.12.2006	31.12.2007
	$	$
Stock	13,862	15,144
Creditors for goods	5,624	7,389
Debtors for goods	9,031	8,624
Rates prepaid	210	225
Rent owing	150	–
Fixtures at valuation	2,500	2,250

You are to draw up a set of final accounts for the year ended 31 December 2007. Show all of your workings.

(20 marks)

Section II

Answer *two* questions *only* from this section.

4 T. Lee is in business as an accountant. From the figures below, prepare his profit and loss account for the year ended 30 June 2006 and a balance sheet as at that date using the vertical style.

	Dr.	*Cr.*
	$	$
Fixtures	16,000	
Equipment	39,500	
Provisions for depreciation		
Fixtures		5,200
Equipment		14,100
Debtors	11,100	
Cash at bank	8,090	
Cash in hand	120	
Fees charged		88,600
Pay	31,960	
Postage and stationery	2,140	
Telephone	1,250	
Computer running expenses	2,190	
Travel expenses	1,620	
Insurance	890	
Rent	3,000	
Sundry expenses	520	
Drawings	29,200	
Capital		39,680
	147,580	147,580

The following items need to be taken into consideration:

1 Rent of $600 was prepaid at 30 June 2006, and insurance of $170;
2 accruals needed at 30 June 2006: stationery, $220; pay, $2,320;
3 depreciation is at the following rates: fixtures, 20%, on the reducing balance basis; equipment, 20%, on the straight line basis;
4 10% of travel expenses is to be treated as for private use.

(20 marks)

5 The bank columns in the cash book of G. Grant for the month of December 2006 appeared as follows.

Dr.		*Cr.*	
2006	$	2006	$
Dec 1 Balance b/f	104	Dec 2 C. Masters	159
Dec 6 T. Smith	208	Dec 11 I. Howe	115
Dec 19 Cash	160	Dec 24 D. Lee	87
Dec 31 P. Stephens	83	Dec 29 T. Moore	15
Dec 31 T. Avon	109	Dec 31 Balance c/d	288
	664		664

The following bank statement was obtained by him.

	Dr.	*Cr.*	*Balance*
2006	$	$	$
Dec 1 Balance b/f			104
Dec 5 C. Masters	159		55 O/D
Dec 6 Cheque		208	153
Dec 15 I. Howe	115		38
Dec 19 Cash		160	198
Dec 29 International: standing order	50		148
Dec 30 C. Stanley: trader's credit		89	237
Dec 31 Bank charges	48		189

You should:

(*a*) write the cash book up to date to take the above into account.

(*b*) prepare a bank reconciliation statement as on 31 December 2006.

(c) A company has an overdraft per its bank statement of $89,656. The only differences between the bank statement and the cash book of the company are that:

1 there were upresented cheques of $6,280;

2 the banking of $17,777 had not yet appeared on the bank statement.

Show your calculation of the balance that would appear in the cash book.

(20 marks)

6 J. Hendry started a firm on 1 January 2003. As economic conditions changed he altered his bad debt provisions. The debtors, after bad debts had been written off, and the requisite percentage provision required were as follows.

	Debtors	*% provision*
Dec 31 2003	$64,000	5%
Dec 31 2004	$80,000	3%
Dec 31 2005	$100,000	3%
Dec 31 2006	$90,000	4%

Bad debts written off were the following.

Year to:

Dec 31 2003	$3,720
Dec 31 2004	$3,690
Dec 31 2005	$4,862
Dec 31 2006	$3,909

(*a*) Write up the following in respect of the above for each of the four years to 31 December 2006:

1 bad debts account;

2 provision for bad debts account;

3 profit and loss account extracts;

4 balance sheet extracts.

(*b*) Show the balance sheet extract of a company with debtors of $156,600, a bad debts provision of $6,600 and a provision for discounts allowed of 2 per cent.

(20 marks)

7 (*a*) From the following balances prepare the purchase and sales ledger control accounts.

2005		$
Jan 1	Purchases ledger balances	3,200
Jan	Sales ledger balances	4,720
Dec 31	Totals for the year 2005:	
	Purchases journal	8,550
	Sales journal	9,360
	Returns outwards journal	150
	Returns inwards journal	210
	Cheques paid to suppliers	7,820
	Petty cash paid to suppliers	30
	Cheques and cash received from customers	7,945
	Discounts allowed	105
	Discounts received	200
	Bad debts written off	130
	Balances on the sales ledger set off against balances in the purchases ledger	550
Dec 31	The list of balances from the purchases ledger shows a total of $3,000 and that from the sales ledger a total of $5,140.	

(*b*) State two advantages that may be gained from the use of control accounts.

(20 marks)

Answers to Exercises

2.1 (*a*) 10,700 (*b*) 23,100 (*c*) 4,300 (*d*) 3,150 (*c*) 25,500 (*f*) 51,400

2.3 (*a*) Asset (*b*) Liability (*c*) Asset (*d*) Asset (*e*) Liabilities (*f*) Asset

2.5 Wrong: Assets: Loan from C. Smith; Creditors; Liabilities: Stock of goods; Debtors.

2.7 Assets: motor, 2,000, premises, 5,000, stock, 1,000, bank, 700, cash, 100 = total 8,800; Liabilities: loan from Bevan, 3,000; Creditors, 400 = total, 3,400; Capital, 8,800 – 3,400 = 5,400

2.9

A. Foster
Balance Sheet as at 31 December 2004

Fixtures	5,500	Capital	23,750
Motor vehicles	5,700	Creditors	2,450
Stock of goods	8,800		
Debtors	4,950		
Cash at bank	1,250		
	26,200		26,200

2.11

Assets	*Liabilities*	*Capital*
(*a*) – Cash	– Creditors	
(*b*) – Bank		
+ Fixtures		
(*c*) + Stock	+ Creditors	
(*d*) + Cash		+ Capital
(*e*) + Cash	+ Loan from J. Walker	
(*f*) + Bank		
– Debtors		
(*g*) – Stock	– Creditors	
(*h*) + Premises		
– Bank		

2.9

C. Sangster
Balance Sheet as at 7 May 2004

Assets	$	*Capital and liabilities*	$
Fixtures	4,500	Capital	18,900
Motor vehicle	4,200	Loan from T. Sasso	2,000
Stock	5,720	Creditors	2,370
Debtors	3,000		
Bank	5,450		
Cash	400		
	23,270		23,270

3.1

	Debited	*Credited*		*Debited*	*Credited*
(*a*)	Motor van	Cash	(*b*)	Office machinery	J. Grant and Son
(*c*)	Cash	Capital	(*d*)	Bank	J. Beach
(*e*)	A. Barrett	Cash			

3.2

	Debited	*Credited*		*Debited*	*Credited*
(*a*)	Machinery	A. Jackson and Son	(*b*)	A. Jackson and Son	Machinery
(*c*)	Cash	J. Brown	(*d*)	Bank	J. Smith (loan)
(*e*)	Cash	Office machinery			

3.5

Cash

	$		$
(1) Capital	1,000	(14) Office machinery	60
		(31) Speed and Sons	698

Motor Lorry

(3) Speed and Sons	698		

Capital

	$		$
		(1) Cash	1,000

Speed and Sons

(31) Cash	698	(3) Motor lorry	698

Office Machinery

(14) Cash	60		

3.6

Bank

	$		$
(1) Capital	2,500	(2) Office furniture	150
		(5) Motor van	600
		(15) Planers	750
		(31) Machinery	280

Capital

		(1) Bank	2,500

Office Furniture

(2) Bank	150	(8) J. Walker	60

Machinery

(3) Planers Ltd	750		
(31) Bank	280		

Cash

	$		$
(23) J. Walker	60		

Planers Ltd

(15) Bank	750	(3) Machinery	750

Motor Van

(5) Bank	600		

J. Walker and Sons

(8) Office furniture	60	(23) Cash	60

37

Cash

	$		$
(1) Capital	2,000	(2) Bank	1,800
(25) Works machinery	75		
(28) Bank	100		

Capital

		(1) Cash	2,000

Office Furniture

(5) Betta-Built	120	(18) Betta-Built	62

Motor Van

(8) Bank	950		

Works Machinery

(12) Evans and Sons	560	(25) Cash	75

Bank

	$		$
(2) Cash	1,800	(8) Motor van	950
(30) J. Smith	500	(26) Betta-Built	58
		(28) Cash	100

Betta-Built Ltd

(18) Office furniture	62	(5) Office furniture	120
(26) Bank	58		

Evans and Sons

		(12) Works machinery	560

J. Smith (Loan)

		(30) Bank	500

4.1 (*a*) *Dr*. Purchases, *Cr*. Cash.
(*b*) *Dr*. Purchases, *Cr.* E. Flynn.
(*c*) *Dr*. C. Grant, *Cr.* Sales.
(*d*) *Dr*. Cash, *Cr*. Motor van.
(*e*) *Dr.* Cash, *Cr.* Sales.

4.2 (*a*) *Dr*. H Fong, *Cr.* Returns outwards.
(*b*) *Dr.* Purchases, *Cr.* P. Franklin.
(*c*) *Dr.* S. Mullings, *Cr.* Sales.
(*d*) *Dr.* Returns Inwards, *Cr*. M. Patterson.
(*e*) *Dr.* Purchases, *Cr.* Bank.

4.5

Purchases

		$			$
(1)	C. Blake	72			
(3)	C. Foster	90			
(30)	A. Price	145			

Sales

		$			$
			(19)	Cash	25
			(21)	E. Rose	64

Return Outwards

		$			$
			(5)	C. Blake	15

C. Blake

		$			$
(5)	Returns	15	(1)	Purchases	72

C. Foster

		$			$
			(3)	Purchases	90

A. Price

		$			$
			(30)	Purchases	145

E. Rose

		$			$
(21)	Sales	64			

Cash

		$			$
(19)	Sales	25			

4.6

Cash

		$			$
(1)	Capital	500	(3)	Purchases	85
(10)	Sales	42	(25)	E, Morgan	88
(31)	A. Knight	55			

Purchases

		$			$
(3)	Cash	85			
(7)	E. Morgan	116			
(18)	A. Moses	98			

Sales

		$			$
			(10)	Cash	42
			(24)	A. Knight	55

Returns Outwards

		$			$
			(14)	E. Morgan	28
			(21)	A. Moses	19

A. Knight

		$			$
(24)	Sales	55	(31)	Cash	55

E. Morgan

		$			$
(14)	Returns	28	(7)	Purchases	116
(25)	Cash	88			

A. Moses

		$			$
(21)	Returns	19	(18)	Purchases	98

Capital

		$			$
			(1)	Cash	500

4.7

Cash

		$			$
(1)	Capital	1,000	(2)	Bank	900
(19)	Sales	28	(7)	Purchases	55

Purchases

		$			$
(4)	S. Holmes	78			
(7)	Cash	55			

Returns Outwards

		$			$
			(12)	S. Holmes	18

S. Holmes

		$			$
(12)	Returns	18	(4)	Purchases	78
(29)	Bank	60			

D. Moore

		$			$
(10)	Sales	98			

Bank

		$			$
(2)	Cash	900	(5)	Motor van	500
(24)	D. Watson (Loan)	100	(29)	S. Holmes	60
			(31)	Kingston Equipment	150

Sales

		$			$
			(10)	D. Moore	98
			(19)	Cash	28

Fixtures

		$			$
(22)	Kingston Equipment	150			

Motor Van

		$			$
(5)	Bank	500			

D. Watson (Loan)

		$			$
			(24)	Bank	100

Kingston Equipment

		$			$
(31)	Bank	150	(22)	Fixtures	150

Capital

		$			$
			(1)	Cash	1,000

4.8

Bank

		$			$
(1)	Capital	10,000	(25)	F. Jones	1,070
(6)	Cash	250	(29)	Montego Motors	2,600

Sales

		$			$
			(4)	Cash	200
			(8)	C. Chin	180
			(10)	J. Newman	220
			(14)	H. Morgan	190
			(14)	J. Peat	320
			(24)	Cash	70

Cash

		$			$
(2)	T. Cooper (loan)	400	(6)	Bank	250
(4)	Sales	200	(20)	Purchases	220
(24)	Sales	70	(31)	Office furniture	100
(28)	Capital	500			

Purchases

		$			$
(3)	F. Jones	840			
(3)	S. Chang	3,600			
(11)	F. Jones	370			
(20)	Cash	220			

(Cont'd)

Returns Inwards

	$		$
(12) C. Chin	40		
(26) H. Morgan	30		

Motor Van

(17) Montego Motors	2,600		

Office Furniture

(18) Faster Supplies	600	(27) Faster Supplies	160
(31) Cash	100		

Capital

		(1) Bank	10,000
		(28) Cash	500

J. Newman

(10) Sales	220		

H. Morgan

(14) Sales	190	(26) Returns	30

C. Chin

(8) Sales	180	(12) Returns	40

J. Peat

(14) Sales	320		

Returns Outwards

	$		$
		(15) F. Jones	140
		(19) S. Chang	110

MontegoMotors

(29) Bank	2,600	(17) Motor van	2,600

Faster Supplies Ltd.

(27) Office furniture	160	(18) Office furniture	600

F. Jones

(15) Returns	140	(3) Purchases	840
(25) Bank	1,070	(11) Purchases	370

S. Chang

(19) Returns	110	(3) Purchases	3,600

T. Cooper (Loan)

		(2) Cash	400

5.1

	Account to be debited:	*Account to be credited:*
(*a*)	Rates	Bank
(*b*)	Pay	Cash
(*c*)	Bank	Rent received
(*d*)	Bank	Insurance
(*e*)	General expenses	Cash

5.2

	Account to be debited:	*Account to be credited:*
(*a*)	Rent	Cash
(*b*)	Purchases	Cash
(*c*)	Bank	Rates
(*d*)	General expenses	Bank
(*e*)	Cash	Commissions received
(*f*)	T. Jones	Returns outwards
(*g*)	Cash	Sales
(*h*)	Office fixtures	Bank
(*i*)	Pay	Cash
(*j*)	Drawings	Cash

5.5

Bank

	$		$
(1) Capital	200	(5) Motor van	250
(2) U. Surer (Loan)	1,000	(12) Insurance	22
		(31) Electricity	17

Capital

		(1) Bank	200

U. Surer (Loan)

		(2) Bank	1,000

Motor Van

(5) Bank	250		

Insurance

(12) Bank	22		

Electricity

(31) Bank	17		

Motor Expenses

(7) Cash	15		

Cash

	$		$
(6) Sales	105	(7) Motor expenses	15
(15) Commission	15	(8) Pay	18

Purchases

(3) T. Parkin	296		
(10) C. Moore	85		

Sales

		(6) Cash	105

T. Parkin

		(3) Purchases	296

C. Moore

		(10) Purchases	85

Commission

		(15) Cash	15

Pay

(8) Cash	18		

5.6

Bank

	$		$
(1) Capital	2,000	(3) Fixtures	150
(21) Rent	5	(24) Motor van	300

Cash

(5) Sales	275	(10) Rent	15
		(12) Stationery	27
		(30) Pay	117
		(31) Drawings	44

Purchases

(2) M. Mills	175		
(6) S. Wong	114		

Sales

		(5) Cash	275
		(23) U. Henry	77

Fixtures

(3) Bank	150		

Rent

(10) Cash	15		

Capital

	$		$
		(1) Bank	2,000

M. Mills

(18) Returns out	23	(2) Purchases	175

S. Wong

		(6) Purchases	114

U. Henry

(23) Sales	77		

Rent Received

		(21) Bank	5

Stationery

(12) Cash	27		

Returns Outwards

		(18) M. Mills	23

Motor Van

(24) Bank	300		

Pay

(30) Cash	117		

Drawings

(31) Cash	44		

5.7

Cash

	$		$
(1) Capital	1,500	(3) Rent	28
(11) Sales	49	(4) Bank	1,000
		(20) Building repairs	18
		(28) Purchases	125
		(30) Motor expenses	15

Bank

(4) Cash	1,000	(7) Stationery	15
		(27) A. Chang	279
		(29) Motor van	395

Purchases

(2) A. Chang	296		
(28) Cash	125		

Sales

		(5) E. Linton	54
		(11) Cash	49
		(17) S. Morgan	29

Stationery

(7) Bank	15		

Return Outwards

		(14) A. Chang	17

Fixtures

(31) A. Webster	120		

Capital

	$		$
		(1) Cash	1,500

Rent

(3) Cash	28		

Building Repairs

(20) Cash	18		

Motor Expenses

(30) Cash	15		

Motor Van

(29) Bank	395		

A. Chang

(14) Returns inwards	17	(2) Purchases	296
(27) Bank	279		

E. Linton

(5) Sales	54	(22) Returns inwards	14

S. Morgan

(17) Sales	29		

Returns Inwards

(22) E. Linton	14		

A. Webster

		(31) Fixtures	120

6.1

H. Harvey

	$		$
(1) Sales	690	(10) Returns	40
(4) Sales	66	(24) Cash	300
		(31) Balance c/d	416
	756		756
(1) Balance b/d	416		

L. Masters

(4) Sales	418	(31) Balance c/d	621
(31) Sales	203		
	621		621
(1) Balance b/d	621		

N. Morgan

	$		$
(1) Sales	153	(18) Bank	153

J. Lindo

(1) Sales	420	(10) Returns	20
		(20) Bank	400
	420		420

6.2

J. Young

	$		$
(10) Returns	55	(1) Purchases	458
(28) Cash	250	(15) Purchases	80
(30) Balance c/d	233		
	538		538
		(1) Balance b/d	233

G. Norman

	$		$
(10) Returns	22	(1) Purchases	708
(30) Balance c/d	686		
	708		708
		(1) Balance b/d	686

L. Williams

	$		$
(30) Returns	17	(1) Purchases	120
(30) Balance c/d	180	(3) Purchases	77
	197		197
		(1) Balance b/d	180

T. Harris

	$		$
(19) Bank	880	(3) Purchases	880

6.3

D. Williams

	$		$
(1) Sales	458	(24) Bank	300
		(28) Cash	100
		(30) Balance c/d	58
	458		458
(1) Balance b/d	58		

J. Moore

	$		$
(1) Sales	235	(12) Returns	26
(8) Sales	444	(20) Balance c/d	653
	679		679
(1) Balance b/d	653		

G. Grant

	$		$
(1) Sales	98	(12) Returns	9
		(30) Balance c/d	89
	98		98
(1) Balance b/d	89		

F. Franklin

	$		$
(8) Sales	249	(30) Bank	249

A. White

	$		$
(20) Bank	77	(2) Purchases	77

H. Samuels

	$		$
(17) Returns	24	(2) Purchases	231
(30) Balance c/d	219	(10) Purchases	12
	243		243
		(1) Balance b/d	219

P. Owen

			$
		(2) Purchases	65

O. Oliver

	$		$
(17) Returns	12	(10) Purchases	222
(26) Cash	210		
	222		222

7.1

Cash

	$		$
(1) Capital	250	(6) Rent	12
		(15) Carriage	23
		(31) Balance c/d	215
	250		250

Bank

	$		$
(9) C. Bailey	43	(12) K. Gibson	25
(10) H. Spencer	150	(12) D. Ellis	54
		(31) Rent	18
		(31) Balance c/d	96
	193		193

Capital

			$
		(1) Cash	250

Rent

	$		
(6) Cash	12		
(31) Bank	18		

Carriage

	$		
(15) Cash	23		

D. Ellis

	$		$
(12) Bank	54	(2) Purchases	54

C. Mendez

			$
		(2) Purchases	87
		(18) Purchases	43

K. Gibson

	$		$
(12) Bank	25	(2) Purchases	25

D. Booth

			$
		(2) Purchases	76
		(18) Purchases	110

L. Lowe

			$
		(2) Purchases	64

C. Bailey

	$		$
(4) Sales	43	(9) Bank	43

B. Hughes

	$		
(4) Sales	62		
(21) Sales	67		

H. Spencer

	$		$
(4) Sales	176	(10) Bank	150

Purchases

	$		
(2) D. Ellis	54		
(2) C. Mendez	87		
(2) K. Gibson	25		
(2) D. Booth	76		
(2) L. Lowe	64		
(18) C. Mendez	43		
(18) D. Booth	110		

Sales

			$
		(4) C. Bailey	43
		(4) B. Hughes	62
		(4) H. Spencer	176
		(21) H. Hughes	67

Trial Balance as at 31 May 2008

	Dr. $	*Cr.* $
Cash	215	
Bank	96	
Capital		250
Rent	30	
Carriage	23	
C. Mendez		130
D. Booth		186
L. Lowe		64
B. Hughes	129	
H. Spencer	26	
Purchases	459	
Sales		348
	978	978

7.2

Bank

	$		$
(1) Capital	800	(17) M. Hyatt	84
(24) J. Carvalho	95	(21) Betta Ltd	50
		(31) Motor van	400
		(31) Balance c/d	361
	895		895

Cash

	$		$
(5) Sales	87	(6) Pay	14
(30) J. King		(9) Purchases	46
(Loan)	60	(12) Pay	14
		(31) Balance c/d	73
	147		147

Capital

			$
		(1) Bank	800

Motor Van

	$		
(31) Bank	400		

Pay

	$		
(6) Cash	14		
(12) Cash	14		

Shop Fixtures

	$		
(15) Betta Ltd	50		

J. King (Loan)

			$
		(30) Cash	60

H. Elliott

	$		
(7) Sales	35		

L. Lindo

	$		
(7) Sales	42		
(13) Sales	32		

J. Carvalho

	$		$
(7) Sales	72	(24) Bank	95
(13) Sales	23		

K. Henriques

	$		$
(27) Returns	24	(2) Purchases	76

M. Hyatt

	$		$
(17) Bank	84	(2) Purchases	27
		(10) Purchases	57

T. Braham

	$		$
(18) Returns	20	(2) Purchases	56
		(10) Purchases	98

Betta Ltd

	$		$
(21) Bank	50	(15) Shop fixtures	50

Sales

			$
		(5) Cash	87
		(7) H. Elliott	35
		(7) L. Lindo	42
		(7) J. Carvalho	72
		(13) L. Lane	32
		(13) J. Carvalho	23

Purchases

	$		
(2) K. Henriques	76		
(2) M. Hyatt	27		
(2) T. Braham	56		
(9) Cash	46		
(10) M. Hyatt	57		
(10) T. Braham	98		

Returns Outwards

			$
		(18) T. Braham	20
		(27) K. Henriques	24

Trial Balance as at 31 March 2006

	$	$
Bank	361	
Cash	73	
Capital		800
Motor van	400	
Pay	28	
Shop fixtures	50	
J. King (Loan)		60
H. Elliott	35	
L. Lindo	74	
K. Henriques		52
T. Braham		134
Sales		291
Purchases	360	
Returns outwards		44
	1,381	1,381

7.3

Bank

	$		$
(1) Capital	600	(5) Motor van	256
(25) P. Pitter	43	(7) Motor expenses	12
		(21) N. Moss	62
		(21) O. Hue	46
		Balance	267
	643		643

Cash

	$		$
(1) Capital	50	(4) Purchases	23
(23) H. Henry	66	(15) Motor expenses	5
(26) Sales	34	(20) Drawings	10
		(27) Drawings	24
		(29) Postage	4
		Balance	84
	150		150

Capital

			$
		(1) Bank	600
		(1) Cash	50

Drawings

	$
(20) Cash	10
(27) Cash	24

Sales

			$
		(3) H. Henry	66
		(3) N. Neita	25
		(3) P. Pitter	43
		(9) B. Barnes	24
		(9) K. Lyn	26
		(9) M. Moore	65
		(26) Cash	34
		(30) N. Neita	43
		(30) M. Edgar	67
		(30) K. Lyn	45

Purchases

	$
(2) C. Jones	500
(4) Cash	23
(11) C. Jones	240
(11) N. Moss	62
(11) O. Hue	46

Returns Inwards

	$
(19) N. Neita	11

Returns Outwards

			$
		(13) C. Jones	25
		(28) C. Jones	42

Motor Van

	$
(5) Bank	256

Motor Expenses

	$
(7) Bank	12
(15) Cash	5

Postage

	$
(29) Cash	4

H. Henry

	$		$
(3) Sales	66	(23) Cash	66

N. Neita

	$		$
(3) Sales	25	(19) Returns inwards	11
(30) Sales	43		

P. Pitter

	$		$
(3) Sales	43	(25) Bank	43

B. Barnes

	$
(9) Sales	24

K. Lyn

	$
(9) Sales	26
(30) Sales	45

M. Moore

	$
(9) Sales	65

M. Edgar

	$
(30) Sales	67

C. Jones

	$		$
(13) Returns outwards	25	(2) Purchases	500
(28) Returns outwards	42	(11) Purchases	240

N. Moss

	$		$
(21) Bank	62	(11) Purchases	62

O. Hue

	$		$
(21) Bank	46	(11) Purchases	46

Trial Balance 30 June 2008

	$	$
Bank	267	
Cash	84	
Capital		650
Drawings	34	
Sales		438
Purchases	871	
Returns inwards	11	
Returns outwards		67
Motor van	256	
Motor expenses	17	
Postage	4	
N. Neita	57	
B. Barnes	24	
K. Lyn	71	
M. Moore	65	
M. Edgar	67	
C. Jones		673
	1,828	1,828

8.1 (Horizontal)

B. Charles
Trading and Profit and Loss Account for the year ended 31 December 2006

	$		$
Purchases	14,629	Sales	18,462
Less Closing stock	2,548		
Cost of goods sold	12,081		
Gross profit c/d	6,381		
	18,462		18,462
Pay	2,150	Gross profit b/d	6,381
Motor expenses	520		
Rent and rates	670		
Insurance	111		
General expenses	105		
Net profit	2,825		
	6,381		6,381

(Vertical)

B. Charles
Trading and Profit and Loss Account for the year ended 31 December 2006

	$	$
Sales		18,462
Less Cost of goods sold:		
Purchases	14,629	
Less Closing stock	2,548	12,081
Gross profit		6,381
Less Expenses:		
Pay	2,150	
Motor expenses	520	
Rent and rates	670	
Insurance	111	
General expenses	105	3,556
Net profit		2,825

8.2 (Horizontal)

C. Wynter
Trading and Profit and Loss Account for the year ended 30 June 2004

	$		$
Purchases	23,803	Sales	28,794
Less Closing stock	4,166		
Cost of goods sold	19,637		
Gross profit c/d	9,157		
	28,794		28,794
Pay	3,164	Gross profit b/d	9,157
Rent	854		
Lighting	422		
Insurance	105		
Motor expenses	1,133		
Trade expenses	506		
Net profit	2,973		
	9,157		9,157

(Vertical)

C. Wynter
Trading and Profit and Loss Account for the year ended 30 June 2004

	$	$
Sales		28,794
Less Cost of goods sold:		
Purchases	23,803	
Less Closing stock	4,166	19,637
Gross profit		9,157
Less Expenses:		
Pay	3,164	
Rent and rates	854	
Lighting expenses	422	
Insurance	105	
Motor expenses	1,133	
Trade expenses	506	6,184
Net profit		2,973

9.1 (Horizontal)

B. Charles
Balance Sheet as at 31 December 2006

	$	$		$	$
Fixed assets			*Capital*		
Premises		1,500	Balance at 1.1.2006	5,424	
Motors		1,200	*Add* Net profit	2,825	
		2,700		8,249	
Current assets			*Less* Drawings	895	7,354
Stock	2,548				
Debtors	1,950		*Current liabilities*		
Bank	1,654		Creditors		1,538
Cash	40	6,192			
		8,892			8,892

(Vertical)

B. Charles
Balance Sheet as at 31 December 2006

	$	$
Fixed assets		
Premises	1,500	
Motor vehicles	1,200	2,700
Current assets		
Stock	2,548	
Debtors	1,950	
Bank	1,654	
Cash	40	
	6,192	
Less Current liabilities		
Creditors	1,538	
Working capital		4,654
		7,354
Financed by:		
Capital		
Balance at 1.1.2006		5,424
Add Net profit		2,825
		8,249
Less Drawings		895
		7,354

9.2 (Horizontal)

C. Wynter
Balance Sheet as at 30 June 2004

	$	$		$	$
Fixed assets			*Capital*		
Buildings		50,000	Balance at 1.7.2003	65,900	
Fixtures		1,000	*Add* Net profit	2,973	
Motor		5,500		68,873	
		56,500	*Less* Drawings	2,400	66,473
Current assets					
Stock	4,166		*Current liabilities*		
Debtors	3,166		Creditors		1,206
Bank	3,847	11,179			
		67,679			67,679

(Vertical)

C. Wynter
Balance Sheet as at 30 June 2004

	$	$
Fixed assets		
Shop buildings	50,000	
Shop fixtures	1,000	
Motor vans	5,500	56,500
Current assets		
Stock	4,166	
Debtors	3,166	
Bank	3,847	
	11,179	
Less Current liabilities		
Creditors	1,206	
Working capital		9,973
		66,473
Financed by:		
Capital		
Balance at 1.7.2003		65,900
Add Net profit		2,973
		68,873
Less Drawings		2,400
		66,473

10.1 (Horizontal)

J. Grant
Trading Account for the year ended 31 December 2003

	$	$		$	$
Opening stock		6,924	Sales	38,742	
Add Purchases	26,409		*Less* Returns inwards	890	37,852
Less Returns outwards	495	25,914			
Carriage inwards		670			
		33,508			
Less Closing stock		7,489			
Cost of goods sold		26,019			
Gross profit		11,833			
		37,852			37,852

(Cont'd)

(Vertical)

J. Grant
Trading Account for the year ended 31 December 2003

	$	$	$	$
Sales			38,742	
Less Returns inwards			890	37,852
Less Cost of goods sold:				
Opening stock		6,924		
Add Purchases	26,409			
Less Returns outwards	495	25,914	32,838	
Add Carriage inwards			670	
			33,508	
Less Closing stock			7,489	26,019
Gross profit				11,833

10.3 (Horizontal)

R. Mendez
Trading and Profit and Loss Account for the year ended 30 September 2006

	$	$		$	$
Opening stock		2,368	Sales	18,600	
Add Purchases	11,874		*Less* Returns inwards	205	18,395
Less Returns outwards	322	11,552			
Carriage inwards		310			
		14,230			
Less Closing stock		2,946			
Cost of goods sold		11,284			
Gross profit c/d		7,111			
		18,395			18,395
Pay		3,862	Gross profit b/d		7,111
Rent and rates		304			
Carriage outwards		200			
Insurance		78			
Motor expenses		664			
Office expenses		216			
Lighting and heating		166			
General expenses		314			
Net profit		1,307			
		7,111			7,111

Balance Sheet as at 30 September 2006

	$	$		$	$
Fixed assets			*Capital*		
Premises		5,000	Balance at 1.10.2005		12,636
Fixtures		350	*Add* Net profit		1,307
Motor vehicles		1,800			13,943
		7,150	*Less* Drawings		1,200
					12,743
Currents assets					
Stock	2,946		*Current liabilities*		
Debtors	3,896		Creditors		1,731
Bank	482	7,324			
		14,474			14,474

(Cont'd)

(Vertical)

R. Mendez

Trading and Profit and Loss Account for the year ended 30 September 2006

	$	$	$
Sales		18,600	
Less Returns inwards		205	18,395
Less Cost of goods sold:			
Opening stock		2,368	
Add Purchases	11,874		
Less Returns outwards	322	11,552	
Add Carriage inwards		310	
		14,230	
Less Closing stock		2,946	11,284
Gross profit			7,111
Less Expenses:			
Pay		3,862	
Rent and rates		304	
Carriage outwards		200	
Insurance		78	
Motor expenses		664	
Office expenses		216	
Lighting and heating expenses		166	
General expenses		314	5,804
Net profit			1,307

Balance Sheet as at 30 September 2006

	$	$
Fixed assets		
Premises	5,000	
Fixtures and fittings	350	
Motor vehicles	1,800	7,150
Current assets		
Stock	2,946	
Debtors	3,896	
Bank	482	
	7,324	
Less Current liabilities		
Creditors	1,731	
Working capital		5,593
		12,743
Financed by:		
Capital		
Balance at 1.10.2005		12,636
Add Net profit		1,307
		13,943
Less Drawings		1,200
		12,743

10.4 (Horizontal)

B. Rousseau

Trading and Profit and Loss Account for the year ended 30 April 2007

	$	$		$	$
Opening stock		3,776	Sales	18,600	
Add Purchases	11,556		*Less* Returns inwards	440	18,160
Less Returns outwards	355	11,201			
Carriage inwards		234			
		15,211			
Less Closing stock		4,998			
		10,213			
Gross profit c/d		7,947			
		18,160			18,160
Pay		2,447	Gross profit b/d		7,947
Motor expenses		664			
Rent		456			
Rates		120			
Carriage outwards		326			
Sundry expenses		1,202			
Net profit		2,732			
		7,947			7,947

Balance Sheet as at 30 April 2007

	$	$		$	$
Fixed assets			*Capital*		
Fixtures		600	Balance as at 1.5.2006		12,844
Motors		2,400	*Add* Net profits		2,732
		3,000			15,576
Current assets			*Less* Drawings		2,050
Stock	4,998				13,526
Debtors	4,577				
Bank	3,876		*Current liabilities*		
Cash	120	13,571	Creditors		3,045
		16,571			16,571

(Vertical)

B. Rousseau

Trading and Profit and Loss Account for the year ended 30 April 2007

	$	$	$
Sales		18,600	
Less Returns inwards		440	18,160
Less Cost of goods sold:			
Opening stock		3,776	
Add Purchases	11,556		
Less Returns outwards	355	11,201	
Add Carriage inwards		234	
		15,211	
Less Closing stock		4,998	10,213
Gross profit			7,947
Less Expenses:			
Pay		2,447	
Motor expenses		664	
Rent		456	
Rates		120	
Carriage outwards		326	
Sundry expenses		1,202	5,215
Net profit			2,732

Balance Sheet as at 30 April 2007

	$	$
Fixed assets		
Fixtures and fittings	600	
Motor vehicles	2,400	3,000
Current assets		
Stock	4,998	
Debtors	4,577	
Bank	3,876	
Cash	120	
	13,571	
Less Current liabilities		
Creditors	3,045	
Working capital		10,526
		13,526
Financed by:		
Capital		
Balance as at 1.5.2006		12,844
Add Net profit		2,732
		15,576
Less Drawings		2,050
		13,526

12.1

Sales Journal

	$
(1) J. Gordon	187
(3) G. Abrahams	166
(6) V. White	12
(10) J. Gordon	55
(17) F. Williams	289
(19) U. Richards	66
(27) V. Wong	28
(31) L. Singh	78
	881

Sales Ledger

	$
	J. Gordon
(1) Sales	187
(10) Sales	55
	G. Abrahams
(3) Sales	166
	V. White
(6) Sales	12
	F. Williams
(17) Sales	289
	U. Richards
(19) Sales	66
	V. Wong
(27) Sales	28
	L. Singh
(31) Sales	78

General Ledger
Sales Account

	$
(31) Total for month	881

12.3 Workings for invoices.

		$	$	$
(1) F. Gomez	3 rolls white tape × 10 =	30		
	5 sheets blue cotton × 6 =	30		
	1 dress length × 20 =	20	80	
	Less Trade discount 25%		20	60
(4) A. Gray	6 rolls white tape × 10 =	60		
	30 metres green baize × 4 =	120	180	
	Less Trade discount × 33⅓%		60	120
(8) E. Hosein	1 dress length black silk × 20 =			20
(20) M. Ali	10 rolls white tape × 10 =	100		
	6 sheets blue cotton × 6 =	36		
	3 dress lengths black silk × 20 =	60		
	11 metres green baize × 4 =	44	240	
	Less Trade discount × 25%		60	180
(31) B. Cooper	12 rolls white tape × 10 =	120		
	14 sheets blue cotton × 6 =	84		
	9 metres green baize × 4 =	36	240	
	Less Trade discount 33⅓%		80	160

(Cont'd)

Sales Journal

	$
(1) F. Gomez	60
(4) A. Gray	120
(8) E. Hosein	20
(20) M. Ali	180
(31) B. Cooper	160
	540

Sales Ledger

	$
	J. Gomez
(1) Sales	60
	A. Gray
(4) Sales	120
	E. Hosein
(8) Sales	20
	M. Ali
(20) Sales	180
	H. Cooper
(31) Sales	160

General Ledger
Sales Account

	$
(31) Total for month	540

13.1 Working for purchases invoices.

		$	$	$
(1) K. Khan	4 radios × 30 =	120		
	3 music centres × 160 =	480	600	
	Less Trade discount 25%		150	450
(3) A. Bell	2 washing machines × 200 =	400		
	5 vacuum cleaners × 60 =	300		
	2 dish dryers × 150 =	300	1,000	
	Less Trade discount 20%		200	800
(15) J. Kelly	1 music centre × 300 =	300		
	2 washing machines × 250 =	500	800	
	Less Trade discount 25%		200	600
(20) B. Powell	6 radios × 70		420	
	Less Trade discount 33⅓%		140	280
(30) B. Lewis	4 dish dryers × 200		800	
	Less Trade discount 20%		160	640

Purchases Journal

	$
(1) K. Khan	450
(3) A. Bell	800
(15) J. Kelly	600
(20) B. Powell	280
(30) B. Lewis	640
	2,770

General Ledger
Purchases Account

	$
(31) Total for month	2,770

Purchases Ledger

		$
K. Khan		
	(1) Purchases	450
A. Bell		
	(3) Purchases	800
J. Kelly		
	(15) Purchases	600
B. Powell		
	(20) Purchases	280
B. Lewis		
	(30) Purchases	640

13.3

Purchases Journal

	$
(1) Smith Stores	90
(23) C. Kelly	105
(31) J. Hamilton	180
	375

Sales Journal

	$
(8) A. Grantley	72
(15) A. Henry	240
(24) D. Sangster	81
	393

Purchases Ledger

		$
Smith Stores		
	(1) Purchases	90
C. Kelly		
	(23) Purchases	105
J. Hamilton		
	(31) Purchases	180

Sales Ledger

	$	
A. Grantley		
(8) Sales	72	
A. Henry		
(15) Sales	240	
D. Sangster		
(24) Sales	81	

General Ledger
Sales Account

		$
	(31) Total for month	393

Purchases Account

(31) Total for month	375	

14.1

Purchases Journal

	$
(1) H. Lloyd	119
(4) D. Scott	98
(4) A. Simpson	114
(4) A. Williams	25
(4) S. Wood	56
(10) A. Simpson	59
(18) M. White	89
(18) J. Wong	67
(18) H. Miller	196
(18) H. Lewis	119
(31) A. Williams	56
(31) C. Cooper	98
	1,096

Returns Outwards Journal

	$
(7) H. Lloyd	16
(7) D. Scott	14
(25) J. Wong	5
(25) A. Simpson	11
	46

General Ledger
Purchases Account

	$		
(31) Total for month	1,096		

Returns Outwards account

		(31) Total for month	46

Purchases Ledger

	$		$
H. Lloyd			
(7) Returns	16	(1) Purchases	119
D. Scott			
(7) Returns	14	(4) Purchases	98
A. Simpson			
(25) Returns	11	(4) Purchases	114
		(10) Purchases	59
A. Williams			
		(4) Purchases	25
		(31) Purchases	56
S. Wood			
		(4) Purchases	56
M. White			
		(18) Purchases	89
J. Wong			
(25) Returns	5	(18) Purchases	67
H. Miller			
		(18) Purchases	196
H. Lewis			
		(18) Purchases	119
C. Cooper			
		(31) Purchases	98

14.3

Sales Journal

	$
(1) T. Thompson	56
(1) L. Rodriguez	148
(1) K. Barton	145
(7) K. Kelly	89
(7) N. Mendes	78
(7) N. Lee	257
(24) K. Mohammed	57
(24) K. Kelly	65
(24) O. Green	112
(31) N. Lee	55
	1,062

Purchases Journal

	$
(3) P. Potter	144
(3) H. Harris	25
(3) B. Spencer	76
(9) B. Perkins	24
(9) H. Harris	58
(9) H. Miles	123
(17) H. Harris	54
(17) B. Perkins	65
(17) L. Nixon	75
	644

Returns Inwards Journal

	$
(14) T. Thompson	5
(14) K. Barton	11
(14) K. Kelly	14
(28) N. Mendes	24
	54

Returns Outwards Journal

	$
(11) P. Potter	12
(11) B. Spencer	22
(20) B. Spencer	14
	48

Sales Ledger

	$		$
	T. Thompson		
(1) Sales	56	(14) Returns	5
	L. Rodriguez		
(1) Sales	148		
	K. Barton		
(1) Sales	145	(14) Returns	11
	K. Kelly		
(7) Sales	89	(14) Returns	14
(24) Sales	65		
	N. Mendes		
(7) Sales	78	(28) Returns	24
	N. Lee		
(7) Sales	257		
(31) Sales	55		
	K. Mohammed		
(24) Sales	57		
	O. Green		
(24) Sales	112		

Purchases Ledger

	$		$
	P. Potter		
(11) Returns	12	(3) Purchases	144
	H. Harris		
		(3) Purchases	25
		(9) Purchases	58
		(17) Purchases	54
	B. Spencer		
(11) Returns	22	(3) Purchases	76
(20) Returns	14		
	B. Perkins		
		(9) Purchases	24
		(17) Purchases	65
	H. Miles		
		(9) Purchases	123
	L. Nixon		
		(17) Purchases	75

General Ledger

	$		$
	Sales		
		(30) Total for month	1,062
	Purchases		
(30) Total for month	644		
	Returns Inwards		
(30) Total for month	54		
	Returns Outwards		
		(30) Total for month	48

14.4

Sales Ledger

K. King

	$		$
(1) Sales	196	(16) Returns	21
		(30) Balance c/d	175
	196		196

R. Jones

	$		$
(6) Sales	490	(30) Balance c/d	490

N. English

	$		$
(20) Sales	400	(30) Balance c/d	400

Purchases Ledger

E. T. Ltd

	$		$
(24) Returns	160	(11) Purchases	1,440
(30) Balance c/d	1,280		
	1,440		1,440

A. Richards

	$		$
(30) Balance c/d	400	(30) Purchases	400

Sales Journal

	$
(1) K. King	196
(6) R. Jones	490
(20) N. English	400
	1,086

Purchases Journal

	$
(11) E. T. Ltd	1,440
(30) A. Richards	400
	1,840

Returns Inwards Journal

	$
(16) K. King	21
	21

Returns Outwards Journal

	$
(24) E. T. Ltd	160
	160

General Ledger

Sales Account

	$		$
		(30) Sales	1,086

Purchases Account

	$		$
(30) Purchases	1,840		

Returns Inwards Account

	$		$
(30) Returns inwards	21		

Returns Outwards Account

	$		$
		(30) Returns outwards	160

Trial Balance as at 30 June 2002

	Dr. $	*Cr.* $
K. King	175	
R. Jones	490	
N. English	400	
E. T. Ltd		1,280
A. Richards		400
Sales		1,086
Purchases	1,840	
Returns inwards	21	
Returns outwards		160
	2,926	2,926

16.1

Cash Book

	Cash	Bank		Cash	Bank
	$	$		$	$
(1) Capital	100		(2) Rent	10	
(3) F. Lai (loan)		500	(4) B. McKenzie		65
(5) Sales	98		(9) B. Burton	22	
(7) N. Miller		62	(16) Bank C	50	
(11) Sales		53	(19) F. Lai (loan)		100
(15) G. Motta	65		(26) Motor expenses		12
(16) Cash C		50	(30) Cash C		100
(22) Sales		66	(31) Pay	97	
(30) Bank C	100		(31) Balances c/d	184	454
	363	731		363	731

16.2

Cash Book

	Cash	Bank		Cash	Bank
	$	$		$	$
(1) Balances b/d	56	2,356	(2) Rates		156
(5) Sales	74		(3) Postages	5	
(7) Cash C		60	(7) Bank C	60	
(12) J. Moores	50	100	(8) T. Lee		75
(20) P. Jones		79	(10) C. Brooks	2	
(22) Bank C	200		(17) Drawings	20	
(31) Sales		105	(22) Cash C		200
			(24) Motor van	195	
			(28) Rent		40
			(31) Balance c/d	98	2,229
	380	2,700		380	2,700

17.1

Cash Book

	Discount	Cash	Bank		Discount	Cash	Bank
	$	$	$		$	$	$
(1) Capital			6,000	(1) Fixtures			950
(3) Sales		407		(2) Purchases			1,240
(5) N. Morgan	10		210	(4) Rent		200	
(9) S. Cooper	20		380	(7) S. Thompson			
(14) L. Curtis			115	and Co.	4		76
(20) P. Exeter	2		78	(12) Rates			410
(31) Sales			88	(16) M. Monroe	6	114	
				(31) Balance c/d		93	4.195
	32	407	6,871		10	407	6,871

In general ledger:

debit discounts allowed 32; credit discounts received 10.

17.2

Cash Book

	Discount	Cash	Bank		Discount	Cash	Bank
	$	$	$		$	$	$
(1) Balance b/d		230	4,756	(4) Rent			120
(2) R. Burton	7		133	(8) N. Black	9		351
(2) E. Taylor	11		209	(8) P. Towers	12		468
(2) R. Harris	15		285	(8) C. Rowse	20		780
(6) J. Cotton: loan			1,000	(10) Motor expenses		44	
(12) H. Hankins	3		74	(15) Pay		160	
(18) C. Winston	13		247	(21) Cash			350
(18) R. Wilson and Son	17		323	(24) Drawings		120	
(18) H. Winter	23		437	(25) T. Briers	7	133	
(21) Bank		350		(29) Fixtures			650
(31) Commission			88	(31) Balances c/d		123	4,833
	89	580	7,552		48	580	7,552

Discounts Received

		$
	(31) Total for months	48

Discounts Allowed

(31) Total for month	89

17.3

Cash Book

	Discount	Cash	Bank		Discount	Cash	Bank
	$	$	$		$	$	$
(1) Balances b/f		211	3,984	(2) T. Adams	4		76
(4) C. Potts			98	(2) C. Bibby	13		247
(6) Sales			49	(2) D. Clarke	22		418
(9) R. Smiley	4		156	(7) Insurance		65	
(9) J. Turner	16		624	(12) Motor expenses		100	
(9) R. Pimlot	13		507	(21) Pay			120
(18) Sales		98		(23) Rent		60	
(28) R. Godfrey (loan)			500	(31) Stationery			27
				(31) Balances c/d		84	5,030
	33	309	5,918		39	309	5,918

Discounts Received

		$
	(31) Total for months	39

Discounts Allowed

(31) Total for month	33

18.1

The Journal

		$	$
(1)	Premises	2,000	
	Motor van	450	
	Fixtures	600	
	Stock	1,289	
	Debtors: N. Hardy	40	
	M. Nelson	180	
	Bank	1,254	
	Cash	45	
	Creditors: B. Blake		60
	V. Rodriguez		200
	Capital		5,598
		5,858	5,858
(14)	Motor van	300	
	Better Motors		300

Returns Inwards Journal

(11)	K. O'Connor	16
(11)	L. Singh	18
		34

Returns Outwards Journal

(19)	N. Lopez	9

Purchases Journal

		$
(2)	B. Blake	20
(2)	C. Harris	56
(2)	H. Gordon	38
(2)	N. Lopez	69
(22)	J. Johnson	89
(22)	T. Baptiste	72
		344

Sales Journal

		$
(3)	K. O'Connor	56
(3)	M. Benjamin	78
(3)	L. Singh	98
(3)	N. Duffy	48
(3)	B. Green	118
(3)	M. Nelson	40
(9)	M. Benjamin	22
(9)	L. Pearson	67
		527

Cash Book

		Discount $	*Cash* $	*Bank* $			*Discount* $	*Cash* $	*Bank* $
(1)	Balances		45	1,254	(1)	Rent			15
(16)	N. Hardy	2		38	(4)	Motor expenses		13	
(16)	M. Nelson	11		209	(7)	Drawings		20	
(16)	K. O'Connor	2		38	(24)	B. Blake	4		76
(16)	L. Singh	4		76	(24)	V. Rodriguez	10		190
					(24)	N. Lopez	3		57
					(27)	Pay			56
					(30)	Rates			66
					(31)	Better Motors			300
					(31)	Balance c/d		12	855
		19	45	1,615			17	45	1,615

(Cont'd)

Purchases Ledger

B. Blake

	$		$
(24) Bank	76	(1) Balance	60
(24) Discount	4	(2) Purchases	20
	80		80

V. Rodriguez

(24) Bank and discount	200	(1) Balance b/d	200

C. Harris

		(2) Purchases	56

H. Gordon

		(2) Purchases	38

N. Lopez

(19) Returns	9	(2) Purchases	69
(24) Bank and discount	60		—
	69		69

M. Benjamin

	$		$
(3) Sales	78		
(9) Sales	22		

L. Singh

(3) Sales	98	(11) Returns	18
	—	(16) Bank and discount	80
	98		98

N. Duffy

(3) Sales	48		

B. Green

(3) Sales	118		

L. Pearson

(9) Sales	67		

Better Motors

(31) Bank	300	(14) Motor van	300

J. Johnson

		(22) Purchases	89

T. Baptiste

		(22) Purchases	72

General Ledger

Capital

	$		$
		(1) Balance	5,598

Rent

(1) Bank	15		

Motor Expenses

(4) Cash	13		

Drawings

(7) Cash	20		

Pay

(27) Bank	56		

Rates

(30) Bank	66		

Sales

		(31) Total for month	527

Purchases

(31) Total for month	344		

Returns Inwards

	$		$
(31) Total for month	34		

Returns Outwards

		(31) Total for month	9

Premises

(1) Balance	2,000		

Motor Vans

(1) Balance	450		
(14) Better Motors	300		

Fixtures

(1) Balance	600		

Stock

(1) Balance	1,289		

Discounts Allowed

(31) Total for month	19		

Discounts Received

		(31) Total for month	17

(Cont'd)

Sales Ledger

N. Hardy

	$		$
(1) Balance	40	(16) Bank and discount	40

M. Nelson

	$		$
(1) Balance	180	(16) Bank and discount	220
(3) Sales	40		
	220		220

K. O'Connor

	$		$
(3) Sales	56	(11) Returns	16
		(16) Bank and discount	40
	56		56

Trial Balance as at 31 May 2006

	$	$
C. Harris		56
H. Gordon		38
J. Johnson		89
T. Baptiste		72
M. Benjamin	100	
N. Duffy	48	
B. Green	118	
L. Pearson	67	
Capital		5,598
Rent	15	
Motor expenses	13	
Drawings	20	
Pay	56	
Rates	66	
Sales		527
Purchases	344	
Returns inwards	34	
Returns outwards		9
Premises	2,000	
Motor vans	750	
Fixtures	600	
Stock	1,289	
Discounts allowed	19	
Discounts received		17
Bank	855	
Cash	12	
	6,406	6,406

18.2

			$				$
(i)	Motor Vehicles	Dr.	6,790	:	Kingston	Cr.	6,790
(ii)	Machinery	Dr.	980	:	Systems Accelerated	Cr.	980
(iii)	Unique Offices	Dr.	490	:	Office furniture	Cr.	490
(iv)	Office furniture	Dr.	150	:	W. Charles	Cr.	150
(v)	Drawings	Dr.	45	:	Purchases	Cr.	45
(vi)	Drawings	Dr.	76	:	Insurance	Cr.	76

19.1

Sales Ledger Control

2004		$	2004		$
May 1	Balances b/f	4,560	May 31	Returns in	460
May 31	Sales	10,870	May 31	Bank and cash	9,615
			May 31	Discounts	305
			May 31	Balances c/d	5,050
		15,430			15,430

19.2

Sales Ledger Control

2008		$	2008		$
Mar 1	Balances b/f	6,708	Mar 31	Discounts	300
Mar 31	Sales	11,500	Mar 31	Bank and cash	8,970
			Mar 31	Bad debts	115
			Mar 31	Returns in	210
			Mar 31	Balances c/d	8,613
		18,208			18,208

19.5

Sales Ledger Control

2005		$	2005		$
May 1	Balances b/f	6,420	May 31	Cash and bank	10,370
May 31	Sales	12,800	May 31	Discounts allowed	395
May 31	Balances c/d	50	May 31	Set-offs: purchase ledger	145
			May 31	Balances c/d	8,360
		19,270			19,270

20.1

Straight Line	$	Reducing Balance	$
Cost	4,000	Cost	4,000
Yr 1 Depreciation	700	Yr 1 Depreciation 40% of 4,000	1,600
	3,300		2,400
Yr 2 Depreciation	700	Yr 2 Depreciation 40% of 2,400	960
	2,600		1,440
Yr 3 Depreciation	700	Yr 3 Depreciation 40% of 1,440	576
	1,900		864
Yr 4 Depreciation	700	Yr 4 Depreciation 40% of 864	346
	1,200		518
Yr 5 Depreciation	700	Yr 5 Depreciation 40% of 518	207
	500		311

4,000 – 500 = 3,500 ÷ 5 = 700

20.2

Straight Line	$	Reducing Balance	$
Cost	12,500	Cost	12,500
Yr 1 Depreciation	1,845	Yr 1 Depreciation 20% of 12,500	2,500
	10,655		10,000
Yr 2 Depreciation	1,845	Yr 2 Depreciation 20% of 10,000	2,000
	8,810		8,000
Yr 3 Depreciation	1,845	Yr 3 Depreciation 20% of 8,000	1,600
	6,965		6,400
Yr 4 Depreciation	1,845	Yr 4 Depreciation 20% of 6,400	1,280
	5,120		5,120

$$\frac{12{,}500 - 5{,}120}{4} = 1{,}845$$

20.3

Reducing Balance	$	Straight Line	$
Cost	6,400	Cost	6,400
Yr 1 Depreciation 50% of 6,400	3,200	Yr 1 Depreciation	1,240
	3,200		5,160
Yr 2 Depreciation 50% of 3,200	1,600	Yr 2 Depreciation	1,240
	1,600		3,920
Yr 3 Depreciation 50% of 1,600	800	Yr 3 Depreciation	1,240
	800		2,680
Yr 4 Depreciation 50% of 800	400	Yr 4 Depreciation	1,240
	400		1,440
Yr 5 Depreciation 50% of 400	200	Yr 5 Depreciation	1,240
	200		200

$$\frac{6{,}400 - 200}{5} = 1{,}240$$

21.1 Old method (to nearest $)

Motor Delivery Van Account

(*a*) 2002			$	2003			$
Jul 1	Bank		4,000	Jun 30	Depreciation		800
				Jun 30	Balance	c/d	3,200
			4,000				4,000
2003				2004			
Jul 1	Balance	b/d	3,200	Jun 30	Depreciation		640
				Jun 30	Balance	c/d	2,560
			3,200				3,200
2004				2005			
Jul 1	Balance	b/d	2,560	Jun 30	Depreciation		512
				Jun 30	Balance	c/d	2,048
			2,560				2,560
2005				2006			
Jul 1	Balance	b/d	2,048	Jun 30	Depreciation		410
				Jun 30	Balance	c/d	1,638
			2,048				2,048

(*b*) Per text

21.2 **Straight line**

Motor Van

2003			$	2003			$
Jan 1	Bank		7,500	Dec 31	Depreciation		1,500
				Dec 31	Balance	c/d	6,000
			7,500				7,500
2004				2004			
Jan 1	Balance	b/d	6,000	Dec 31	Depreciation		1,500
				Dec 31	Balance	c/d	4,500
			6,000				6,000
2005				2005			
Jan 1	Balance	b/d	4,500	Dec 31	Depreciation		1,500
				Dec 31	Balance	c/d	3,000
			4,500				4,500

Reducing or diminishing balance

Motor Van

2003			$	2003			$
Jan 1	Bank		7,500	Dec 31	Depreciation		1,500
				Dec 31	Balance	c/d	6,000
			7,500				7,500
2004				2004			
Jan 1	Balance	b/d	6,000	Dec 31	Depreciation		1,200
				Dec 31	Balance	c/d	4,800
			6,000				6,000
2005				2005			
Jan 1	Balance	b/d	4,800	Dec 31	Depreciation		960
				Dec 31	Balance	c/d	3,840
			4,800				4,800

21.6 Straight line depreciation method

Fixed asset

	$		$
Year 1 Bank	10,000	Year 3 Asset disposals	10,000

Provision for depreciation

	$		$
		Year 1 Profit and loss	2,000
Year 2 Balance c/d	4,000	Year 2 Profit and loss	2,000
	4,000		4,000
Year 3 Asset disposals	4,000	Year 3 Balance b/d	4,000

Asset disposals

	$		$
Year 3 Fixed asset	10,000	Year 5 Bank	5,000
		Year 5 Provision for depreciation	4,000
		Year 5 Profit and loss	1,000
	10,000		10,000

Reducing balance method

Fixed asset

	$		$
Year 1 Bank	10,000	Year 3 Asset disposals	10,000

Provision for depreciation

	$		$
		Year 1 Profit and loss	4,000
Year 2 Balance c/d	6,400	Year 2 Profit and loss	2,400
	6,400		6,400
Year 3 Asset disposals	6,400	Year 3 Balance b/d	6,400

Asset disposals

	$		$
Year 3 Fixed asset	10,000	Year 3 Bank	5,000
Year 3 Profit and loss	1,400	Year 3 Provision for depreciation	6,400
	11,400		11,400

(*b*) (*i*) The purpose of depreciation provisions is to apportion the cost of a fixed asset over the useful years of its life to the organization.

The matching concept concerns the matching of costs against the revenues which those costs generate. If the benefit to be gained is equal in each year, then the straight line method is to be preferred. If the benefits are greatest in year 1 and then falling year by year, then the reducing balance method would be preferred. The impact of maintenance costs of the fixed asset, if heavier in later years, may also give credence to the reducing balance method.

(*ii*) The net figure at the end of year 2 is the amount of original cost not yet expensed against revenue.

22.1

D. Fung

2007		$	2007	$
Jan 1 Balance	b/f	200	Feb 1 Cash	150
			Feb 1 Bad debts	50
		200		200

(Cont'd)

C. Manley

		$		$
2007			2007	
Jan 1 Balance	b/f	120	Mar 10 Cash	36
			Mar 10 Bad debts	84
		120		120

Bad Debts

	$		$
2007		2007	
Feb 1 D. Fung	50	Jun 30 Profit and loss	134
Mac 10 C. Manley	84		
	134		134

22.2 (*a*) **Provision for Bad Debts**

		$		$
2008			2007	
Sept 30 Profit and loss		186	Sept 30 Profit and loss	1,186
Sept 30 Balance	c/d	1,000		
		1,186		1,186

(*b*) **Profit and Loss Accounts**

		$			$
(2007)	Bad debts	140			
	Provision for bad debts	1,186			
(2008)	Bad debts	?	(2008)	Reduction in provision for bad debts	186

(*c*) **Balance Sheets**

		$	$
2007	Debtors	11.860	
	Less Provision for bad debts	1,186	10,674
2008	Debtors	10,000	
	Less Provision for bad debts	1,000	9,000

23.1 (*a*)

Rent

	$		$
2001		2001	
Dec 31 Bank	3,300	Dec 31 Profit and loss	3,600
Dec 31 Owing c/d	300		
	3,600		3,600

(*b*)

Telephone

	$		$
2001		2001	
Dec 31 Bank	589	Dec 31 Profit and loss	696
Dec 31 Owing c/d	107		
	696		696

(*c*)

Pay

	$		$
2001		2001	
Dec 31 Bank	14,690	Dec 31 Profit and loss	15,020
Dec 31 Owing c/d	330		
	15,020		15,020

(Cont'd)

(*d*)

Rates

2001		$	2001		$
Dec 31	Bank	5,250	Dec 31	Profit and loss	4,200
			Dec 31	Prepaid c/d	1,050
		5,250			5,250

(*e*)

Insurance

2001		$	2001		$
Dec 31	Bank	1,200	Dec 31	Profit and loss	800
			Dec 31	Prepaid c/d	400
		1,200			1,200

23.3 (*a*)

Insurance Commission

2006			2006		
Dec 31	Profit and loss	1,491	Dec 31	Bank	1,377
			Dec 31	Owing c/d	114
		1,491			1,491

(*b*)

Rent Received

2006			2006		
Dec 31	Profit and loss	4,800	Dec 31	Bank	5,600
Dec 31	In advance c/d	800			
		5,600			5,600

(*c*)

Advertising Revenue

2006			2006		
Dec 31	Profit and loss	270	Dec 31	Bank	248
			Dec 31	Owing c/d	22
		270			270

(*d*)

Deck Chair Hire

2006			2006		
Dec 31	Profit and loss	3,167	Dec 31	Bank	3,122
			Dec 31	Owing c/d	45
		3,167			3,167

23.5

Motor Expenses

2006		$	2006		$
Dec 31	Cash and bank	744	Dec 31	Profit and loss	772
Dec 31	Owing c/d	28			
		772			772

Insurance

2006		$	2006		$
Dec 31	Cash and bank	420	Dec 31	Prepaid c/d	35
			Dec 31	Profit and loss	385
		420			420

Rent

2006		$	2006		$
Dec 31	Cash and bank	1,800	Jan 1	Owing b/f	250
Dec 31	Owing c/d	490	Dec 31	Profit and loss	2,040
		2,290			2,290

(Cont'd)

Rates

2006		$	2006		$
Jan 1	Prepaid b/f	220	Dec 31	Prepaid c/d	290
Dec 31	Cash and bank	950	Dec 31	Profit and loss	880
		1,170			1,170

Rent Received

2006		$	2006		$
Jan 1	Owing b/f	180	Dec 31	Cash and bank	550
Dec 31	Profit and loss	580	Dec 31	Owing c/d	210
		760			760

23.7

Rates

2006		$	2006		$
Jan 1	Prepaid b/f	150	Dec 31	Profit and loss	750
May 11	Bank	400	Dec 31	Prepaid c/d	200
Nov 23	Bank	400			
		950			950

23.11

J. Brown
Trading and Profit and Loss Account for the year ended 31 December 2007

	$	$	$
Sales		40,000	
Less Returns in		500	39,500
Less Cost of goods sold:			
Stock at 1.1.2007		10,000	
Add Purchases	35,000		
Less Returns out	620	34,380	
		44,380	
Less Stock at 31.12.2007		12,000	32,380
Gross profit			7,120
Less Pay		3,500	
Rates		550	
Telephone		122	
Bad debts		20	
Provision for bad debts		18	
Depreciation:			
Shop fittings		400	
Van		600	5,210
Net profit			1,910

Balance Sheet as at 31 December 2007

	$	$	$
Fixed assets			
Shop fittings at cost		4,000	
Less Depreciation		400	3,600
Van at cost		3,000	
Less Depreciation		600	2,400
			6,000

(Cont'd)

Current assets			
Stock		12,000	
Debtors	980		
Less Provision	98	882	
Prepayments		50	
Bank		300	
		13,232	
Less Current liabilities			
Creditors	700		
Expenses accrued	522	1,222	
Working capital			12,010
			18,010
Financed by:			
Capital			
Balance as at 1.1.2007			17,900
Add Net profit			1,910
			19,810
Less Drawings			1,800
			18,010

23.12

J. Graham
Trading and Profit and Loss Account for the year ended 30 September 2008

	$	$	$
Sales		130,900	
Less Returns inwards		550	130,350
Less Cost of goods sold:			
Opening stock		23,910	
Add Purchases	92,100		
Less Returns outwards	307	91,793	
Carriage inwards		215	
		115,918	
Less Closing stock		27,475	88,443
Gross profit			41,907
Less Expenses:			
Pay		12,810	
Carriage outwards		309	
Motor expenses		1,630	
Rent and rates (2,970 + 300 – 405)		2,865	
Telephone (405 + 85)		490	
Insurance (492 – 105)		387	
Office expenses		1,377	
Sundry expenses		284	
Depreciation:			
Motor van		1,200	
Office equipment		1,600	22,952
Net profit			18,955

(Cont'd)

Balance Sheet as at 30 September 2008

	$	$	$
Fixed assets			
Office equipment at cost		8,000	
Less Depreciation to date		3,350	4,650
Motor van at cost		6,000	
Less Depreciation to date		3,100	2,900
			7,550
Current assets			
Stock		27,475	
Debtors		12,300	
Prepayments		510	
Cast at bank		3,115	
Cash in hand		295	
		43,695	
Less Current liabilities			
Creditors	9,370		
Expenses owing	385	9,755	
Working capital			33,940
			41,490
Less Long-term liabilities			
Loan from P. Parkin			5,000
			36,490
Financed by:			
Capital			
Balance as at 1.10.2007			25,955
Add Net profit			18,955
			44,910
Less Drawings			8,420
			36,490

23.13

J. Webster
Trading and Profit and Loss Account for the year ended 31 December 2003

	$	$	$
Sales		91,400	
Less Returns inwards		1,200	90,200
Less Cost of goods sold:			
Opening stock		31,630	
Add Purchases	60,800		
Less Returns outwards	1,350	59,450	
Carriage inwards		450	
		91,530	
Less Closing stock		36,530	55,000
Gross profit			35,200
Add Discounts received			210
			35,410

(Cont'd)

Less Expenses:			
Pay (5,310 + 506)		5,816	
Motor expenses		1,864	
Carriage outwards		310	
Discounts allowed		309	
Rent and rates		810	
Insurance (204 – 44)		160	
Bad debts		1,516	
Increase in provision for bad debts		75	
Depreciation:			
Fixtures		2,200	
Motor vans		1,620	14,680
Net profit			20,730

Balance Sheet as at 31 December 2003

	$	$	$
Fixed assets			
Fixtures at cost		11,000	
Less Depreciation to date		6,600	4,400
Motor vans at cost		9,400	
Less Depreciation to date		3,980	5,420
			9,820
Current assets			
Stock		36,530	
Debtors	22,460		
Less Provision for bad debts	880	21,580	
Prepayments		44	
Bank		5,850	
Cash		150	
		64,154	
Less Current liabilities			
Creditors	11,960		
Expenses owing	506	12,466	
Working capital			51,688
			61,508
Financed by:			
Capital			
Balance as at 1.1.2003			47,933
Add Net profit			20,730
			68,663
Less Drawings			7,155
			61,508

23.16

H. Brown

Trading and Profit and Loss Account for the year ended 31 December 2004

	$	$	$
Sales			14,260
Less Cost of goods sold:			
Opening stock		910	
Add Purchases		11,100	
		12,010	
Less Closing stock		1,820	10,190
Gross profit			4,070
Less Expenses:			
Pay		1,560	
Motor expenses (310 + 26)		336	
Rates and insurance (160 – 12)		148	
Sundry expenses (106 – 15)		91	
Provision for doubtful debts		41	
Depreciation:			
Motors		240	2,416
Net profit			1,654

Balance Sheet as at 31 December 2004

	$	$	$
Fixed assets			
Land and buildings			5,000
Motor vehicles at cost		1,200	
Less Depreciation		840	360
			5,360
Current assets			
Stock		1,820	
Debtors	820		
Less Provision for doubtful debts	41	779	
Prepaid expenses		12	
		2,611	
Less Current liabilities			
Creditors (1,210 – 250)	960		
Expenses owing	26		
Bank overdraft (96 + 250)	346	1,332	1,279
			6,639
Financed by:			
Capital			
Balance at 1.1.2004			6,400
Add Net profit			1,654
			8,054
Less Drawings (1,400 + 15)			1,415
			6,639

25.1 (*a*)

Cash Book

		$			$
2005	(Totals so far)	2,328	2005	(Totals so far)	497
Dec 31	J. Walters	54	Dec 31	Bank charges	22
			Dec 31	Balance c/d	1,863
		2,382			2,382

(*b*) **Bank Reconciliation Statement as at 31 December 2005**

	$
Balance per cash book	1,863
Add Unpresented cheque	115
	1,978
Less Bankings not yet on bank statement (249 + 178)	427
Balance per bank statement	1,551

or

Bank Reconciliation Statement as at 31 December 2005

	$
Balance per bank statement	1,551
Add Bankings not yet on bank statement (249 + 178)	427
	1,978
Less Unpresented cheque	115
Balance per cash book	1,863

Note for teachers:
Both in theory and in practice, you can start with the cash book balance working to the bank statement balance, or you can reverse this method. Many teachers have their preferences, but this is a personal matter only. Examiners sometimes ask for them using one way, sometimes the other. Students should therefore be able to tackle them both ways.

25.3 (*a*)

C. Grant: Cash Book

2007		$	2007		$
June 1	Balance b/f	2,379	June 5	D. Blake	150
June 7	P. Green	158	June 12	J. Gray	433
June 16	A. Silver	93	June 16	B. Stephens	88
June 28	M. Brown	307	June 29	Orange Club	57
June 30	K. Black	624	June 29	U.D.T.	44
June 30	Johnson	90	June 30	Bank charges	70
			June 30	Balance c/d	2,809
		3,651			3,651

(*b*) **C. Grant: Bank Reconciliation Statement as on 30 June 2007**

	$
Balance in hand per cash book	2,809
Add Unpresented cheque	57
	2,866
Less Bank lodgement not yet entered on bank statement	624
Balance in hand as per bank statement	2,242

25.5 (*a*)

Cash Book (bank columns)

2001		$	2001		$
May 7	Sales	1,630	May 1	Balance b/f	3,340
May 10	Capital	10,000	May 4	Motor van	5,000
May 29	A. B. Ltd	555	May 18	D. Marple Ltd	237
May 31	Dividend J.G. Ltd	280	May 30	Pay	470
			May 31	Sales (dishonoured cheque)	75
			May 31	Insurance	920
			May 31	Bank charges	110
			May 31	Balance c/d	2,313
		12,465			12,465

(*b*)

Bank Reconciliation Statement as at 31 May 2001

	$
Balance per cash book	2,313
Add Unpresented cheque	237
	2,550
Less Lodgement not entered	555
Balance per bank statement	1,995

(*c*) Per text.

26.1

Petty Cash Book

Receipts $		*Total* $	*Motor expenses* $	*Post and stationery* $	*Cleaning* $	*Sundry expenses* $	*Ledger* $
1,000	(1) Balance b/d						
	(1) Cleaning	36			36		
	(3) Speedy Garage	24	24				
	(4) Postage	55		55			
	(5) Envelopes	17		17			
	(6) Poison licence	18				18	
	(8) Unique Garage	57	57				
	(9) Corner Garage	64	64				
	(11) Postage	58		58			
	(12) F. Lee	99					99
	(13) H. Norman	44					44
	(15) Sweeping brush	23			23		
	(16) Bends Garage	77	77				
	(17) K. King	65		65			
	(19) Driving licences	11	11				
	(21) C. Hope	72					72
	(25) Cleaning	68			68		
	(27) Dog licences	12				12	
	(28) Guard dog food	29				29	
	(31) Corner Garage	54	54				
		883	287	195	127	59	215
883	(31) Cash						
	(31) Balance c/d	1,000					
1,883		1,883					
1,000	(1) Balance c/d						

26.2

Petty Cash Book

Receipts			Total	Office expenses	Motor expenses	Cleaning expenses	Casual labour
$			$	$	$	$	$
500	(1)	Balance b/d					
	(1)	H. Sangster	13				13
	(2)	Letterheaded stationery	22	22			
	(2)	Unique Motors	30		30		
	(3)	Cleaning materials	16			16	
	(6)	Envelopes	14	14			
	(8)	Petrol	28		28		
	(11)	J. Hogan	15				15
	(12)	Paper-clips	12	12			
	(12)	Mrs. Bell	27			27	
	(14)	Petrol	11		11		
	(16)	Typewritter ribbons	31	31			
	(16)	Petrol	29		29		
	(21)	Motor taxation	50		50		
	(22)	T. Cooke	21				21
	(23)	Mrs Bell	10			10	
	(24)	P. King	19				19
	(25)	Copy paper	27	27			
	(26)	Flat Cars	21		21		
	(29)	Petrol	12		12		
	(30)	J. Young	16				16
			424	106	181	53	84
424	(30)	Cash					
	(30)	Balance b/d	500				
924			924				
500	(1)	Balance b/d					

Motor Expenses			*Office Expenses*		
(30)	Petty cash	181	(30)	Petty cash	106

27.1

		$				$
(*a*) J. Harris	*Dr.*	678	:	J. Hart	*Cr.*	678
(*b*) Machinery	*Dr.*	4,390	:	L. Pyle	*Cr.*	4,390
(*c*) Motor van	*Dr.*	3,800	:	Motor expenses	*Cr.*	3,800
(*d*) E. Fitzwilliam	*Dr.*	9	:	Sales	*Cr.*	9
(*e*) Sales	*Dr.*	257	:	Commissions received	*Cr.*	257

27.3

A. Smith
Balance Sheet as at 31 December 2006

	Cost	Depreciation	Net book value
	$	$	$
Fixed assets			
Goodwill	14,000	–	14,000
Premises	182,000	–	182,000
Furniture and equipment	97,400	5,000	92,400
	293,400	5,000	288,400

(Cont'd)

Current assets				
Stock		38,500		
Debtors	43,200			
Less Provision	2,160	41,040		
Prepaid expenses		1,000		
Cash in hand		1,000	81,540	
Less Current liabilities				
Creditors		39,680		
Bank overdraft		9,000		
Expenses accrued		1,260	49,940	
Working capital				31,600
				320,000
Financed by:				
Capital				
Balance as at 1.1.1999				310,000
Add Net profit				30,000
				340,000
Less Drawings				20,000
				320,000

28.1 **The Journal**

	Dr. $	*Cr.* $
(*a*) T. Thomas	900	
Bank		900
(*b*) C. Charles	35	
Discounts allowed		35
(*c*) Office equipment	6,000	
Motor vehicles		6,000
(*d*) J. Graham	715	
Sales		715
(*e*) Pay	210	
Drawings	210	
Suspense		420

28.2

(*a*)	*No effect*	*Debit side exceeds credit side by:* $	*Credit side exceeds debit side by:* $
1	✔	–	–
2		298	
3	✔ (each side 36, short)		
4		100	
5	✔		

(*b*) 1:3:4

(*c*) 3

(*d*) (i) Principle 1; (ii) Commission 5; (iii) Original entry 3.

(Cont'd)

(*e*) **The Journal**

		Dr. $	*Cr.* $
1	Equipment	2,500	
	General expenses		2,500
2	Suspense	298	
	E. Grey		298
3	J. Crook	36	
	Sales		36
4	Suspense	100	
	Discount allowed		100
5	B. B. Ltd	135	
	D. D. Ltd		135

28.4 **Trial Balance as at 31 January 2009**

	Dr. $	*Cr.* $
Drawings	2,800	
Stock	2,597	
Debtors (2,130 – 6)	2,124	
Furniture (1,750 + 120)	1,870	
Cash	1,020	
Returns inwards	85	
Business expenses	950	
Purchases (4,380 – 120)	4,260	
Discounts allowed	38	
Capital		5,500
Creditors (2,735 – 75)		2,660
Sales (7,430 + 108)		7,538
Discounts received		46
	15,744	15,744

29.1 **J. Jackson**
Trading Account for the year ended 31 July 2003

		$		$
Stock 1.8.2002		4,936	Sales	30,000
Add Purchases	(C)	25,374		
	(B)	30,310		
Less Closing stock 31.7.2003		6,310		
Cost of goods sold	(A)	24,000		
Gross profit		6,000		
		30,000		30,000

Mark-up is 25%, therefore margin is 20%, consequently gross profit is 20% × 30,000 = 6,000.
(A) (B) and (C) are then found, in that order, by normal arithmetical deduction.

29.2

P. R. Masters
Trading Account for the year ended 31 August 2009

		$		$
Stock 1.9.2008		2,000	Sales	21,000
Add Purchases		18,000		
		20,000		
Less Stock 30.8.2009	(A)	6,000		
Cost of goods sold		14,000		
Gross profit		7,000		
		21,000		21,000

Average stock = 4,000.

Therefore $\frac{(2{,}000 + (A))}{2}$ = 4,000 and (A) is found to be 6,000.

Cost of goods sold is then calculated as 14,000. Mark-up is 50%, so sales = 14,000 + 50% = 21,000. If net profit on sales is not to be less than 10% of sales = 2,100, this means that he can afford up to 4,900 expenses; i.e., gross profit 7,000 – 4,900 expenses = 2,100 net profit.

30.1

S. Phillips
Balance Sheet as at 31 July 2007

	$	$		$
Fixed assets				
Furniture		900		
Less Depreciation		100		800
Motor vehicles		2,100		
Less Depreciation		500		1,600
				2,400
Current assets				
Stock	2,700			
Debtors	1,600			
Cash	50	4,350		
Less Current liabilities				
Creditors	3,300			
Bank overdraft	1,000	4,300		
Working capital				50
				2,450
Less Long-term liability				
Loan: B. Smith				200
				*2,250
Financed by:				
Capital				1,000
Add Net profit			(C)	4,250
			(B)	5,250
Less Drawings				3,000
			(A)	2,250

Workings:

(A) (B) and (C) found in that order by filling in figures needed to balance the balance sheet figures.

(A) Equals the total of the balance sheet see*

(B) is 2,250 + 3,000 = 5,250

(C) is 5,250 – 1,000 = 4,250 = net profit

30.2

J. Marcano
Statement of Affairs as at 31 August 2006

	$	$
Fixed assets		
Fixtures		3,500
Motor van		3,500
		7,000
Current assets		
Stock	16,740	
Debtors	11,890	
Bank	2,209	
Cash	115	
	30,954	
Less Current liabilities		
Creditors	9,952	21,002
		28,002

Statement of Affairs as at 31 August 2007

	$	$	$
Fixed assets			
Fixtures		5,500	
Less Depreciation		300	5,200
Motor van		3,500	
Less Depreciation		700	2,800
			8,000
Current assets			
Stock		24,891	
Debtors		15,821	
Prepaid expenses		72	
Cash		84	
		40,868	
Less Current liabilities			
Trade creditors	6,002		
Expenses owing	236		
Bank overdraft	165	6,403	
Net current assets			34,465
			42,465
Capital			
Balance as at 31.8.2006			28,002
Add Cash introduced			12,800
Add Net profit		(C)	9,223
		(B)	50,025
Less Drawings			7,560
		(A)	42,465

(A) Found as figure to make balance sheet totals agree 42,465.
(B) Less 7,560 = (A) 42,465, therefore (B) is 50,025.
(C) Missing figure to total 50,025 = 9,223.

30.5 (*a*)

Total Debtors

	$		$
Balances b/f	2,980	Cash	10,820
Sales	11,520	Balances (difference) c/d	3,680
	14,500		14,500

Total Creditors

	$		$
Cash	7,780	Balances b/f	1,880
Balances (difference) c/d	2,220	Purchases	8,120
	10,000		10,000

(*a*) Capital

	31.3.2008	*31.3.2009*
	$	$
Bank	1,460	1,740
Furniture	600	500
Stock	2,320	2,620
Cash	60	80
Debtors	2,980	3,680
	7,420	8,620
Less Creditors	1,880	2,220
Capital	5,540	6,400

(*c*)

		$
Capital as at 31.3.2008		5,540
Add Net profit	(B)	____
	(A)	
Less Drawings		2,540
Capital as at 31.3.2009		6,400

By arithmetical deduction, (A) is 8,940. Thus, 5,540 + (B) = 8,940; i.e., (B) is 3,400.

30.7 (*a*)

Workings

Capital as at 31.12.2003	$	*Purchases*	$	*Sales*	$
Bank	1,890	Bank	31,695	Bank	44,656
Cash	48	Cash	642	Cash	698
Stock	11,163		32,337		45,354
Debtors	6,013	*Less* Opening Crs.	4,896	*Less* Opening Drs.	6,013
Rates prepaid	282		27,441		39,341
Motor van	2,800	*Add* Closing Crs.	5,091	*Add* Closing Drs.	7,132
	22,196		32,532		46,473
Less Creditors	4,896				
	17,300				

(Cont'd)

(*b*) **Workings**

	Cash	*Bank*		*Cash*	*Bank*
	$	$		$	$
Balance b/f	48	1,890	Cash C		5,400
Receipts from debtors		44,656	Trade creditors	642	31,695
Cash sales	698		Rent		2,750
Loan from Carter		2,000	Rates		1,316
Bank C	5,400		Drawings	5,289	3,095
			Sundry expenses	122	1,642
			Balance c/f	93	2,648
	6,146	48,546		6,146	48,546

(*c*) **J. Evans**

Trading and Profit and Loss Account for the year ended 31 December 2004

	$	$
Sales		46,473
Less Cost of goods sold:		
Opening stock	11,163	
Add Purchases	32,532	
	43,695	
Less Closing stock	13,021	30,674
Gross profit		15,799
Less Expenses:		
Rent (2,750 + 250)	3,000	
Rates (1,316 + 282 – 312)	1,286	
Sundry expenses	1,764	
Depreciation:		
Van	400	6,450
Net profit		9,349

31.1

Capital: (*a*) (*c*) (*d*) (*f*) (*j*) (*l*).
Revenue: (*b*) (*e*) (*g*) (*h*) (*i*) (*k*).

31.3

Capital: (*a*) (*b*) (*e*).
Revenue: (*c*) (*d*).

32.1 **Marabella Town Sports Club**

Bar Trading Account for the year ended 31 March 2008

	$	$
Sales		15,270
Less Cost of goods sold:		
Opening stock	2,190	
Add Purchases	9,540	
	11,730	
Less Closing stock	2,460	9,270
Gross profit to income and expenditure account		6,000

(Cont'd)

Marabella Town Sports Club
Income and Expenditure Accounts for the year ended 31 March 2008

	$	$
Income:		
Subscriptions (8,640 + 90)		8,730
Gross profit on bar		6,000
		14,730
Less Expenditure:		
Secretary's pay	3,600	
Staff pay	5,280	
Postage and telephone	870	
Rates and insurance (1,230 – 60)	1,170	
Sundry expenses	840	
Depreciation:		
Sports equipment	600	
Office furniture	120	12,480
Surplus of income over expenditure		2,250

Marabella Town Sports Club
Balance Sheet as at 31 March 2008

	$	$
Fixed assets		
Club premises		13,500
Sports equipment	5,100	
Less Depreciation to date	600	4,500
Office furniture	1,200	
Less Depreciation to date	120	1,080
		19,080
Current assets		
Bar stock	2,460	
Subscriptions owing	90	
Prepaid rates	60	
Bank	2,790	
Cash	60	5,460
		24,540
Accumulated fund		
Balance as at 1.4.2007		22,290
Add Surplus of income over expenditure		2,250
		24,540

32.2 (*a*)

East Point Social Club
Receipts and Payments Account for the year ended 31 December 2004

	$		$
Subscriptions received	30,100	Bank overdraf b/f	1,650
Bar takings	8,960	Bar purchases	6,150
Donations	4,240	Rent	5,000
		Bar staff pay	1,880
		Equipment	8,900
		Insurance	1,570
		Affiliation fees	360
		Transport	7,140
		Ground staff pay	9,370
		Balance c/f	1,280
	43,300		43,300

(*b*)

East Point Social Club
Refreshment Bar and Trading Account for the year ended 31 December 2004

	$	$
Takings		8,600
Less Cost of goods sold:		
Opening bar stock	550	
Add Purchases	6,150	
	6,700	
Less Closing stock	940	
	5,760	
Staff profit	1,880	7,640
Bar profit		1,320

(*c*)

East Point Social Club
Income and Expenditure Account for the year ended 31 December 2004

	$	$
Income		
Subscriptions		30,000
Donations received		4,240
Bar profits		1,320
		35,560
Less Expenditure		
Wages of staff	9,370	
Rent	6,000	
Insurance	1,360	
Affiliation fees	360	
Transport expenses	7,140	
Depreciation of equipment	5,000	29,320
Excess of income over expenditure		6,330

(Cont'd)

(*d*) **Accumulated Fund as at 31 December 2004**

	$	$
Equipment	16,100	
Fixtures	2,100	
Bar stocks	550	
Subscriptions owing	1,200	19,950
Less Overdraft		1,650
		18,300

34.1

Stephens, Owen and Jones
Appropriation Account for the year ended 31 December 2006

		$	$	$
Net profit b/d				25,200
Less Pay:	Owen	3,000		
	Jones	1,000	4,000	
Interest on capital:	Stephens	600		
	Owen	400		
	Jones	200	1,200	5,200
				20,000
Balance of profits shared:	Stephens ⅖		8,000	
	Owen ⅖		8,000	
	Jones ⅕		4,000	20,000

34.2

Williams, Powell and Howe
Appropriation Account for the year ended 31 December 2007

			$	$	$
Net profit b/d					30,350
Add Interest on drawings:	Williams			240	
	Powell			180	
	Howe			130	550
					30,900
Less Interest on Capital:	Williams		2,000		
	Powell		1,500		
	Howe		900	4,400	
Salaries:	Powell		2,000		
	Howe		3,500	5,500	9,900
					21,000
Balance of profits shared:	Williams	50%		10,500	
	Powell	30%		6,300	
	Howe	20%		4,200	21,000

Balance Sheet as at 31 December 2007 (extracts)

		$	$
Capital:	Williams	40,000	
	Powell	30,000	
	Howe	18,000	88,000

(Cont'd)

Current accounts:

	Williams	*Powell*	*Howe*	
	$	$	$	
Balances 1.12007	1,860	946	717	
Add Share of profits	10,500	6,300	4,200	
Salary		2,000	3,500	
Interest on capital	2,000	1,500	900	
	14,360	10,746	9,317	
Less Interest on drawings	240	180	130	
Drawings	9,200	7,100	6,900	
	4,920	3,466	2,287	10,673

34.4

Mendez and Marshall
Trading and Profit and Loss Account for the year ended 30 June 2006

	$	$	$
Sales			123,650
Less Cost of goods sold:			
Opening stock		41,979	
Add Purchases		85,416	
		127,395	
Less Clossing stock		56,340	71,055
Gross profit			52,595
Add Reduction in provision for bad debts			80
			52,675
Less Pay (18,917 + 200)		19,117	
Office expenses (2,416 + 96)		2,512	
Carriage outwards		1,288	
Discounts allowed		115	
Bad debts		503	
Loan interest		4,000	
Depreciation:			
Fixtures	770		
Buildings	1,000	1,770	29,305
Net profit			23,370
Add Interest on drawings:			
Mendez		180	
Marshall		120	300
			23,670
Less Interest on capital:			
Mendez	3,500		
Marshall	2,950	6,450	
Salary Mendez		800	7,250
			16,420
Balance of profits shared:			
Mendez		8,210	
Marshall		8,210	16,420

Balance Sheet as at 30 June 2006

Fixed assets	*Cost*	*Depreciation*	*Net*
	$	$	$
Buildings	75,000	26,000	49,000
Fixtures	11,000	4,070	6,930
	86,000	30,070	55,930
Current assets			
Stock		56,340	
Debtors	16,243		
Less Provision for bad debts	320	15,923	
Bank		677	
		72,940	
Less Current liabilities			
Creditors	11,150		
Expenses owing	296	11,446	
Working capital			61,494
			117,424
Less Long-term liability			
Loan from J. Khan			40,000
			77,424
Financed by:			
Capital:			
Mendez		35,000	
Marshall		29,500	64,500
Current accounts	*Mendez*	*Marshall*	
Balance 1.7.2005	1,306	298	
Add Interest on capital	3,500	2,950	
Add Salary	800		
Add Balance of profit	8,210	8,210	
	13,816	11,458	
Less Drawings	6,400	5,650	
Less Interest on drawings	180	120	
	7,236	5,688	12,924
			77,424

34.6 (*a*) **Opening Capital**

		Q		P
	$	$	$	$
Equipment		7,000		8,500
Premises		15,000		–
Stock		12,000		9,000
Debtors		2,100		3,900
Motor van		–		7,200
Prepaid expenses		300		230
		36,400		28,830
Less Creditors	1,970		2,040	
Expenses owing	430	2,400	790	2,830
		34,000		26,000

(*b*) **O and P**

Profit and Loss Appropriation Account for the year ended 31 December 2005

	$	$	$
Net profit b/d			23,680
Add Interest on drawings:			
Q		120	
P		200	320
			24,000
Less Salary: P		2,000	
Interest on capital:			
Q	3,600		
P	2,400	6,000	
Balance of profits shared:			
Q ½	8,000		
P ½	8,000	16,000	24,000

(*c*) **Balance Sheet (extracts)**

Capital		Q		P
	$	$	$	$
Opening balances		34,000		26,000
Add Share of profit		8,000		8,000
Add Salary				2,000
Add Interest on capital		3,400		2,600
		45,400		38,600
Less Drawings	5,200		8,400	
Interest on drawings	120	5,320	200	8,600
		40,080		30,000

35.1 Average sales = (240,000 + 280,000 + 275,000 = 795,000) ÷ 3 = 265,000. Goodwill = 4 × 265,000 = 1,060,000.

35.3 Average fees = (163,500 + 181,000 + 178,500 + 201,000 = 724,000) ÷ 4 = 181,000. Goodwill = 5 × 181,000 = 905,000.

35.5

	$	$
Annual net profits		110,000
Less Remuneration possible elsewhere	60,000	
Alternative investment income	24,000	84,000
Annual super profits		26,000

Goodwill = 5 × 26,000 = 130,000

35.7

Marshall, Russell and Sangster
Balance Sheet as at 31 December 2004

		(a)		(b)		(c)
Fixed assets	$	$		$		$
Goodwill		–		–		12,000
Buildings		11,000		11,000		11,000
						23,000
Current assets						
Stock	6,000		6,000		6,000	
Debtors	2,000		2,000		2,000	
Bank	12,000		9,000		9,000	
	20,000		17,000		17,000	
Less Current liabilities						
Creditors	2,000		2,000		2,000	
Working capital		18,000		15,000		15,000
		29,000		26,000		38,000
Capital						
Marshall	12,000		10,000		18,000	
Russell	9,000		8,000		12,000	
Sangster	8,000	29,000	8,000	26,000	8,000	38,000

36.1

Purchases Analysis Book

2009	*Invoice no.*	*Total*	*A – G*	*H – M*	*N – Z*
		$	$	$	$
Feb 1 F. Archer	21	960	960		
Feb 2 J. Potter	22	360			360
Feb 3 J. Harris	23	575		575	
Feb 4 C. Cooper	24	106	106		
Feb 5 B. Singh	25	91			91
Feb 6 F. Lewis	26	450		450	
		2,542	1,066	1,025	451

36.3

Sales Journal

2006	*Total*	*Britain*	*Far East*	*USA*
	$	$	$	$
May 1 H. K. Hiram	119			119
May 3 P. Osaki	288		288	
May 5 B. Hardcastle	249	249		
May 10 A. Smith	44	44		
May 15 T. Roosevelt	387			387
May 17 L. Nakamura	84		84	
May 19 C. Rockefeller	219			219
May 28 I. Aoki	188		188	
May 31 S. Chang	572		572	
	2,150	293	1,132	725

37.1

Super Shoes
Manufacturing, Trading and Profit and Loss Account
for the year ended 31 May 2005

	$	$
Opening stock of raw materials 1.6.2004		7,800
Add Purchases		10,100
		17,900
Less Closing stock of raw materials		4,950
(i) Cost of raw materials consumed		12,950
Machine operators' pay		16,340
(ii) Prime cost		29,290
(iii) Factory overheads:		
Manager's pay	2,460	
Light and power (75%)	660	
Rent of factory	770	
Depreciation	4,800	8,690
(iv) Production cost of goods completed c/d		37,980
Sales		52,000
(iv) Production cost of goods completed b/d		37,980
(v) Gross profit		14,020
Less Expenses:		
Salesforce's pay	4,620	
Bookkeeper's pay	1,950	
Light and power (25%)	220	
General expenses	390	7,180
(vi) Net profit		6,840

37.3

G. C. and Co.
Manufacturing, Trading and Profit and Loss Account
for the year ended 31 December 2004

	$	$
Stock: raw materials 1.1.2004		12,600
Add Purchases		44,000
Add Freight and carriage		1,760
		58,360
Less Stock: raw materials 31.12.2004		10,160
Cost of raw materials consumed		48,200
Production on staff pay		44,000
		92,200
Factory overheads:		
Rent and rates	1,500	
Gas and fuel	2,700	
Depreciation:		
Machinery	3,600	7,800
		100,000

(Cont'd)

Add Work-in-progress 1.1.2004		16,000
		116,000
Less Work-in-progress 31.12.2004		36,000
Production cost of goods completed c/d		80,000
Sales		147,200
Less Production cost of goods sold:		
Stock of finished goods 1.1.2004	12,000	
Add Production cost of goods completed b/d	80,000	
	92,000	
Less Stock of finished goods 31.12.2004	10,000	82,000
Gross profit		65,200
Less Expenses:		
Rent and rates	500	
Gas and fuel	900	
Office staff pay	4,600	6,000
Net profit		59,200

37.4

R. B. Manufacturing Co.
Manufacturing Account for the year ended 31 December 2006

	$	$
Stock raw materials 1.1.2006		3,777
Add Purchases		48,917
Add Carriage inwards		2,800
		55,494
Less Stock of raw materials 31.12.2006		4,394
(i) Cost of raw materials used		51,100
Factory staff pay		39,600
(ii) Prime cost		90,700
(iii) Factory overheads:		
Maintenance (3,950 + 220)	4,170	
Factory power	1,694	
Factory staff pay	7,146	
Factory rent	4,800	
Depreciation	3,490	21,300
		112,000
Add Work-in-progress 1.1.2006		5,500
		117,500
Less Work-in-progress 31.12.2006		7,500
(iv) Production cost of goods completed		110,000

(*b*) Unit cost of production: $\frac{110{,}000}{1{,}000}$ = \$110 per unit.

(*c*) We can manufacture each unit more cheaply than we could buy it elsewhere. Therefore we should carry on production ourselves.

38.1

Time sheet								
Name of company: Engineering Associates				*Week commencing*: 15 May 2005				
Name of employee: Jones, S.					*Works no.* 15		*Dept.* Works	
Day	*a.m.* *In*	*Out*	*p.m.* *In*	*Out*	*Normal hours*	*Overtime hours*	*Total hours*	
Mon	0800	1200	1300	1700	8		8	
Tues	0800	1200	1300	1800	8	1	9	
Wed	0800	1200	1300	1830	8	1½	9½	
Thur	0800	1200	1300	1930	8	2½	10½	
Fri	0800	1200	1300	1700	8		8	
Sat								
Sun								
				Total	40	5	45	

Time sheet								
Name of company: Engineering Associates				*Week commencing*: 15 May 2005				
Name of employee: Thomas, R.					*Works no.* 17		*Dept.* Works	
Day	*a.m.* *In*	*Out*	*p.m.* *In*	*Out*	*Normal hours*	*Overtime hours*	*Total hours*	
Mon	0800	1200	1300	1800	8	1	9	
Tues	0800	1200	1300	1800	8	1	9	
Wed	0800	1200	1300	1700	8		8	
Thur	0800	1200	1300	1900	8	2	10	
Fri	0800	1200	1300	1700	8		8	
Sat								
Sun								
				Total	40	4	44	

Time sheet								
Name of company: Engineering Associates				*Week commencing*: 15 May 2005				
Name of employee: Wallace, V.					*Works no.* 22		*Dept.* Design	
Day	*a.m.* *In*	*Out*	*p.m.* *In*	*Out*	*Normal hours*	*Overtime hours*	*Total hours*	
Mon	0830	1200	1300	1900	7½	2	9½	
Tues	0830	1200	1300	1900	7½	2	9½	
Wed	0830	1200	1300	1900	7½	2	9½	
Thur	0830	1200	1300	1700	7½		7½	
Fri	0830	1200	1300	1700	7½		7½	
Sat								
Sun								
				Total	37½	6	43½	

Cont'd

Time sheet							
Name of company: Engineering Associates				*Week commencing*: 15 May 2005			
Name of employee: Worrall, W.					*Works no.* 24		*Dept.* Office
Day	*a.m.* *In*	*a.m.* *Out*	*p.m.* *In*	*p.m.* *Out*	*Normal hours*	*Overtime hours*	*Total hours*
Mon	0830	1200	1300	1700	7½		7½
Tues	0830	1200	1300	1800	7½	1	8½
Wed	0830	1200	1300	1700	7½		7½
Thur	0830	1200	1300	1800	7½	1	8½
Fri	0830	1200	1300	1900	7½	2	9½
Sat							
Sun							
				Total	37½	4	41½

38.2

(*a*)

Payroll Register: Week commencing 15 May 2005											
Employee	*Total hours*	*Regular* $	*Over-time* $	*Gross* $	*Year to date earnings* $	*Nat. ins.* $	*Income tax* $	*Life ins.* $	*Credit union* $	*Total* $	*Net pay* $
Jones, S.	45	240	45	285	1,672	17	48	15	20	100	185
Thomas, R.	44	240	36	276	1,764	16	59	15	20	110	166
Wallace, V.	43½	300	64	364	2,296	26	85	15	28	154	210
Worrall, W.	41½	225	30	255	1,567	14	37	15	28	94	161

(*b*)

Employees earnings record: R. Thomas										
Period ended	*Year to date earnings* $	*Regular* $	*Overtime* $	*Gross* $	*Nat. ins.* $	*Income tax* $	*Life ins.* $	*Credit union* $	*Total* $	*Net pay* $
Week 6	1,764	240	36	276	16	59	15	20	110	166
Week 7	2,022	240	18	258	15	55	15	20	105	153
Week										

(*c*)

V. Wallace
Payslip for week commencing 15 May 2005

	$	$
Gross pay		364
Less National insurance	26	
Income tax	85	
Life insurance	15	
Credit union	28	154
		210

38.5

H. Smith
Payslip for week ended 18 May 2005

	$	$
40 hours × 6		240
Less Income tax	10	
Less Social security 5%	12	22
Net pay		218

38.6

B. Charles
Payslip for week ended 12 March 2006

	$	$
40 hours × 4		160
20 hours × 6		120
		280
Less income tax 30% × (280 – 240) = 30% × 40	12	
Less Social security 5%	14	26
Net pay		254

39.1

R. O. Limited
Balance Sheet as at 31 December 2004

	Cost $	*Depreciation* $	*Net* $
Fixed assets			
Premises	45,000	18,000	27,000
Machinery	24,000	7,200	16,800
Fixtures	12,000	4,800	7,200
	81,000	30,000	51,000
Current assets			
Stock		18,000	
Debtors		9,000	
Bank		6,000	
		33,000	
Less Current liabilities			
Creditors	9,000		
Proposed dividend	3,000	12,000	
Working capital			21,000
			72,000
Less Long-term liabilities			
10% debentures			18,000
			54,000
Financed by:			
Share capital			
Authorized 60,000 ordinary shares at $1 each		60,000	
Issued 36,000 ordinary shares at $1 each			36,000
Reserves			
General reserve		15,000	
Retained profits per profit and loss account		(C) ?	(B) ?
			(A) ?

(A) is the figure needed to make the balance sheet total agree, i.e. 54,000.
(B) is the figure needed to add up to 54,000 = 18,000.
(C) As (B) is 18,000, (C) must be the missing figure of 3,000.

39.3

C. A. Company Limited
Profit and Loss Appropriation Account for the year ended 31 December 2002

	$	$
Net profit brought down		210,000
Add Retained profits from last year		17,000
		227,000
Less Transfer to general reserve	30,000	
Transfer to foreign exchange reserve	5,000	
Goodwill written off	11,000	
Preference dividend paid	25,000	
Proposed ordinary dividends 10%	100,000	171,000
Retained profits carried forward to next year		56,000

39.5

B. B. C. Ltd
Trading and Profit and Loss Account for the year ended 31 December 2003

	$	$	$
Sales			97,500
Less Cost of goods sold			
Stock 1.1.2003		41,419	
Add Purchases		51,380	
		92,795	
Less Stock 31.12.2003		54,300	38,495
Gross profit			59,005
Less Expenses			
Pay		11,372	
Motor expenses		8,589	
Machinery repairs		2,308	
Sundries		1,076	
Depreciation:			
Machinery		5,400	
Motors		3,080	
Directors' remuneration		6,200	38,025
Net profit			20,980
Add Retained profit brought forward from last year			6,138
			27,118
Less Appropriations			
Proposed dividend		15,000	
General reserve		2,000	17,000
Retained profits carried forward to next year			10,118

Balance Sheet as at 31 December 2003

Fixed assets	*Cost* $	*Depreciation* $	*Net* $
Machinery	45,000	23,400	21,600
Motors	28,000	15,680	12,320
	73,000	39,080	33,920
Current assets			
Stock		54,300	
Debtors		28,560	
Bank		16,255	
		99,115	

(Cont'd)

Less Current liabilities			
Creditors	22,472		
Expenses owing	445		
Proposed dividend	15,000	37,917	
Working capital			61,198
			95,118
Financed by:			
Capital and reserves			
Called-up share capital			75,000
General reserve		10,000	
Profit and loss account		10,118	20,118
			95,118

40.1

(*a*) (i) 22121250 (ii) 30711065 (iii) 13321195 (iv) 40541035

(*b*) (i) Ladies' black shoes, short black laces, synthetic uppers, synthetic soles, no guarantee, size 4½.

(ii) Boy's white shoes, long white laces, canvas uppers, rubber soles, no guarantee, size 6.

(iii) Men's dark brown shoes, no laces, synthetic uppers, synthetic soles, no guarantee, size 8½.

(iv) Girl's green shoes, no laces, leather uppers, rubber soles, one year guarantee, size 2.

(*c*) Digit-three range will be given number 8 for red colour.

(*d*) Digit-one range will be extended as men's boots 5, boy's boots 6, ladies' boots 7, girl's boots 8.

(*e*) Probably useful to know whether they are high-heel, medium heel or flat heel.

(*f*) Digits 7 and 8 cover size. 9½ is 95 and there is no room left in range of digits 7 and 8. Would either have to extend to a nine-digit system or completely alter present system. Otherwise size ten (10) would be completely indistinguishable from size one (10), and size 10½ could not be accommodated.

40.2

(*a*) Omission
(*b*) Double transposition
(*c*) Transposition
(*d*) Addition
(*e*) Transcription
(*f*) Random

41.1

Item no. 24 *Date*	*Ref.*	*In*	*Out*	*Balance*
2009		$	$	$
May 1	Opening balance			500
May 2	Starlight Co. Ltd	300		800
May 8	740		173	627
May 8	Moonbeam & Sons	200		827
May 10	810		294	533
May 14	976		104	429
May 24	Starlight Co. Ltd	350		779
May 28	981		206	573

41.2

Henriques
Valuation of Stock-in-trade as on 31 January 2004

	$	$
Stock as on 7 February 2004		2,830
Add Sales between 31 January and 7 February, at cost: 460 – 20% profit	368	
Goods taken for own use between 31 January and 7 February	38	406
		3,236
Less Good bought since 31 January 2004 and received: 296 – 54	242	
Reduction to market price: 120 – 97	23	265
Stock as on 31 January 2004		2,971

41.5

(*a*) (i) *FIFO*

	Received	*Issued*	*Stock after each transaction*	$	$
January	20 at $30 each		20 at $30 each		600
May	10 at $33 each		20 at $30 each	600	
			10 at $ 33 each	330	930
June		6 at $30 each	14 at $30 each	420	
			10 at $33 each	330	750
July	16 at $38.5 each		14 at $30 each	420	
			10 at $33 each	330	
			16 at $38.5 each	616	1,366
August		14 at $30 each	2 at $33 each	66	
		8 at $33 each	16 at $38.5 each	616	682
		22			
October	12 at $39 each		2 at $33 each	66	
			16 at $38.5 each	616	
			12 at $39 each	468	1,150
December		2 at $33 each	8 at $38.5 each	308	
		8 at $38.5 each	12 at $39 each	468	776

(ii) *LIFO*

	Received	*Issued*	*Stock after each transaction*	$	$
January	20 at $30 each		20 at $30 each		600
May	10 at $33 each		20 at $30 each	600	
			10 at $33 each	330	930
June		6 at $33 each	20 at $30 each	600	
			4 at $33 each	132	732
July	16 at $38.5 each		20 at $30 each	600	
			4 at $33 each	132	
			16 at $38.5 each	616	1,348
August		16 at $38.5 each			
		4 at $33 each			
		2 at $30 each	18 at $30 each		540
October	12 at $39 each		18 at $30 each	540	
			12 at $39 each	468	1,008
December		10 at $39 each	18 at $30 each	540	
			2 at $39 each	78	618

(iii) *AVCO*	*Received*	*Issued*	*Average cost per unit of stock held*	*Number of units of stock*	*Total value of stock* $
January	20 at $30		$30	20	600
May	10 at $33		$31	30	930
June		6 at $31	$31	24	744
July	16 at $38.5		$34	40	1,360
August		22 at $34	$34	18	612
October	12 at $39		$36	30	1,080
December		10 at $36	$36	20	720

(*b*) **Trading Account for the year ended 31 December 2002**

	FIFO		*LIFO*		*AVCO*	
	$	$	$	$	$	$
Sales		1,762		1,762		1,762
Less Cost of goods sold:						
Purchases	2,014		2,014		2,014	
Less Closing stock	776	1,238	618	1,396	720	1,294
Gross profit		524		366		468

42.1

	A	B
(*a*) (i) Gross profit as % of sales:	$\frac{20,000}{80,000} \times \frac{100}{1} = 25\%$	$\frac{24,000}{120,000} \times \frac{100}{1} = 20\%$
(ii) Net profit as % of sales:	$\frac{10,000}{80,000} \times \frac{100}{1} = 12.5\%$	$\frac{15,000}{120,000} \times \frac{100}{1} = 12.5\%$
(iii) Expenses as % of sales:	$\frac{10,000}{80,000} \times \frac{100}{1} = 12.5\%$	$\frac{9,000}{120,000} \times \frac{100}{1} = 7.5\%$
(iv) Stockturn:	$\frac{60,000}{(25,000 + 15,000) \div 2} = 3$ times	$\frac{96,000}{(22,500 + 17,500) \div 2} = 4.8$ times
(v) Rate of return on capital employed:	$\frac{10,000}{(38,000 + 42,000) \div 2} \times \frac{100}{1}$ = 25%	$\frac{15,000}{(36,000 + 44,000) \div 2} \times \frac{100}{1}$ = 37.5%
(vi) Current ratio:	$\frac{45,000}{5,000} = 9$	$\frac{40,000}{10,000} = 4$
(vii) Acid test ratio:	$\frac{30,000}{5,000} = 6$	$\frac{22,500}{10,000} = 2.25$
(viii) Debtor: sales ratio:	$\frac{25,000}{80,000} \times 12 = 3.75$ months	$\frac{20,000}{120,000} \times 12 = 2$ months
(ix) Creditor: Purchases ratio:	$\frac{5,000}{50,000} \times 12 = 1.2$ months	$\frac{10,000}{91,000} \times 12 = 1.3$ months approx.

(*b*) Business B is the most profitable, both in terms of actual net profits ($15,000 compared to $10,000) and in terms of capital employed, where B has managed to achieve a return of $37.50 for every $100 invested, i.e. 37.5%, and A has managed a lower return of 25%.

Reasons (suppositions only, as not until you know more about the business could you give a definite answer):

(i) Possibly managed to sell far more merchandise because of lower prices, i.e. took only 20% margin as compared with A's 25% margin.

(ii) Maybe more efficient use of mechanized means in the business. Note B has more equipment, and perhaps as a consequence kept other expenses down to 6,000 as compared with A's 9,000.

(Cont'd)

(iii) Did not have as much stock lying idle: turned over stock 4.8 times in the year as compared with 3 for A.
(iv) A's current ratio of 9 far greater than normally needed. B kept it down to 4. A therefore had too much money lying idle and not doing anything.
(v) Following on from (iv), the acid test ratio for A is also higher than necessary.
(vi) Part of the reasons for (iv) and (v) is that A waited (on average) 3.75 months to be paid by his customers, where B managed to collect them on a 2-month average. Money represented by debts is money lying idle.
(vii) A also paid his creditors quicker than did B, but not by much.

Put all these factors together, and it is obvious that B is running his business far more efficiently, and is more profitable as a consequence.

43.1

Farmers' Cooperative Ltd
Appropriation Account for the year ended 31 December 2003

	$		$
Transfer to statutory reserve	24,000	Surplus for the year b/d	80,000
Transfer to special reserve	5,600	Undistributed surplus brought forward from last year	11,170
Proposed dividend 5%	20,000		
Undistributed surplus carried to next year	41,570		
	91,170		91,170

43.2

Teachers' Cooperative Credit Union Ltd
Appropriation Account for the year ended 31 December 2002

	$		$
Honorarium to retiring secretary	20,000	Undistributed surplus brought froward from last year	50,000
Transfers to reserves:		Surplus for the year b/d	150,000
Statutory reserve	30,000		
Special reserve	12,000		
Proposed dividends	75,000		
Undistributed surplus carried forward to next year	63,000		
	200,000		200,000

Balance Sheet as at 31 December 2002

	$	$		$	$
Employment of capital			*Capital employed*		
Fixed assets	150,000		Share capital		250,000
Investments	50,000		Statutory reserve		102,000
Loans to members	199,500	399,500	Special reserve		12,000
			Undistributed surplus		63,000
					427,000
Current assets					
Cash and bank	122,500				
Interest receivable	15,000	137,500	*Long-term liabilities*		
			Mortgage		23,000
			Current liabilities		
			Members' deposits	7,000	
			Accrued expenses	5,000	
			Proposed dividends	75,000	87,000
		537,000			537,000

Principles of Accounts: Specimen Paper 1
Multiple-choice Questions

1 B	2 C	3 C	4 C	5 A
6 D	7 D	8 A	9 A	10 C
11 C	12 A	13 B	14 D	15 A
16 D	17 A	18 D	19 C	20 C
21 D	22 B	23 A	24 A	25 B
26 C	27 C	28 B	29 C	30 B
31 A	32 D	33 B	34 B	35 C
36 C	37 A	38 D	39 B	40 A
41 C	42 B	43 D	44 D	45 D
46 A	47 C	48 C	49 A	50 C
51 D	52 D	53 B	54 A	55 D
56 C	57 D	58 B	59 B	60 A

Answers to Principles of Accounts Specimen Paper 2 (General Proficiency)

1 (*a*) **Suspense**

	$		$
Balance as per trial balance	1,134	(1) Sales overcast	350
(4) Creditor	166	(2) Discounts undercast	100
		(3) Fixtures omitted	850
	1,300		1,300

(*b*) **K. King**
Trial Balance as at 30 June 2008

	Dr. $	*Cr.* $
Sales (87,050 – 350)		86,700
Purchases	62,400	
Discounts allowed and received	405	410
Pay	3,168	
General expenses	595	
Fixtures (10,000 + 850)	10,850	
Stock 1 July 2007	12,490	
Debtors and creditors	8,120	4,721
Bank	6,790	
Drawings (4,520 – 490)	4,030	
Capital		17,017
	108,848	108,848

Note: Discounts allowed 305 + (2)100 = 405
Creditors 5,045 + (4)166 – (5)490 = 4,721

(*c*) **K. King**
Calculation of corrected net profits

	$	$
Net profit per accounts		19,000
Less (1) Sales overcast	350	
(2) Discounts undercast	100	
(3) Depreciation on fixtures 10%	85	535
Corrected figure of net profit		18,465

2 (*a*) **Trading and Profit and Loss Account for …**

	$		$
Opening stock	50,000		480,000
Add Purchases	380,000		
	430,000		
Less Closing stock	70,000		
Cost of goods sold	360,000		
Gross profit c/d	120,000		
	480,000		480,000
Commission paid	36,000	Gross profit b/d	120,000
General expenses	22,700		
Net profit	61,300		
	120,000		120,000

(D) Mark-up is 33 1/3%, therefore margin is 25% = 120,000: (C) is difference 360,000: (B) is difference: (A) is difference: (E) Balance b/d: (G) 7.5% of 480,000 = 36,000: (H) is difference 22,700

(*b*) $\frac{\text{Cost of goods sold}}{\text{Average stock}} = \frac{360{,}000}{(50{,}000 + 70{,}000) \div 2}$ = Stockturn 6 times per annum

(*c*) $\frac{120{,}000}{480{,}000} \times 100 = 25\%$

(*d*) $\frac{61{,}300}{480{,}000} \times 100 = 12.8$ (rounded up)

(*e*) Any from:

- cut prices to increase sales
- had to pay more for purchases but could not increase selling prices
- thefts by staff or customers
- wastage of goods when being stored or handled
- cut prices because of competition
- errors in pricing
- frauds by staff.

It is possible to think of more examples.

3 **Kelly**

Trading and Profit and Loss Account for the year ended 31 December 2007

	$	$	$
Sales			47,159
Less Cost of goods sold:			
Opening stock		13,862	
Add Purchases		34,246	
		48,108	
Less Closing stock		15,144	32,964
Gross profit			14,195
Less Expenses:			
Pay		5,472	
Rent (1,650 – 150)		1,500	
Rates (890 + 210 – 225)		875	
Sundry expenses		375	
Depreciation: Fixtures		250	8,472
Net profit			5,723

Kelly
Balance Sheet as at 31 December 2007

	$	$	$
Fixed assets			
Fixtures at valuation		2,500	
Less Depreciation		250	2,250
Current assets			
Stock		15,144	
Debtors		8,624	
Prepayments		225	
		23,993	
Less Current liabilities			
Trade creditors	7,389		
Bank overdraft	602	7,991	
Working capital			16,002
			18,252
Capital			
Balance at 1.1.2007			20,234
Add Net profit			5,723
			25,957
Less Drawings (1,164 + 6,541)			7,705
			18,252

3 *Workings:*

	$		$
Purchases		*Sales*	
Bank	29,487	Banked	37,936
Cash	2,994	Cash	9,630
	32,481		47,566
– Creditors 31.12.2006	5,624	– Debtors 31.12.2006	9,031
	26,857		38,535
+ Creditors 31.12.2007	7,389	+ Debtors 31.12.2007	8,624
Purchases for 2007	34,246	Sales for 2007	47,159

	$	$
Opening capital		
Bank	405	
Stock	13,862	
Debtors	9,031	
Rates prepaid	210	
Fixtures	2,500	26,008
Less Creditors	5,624	
Rent owing	150	5,774
		20,234

4

T. Lee
Profit and Loss Account for the year ended 30 June 2006

	$	$
Fees charged		88,600
Less Expenses:		
Pay (31,960 + 2,320)	34,280	
Postage and stationery (2,140 + 220)	2,360	
Telephone	1,250	
Computer running expenses	2,190	
Travel expenses (1,620 – 162)	1,458	
Insurance (890 – 170)	720	
Rent (3,000 – 600)	2,400	
Sundry expenses	520	
Depreciation:		
Fixture	2,160	
Equipment	7,900	55,238
Net profit		33,362

T. Lee
Balance Sheet as at 30 June 2006

	$	$
Fixed assets		
Fixture at cost	16,000	
Less Depreciation to date	7,360	8,640
Equipment	39,500	
Less Depreciation to date	22,000	17,500
		26,140
Current assets		
Debtors	11,100	
Prepayments (600 + 170)	770	
Bank	8,090	
Cash	120	
	20,080	
Less Current liabilities		
Expenses owing (220 + 2,320)	2,540	
Net current assets		17,540
		43,680
Financed by:		
Capital		
Balance as at 1.7.2005		39,680
Add Net profit		33,362
		73,042
Less Drawings (29,200 + 162)		29,362
		43,680

5 (*a*)

Cash Book

2006		$	2006		$
Dec 31	Balance b/d	288	Dec 29	International	50
Dec 30	C. Stanley	89	Dec 31	Bank charges	48
			Dec 31	Balance c/d	279
		377			377

(Cont'd)

(*b*)

C. Grant
Bank Reconciliation Statement as at 31 December 2006

	$
Balance per cash book	279
Add Unpresented cheques (87 + 15)	102
	381
Less Bank lodgements not on bank statement (83 + 109)	192
Balance per bank statement	189

(*c*)

Bank Reconciliation Statement

	$
Bank overdraft per bank statement	89,656
Add Unpresented cheques	6,280
	95,936
Less Bankings not on bank statement	17,777
Bank overdraft per cash book	78,159

6 (*a*)

Bad Debts

		$			$
2003			2003		
Dec 31	Various debtors	3,720	Dec 31	Profit and loss	3,720
2004			2004		
Dec 31	Various debtors	3,690	Dec 31	Profit and loss	3,690
2005			2005		
Dec 31	Various debtors	4,862	Dec 31	Profit and loss	4,862
2006			2006		
Dec 31	Various debtors	3,909	Dec 31	Profit and loss	3,909

Provision for Bad Debts

2004			2003		
Dec 31	Profit and loss	800	Dec 31	Profit and loss	3,200
Dec 31	Balance c/d	2,400			
		3,200			3,200
2005			2005		
Dec 31	Balance c/d	3,000	Jan 1	Balance b/d	2,400
			Dec 31	Profit and loss	600
		3,000			3,000
2006			2006		
Dec 31	Balance c/d	3,600	Jan 1	Balance b/d	3,000
			Dec 31	Profit and loss	600
		3,600			3,600

Profit and Loss Accounts

2003	Bad debts	3,720			
	Provision for bad debts	3,200			
2004	Bad debts	3,690	2004	Provision for bad debts (reduction)	800
2005	Bad debts	4,862			
	Provision for bad debts	600			
2006	Bad debts	3,909			
	Provision for bad debts	600			

(*Cont'd*)

(*b*)	$	$
Debtors		156,600
Less provision for bad debts	6,600	
Less Provision for discounts allowed	3,000	9,600
		147,000

7 (*a*)

Purchases Ledger Control

2005		$	2005		$
Jan 31	Returns outwards	150	Jan 1	Balances b/f	3,200
Jan 31	Bank	7,820	Jan 31	Purchases	8,550
Jan 31	Petty cash	30			
Jan 31	Discounts received	200			
Jan 31	Set-offs: sales ledger	550			
Jan 31	Balances c/d	3,000			
		11,750			11,750

Sales Ledger Control

2005		$	2005		$
Jan 1	Balances b/d	4,720	Jan 31	Returns inwards	210
Jan 31	Sales	9,360	Jan 31	Bank and cash	7,945
			Jan 31	Discounts allowed	105
			Jan 31	Bad debts	130
			Jan 31	Set-offs: purchases ledger	550
			Jan 31	Balances c/d	5,140
		14,080			14,080

(*b*) Any two from:

- check on accuracy of sales and purchases ledgers
- enable quick calculation of debtors and creditors without waiting to extract individual balances from sales and purchases ledgers
- locate any errors to a particular ledger.

Index